PACIFIC
PRESS
PUB
ASSN

TESTIMONY TREASURES

Counsels for the Church
as Selected From
the Testimonies

Testimony Treasures

Counsels for the Church
as Selected From
the Testimonies

by
ELLEN G. WHITE

Volume I

PACIFIC PRESS PUBLISHING ASSOCIATION
Mountain View, California
Portland, Oregon Omaha, Nebraska

Third printing

Foreword

THE possession of the spirit of prophecy is one of the two distinguishing features of the remnant church, as foretold in the book of the Revelation. From the very beginning days this gift has played an important role in the experience of Seventh-day Adventists and in the development of the church. Through it the church has been admonished, guided, encouraged, as well as reproved and corrected.

As from time to time the *Testimonies* came from the press, they were eagerly secured, their contents prayerfully studied, and the instruction heeded. Through the years some of these testimonies have also been provided for believers who read languages other than English. Largely to these messages may be traced the present-day strength, unity, and high standards of the church.

Now, through this world edition of *Testimony Treasures,* these counsels which have wielded so large an influence are being made available to Seventh-day Adventists the world around. It is, however, only by presenting a selection of articles that it is possible to publish them in this compact, easily handled, and widely distributed form.

These three volumes present a well-balanced and fully representative selection of articles, chosen by able committees of experienced workers, under the direction of, and in collaboration with the Board of Trustees of the Ellen G. White Publications, the agency established by Mrs. E. G. White to carry the responsibility of the continuing publication of her writings. They constitute an integral part of the Introductory Spirit of Prophecy Library—twelve spirit of prophecy volumes designated for early publication in the principal languages of the world.

The full nine volumes of the *Testimonies for the Church* are composed of a series of independently written articles and letters often on unrelated topics. The first collection, in pamphlet form, was published late in 1855. Others soon followed, until there were thirty-seven consecutively numbered pamphlets and books issued over a period of fifty-five years. The messages were both general and specific in character, interspersed with personal testimonies dealing with problems others might face.

Written as they were over a long period of time, to meet the current needs of the church, there was naturally considerable repetition of subject matter. Moreover, much of the counsel applied especially to local and sometimes isolated conditions that existed at the time of writing. Such repetition of counsel, and messages of local import, while of great value, are not of present-day service to the church outside North America. A selection of articles of general and universal application is therefore feasible and advisable as the testimony counsel is made available to the church throughout the world. The making of such a selection is in full harmony with a policy outlined by Mrs. White herself in 1864 in reprinting the first ten numbers of the *Testimonies*. To make this clear we quote her introductory statement:

"During the last nine years, from 1855 to 1864, I have written ten small pamphlets, entitled *Testimony for the Church*, which have been published and circulated among Seventh-day Adventists. The first edition of most of these pamphlets being exhausted, and there being an increasing demand for them, it has been thought best to reprint them, as given in the following pages, omitting local and personal matters, and giving those portions only which are of practical and general interest and importance."—*Testimony for the Church, Nos. 1-10, as Republished in Spiritual Gifts, volume 4.*

Although later English editions embodied the full presentation of the earlier pamphlets, these principles enunciated by Mrs. White have guided in preparing this uniform world edition of *Testimony Treasures*.

The *Testimonies for the Church* published in English aggregate 4,737 pages. There are 1,500 pages of text in these three volumes of *Testimony Treasures,* or about one third of the content of the nine volumes. An endeavor has been made to include all of the articles which have appeared in the two basic *Selections From the Testimonies* which have in the past been published in languages other than English—the two-volume 650-page edition published in Central Europe and the three-volume 1,100-page edition published in some of the Latin languages. In a few cases when paralleling articles in the above-named *Selections* would result in duplication or a close repetition of subject matter in this three-volume set or within the Introductory Spirit of Prophecy Library, such articles have been omitted.

As a rule, articles are used in their entirety. In some cases, however, in order to conserve space and thus open the way for a broad selection of subject matter, some portions of long articles are omitted. In each case, deletions in the text are indicated. Aside from the articles which are selected, some outstanding paragraphs, presenting vital points of truth, have been taken from other chapters. In each case the original source is clearly indicated. There have also been included a few important articles of a testimony character, dealing with vital topics not represented in the *Testimonies,* but which appear elsewhere in the English editions of the E. G. White books not available in other languages.

The articles will be found in their chronological order as they appear in the full nine-volume set, with the exception of a few cases where rearrangement seemed advisable to make appropriate openings for the three volumes. Subheadings have been added, and in some cases long paragraphs have been divided. Modern forms of punctuation and spelling have been employed, but there has been no editing or changing of the text. The date of first publication, together with the source of the article and the original chapter title, if a change in title has been made, is given as a footnote in connection with each article.

In a very few cases references which are obscure because of the deletion of preceding chapters are clarified by explanatory footnotes. It will be observed that in the personal testimonies the names of those concerned do not appear, the initials "A," "B," "C," etc., being used instead. The initial used in the testimony, therefore, bears no relation to the name of the individual for whom the message was given.

These volumes in the English are not designed to replace the full nine-volume set of *Testimonies for the Church*. That standard edition will always be in large demand. *Testimony Treasures* in the English will, however, greatly broaden the distribution of important testimony counsels, making them available in convenient and less expensive form for English readers in the Americas and abroad.

As rapidly as these volumes are made available in other leading languages, they will carry the important testimony messages of admonition and encouragement to the homes of Seventh-day Adventists throughout the world. The uniformity of content of *Testimony Treasures* as published in all languages, will bring large advantage to the people of God who are one in interest, objective, faith, and hope throughout the world. That this counsel, vital to the welfare of the church, may be effectual in "the perfecting of the saints" and "the edifying of the body of Christ," is the earnest prayer of the General Conference Committee, the publishers, and—

THE TRUSTEES OF THE
ELLEN G. WHITE PUBLICATIONS.

Contents

Ellen G. White

A Brief Biographical Sketch

Ellen G. Harmon and her twin sister were born November 26, 1827, at Gorham, near Portland, Maine, in northern New England. When nine years of age, Ellen was involved in an accident in which a stone was thrown by a thoughtless classmate. The severe face injury nearly cost her life and left her much weakened. Soon it was evident that she was physically unable to continue her schooling.

At the age of eleven, while attending a Methodist camp meeting with her parents, Robert and Eunice Harmon, Ellen gave her heart to God. Shortly thereafter she was baptized by immersion in the sea and was received as a member of the Methodist Church. With other members of her family she attended the Adventist meetings in Portland, which began in 1840. She accepted fully the views of the nearness of the second advent of Christ presented by William Miller and his associates, and confidently looked for the Saviour's imminent return.

The keenness of the great disappointment of October 22, 1844, was not lessened by Ellen's youth. She, with others, in the succeeding days of perplexity, sought God earnestly for light and guidance. One morning in December, 1844, while praying with four women, the power of God rested upon her. At first she was lost to earthly things; then in a figurative revelation she witnessed the travels of the Advent people to the city of God. She was also shown the reward of the faithful. With trembling, the seventeen-year-old girl related this and succeeding visions to her fellow believers in Portland. Then, as opportunity afforded, she recounted them to companies of Adventists in Maine and near-by states.

In August, 1846, Ellen Harmon was united in marriage with James White, a youthful Adventist minister. Through the next thirty-five years Mrs. White's life was closely linked with that of her husband in strenuous gospel work until his death, August 6, 1881. They traveled extensively in the United States, preaching and writing, planting and building, organizing and administering. Time and test have proved how broad and firm were the foundations they laid, and how wisely and well they built. They led out among Sabbathkeeping Adventists in inaugurating the publishing work in 1849 and 1850, and in developing church organization with a sound system of church finance in the late fifties. This was culminated by the organization of the General Conference of Seventh-day Adventists in 1863. The middle sixties marked the beginnings of our medical work, and the great educational work of the denomination had its inception in the early seventies. The plan of holding annual camp meetings was developed in 1868, and in 1874 Seventh-day Adventists sent their first missionary abroad from the United States.

Leading in all of these advancements, as well as in the full development and operation of these lines of endeavor, were the messages of counsel, instruction, and encouragement which came to the church in oral discourse and from the tireless pen of Ellen G. White. At first the communications to the church reached the members by individual letters, or through articles in *Present Truth*. Then in 1851 Mrs. White issued her first book, a sixty-four-page work entitled, *A Sketch of the Christian Experience and Views of Ellen G. White*. Beginning with 1855 a series of numbered pamphlets was published, each bearing the title of *Testimony for the Church*. These made available messages of instruction and correction which, from time to time, God chose to send to bless, reprove, and guide His people. To meet the continued demand for this instruction, it was republished in 1885 in four bound books, and with the addition of other volumes, which appeared from

1889 to 1909, constitutes a set of nine volumes of *Testimonies for the Church.*

Though much of their time was spent in travel and public labor, Elder and Mrs. White resided in the Eastern states until 1855. For the next seventeen years they made their home in the State of Michigan. From 1872 to the time of Elder White's death in 1881, they resided largely in California. Although never too strong, Mrs. White through middle life enjoyed good health.

Four children were born to the Whites. The eldest boy, Henry, lived to the age of sixteen, the youngest boy, Herbert, died at the age of three months. The two middle boys, Edson and William, lived to maturity and each engaged actively in the work of the Seventh-day Adventist denomination.

In response to the request of the General Conference, Mrs. White went to Europe in the summer of 1885. There she spent two years in strengthening the newly developed work on the Continent. Making her home at Basel, Swizerland, she traveled extensively through Southern, Central, and Northern Europe, attending the general gatherings of the church and meeting with believers in their congregations. Four years were then spent in the United States. In 1891, in response to the call of the General Conference, she sailed to Australia. There she resided for nine years and aided in pioneering and developing the work, especially in educational and medical lines, in the great Australasian field. Mrs. White returned to the United States in 1900 and made her home on the West Coast at St. Helena, California, until her death in 1915.

During her entire lifetime of service Mrs. White's influence was felt throughout the ranks of Seventh-day Adventists. She visited churches, took part in the General Conference sessions, and, when possible, the camp meetings. Often such labor took her from one camp meeting to another through an entire season, when she addressed the church members and large gatherings of the general public.

For several decades articles from her pen appeared regularly in the journals of the denomination. These weekly, inspired messages exerted a quiet but large molding influence. From time to time her books came from the press to be eagerly read and reread. The task of setting before the church and the world the instruction and the information which had been imparted to her through vision was a lifetime work. The visions continued all through her life's experience. Early among these, in 1858, was the comprehensive basic vision of *The Great Controversy*. Within six months of the revelation, the matter was ready for the public in the form of the little book *Spiritual Gifts,* volume 1, "The Great Controversy Between Christ and His Angels and Satan and His Angels" *(Early Writings,* part 3). In many succeeding visions the great controversy account was opened up in greater detail, and Mrs. White rewrote it, first in the seventies and eighties in the four volumes of the *Spirit of Prophecy* and later in the volumes of the Conflict of the Ages Series—*Patriarchs and Prophets, Prophets and Kings, The Desire of Ages, Acts of the Apostles,* and *The Great Controversy*. Other works from Mrs. White's pen which have exerted a wide, molding influence are *The Ministry of Healing, Christ's Object Lessons, Education, Thoughts From the Mount of Blessing,* and half a score of volumes devoted to special lines of counsel, as *Gospel Workers, Colporteur Evangelist, Counsels to Parents, Teachers, and Students,* etc. The well-known work *Steps to Christ* has been read by millions in sixty languages.

In 1909 Mrs. White, at the age of eighty-one, attended the General Conference session held in Washington, D. C. This was her last transcontinental journey. The succeeding five years were devoted to the preparing of articles for the denominational journals and to the publication of her books. Near the close of her life she declared: "Whether or not my life is spared, my writings will constantly speak, and their work will go forward as long as time shall last."—*Writing and Sending Out of the Testimonies for the Church,* pages 12, 13.

Although Mrs. White remained active in literary work until early 1915, she did not, during the last three years of her life, labor under the great burden of writing which had characterized her work through the long years of her life. With undaunted courage and in full confidence in her Redeemer, she fell asleep at her own home, July 16, 1915, and was laid to rest by the side of her husband and children at the Oak Hill Cemetery in Battle Creek, Michigan.

Seventh-day Adventists understood, and today understand, Mrs. White's ministry as the "messenger of the Lord" to be in fulfillment of the prophecy of Revelation 12:17 and 19:10, that the remnant church "which keep the commandments of God" was to "have the testimony of Jesus"—"the spirit of prophecy." They see in her work the gift of prophecy of which Paul speaks in Ephesians 4:9-13 placed with other gifts in the church "for the perfecting of the saints" and "the edifying of the body of Christ: till we all come in the unity of the faith."

The revelations given to her through her long life were in harmony with God's appointed means declared to Israel: "If there be a prophet among you, I the Lord will make Myself known unto him in a vision, and will speak unto him in a dream." Numbers 12:6. In character her work was much like that of the leader of Israel of old, of whom it is recorded in Hosea 12:13: "By a prophet the Lord brought Israel out of Egypt, and by a prophet was he preserved."

Mrs. White was known by her neighbors and friends as an earnest, godly, Christian woman. For an appraisal of her life and work as it was known by those about her, we turn to the *American Biographical History* and find its editor in 1878 stating:

"Mrs. White is a woman of singularly well-balanced mental organization. Benevolence, spirituality, conscientiousness, and ideality are the predominating traits. Her personal qualities are such as to win for her the warmest friendship of all with whom she comes in contact, and to inspire them with the utmost confidence in her sincerity. . . . Notwithstanding her many years of public labor, she has retained all the simplicity and honesty which characterized her early life.

"As a speaker, Mrs. White is one of the most successful of the few ladies who have become noteworthy as lecturers, in this country, during the last twenty years. Constant use has so strengthened her vocal organs as to give her voice rare depth and power. Her clearness and strength of articulation are so great that, when speaking in the open air, she has frequently been distinctly heard at the distance of a mile. Her language, though simple, is always forcible and elegant. When inspired with her subject, she is often marvelously eloquent, holding the largest audiences spellbound for hours without a sign of impatience or weariness.

"The subject matter of her discourses is always of a practical character, bearing chiefly on fireside duties, the religious education of children, temperance, and kindred topics. On revival occasions she is always the most effective speaker. She has frequently spoken to immense audiences, in the large cities, on her favorite themes, and has always been received with great favor. On one occasion, in Massachusetts, twenty thousand persons listened to her, with close attention, for more than an hour.

"Mrs. White is the author of numerous works which have had a wide circulation. Her writings are characterized by the same simplicity and practical nature which are conspicuous in her speaking. They enter into the home life of the family circle in a manner which rivets the attention of the candid reader, and cannot fail to instruct in the solemn duties of practical life."—*American Biographical History of Eminent and Self-Made Men of the State of Michigan (Third Congressional District)*, page 108.

By her fellow workers, the church, and the members of

her family, Mrs. White was esteemed and honored as a devoted mother and as an earnest, generous, tireless religious worker. She never held official church office. Never did she ask others to look to her, nor did she ever use her gift to build herself financially or in popularity. Her life and all that she had was dedicated to the cause of God.

On her death the editor of a popular weekly magazine closed his comments on her fruitful life with these words: "She was absolutely honest in her belief in her revelations. Her life was worthy of them. She showed no spiritual pride, and she sought no filthy lucre. She lived the life and did the work of a worthy prophetess."—*The Independent,* Aug. 23, 1915.

For a more detailed account of Mrs. White's life and work the reader is directed to *The Christian Experience and Teachings of Ellen G. White.*

THE TRUSTEES OF THE
ELLEN G. WHITE PUBLICATIONS.

Faith in God

When at Battle Creek, Michigan, May 5, 1855, I saw that there was a great lack of faith with the servants of God, as well as with the church. They were too easily discouraged, too ready to doubt God, too willing to believe that they had a hard lot and that God had forsaken them. I saw that this was cruel. God so loved them as to give His dearly beloved Son to die for them, and all heaven was interested in their salvation; yet after all that had been done for them, it was hard to believe and trust so kind and good a Father. He has said that He is more willing to give the Holy Spirit to them that ask Him, than earthly parents are to give good gifts to their children. I saw that the servants of God and the church were too easily discouraged. When they asked their Father in heaven for things which they thought they needed, and these did not immediately come, their faith wavered, their courage fled, and a murmuring feeling took possession of them. This, I saw, displeased God.

Every saint who comes to God with a true heart, and sends his honest petitions to Him in faith, will have his prayers answered. Your faith must not let go of the promises of God, if you do not see or feel the immediate answer to your prayers. Be not afraid to trust God. Rely upon His sure promise: "Ask, and ye shall receive." John 16:24. God is too wise to err, and too good to withhold any good thing from His saints that walk uprightly. Man is erring, and although his petitions are sent up from an honest heart, he does not always ask for the things that are good for himself, or that will glorify God. When this is so, our wise and good Father

1855, vol. 1, pp. 120, 121.

hears our prayers, and will answer, sometimes immediately; but He gives us the things that are for our best good and His own glory. God gives us blessings; if we could look into His plan, we would clearly see that He knows what is best for us and that our prayers are answered. Nothing hurtful is given, but the blessing we need, in the place of something we asked for that would not be good for us, but to our hurt.

I saw that if we do not feel immediate answers to our prayers, we should hold fast our faith, not allowing distrust to come in, for that will separate us from God. If our faith wavers, we shall receive nothing from Him. Our confidence in God should be strong; and when we need it most, the blessing will fall upon us like a shower of rain.

When the servants of God pray for His Spirit and blessing, it sometimes comes immediately; but it is not always then bestowed. At such times, faint not. Let your faith hold fast the promise that it will come. Let your trust be fully in God, and often that blessing will come when you need it most, and you will unexpectedly receive help from God when you are presenting the truth to unbelievers, and will be enabled to speak the word with clearness and power.

It was represented to me like children asking a blessing of their earthly parents who love them. They ask something that the parent knows will hurt them; the parent gives them the things that will be good and healthful for them, in the place of that which they desired. I saw that every prayer which is sent up in faith from an honest heart will be heard of God and answered, and the one that sent up the petition will have the blessing when he needs it most, and it will often exceed his expectations. Not a prayer of a true saint is lost if sent up in faith from an honest heart.

Prepare to Meet the Lord

I SAW that we should not put off the coming of the Lord. Said the angel: "Prepare, prepare, for what is coming upon the earth. Let your works correspond with your faith." I saw that the mind must be stayed upon God, and that our influence should tell for God and His truth. We cannot honor the Lord when we are careless and indifferent. We cannot glorify Him when we are desponding. We must be in earnest to secure our own soul's salvation, and to save others. All importance should be attached to this, and everything besides should come in secondary.

I saw the beauty of heaven. I heard the angels sing their rapturous songs, ascribing praise, honor, and glory to Jesus. I could then realize something of the wondrous love of the Son of God. He left all the glory, all the honor which He had in heaven, and was so interested for our salvation that He patiently and meekly bore every indignity and slight which man could heap upon Him. He was wounded, smitten, and bruised; He was stretched on Calvary's cross and suffered the most agonizing death to save us from death, that we might be washed in His blood and be raised up to live with Him in the mansions He is preparing for us, to enjoy the light and glory of heaven, to hear the angels sing, and to sing with them.

I saw that all heaven is interested in our salvation; and shall we be indifferent? Shall we be careless, as though it were a small matter whether we are saved or lost? Shall we slight the sacrifice that has been made for us? Some have done this. They have trifled with offered mercy, and the

1855, vol. 1, pp. 123-126.

frown of God is upon them. God's Spirit will not always be grieved. It will depart if grieved a little longer. After all has been done that God could do to save men, if they show by their lives that they slight Jesus' offered mercy, death will be their portion, and it will be dearly purchased. It will be a dreadful death; for they will have to feel the agony that Christ felt upon the cross to purchase for them the redemption which they have refused. And they will then realize what they have lost—eternal life and the immortal inheritance. The great sacrifice that has been made to save souls shows us their worth. When the precious soul is once lost, it is lost forever.

THE ANGEL WITH THE SCALES

I have seen an angel standing with scales in his hands weighing the thoughts and interest of the people of God, especially the young. In one scale were the thoughts and interest tending heavenward; in the other were the thoughts and interest tending to earth. And in this scale were thrown all the reading of storybooks, thoughts of dress and show, vanity, pride, etc. Oh, what a solemn moment! the angels of God standing with scales, weighing the thoughts of His professed children—those who claim to be dead to the world and alive to God. The scale filled with thoughts of earth, vanity, and pride quickly went down, notwithstanding weight after weight rolled from the scale. The one with the thoughts and interest tending to heaven went quickly up as the other went down, and oh, how light it was! I can relate this as I saw it; but never can I give the solemn and vivid impression stamped upon my mind, as I saw the angel with the scales weighing the thoughts and interest of the people of God. Said the angel: "Can such enter heaven? No, no, never. Tell them the hope they now possess is vain, and unless they speedily repent, and obtain salvation, they must perish."

A form of godliness will not save any. All must have a deep and living experience. This alone will save them in the time of trouble. Then their work will be tried of what sort it is; and if it is gold, silver, and precious stones, they will be hid as in the secret of the Lord's pavilion. But if their work is wood, hay, and stubble, nothing can shield them from the fierceness of Jehovah's wrath.

The young, as well as those who are older, will be required to give a reason for their hope. But the mind, designed by God for better things, formed to serve Him perfectly, has dwelt upon foolish things, instead of eternal interests. That mind which is left to wander here and there is just as well able to understand the truth, the evidence from the word of God for keeping the Sabbath, and the true foundation of the Christian's hope, as to study the appearance, the manners, the dress, etc. And those who give up the mind to be diverted with foolish stories and idle tales, have the imagination fed, but the brilliancy of God's word is eclipsed to them. The mind is led directly from God. The interest in His precious word is destroyed.

OUR GUIDEBOOK

A book has been given us to guide our feet through the perils of this dark world to heaven. It tells us how we can escape the wrath of God, and also tells of the sufferings of Christ for us, the great sacrifice that has been made that we might be saved and enjoy the presence of God forever. And if any come short at last, having heard the truth as they have in this land of light, it will be their own fault; they will be without excuse. The word of God tells us how we may become perfect Christians and escape the seven last plagues. But they took no interest to find this out. Other things diverted the mind, idols were cherished by them, and God's Holy Word was neglected and slighted. God has been trifled with by professed Christians, and when His Holy Word shall judge them in the last day, they will be found wanting. That word which they have neglected for foolish storybooks, tries their lives. That is the standard; their motives, words, works, and the manner in which they use their time are all compared with the written word of God; and if they come short then, their cases are decided forever.

OUR ONLY PATTERN

I saw that many measure themselves among themselves, and compare their lives with the lives of others. This should not be. No one but Christ is given us as an example. He is our true Pattern, and each should strive to excel in imitating Him. We are co-workers with Christ, or co-workers with the enemy. We either gather with Christ or scatter abroad. We are decided, wholehearted Christians, or none at all. Says Christ: "I would thou wert cold or hot. So then because thou art lukewarm, and neither cold nor hot, I will spew thee out of My mouth." Revelation 3:15, 16.

I saw that some hardly know as yet what self-denial or sacrifice is, or what it is to suffer for the truth's sake. But none will enter heaven without making a sacrifice. A spirit of self-denial and sacrifice should be cherished. Some have not sacrificed themselves, their own bodies, on the altar of God. They indulge in hasty, fitful temper, gratify their appetites, and attend to their own self-interest, regardless of the cause of God. Those who are willing to make any sacrifice for eternal life, will have it; and it will be worth suffering for, worth crucifying self for, and sacrificing every idol for. The far more exceeding and eternal weight of glory swallows up everything and eclipses every earthly pleasure.

Parental Responsibility

I SAW that great responsibility rests upon parents. They must not be led by their children, but must lead them. I was referred to Abraham. He was faithful in his house. He commanded his household after him, and it was remembered of God.

I was then referred to the case of Eli. He restrained not his children, and they became wicked and vile, and by their wickedness led Israel astray. When God had made known to Samuel their sins, and the heavy curse that was to follow because Eli restrained them not, He said that their sins should not be purged with sacrifice nor offering forever. When told by Samuel what the Lord had shown him, Eli submitted, saying: "It is the Lord: let Him do what seemeth Him good." 1 Samuel 3:18. The curse of God soon followed. Those wicked priests were slain, and thirty thousand of Israel were also slain, and the ark of God was taken by their enemies. And when Eli heard that the ark of God was taken, he fell backward and died. All this evil resulted from Eli's neglect to restrain his sons. I saw that if God was so particular as to notice such things anciently, He will be no less particular in these last days.

Parents must govern their children, correct their passions, and subdue them, or God will surely destroy the children in the day of His fierce anger, and the parents who have not controlled their children will not be blameless. Especially should the servants of God govern their own families and have them in good subjection. I saw that they are not prepared to judge or decide in matters of the church, unless they

1855, vol. 1, pp. 118-120.

can rule well their own house. They must first have order at home, and then their judgment and influence will tell in the church.

I saw that the reason why visions have not been more frequent of late, is, they have not been appreciated by the church. The church have nearly lost their spirituality and faith, and the reproofs and warnings have had but little effect upon them. Many of those who have professed faith in them have not heeded them.

Some have taken an injudicious course; when they have talked their faith to unbelievers, and the proof has been asked for, they have read a vision, instead of going to the Bible for proof. I saw that this course was inconsistent, and prejudiced unbelievers against the truth. The visions can have no weight with those who have never seen them and know nothing of their spirit. They should not be referred to in such cases.

Thy Brother's Keeper

November 20, 1855, while in prayer, the Spirit of the Lord came suddenly and powerfully upon me, and I was taken off in vision.

I saw that the Spirit of the Lord has been dying away from the church. The servants of the Lord have trusted too much to the strength of argument, and have not had that firm reliance upon God which they should have. I saw that the mere argument of the truth will not move souls to take a stand with the remnant; for the truth is unpopular. The servants of God must have the truth in the soul. Said the angel: "They must get it warm from glory, carry it in their bosoms, and pour it out in the warmth and earnestness of the soul to those that hear." A few that are conscientious are ready to decide from the weight of evidence; but it is impossible to move many with a mere theory of the truth. There must be a power to attend the truth, a living testimony to move them.

I saw that the enemy is busy to destroy souls. Exaltation has come into the ranks; there must be more humility. There is too much of an independence of spirit indulged in among the messengers. This must be laid aside, and there must be a drawing together of the servants of God. There has been too much of a spirit to ask, "Am I my brother's keeper?" Genesis 4:9. Said the angel: "Yea, *thou art* thy brother's keeper. Thou shouldest have a watchful care for thy brother, be interested for his welfare, and cherish a kind, loving spirit toward him. Press together, press together." God designed that man should be openhearted and honest, without affectation, meek, humble, with simplicity. This is the principle of

1855, vol. 1, pp. 113-115.

heaven; God ordered it so. But poor, frail man has sought out something different—to follow his own way, and carefully attend to his own self-interest.

I asked the angel why simplicity had been shut out from the church, and pride and exaltation had come in. I saw that this is the reason why we have almost been delivered into the hand of the enemy. Said the angel: "Look ye, and ye shall see that this feeling prevails: Am I my brother's keeper?" Again said the angel: "Thou art thy brother's keeper. Thy profession, thy faith, requires thee to deny thyself and sacrifice to God, or thou wilt be unworthy of eternal life; for it was purchased for thee dearly, even by the agony, the sufferings, and blood of the beloved Son of God."

SHACKLED BY EARTHLY POSSESSIONS

I saw that many in different places, East and West, were adding farm to farm, and land to land, and house to house, and they make the cause of God their excuse, saying they do this that they may help the cause. They shackle themselves so that they can be of but little benefit to the cause. Some buy a piece of land, and labor with all their might to pay for it. Their time is so occupied that they can spare but little time to pray, and serve God, and gain strength from Him to overcome their besetments. They are in debt, and when the cause needs their help they cannot assist; for they must get free from debt first. But as soon as they are free from debt they are farther from helping the cause than before; for they again involve themselves by adding to their property. They flatter themselves that this course is right, that they will use the avails in the cause, when they are actually laying up treasure here. They love the truth in word, but not in work. They love the cause just as much as their works show. They love the world more and the cause of God less; the attraction to earth grows stronger and the attraction to heaven weaker. Their heart is with their treasure. By their example they say to those around them that they are intending to stay here, that this world is their home. Said the angel: "Thou art thy brother's keeper."

Many have indulged in needless expense, merely to gratify the feelings, the taste, and the eye, when the cause needed the very means thus used, and when some of the servants of God were poorly clothed and were crippled in their labor for lack of means. Said the angel: "Their time to do will soon be past. Their works show that self is their idol, and to it they sacrifice." Self must first be gratified; their feeling is: "Am I my brother's keeper?" Warning after warning many have received, but heeded not. Self is the main object, and to it everything must bow.

I saw that the church has nearly lost the spirit of self-denial and sacrifice; they make self and self-interest first, and then they do for the cause what they think they can as well as not. Such a sacrifice, I saw, is lame, and not accepted of God. All should be interested to do their utmost to advance the cause. I saw that those who have no property, but have strength of body, are accountable to God for their strength. They should be diligent in business and fervent in spirit; they should not leave those that have possessions to do all the sacrificing. I saw that they can sacrifice, and that it is their duty to do so, as well as those who have property. But often those that have no possessions do not realize that they can deny themselves in many ways, can lay out less upon their bodies, and to gratify their tastes and appetites, and find much to spare for the cause, and thus lay up a treasure in heaven. I saw that there is loveliness and beauty in the truth; but take away the power of God, and it is powerless.

The Two Ways

At the Conference at Battle Creek, May 27, 1856, I was shown in vision some things that concern the church generally. The glory and majesty of God were made to pass before me. Said the angel: "He is terrible in His majesty, yet ye realize it not; terrible in His anger, yet ye offend Him daily. 'Strive to enter in at the strait gate;' 'for wide is the gate, and broad is the way, that leadeth to destruction, and many there be which go in thereat: because strait is the gate, and narrow is the way, which leadeth unto life, and few there be that find it.'" Luke 13:24; Matthew 7:13, 14. These roads are distinct, separate, in opposite directions. One leads to eternal life, the other to eternal death. I saw the distinction between these roads, also the distinction between the companies traveling them. The roads are opposite; one is broad and smooth, the other narrow and rugged. So the parties that travel them are opposite in character, in life, in dress, and in conversation.

Those who travel in the narrow way are talking of the joy and happiness they will have at the end of the journey. Their countenances are often sad, yet often beam with holy, sacred joy. They do not dress like the company in the broad road, nor talk like them, nor act like them. A pattern has been given them. A man of sorrows and acquainted with grief opened that road for them, and traveled it Himself. His followers see His footsteps, and are comforted and cheered. He went through safely; so can they, if they follow in His footsteps.

In the broad road all are occupied with their persons, their dress, and the pleasures in the way. They indulge freely in

1856, vol. 1, pp. 127-131.

hilarity and glee, and think not of their journey's end, of the certain destruction at the end of the path. Every day they approach nearer their destruction; yet they madly rush on faster and faster. Oh, how dreadful this looked to me!

I saw many traveling in this broad road who had the words written upon them: "Dead to the world. The end of all things is at hand. Be ye also ready." They looked just like all the vain ones around them, except a shade of sadness which I noticed upon their countenances. Their conversation was just like that of the gay, thoughtless ones around them; but they would occasionally point with great satisfaction to the letters on their garments, calling for the others to have the same upon theirs. They were in the broad way, yet they professed to be of the number who were traveling the narrow way. Those around them would say: "There is no distinction between us. We are alike; we dress, and talk, and act alike."

AN UNAPPRECIATED BLESSING

Then I was pointed back to the years 1843 and 1844. There was a spirit of consecration then that there is not now. What has come over the professed peculiar people of God? I saw the conformity to the world, the unwillingness to suffer for the truth's sake. I saw a great lack of submission to the will of God. I was pointed back to the children of Israel after they left Egypt. God in mercy called them out from the Egyptians, that they might worship Him without hindrance or restraint. He wrought for them in the way by miracles, He proved and tried them by bringing them into strait places. After the wonderful dealings of God with them, and their deliverance so many times, they murmured when tried or proved by Him. Their language was: "Would to God we had died by the hand of the Lord in the land of Egypt." Exodus 16:3. They lusted for the leeks and onions there.

I saw that many who profess to believe the truth for these

last days think it strange that the children of Israel murmured as they journeyed; that after the wonderful dealings of God with them, they should be so ungrateful as to forget what He had done for them. Said the angel: "Ye have done worse than they." I saw that God has given His servants the truth so clear, so plain, that it cannot be resisted. Wherever they go, they have certain victory. Their enemies cannot get round the convincing truth. Light has been shed so clear that the servants of God can stand up anywhere and let truth, clear and connected, bear away the victory. This great blessing has not been prized, or even realized. If any trial arises, some begin to look back and think they have a hard time. Some of the professed servants of God do not know what purifying trials are. They sometimes make trials for themselves, imagine trials, and are so easily discouraged, so easily hurt, self-dignity is so quick to feel, that they injure themselves, injure others, and injure the cause. Satan magnifies their trials and puts thoughts into their minds that if given way to, will destroy their influence and usefulness.

Some have felt tempted to take themselves from the work, to labor with their hands. I saw that if the hand of God should be taken from them, and they be left subject to disease and death, then they would know what trouble is. It is a fearful thing to murmur against God. They do not bear in mind that the way which they are traveling is a rugged, self-denying, self-crucifying way, and they must not expect everything to move on as smoothly as though they were traveling in the broad road.

I saw that some of the servants of God, even ministers, are so easily discouraged, self is so quickly hurt, that they imagine themselves slighted and injured when it is not so. They think their lot hard. Such realize not how they would feel should the sustaining hand of God be withdrawn, and they pass through anguish of soul. They would then find their lot tenfold harder than it was before, while they were employed in the work of God, suffering trials and privations, yet withal having the Lord's approbation. Some that are laboring in the cause of God know not when they do have an easy time. They have had so few privations and know so little of want or wearing labor or burden of soul that when they have an easy time, when they are favored of God and almost entirely free from anguish of spirit, they know it not and think their trials great. I saw that unless such have a spirit of self-sacrifice, and are ready to labor cheerfully, not sparing themselves, God will release them. He will not acknowledge them as His self-sacrificing servants, but will raise up those who will labor, not slothfully, but in earnest, and will know when they have an easy time. God's servants must feel the burden of souls and weep between the porch and the altar, crying: "Spare Thy people, O Lord." Joel 2:17.

Some of the servants of God have given up their lives to spend and be spent for the cause of God, until their constitutions are broken down, and they are almost worn out with mental labor, incessant care, toil, and privations. Others have not had and would not take the burden upon them. Yet just such ones think they have a hard time, because they have never experienced hardships. They never have been baptized into the suffering part, and never will be as long as they manifest so much weakness and so little fortitude, and love their ease so well. From what God has shown me, there needs to be a scourging among the ministers, that the slothful, dilatory, and self-caring ones may be scourged out, and there remain a pure, faithful, and self-sacrificing company who will not study their ease, but will minister faithfully in word and doctrine, willing to suffer and endure all things for Christ's sake, and to save those for whom He died. Let these servants feel the woe upon them if they preach not the gospel, and it will be enough; but all do not feel this.

Wives of Ministers

I SAW the wives of the ministers. Some of them are no help to their husbands, yet they profess the third angel's message. They think more of studying their own wishes and pleasure than the will of God, or how they can hold up the hands of their husbands by their faithful prayers and careful walk. I saw that some of them take so willful and selfish a course that Satan makes them his instruments and works through them to destroy the influence and usefulness of their husbands. They feel at liberty to complain and murmur if they are brought through any strait places. They forget the sufferings of the ancient Christians for the truth's sake and think that they must have their wishes and way, and follow their own will. They forget the suffering of Jesus, their Master. They forget the Man of Sorrows, who was acquainted with grief—He who had not where to lay His head. They do not care to remember that holy brow, pierced with a crown of thorns. They forget Him, who, bearing His own cross to Calvary, fainted beneath its burden. Not merely the burden of the wooden cross, but the heavy burden of the sins of the world, was upon Him. They forget the cruel nails driven through His tender hands and feet, and His expiring, agonizing cries: "My God, My God, why hast Thou forsaken Me?" Matthew 27:46; Mark 15:34. After all this suffering endured for them, they feel a strong unwillingness to suffer for Christ's sake.

These persons, I saw, are deceiving themselves. They have no part nor lot in the matter. They have hold of the truth; but the truth has not hold of them. When the truth, the

1856, vol. 1, pp. 137-140.

solemn, important truth, gets hold of them, self will die; then the language will not be, "I will go there, I will not stay here;" but the earnest inquiry will be, "Where does God want me to be? Where can I best glorify Him, and where can our united labors do the most good?" Their will should be swallowed up in the will of God. The willfullness and lack of consecration that some of the ministers' wives manifest will stand in the way of sinners; the blood of souls will be upon their garments. Some of the ministers have borne a strong testimony in regard to the duty and the wrongs of the church; but it has not had its designed effect, for their own companions needed all the straight testimony that had been borne, and the reproof came back upon themselves with great weight. They let their companions affect them and drag them down, prejudicing their minds, and their usefulness and influence are lost; they feel desponding and disheartened, and realize not the true source of the injury. It is close at home.

WIVES AS CO-WORKERS

These sisters are closely connected with the work of God if He has called their husbands to preach the present truth. These servants, if truly called of God, will feel the importance of the truth. They are standing between the living and the dead, and must watch for souls as they that must give an account. Solemn is their calling, and their companions can be a great blessing or a great curse to them. They can cheer them when desponding, comfort them when cast down, and encourage them to look up and trust fully in God when their faith fails. Or they can take an opposite course, look upon the dark side, think they have a hard time, exercise no faith in God, talk their trials and unbelief to their companions, indulge a complaining, murmuring spirit, and be a dead weight and even a curse to them.

I saw that the wives of the ministers should help their

husbands in their labors and be exact and careful what influence they exert, for they are watched, and more is expected of them than of others. Their dress should be an example. Their lives and conversation should be an example, savoring of life rather than of death. I saw that they should take a humble, meek, yet exalted stand, not having their conversation upon things that do not tend to direct the mind heavenward. The great inquiry should be: "How can I save my own soul, and be the means of saving others?" I saw that no half-hearted work in this matter is accepted of God. He wants the whole heart and interest, or He will have none. Their influence tells, decidedly, unmistakably, in favor of the truth or against it. They gather with Jesus, or scatter abroad. An unsanctified wife is the greatest curse that a minister can have. Those servants of God that have been and are still so unhappily situated as to have this withering influence at home, should double their prayers and their watchfulness, take a firm, decided stand, and let not this darkness press them down. They should cleave closer to God, be firm and decided, rule well their own house, and live so that they can have the approbation of God and the watchcare of the angels. But if they yield to the wishes of their unconsecrated companions, the frown of God is brought upon the dwelling. The ark of God cannot abide in the house, because they countenance and uphold them in their wrongs.

Our God is a jealous God. It is a fearful thing to trifle with Him. Anciently, Achan coveted a golden wedge and a Babylonish garment, and secreted them, and all Israel suffered; they were driven before their enemies. And when Joshua inquired the cause, the Lord said: "Up, sanctify the people, and say, Sanctify yourselves against tomorrow: for thus saith the Lord God of Israel, There is an accursed thing in the midst of thee, O Israel: thou canst not stand before thine enemies, until ye take away the accursed thing from among you." Joshua 7:13. Achan had sinned, and God destroyed him and all his household, with all they possessed, and wiped the curse from Israel.

I saw that the Israel of God must arise and renew their strength in God by renewing and keeping their covenant with Him. Covetousness, selfishness, love of money, and love of the world, are all through the ranks of Sabbathkeepers. These evils are destroying the spirit of sacrifice among God's people. Those that have this covetousness in their hearts are not aware of it. It has gained upon them imperceptibly, and unless it is rooted out, their destruction will be as sure as was Achan's. Many have taken the sacrifice from God's altar. They love the world, love its gain and increase, and, unless there is an entire change in them, they will perish with the world. God has lent them means; it is not their own, but God has made them His stewards. And because of this, they call it their own and hoard it up. But, oh, how quick, when the prospering hand of God is removed from them, it is all snatched away in a moment! There must be a sacrificing for God, a denying of self for the truth's sake. Oh, how weak and frail is man! How puny his arm! I saw that soon the loftiness of man is to be brought down, and the pride of man humbled. Kings and nobles, rich and poor, alike shall bow, and the withering plagues of God shall fall upon them.

Be Zealous and Repent

Dear Brethren and Sisters: The Lord has shown me in vision some things concerning the church in its present lukewarm state, which I will relate to you. The church was presented before me in vision. Said the angel to the church: "Jesus speaks to thee, 'Be zealous and repent.'" This work, I saw, should be taken hold of in earnest. There is something to repent of. Worldly-mindedness, selfishness, and covetousness have been eating out the spirituality and life of God's people.

The danger of God's people for a few years past has been the love of the world. Out of this have sprung the sins of selfishness and covetousness. The more they get of this world, the more they set their affections on it; and still they reach out for more. Said the angel: "It is easier for a camel to go through a needle's eye, than for a rich man to enter into the kingdom of God." Luke 18:25. Yet many who profess to believe that we are having the last note of warning to the world, are striving with all their energies to place themselves in a position where it is easier for a camel to go through a needle's eye than for them to enter the kingdom.

These earthly treasures are blessings when rightly used. Those who have them should realize that they are lent them of God and should cheerfully spend their means to advance His cause. They will not lose their reward here. They will be kindly regarded by the angels of God and will also lay up a treasure in heaven.

I saw that Satan watches the peculiar, selfish, covetous

1857, vol. 1, pp. 141-146.

temperament of some who profess the truth, and he will tempt them by throwing prosperity in their path, offering them the riches of earth. He knows that if they do not overcome their natural temperament, they will stumble and fall by loving mammon, worshiping their idol. Satan's object is often accomplished. The strong love of the world overcomes, or swallows up, the love of the truth. The kingdoms of the world are offered them, and they eagerly grasp their treasure and think they are wonderfully prospered. Satan triumphs because his plan has succeeded. They have given up the love of God for the love of the world.

THE LOVE OF THE WORLD

I saw that those who are thus prospered can thwart the design of Satan if they will overcome their selfish covetousness by laying all their possessions upon the altar of God. And when they see where means are needed to advance the cause of truth and to help the widow, the fatherless, and afflicted, they should give cheerfully and thus lay up treasure in heaven.

Heed the counsel of the True Witness. Buy gold tried in the fire, that thou mayest be rich, white raiment that thou mayest be clothed, and eyesalve that thou mayest see. Make some effort. These precious treasures will not drop upon us without some exertion on our part. We must buy—"be zealous and repent" of our lukewarm state. We must be awake to see our wrongs, to search for our sins, and to zealously repent of them.

I saw that the brethren who have possessions have a work to do to tear away from these earthly treasures and to overcome their love of the world. Many of them love this world, love their treasure, but are not willing to see it. They must be zealous and repent of their selfish covetousness, that the love of the truth may swallow up everything else. I saw that many of those who have riches will fail to buy the gold, white raiment, and eyesalve. Their zeal does not possess intensity and earnestness proportionate to the value of the object of which they are in pursuit.

I saw these men while striving for the possessions of earth; what zeal they manifested, what earnestness, what energy to obtain an earthly treasure that must soon pass away! What cool calculations they made! They plan and toil early and late, and sacrifice their ease and comfort for earthly treasure. A corresponding zeal on their part to obtain the gold, white raiment, and eyesalve will bring them in possession of these desirable treasures and life, everlasting life, in the kingdom of God. I saw that if any need eyesalve, it is those who have earthly possessions. Many of them are blind to their own state, blind to their firm grasp upon this world. Oh, that they may see!

"Behold, I stand at the door, and knock: if any man hear My voice, and open the door, I will come in to him, and will sup with him, and he with Me." Revelation 3:20. I saw that many have so much rubbish piled up at the door of their heart that they cannot get the door open. Some have difficulties between themselves and their brethren to remove. Others have evil tempers, selfish covetousness, to remove before they can open the door. Others have rolled the world before the door of their heart, which bars the door. All this rubbish must be taken away, and then they can open the door and welcome the Saviour in.

Oh, how precious was this promise, as it was shown to me in vision! "I will come in to him, and will sup with him, and he with Me." Oh, the love, the wondrous love of God! After all our lukewarmness and sins He says: "Return unto Me, and I will return unto thee, and will heal all thy backslidings." This was repeated by the angel a number of times. "Return unto Me, and I will return unto thee, and will heal all thy backslidings."

Some, I saw, would gladly return. Others will not let this

message to the Laodicean church have its weight upon them. They will glide along, much after the same manner as before, and will be spewed out of the mouth of the Lord. Those only who zealously repent will have favor with God.

"To him that overcometh will I grant to sit with Me in My throne, even as I also overcame, and am set down with My Father in His throne." Revelation 3:21. We can overcome. Yes; fully, entirely. Jesus died to make a way of escape for us, that we might overcome every evil temper, every sin, every temptation, and sit down at last with Him.

It is our privilege to have faith and salvation. The power of God has not decreased. His power, I saw, would be just as freely bestowed now as formerly. It is the church of God that have lost their faith to claim, their energy to wrestle, as did Jacob, crying: "I will not let Thee go, except Thou bless me." Genesis 32:26. Enduring faith has been dying away. It must be revived in the hearts of God's people. There must be a claiming of the blessing of God. Faith, living faith, always bears upward to God and glory; unbelief, downward to darkness and death.

MANUFACTURING TRIALS

I saw that the minds of some of the church have not run in the right channel. There have been some peculiar temperaments that have had their notions by which to measure their brethren. And if any did not exactly agree with them, there was trouble in the camp at once. Some have strained at a gnat and swallowed a camel.

These set notions have been humored and indulged altogether too long. There has been a picking at straws. And when there were no real difficulties in the church, trials have been manufactured. The minds of the church and the servants of the Lord are called from God, truth, and heaven to dwell upon darkness. Satan delights to have such things go on; it feasts him. But these are none of the trials which are to purify the church and that will in the end increase the strength of God's people.

I saw that some are withering spiritually. They have lived some time watching to keep their brethren straight—watching for every fault to make trouble with them. And while doing this, their minds are not on God, nor on heaven, nor on the truth; but just where Satan wants them—on someone else. Their souls are neglected; they seldom see or feel their own faults, for they have had enough to do to watch the faults of others without so much as looking to their own souls or searching their own hearts. A person's dress, bonnet, or apron takes their attention. They must talk to this one or that one, and it is sufficient to dwell upon for weeks. I saw that all the religion a few poor souls have consists in watching the garments and acts of others, and finding fault with them. Unless they reform, there will be no place in heaven for them, for they would find fault with the Lord Himself.

Said the angel: "It is an individual work to be right with God." The work is between God and our own souls. But when persons have so much care of others' faults, they take no care of themselves. These notional, faultfinding ones would often cure themselves of the habit if they would go directly to the individual they think is wrong. It would be so crossing that they would give up their notions rather than go. But it is easy to let the tongue run freely about this one or that one when the accused is not present.

ORDER IN WORSHIP

Some think it is wrong to try to observe order in the worship of God. But I have seen that it is not dangerous to observe order in the church of God. I have seen that confusion is displeasing to the Lord, and that there should be order in praying and also in singing. We should not come to the house of God to pray for our families unless deep feeling shall lead us while the Spirit of God is convicting them.

Generally, the proper place to pray for our families is at the family altar. When the subjects of our prayers are at a distance, the closet is the proper place to plead with God for them. When in the house of God, we should pray for a present blessing and should expect God to hear and answer our prayers. Such meetings will be lively and interesting.

I saw that all should sing with the Spirit and with the understanding also. God is not pleased with jargon and discord. Right is always more pleasing to Him than wrong. And the nearer the people of God can approach to correct, harmonious singing, the more is He glorified, the church benefited, and unbelievers favorably affected.

I have been shown the order, the perfect order, of heaven, and have been enraptured as I listened to the perfect music there. After coming out of vision, the singing here has sounded very harsh and discordant. I have seen companies of angels, who stood in a hollow square, everyone having a harp of gold. At the end of the harp was an instrument to turn to set the harp or change the tunes. Their fingers did not sweep over the strings carelessly, but they touched different strings to produce different sounds. There is one angel who always leads, who first touches the harp and strikes the note, then all join in the rich, perfect music of heaven. It cannot be described. It is melody, heavenly, divine, while from every countenance beams the image of Jesus, shining with glory unspeakable.

God's people are not to be in confusion, lacking order and harmony, consistency and beauty. The Lord is greatly dishonored when disunion exists among His people. Truth is a unit. The unity that God requires must be cultivated day by day if we would answer the prayer of Christ. The disunion that is striving for existence among those who profess to believe the last message of mercy to be given to the world, must find no place; for it would be a fearful hindrance to the advancement of God's work. His servants are to be one, as Christ is one with the Father; their powers, illuminated, inspired, and sanctified, must be united to make a complete whole. Those who love God and keep His commandments are not to draw apart; they are to press together.—1904, vol. 8, pp. 174, 175.

Young Sabbathkeepers

August 22, 1857, at the house of prayer in Monterey, Michigan, I was shown that many have not yet heard the voice of Jesus, and the saving message has not taken hold of the soul and worked a reformation in the life. Many of the young have not the spirit of Jesus. The love of God is not in their hearts, therefore all the natural besetments hold the victory instead of the Spirit of God and salvation.

Those who really possess the religion of Jesus will not be ashamed nor afraid to bear the cross before those who have more experience than they. They will, if they earnestly long to be right, desire all the help they can get from older Christians. Gladly will they be helped by them; hearts that are warmed by love to God will not be hindered by trifles in the Christian course. They will talk out what the Spirit of God works in. They will sing it out, pray it out. It is the lack of religion, lack of holy living, that makes the young backward. Their life condemns them. They know they do not live as Christians should, therefore they have not confidence toward God, or before the church.

Why the young feel more liberty when the older ones are absent is: They are with those of their kind. Each thinks he is as good as the other. All fail of the mark, but measure themselves by themselves, and compare themselves among themselves, and neglect the only perfect and true standard. Jesus is the true Pattern. His self-sacrificing life is our example.

I saw how little the Pattern was studied, how little exalted before them. How little do the young suffer, or deny self,

1857, vol. 1, pp. 154-164.

for their religion! To sacrifice is scarcely thought of among them. They entirely fail of imitating the Pattern in this respect. I saw that the language of their lives is: Self must be gratified, pride must be indulged. They forget the Man of Sorrows, who was acquainted with grief. The sufferings of Jesus in Gethsemane, His sweating as it were great drops of blood in the garden, the platted crown of thorns that pierced His holy brow, do not move them. They have become benumbed. Their sensibilities are blunted, and they have lost all sense of the great sacrifice made for them. They can sit and listen to the story of the cross, hear how the cruel nails were driven through the hands and feet of the Son of God, and it does not stir the depths of the soul.

Said the angel: "If such should be ushered into the city of God, and told that all its rich beauty and glory was theirs to enjoy eternally, they would have no sense of how dearly that inheritance was purchased for them. They would never realize the matchless depths of a Saviour's love. They have not drunk of the cup, nor been baptized with the baptism. Heaven would be marred if such should dwell there. Those only who have partaken of the sufferings of the Son of God, and have come up through great tribulation, and have washed their robes and made them white in the blood of the Lamb, can enjoy the indescribable glory and unsurpassed beauty of heaven."

The want of this necessary preparation will shut out the greater portion of young professors, for they will not labor earnestly and zealously enough to obtain that rest that remains for the people of God. They will not honestly confess their sins, that they may be pardoned and blotted out. These sins in a short time will be revealed in just their enormity. God's eye does not slumber. He knows every sin that is hidden from mortal eye. The guilty know just what sins to confess that their souls may be clean before God. Jesus is now giving them opportunity to confess, to repent in deep humility, and purify their lives by obeying and living out the truth. Now is the time for wrongs to be righted and sins to be confessed, or they will appear before the sinner in the day of God's wrath.

PARENTS UNITED IN DISCIPLINE

Parents generally put too much confidence in their children; for often when the parents are confiding in them, they are in concealed iniquity. Parents, watch your children with a jealous care. Exhort, reprove, counsel them when you rise up and when you sit down, when you go out and when you come in, line upon line, precept upon precept, here a little, and there a little. Subdue your children when they are young. With many parents this is sadly neglected. They do not take as firm and decided a stand as they should in regard to their children. They suffer them to be like the world, to love dress, and associate with those who hate the truth and whose influence is poisonous. By so doing they encourage in their children a worldly disposition.

I saw that there should always be a fixed principle with Christian parents to be united in the government of their children. There is a fault in this respect with some parents—a lack of union. The fault is sometimes with the father, but oftener with the mother. The fond mother pets and indulges her children. The father's labor calls him from home often, and from the society of his children. The mother's influence tells. Her example does much toward forming the character of the children.

Some fond mothers suffer wrongs in their children which should not be allowed in them for a moment. The wrongs of the children are sometimes concealed from the father. Articles of dress or some other indulgence is granted by the mother with the understanding that the father is to know nothing about it, for he would reprove for these things.

Here a lesson of deception is effectually taught the children. Then if the father discovers these wrongs, excuses are made and but half the truth told. The mother is not openhearted. She does not consider as she should that the father has the same interest in the children as herself, and that he should not be kept ignorant of the wrongs or besetments that ought to be corrected in them while young. Things have been covered. The children know the lack of union in their parents, and it has its effect. The children begin young to deceive, cover up, tell things in a different light from what they are to their mother, as well as their father. Exaggeration becomes habit, and blunt falsehoods come to be told with but little conviction or reproof of conscience.

These wrongs commenced by the mother's concealing things from the father, who has an equal interest with her in the character their children are forming. The father should have been consulted freely. All should have been laid open to him. But the opposite course, taken to conceal the wrongs of the children, encourages in them a disposition to deceive, a lack of truthfulness and honesty.

The only hope of these children, whether they profess religion or not, is to be thoroughly converted. Their whole character must be changed. Thoughtless mother, do you know, as you teach your children, that their whole religious experience is affected by their teaching when young? Subdue them young; teach them to submit to you, and the more readily will they learn to yield obedience to the requirements of God. Encourage in them a truthful, honest disposition. Let them never have occasion to doubt your sincerity and exact truthfulness.

I saw that the young profess, but do not enjoy, the saving power of God. They lack religion, lack salvation. And, oh, the idle, unprofitable words they speak! There is a faithful, fearful record kept of them, and mortals will be judged according to the deeds done in the body. Young friends, your deeds and your idle words are written in the book. Your conversation has not been on eternal things, but upon this, that, and the other—common, worldly conversation that Christians should not engage in. It is all written in the book.

GENUINE CONVERSION NEEDED

I saw that unless there is an entire change in the young, a thorough conversion, they may despair of heaven. From what has been shown me, there are not more than half of the young who profess religion and the truth who have been truly converted. If they had been converted they would bear fruit to the glory of God. Many are leaning upon a supposed hope without a true foundation. The fountain is not cleansed, therefore the streams proceeding from that fountain are not pure. Cleanse the fountain, and the streams will be pure. If the heart is right, your words, your dress, your acts, will all be right. True godliness is lacking. I would not dishonor my Master so much as to admit that a careless, trifling, prayerless person is a Christian. No; a Christian has victory over his besetments, over his passions. There is a remedy for the sin-sick soul. That remedy is in Jesus. Precious Saviour! His grace is sufficient for the weakest; and the strongest must also have His grace or perish.

I saw how this grace could be obtained. Go to your closet, and there alone plead with God: "Create in me a clean heart, O God; and renew a right spirit within me." Psalm 51:10. Be in earnest, be sincere. Fervent prayer availeth much. Jacoblike, wrestle in prayer. Agonize. Jesus, in the garden, sweat great drops of blood; you must make an effort. Do not leave your closet until you feel strong in God; then watch, and just as long as you watch and pray you can keep these evil besetments under, and the grace of God can and will appear in you.

God forbid that I should cease to warn you. Young friends, seek the Lord with all your heart. Come with zeal, and when you sincerely feel that without the help of God you perish, when you pant after Him as the hart panteth after the water brooks, then will the Lord strengthen you speedily. Then will your peace pass all understanding. If you expect salvation, you must pray. Take time. Be not hurried and careless in your prayers. Beg of God to work in you a thorough reformation, that the fruits of His Spirit may dwell in you, and you shine as lights in the world. Be not a hindrance or curse to the cause of God; you can be a help, a blessing. Does Satan tell you that you cannot enjoy salvation, full and free? Believe him not.

I saw that it is the privilege of every Christian to enjoy the deep movings of the Spirit of God. A sweet, heavenly peace will pervade the mind, and you will love to meditate upon God and heaven. You will feast upon the glorious promises of His word. But know first that you have begun the Christian course. Know that the first steps are taken in the road to everlasting life. Be not deceived. I fear, yea, I know, that many of you know not what religion is. You have felt some excitement, some emotion, but have never seen sin in its enormity. You have never felt your undone condition and turned from your evil ways with bitter sorrow. You have never died to the world. You still love its pleasures; you love to engage in conversation on worldly matters. But when the truth of God is introduced, you have nothing to say. Why so silent? Why so talkative upon worldly things, and so silent upon the subject that should most concern you—a subject that should engage your whole soul? The truth of God does not dwell in you.

I saw that many are fair in their profession, while within is corruption. Deceive not yourselves, falsehearted professors. God looks at the heart. "Out of the abundance of the heart the mouth speaketh." Matthew 12:34. The world, I saw, is in the heart of such, but the religion of Jesus is not there. If professed Christians love Jesus better than the world, they will love to speak of Him, their best Friend, in whom their highest affections are centered. He came to their aid when they felt their lost and perishing condition. When weary and heavy-laden with sin, they turned unto Him. He removed their burden of guilt and sin, took away their sorrow and mourning, and turned the whole current of their affections. The things they once loved, they now hate; and the things they hated, they now love.

JESUS DEMANDS ALL

Has this great change taken place in you? Be not deceived. I would never name the name of Christ, or I would give Him my whole heart, my undivided affections. We should feel the deepest gratitude that Jesus will accept this offering. He demands all. When we are brought to yield to His claims, and give up all, then, and not till then, will He throw around us His arms of mercy. But what do we give when we give all? A sin-polluted soul for Jesus to purify, to cleanse by His mercy, and to save from death by His matchless love. And yet I saw that some thought it hard to give up all. I am ashamed to hear it spoken of, ashamed to write it.

Do you talk about self-denial? What did Christ give for us? When you think it hard that Christ requires all, go to Calvary, and weep there over such a thought. Behold the hands and feet of your Deliverer torn by the cruel nails that you may be washed from sin by His own blood!

Those who feel the constraining love of God do not ask how little may be given in order to obtain the heavenly reward; they ask not for the lowest standard, but aim at a perfect conformity to the will of their Redeemer. With ardent desire they yield *all,* and manifest zeal proportionate to the value of the object of which they are in pursuit. What is the object? Immortality, eternal life.

Young friends, many of you are sadly deceived. You have been satisfied with something short of pure and undefiled religion. I want to arouse you. The angels of God are trying to arouse you. Oh, that the important truths of the word of God may arouse you to a sense of your danger, and lead you to a thorough examination of yourselves! Your hearts are yet carnal. They are not subject to the law of God, neither indeed can be. These carnal hearts must be changed, and you see such beauty in holiness that you will pant after it as the hart panteth after the water brooks. Then you will love God and love His law. Then the yoke of Christ will be easy and His burden light. Although you will have trials, yet these trials, well borne, only make the way more precious. The immortal inheritance is for the self-denying Christian.

I saw that the Christian should not set too high a value, or depend too much, upon a happy flight of feeling. These feelings are not always true guides. It should be the study of every Christian to serve God from principle, and not be ruled by feeling. By so doing, faith will be brought into exercise, and will increase. I was shown that if the Christian lives a humble, self-sacrificing life, peace and joy in the Lord will be the result. But the greatest happiness experienced will be in doing others good, in making others happy. Such happiness will be lasting.

Many of the young have not a fixed principle to serve God. They do not exercise faith. They sink under every cloud. They have no power of endurance. They do not grow in grace. They appear to keep the commandments of God. They make now and then a formal prayer and are called Christians. Their parents are so anxious for them that they accept anything which appears favorable, and do not labor with them, and teach them that the carnal mind must die. They encourage them to come along and act a part; but they fail to lead them to search their own hearts diligently, to examine themselves, and to count the cost of what it is to be a Christian. The result is, the young profess to be Christians without sufficiently trying their motives.

Says the True Witness: "I would thou wert cold or hot.

So then because thou art lukewarm, and neither cold nor hot, I will spew thee out of My mouth." Revelation 3:15, 16. Satan is willing that you should be Christians in name, for you can suit his purpose better. If you have a form and not true godliness, he can use you to decoy others into the same self-deceived way. Some poor souls will look to you, instead of looking to the Bible standard, and will come up no higher. They are as good as you, and are satisfied.

The young are often urged to do duty, to speak or pray in meeting; urged to die to pride. Every step they are urged. Such religion is worth nothing. Let the carnal heart be changed, and it will not be such drudgery, ye coldhearted professors, to serve God. All that love of dress and pride of appearance will be gone. The time that you spend standing before the glass preparing the hair to please the eye, should be devoted to prayer and searching of heart. There will be no place for outward adornment in the sanctified heart; but there will be an earnest, anxious seeking for the inward adorning, the Christian graces—the fruits of the Spirit of God.

Says the apostle: "Whose adorning let it not be that outward adorning of plaiting the hair, and of wearing of gold, or of putting on of apparel; but let it be the hidden man of the heart, in that which is not corruptible, even the ornament of a meek and quiet spirit, which is in the sight of God of great price." 1 Peter 3:3, 4.

Subdue the carnal mind, reform the life, and the poor mortal frame will not be so idolized. If the heart is reformed, it will be seen in the outward appearance. If Christ be in us the hope of glory, we shall discover such matchless charms in Him that the soul will be enamored. It will cleave to Him, choose to love Him, and in admiration of Him, self will be forgotten. Jesus will be magnified and adored, and self abased and humbled. But a profession, without this deep love, is mere talk, dry formality, and heavy drudgery. Many of you may retain a notion of religion in the head, an outside religion, when the heart is not cleansed. God looks at the heart; "all things are naked and opened unto the eyes of Him with whom we have to do." Hebrews 4:13. Will He be satisfied with anything but truth in the inward parts? Every truly converted soul will carry the unmistakable marks that the carnal mind is subdued.

I speak plainly. I do not think this will discourage a true Christian; and I do not want any of you to come up to the time of trouble without a well-grounded hope in your Redeemer. Determine to know the worst of your case. Ascertain if you have an inheritance on high. Deal truly with your own soul. Remember that a church without spot, or wrinkle, or any such thing, will Jesus present to His Father.

How are you to know that you are accepted of God? Study His word prayerfully. Lay it not aside for any other book. This Book convinces of sin. It plainly reveals the way of salvation. It brings to view a bright and glorious reward. It reveals to you a complete Saviour, and teaches you that through His boundless mercy alone can you expect salvation.

Do not neglect secret prayer, for it is the soul of religion. With earnest, fervent prayer, plead for purity of soul. Plead as earnestly, as eagerly, as you would for your mortal life, were it at stake. Remain before God until unutterable longings are begotten within you for salvation, and the sweet evidence is obtained of pardoned sin.

The hope of eternal life is not to be received upon slight grounds. It is a subject to be settled between God and your own soul—settled for eternity. A supposed hope, and nothing more, will prove your ruin. Since you are to stand or fall by the word of God, it is to that word you must look for testimony in your case. There you can see what is required of you to become a Christian. Do not lay off your armor, or leave the battlefield until you have obtained the victory, and triumph in your Redeemer.

Treasure in Heaven

A STRICTLY honest, honorable course has not been taken by some. Such must take a very different course and work fast to redeem the time. Many Sabbathkeepers are at fault here. Advantage is taken even of their poor brethren, and those who have an abundance exact more than the real worth of things, more than they would pay for the same things, while these same brethren are embarrassed and distressed for want of means. God knows all these things. Every selfish act, every covetous extortion, will bring its reward.

I saw that it is cruel and unjust to have no consideration for a brother's situation. If he is distressed, or poor, yet doing the best he can, allowance should be made for him, and even the full value of things he may purchase of the wealthy should not be exacted; but they should have bowels of compassion for him. God will approve of such kindly acts, and the doer will not lose his reward. But a fearful account stands against many Sabbathkeepers for close, covetous acts.

I was pointed back to a time when there were but few who listened to and embraced the truth. They had not much of this world's goods. The wants of the cause were divided among a very few. Then it was necessary for some to sell their houses and lands, and obtain cheaper to serve them as a shelter, or home, while their means were freely and generously lent to the Lord, to publish the truth, and to otherwise aid in advancing the cause of God. As I beheld these self-sacrificing ones, I saw that they had endured privation for the benefit of the cause. I saw an angel standing by them, pointing them upward, and saying: "Ye have bags in heaven!

1857, vol. 1, pp. 176, 177 (The Rich Young Man).

Ye have bags in heaven that wax not old! Endure unto the end, and great will be your reward."

God has been moving upon many hearts. The truth for which a few sacrificed so much, in order to get it before others, has triumphed, and multitudes have laid hold of it. God in His providence has moved upon those who have means, and has brought them into the truth, that as His work increases, the wants of the cause may be met. Much means has been brought into the ranks of Sabbathkeepers, and I saw that at present God does not call for the houses His people need to live in, unless expensive houses are exchanged for cheaper ones. But if those who have an abundance do not hear His voice, cut loose from the world, and dispose of a portion of their property and lands, and sacrifice for God, He will pass them by, and call for those who are willing to do anything for Jesus, even to sell their homes to meet the wants of the cause. God will have freewill offerings. Those who give must esteem it a privilege to do so.

The Shaking

November 20, 1857, I was shown the people of God, and saw them mightily shaken. Some, with strong faith and agonizing cries, were pleading with God. Their countenances were pale, and marked with deep anxiety, expressive of their internal struggle. Firmness and great earnestness were expressed in their countenances, while large drops of perspiration fell from their foreheads. Now and then their faces would light up with the marks of God's approbation, and again the same solemn, earnest, anxious look would settle upon them.*

Evil angels crowded around them, pressing their darkness upon them, to shut out Jesus from their view, that their eyes

*"Blow the trumpet in Zion, sanctify a fast, call a solemn assembly: gather the people, sanctify the congregation, assemble the elders. . . . Let the priests, the ministers of the Lord, weep between the porch and the altar, and let them say, Spare Thy people, O Lord, and give not Thine heritage to reproach, that the heathen should rule over them: wherefore should they say among the people, Where is their God?" Joel 2:15-17.

"Submit yourselves therefore to God. Resist the devil, and he will flee from you. Draw nigh to God, and He will draw nigh to you. Cleanse your hands, ye sinners; and purify your hearts, ye double-minded. Be afflicted, and mourn, and weep: let your laughter be turned to mourning, and your joy to heaviness. Humble yourselves in the sight of the Lord, and He shall lift you up." James 4:7-10.

"Gather yourselves together, yea, gather together, O nation not desired; before the decree bring forth, before the day pass as the chaff, before the fierce anger of the Lord come upon you, before the day of the Lord's anger come upon you. Seek ye the Lord, all ye meek of the earth, which have wrought His judgment; seek righteousness, seek meekness: it may be ye shall be hid in the day of the Lord's anger." Zephaniah 2:1-3.

1857, vol. 1, pp. 179-184.

might be drawn to the darkness that surrounded them, and they distrust God and next murmur against Him. Their only safety was in keeping their eyes directed upward. Angels of God had charge over His people, and as the poisonous atmosphere from the evil angels was pressed around these anxious ones, the heavenly angels were continually wafting their wings over them, to scatter the thick darkness.

Some, I saw, did not participate in this work of agonizing and pleading. They seemed indifferent and careless. They were not resisting the darkness around them, and it shut them in like a thick cloud. The angels of God left these, and I saw them hastening to the assistance of those who were struggling with all their energies to resist the evil angels, and trying to help themselves by calling upon God with perseverance. But the angels left those who made no effort to help themselves, and I lost sight of them. As the praying ones continued their earnest cries, a ray of light from Jesus would at times come to them, to encourage their hearts, and light up their countenances.

I asked the meaning of the shaking I had seen, and was shown that it would be caused by the straight testimony called forth by the counsel of the True Witness to the Laodiceans. This will have its effect upon the heart of the receiver, and will lead him to exalt the standard and pour forth the straight truth. Some will not bear this straight testimony. They will rise up against it, and this will cause a shaking among God's people.

The testimony of the True Witness has not been half heeded. The solemn testimony upon which the destiny of the church hangs has been lightly esteemed, if not entirely disregarded. This testimony must work deep repentance, and all that truly receive it will obey it and be purified.

Said the angel: "List ye!" Soon I heard a voice that sounded like many musical instruments, all in perfect strains, sweet and harmonious. It surpassed any music I had ever heard. It seemed to be so full of mercy, compassion, and elevating, holy joy. It thrilled through my whole being. Said the angel: "Look ye!" My attention was then turned to the company I had seen, who were mightily shaken. I was shown those whom I had before seen weeping and praying with agony of spirit. The company of guardian angels around them had been doubled, and they were clothed with an armor from their head to their feet. They moved in exact order, firmly, like a company of soldiers. Their countenances expressed the severe conflict which they had endured, the agonizing struggle they had passed through. Yet their features, marked with severe internal anguish, now shone with the light and glory of heaven. They had obtained the victory, and it called forth from them the deepest gratitude, and holy, sacred joy.

The numbers of this company had lessened. Some had been shaken out, and left by the way.* The careless and indifferent, who did not join with those who prized victory and salvation enough to perseveringly plead and agonize for it, did not obtain it, and they were left behind in darkness, but their numbers were immediately made up by others taking hold of the truth and coming into the ranks. Still the evil angels pressed around them, but they could have no power over them.**

---

*"I know thy works, that thou art neither cold nor hot: I would thou wert cold or hot. So then because thou art lukewarm, and neither cold nor hot, I will spew thee out of My mouth. Because thou sayest, I am rich, and increased with goods, and have need of nothing; and knowest not that thou art wretched, and miserable, and poor, and blind, and naked." Revelation 3:15-17.

**"For we wrestle not against flesh and blood, but against principalities, against powers, against the rulers of the darkness of this world, against spiritual wickedness in high places. [Or, "wicked spirits in heavenly places," as in the margin.] Wherefore take unto you the whole armor of God, that ye may be able to withstand in the evil day, and having done all, to stand. Stand therefore, having your loins girt about with truth, and having on the breastplate of righteousness; and your feet shod with the preparation of the

I heard those clothed with the armor speak forth the truth in great power. It had effect. I saw those who had been bound; some wives had been bound by their husbands, and some children had been bound by their parents. The honest who had been held or prevented from hearing the truth, now eagerly laid hold of it. All fear of their relatives was gone. The truth alone was exalted to them. It was dearer and more precious than life. They had been hungering and thirsting for truth. I asked what had made this great change. An angel answered: "It is the latter rain, the refreshing from the presence of the Lord, the loud cry of the third angel."

Great power was with these chosen ones. Said the angel: "Look ye!" My attention was turned to the wicked, or unbelievers. They were all astir. The zeal and power with the people of God had aroused and enraged them. Confusion, confusion was on every side. I saw measures taken against this company, who had the power and light of God. Darkness thickened around them, yet there they stood, approved of God, and trusting in Him. I saw them perplexed. Next I heard them crying unto God earnestly. Through the day and night their cry ceased not.* I heard these words: "Thy will, O God, be done! If it can glorify Thy name, make a way of escape for Thy people! Deliver us from the heathen round about us! They have appointed us unto death; but Thine arm can bring salvation." These are all the words

*"And shall not God avenge His own elect, which cry day and night unto Him, though He bear long with them? I tell you that He will avenge them speedily. Nevertheless when the Son of man cometh, shall He find faith on the earth?" Luke 18:7, 8. See also Revelation 14:14, 15.

---

gospel of peace; above all, taking the shield of faith, wherewith ye shall be able to quench all the fiery darts of the wicked. And take the helmet of salvation, and the sword of the Spirit, which is the word of God: praying always with all prayer and supplication in the Spirit, and watching thereunto with all perseverance and supplication for all saints." Ephesians 6:12-18.

that I can bring to mind. All seemed to have a deep sense of their unworthiness, and manifested entire submission to the will of God. Yet like Jacob, every one, without an exception, was earnestly pleading and wrestling for deliverance.

Soon after they had commenced their earnest cry, the angels, in sympathy, would have gone to their deliverance. But a tall, commanding angel suffered them not. Said he: "The will of God is not yet fulfilled. They must drink of the cup. They must be baptized with the baptism."

Soon I heard the voice of God which shook the heavens and the earth.* There was a mighty earthquake. Buildings were shaken down, and fell on every side. I then heard a triumphant shout of victory, loud, musical, and clear. I looked upon this company, who, a short time before, were in such distress and bondage. Their captivity was turned. A glorious light shone upon them. How beautiful they then looked! All weariness and marks of care were gone; health and beauty were seen in every countenance. Their enemies, the heathen around them, fell like dead men. They could not endure the light that shone upon the delivered, holy ones. This light and glory remained upon them until Jesus was seen in the clouds of heaven, and the faithful, tried company were changed in a moment, in the twinkling of an eye, from glory to glory. The graves were opened and the saints came forth, clothed with immortality, crying: "Victory over death and the grave!" and together with the living saints they were caught up to meet their Lord in the air, while rich, musical shouts of glory and victory proceeded from every immortal tongue.

---

*"The Lord also shall roar out of Zion, and utter His voice from Jerusalem; and the heavens and the earth shall shake: but the Lord will be the hope of His people, and the strength of the children of Israel." Joel 3:16. See also Hebrews 12:26; Revelation 16:17.

God's Proving

God will prove His people. Jesus bears patiently with them, and does not spew them out of His mouth in a moment. Said the angel: "God is weighing His people." If the message had been of as short duration as many of us supposed, there would have been no time for them to develop character. Many moved from feeling, not from principle and faith, and this solemn, fearful message stirred them. It wrought upon their feelings, and excited their fears, but did not accomplish the work which God designed that it should. God reads the heart. Lest His people should be deceived in regard to themselves, He gives them time for the excitement to wear off, and then proves them to see if they will obey the counsel of the True Witness.

God leads His people on, step by step. He brings them up to different points calculated to manifest what is in the heart. Some endure at one point, but fall off at the next. At every advanced point the heart is tested and tried a little closer. If the professed people of God find their hearts opposed to this straight work, it should convince them that they have a work to do to overcome, if they would not be spewed out of the mouth of the Lord.

Said the angel: "God will bring His work closer and closer to test and prove every one of His people." Some are willing to receive one point; but God brings them to another testing point, they shrink from it and stand back, because they find that it strikes directly at some cherished idol. Here they have opportunity to see what is in their hearts that shuts out Jesus. They prize something higher than the truth, and their hearts

1859, vol. 1, pp. 186-190 (The Laodicean Church).

are not prepared to receive Jesus. Individuals are tested and proved a length of time to see if they will sacrifice their idols and heed the counsel of the True Witness. If any will not be purified through obeying the truth, and overcome their selfishness, their pride, and evil passions, the angels of God have the charge: "They are joined to their idols, let them alone," and they pass on to their work, leaving these with their sinful traits unsubdued, to the control of evil angels. Those who come up to every point, and stand every test, and overcome, be the price what it may, have heeded the counsel of the True Witness, and they will receive the latter rain, and thus be fitted for translation. . . .

Oh, that every lukewarm professor could realize the clean work that God is about to make among His professed people! Dear friends, do not deceive yourselves concerning your condition. You cannot deceive God. Says the True Witness: "I know thy works." The third angel is leading up a people, step by step, higher and higher. At every step they will be tested.

Houses of Worship

I SAW that many to whom God has entrusted means feel at liberty to use it freely for their own convenience in fitting up pleasant homes here; but when they build a house in which to worship the great God who inhabiteth eternity, they cannot afford to let Him have the use of the means which He has lent them. Each is not striving to excel the other in showing his gratitude to God for the truth by doing all he can to prepare a suitable place of worship; but some are trying to do just as little as possible; and they feel that the means is as good as lost which they spend in preparing a place for the Most High to visit them. Such an offering is lame, and not acceptable to God. I saw that it would be much more pleasing to God if His people would show as much wisdom in preparing a house for Him, as they do in their own dwellings.

The sacrifices and offerings of the children of Israel were commanded to be without blemish or spot, the best of the flock; and every one of the people was required to share in this work. The work of God for this time will be extensive. If you build a house for the Lord, do not offend and limit Him by casting in your lame offerings. Put the very best offering into a house built for God. Let it be the very best you have; show an interest to make it convenient and comfortable. Some think that this is of no consequence because time is so short. Then carry out the same in your dwellings, and in all your worldly arrangements.

I saw that God could carry on His work without any of man's help; but this is not His plan. The present world is

1859, vol. 1, pp. 196, 197.

designed as a scene of probation for man. He is here to form a character which will pass with him into the eternal world. Good and evil are placed before him, and his future state depends upon the choice he makes. Christ came to change the current of his thoughts and affections. His heart must be removed from his earthly treasure, and placed upon the heavenly. By his self-denial, God can be glorified. The great sacrifice has been made for man, and now he will be tested and proved to see if he will follow the example of Jesus, and make a sacrifice for his fellow man.

Satan and his angels are combined against the people of God; but Jesus is seeking to purify them unto Himself. He requires them to advance His work. God has deposited with His people in this world enough to carry forward His work without embarrassment, and it is His plan that the means which He has entrusted to them be used judiciously. "Sell that ye have, and give alms," (Luke 12:33) is a part of God's Sacred Word. The servants of God must arise, cry aloud, and spare not, "show My people their transgression, and the house of Jacob their sins." Isaiah 58:1. The work of God is to become more extensive, and if His people follow His counsel, there will not be much means in their possession to be consumed in the final conflagration. All will have laid up their treasure where moth and rust cannot corrupt; and the heart will not have a cord to bind it to earth.

Lessons From the Parables

I WAS shown that the parable of the talents has not been fully understood. This important lesson was given to the disciples for the benefit of Christians living in the last days. And these talents do not represent merely the ability to preach and instruct from the word of God. The parable applies to the temporal means which God has entrusted to His people. Those to whom the five and the two talents were given, traded and doubled that which was committed to their trust. God requires those who have possessions here, to put their money out to usury for Him—to put it into the cause to spread the truth. And if the truth lives in the heart of the receiver, he also will aid with his substance in sending it to others; and through his efforts, his influence, and his means, other souls will embrace the truth, and begin also to work for God.

I saw that some of God's professed people are like the man who hid his talent in the earth. They keep their possessions from doing good in the cause of God. They claim that these are their own, and that they have a right to do what they please with their own; and souls are not saved by judicious efforts made by them with their Lord's money. Angels keep a faithful record of every man's work, and as judgment passes upon the house of God, the sentence of each is recorded by his name, and the angel is commissioned to spare not the unfaithful servants, but to cut them down at the time of slaughter. And that which was committed to their trust is taken from them. Their earthly treasure is then swept away, and they have lost all. And the crowns they might have worn, had they been faithful, are

1859, vol. 1, pp. 197-200.

put upon the heads of those saved by the faithful servants whose means was constantly in use for God. And every one they have been the means of saving, adds stars to their crown in glory, and increases their eternal reward.

I was also shown that the parable of the unjust steward was to teach us a lesson. "Make to yourselves friends of the mammon of unrighteousness; that, when ye fail, they may receive you into everlasting habitations." Luke 16:9. If we use our means to God's glory here, we lay up a treasure in heaven; and when earthly possessions are all gone, the faithful steward has Jesus and angels for his friends, to receive him home to everlasting habitations.

ACCOUNTABILITY TO GOD

"He that is faithful in that which is least is faithful also in much." Verse 10. He that is faithful in his earthly possessions, which are least, making a judicious use of what God has lent him here, will be true to his profession. "He that is unjust in the least is unjust also in much." He that will withhold from God that which He has lent him, will be unfaithful in the things of God in every respect. "If therefore ye have not been faithful in the unrighteous mammon, who will commit to your trust the true riches?" Verse 11. If we prove unfaithful in the management of what God lends us here, He will never give us the immortal inheritance. "And if ye have not been faithful in that which is another man's, who shall give you that which is your own?" Verse 12.

Jesus has purchased redemption for us. It is ours; but we are placed here on probation to see if we will prove worthy of eternal life. God proves us by trusting us with earthly possessions. If we are faithful to impart freely of what He has lent us, to advance His cause, God can entrust to us the immortal inheritance. "Ye cannot serve God and mammon." Verse 13; Matthew 6:24. "If any man love the world, the love of the Father is not in him." 1 John 2:15.

God is displeased with the slack, loose manner in which many of His professed people conduct their worldly business. They seem to have lost all sense of the fact that the property they are using belongs to God, and that they must render to Him an account of their stewardship. Some leave their worldly business in perfect confusion. Satan has his eye on it all, and he strikes at a favorable opportunity, and by his management takes much means out of the ranks of Sabbath-keepers. And this means goes into his ranks. Some who are aged are unwilling to make any settlement of their worldly business, and in an unexpected moment they sicken and die. Their children who have no interest in the truth, take the property. Satan has managed it as suited him. "If therefore ye have not been faithful in the unrighteous mammon, who will commit to your trust the true riches? And if ye have not been faithful in that which is another man's, who shall give you that which is your own?" Luke 16:11, 12.

I was shown the awful fact that Satan and his angels have had more to do with the management of the property of God's professed people than the Lord has. Stewards of the last days are unwise. They suffer Satan to control their business matters, and get into his ranks what belongs to, and should be in, the cause of God. God takes notice of you, unfaithful stewards; He will call you to account. I saw that the stewards of God can by faithful, judicious management keep their business in this world square, exact, and straight. And it is especially the privilege and duty of the aged, the feeble, and those who have no children, to place their means where it can be used in the cause of God if they should be suddenly taken away. But I saw that Satan and his angels exult over their success in this matter. And those who should be wise heirs of salvation almost willingly let their Lord's money slip out of their hands into the enemy's ranks. In this way they strengthen Satan's kingdom, and seem to feel very easy about it!

Surety for Unbelievers

I SAW that God was displeased with His people for becoming surety for unbelievers. I was directed to these texts: Proverbs 22:26: "Be not thou one of them that strike hands, or of them that are sureties for debts." Proverbs 11:15: "He that is surety for a stranger shall smart for it: and he that hateth suretyship is sure." Unfaithful stewards! They pledge that which belongs to another,—their heavenly Father,—and Satan stands ready to aid his children to wrench it out of their hands. Sabbathkeepers should not be in partnership with unbelievers. God's people trust too much to the words of strangers, and ask their advice and counsel when they should not. The enemy makes them his agents, and works through them to perplex and take from God's people.

Some have no tact at wise management of worldly matters. They lack the necessary qualifications, and Satan takes advantage of them. When this is the case, such should not remain in ignorance of their task. They should be humble enough to counsel with their brethren, in whose judgment they can have confidence, before they carry out plans. I was directed to this text: "Bear ye one another's burdens." Galatians 6:2. Some are not humble enough to let those who have judgment calculate for them until they have followed their own plans, and have involved themselves in difficulties. Then they see the necessity of having the counsel and judgment of their brethren; but how much heavier the burden then than at first. Brethren should not go to law if it can be possibly avoided; for they thus give the enemy great advantage to entangle and perplex them. It would be better to make a settlement at some loss.

1859, vol. 1, pp. 200, 201.

Oath Taking

I SAW that some of God's children have made a mistake in regard to oath taking, and Satan has taken advantage of this to oppress them, and take from them their Lord's money. I saw that the words of our Lord, "Swear not at all," do not touch the judicial oath. "Let your communication be, Yea, yea; Nay, nay: for whatsoever is more than these cometh of evil." Matthew 5:34, 37. This refers to common conversation. Some exaggerate in their language. Some swear by their own life; others swear by their head—as sure as they live; as sure as they have a head. Some take heaven and earth to witness that such things are so. Some hope that God will strike them out of existence if what they are saying is not true. It is this kind of common swearing against which Jesus warns His disciples.

We have men placed over us for rulers, and laws to govern the people. Were it not for these laws, the condition of the world would be worse than it is now. Some of these laws are good, others are bad. The bad have been increasing, and we are yet to be brought into strait places. But God will sustain His people in being firm and living up to the principles of His word. When the laws of men conflict with the word and law of God, we are to obey the latter, whatever the consequences may be. The law of our land requiring us to deliver a slave to his master, we are not to obey; and we must abide the consequences of violating this law. The slave is not the property of any man. God is his rightful master, and man has no right to take God's workmanship into his hands, and claim him as his own.

I saw that the Lord still has something to do with the

1859, vol. 1, pp. 201-204.

laws of the land. While Jesus is in the sanctuary, God's restraining Spirit is felt by rulers and people. But Satan controls to a great extent the mass of the world, and were it not for the laws of the land, we should experience much suffering. I was shown that when it is actually necessary, and they are called upon to testify in a lawful manner, it is no violation of God's word for His children to solemnly take God to witness that what they say is the truth, and nothing but the truth.

Man is so corrupt that laws are made to throw the responsibility upon his own head. Some men do not fear to lie to their fellow man; but they have been taught, and the restraining Spirit of God has impressed them, that it is a fearful thing to lie to God. The case of Ananias and Sapphira his wife is given for an example. The matter is carried from man to God, so that if one bears false witness, it is not to man, but to the great God, who reads the heart, and knows the exact truth in every case. Our laws make it a high crime to take a false oath. God has often visited judgment upon the false swearer, and even while the oath was on his lips, the destroying angel has cut him down. This was to prove a terror to evildoers.

I saw that if there is anyone on earth who can consistently testify under oath, it is the Christian. He lives in the light of God's countenance. He grows strong in His strength. And when matters of importance must be decided by law, there is no one who can so well appeal to God as the Christian. I was bidden by the angel to notice that God swears by Himself. Genesis 22:16; Hebrews 6:13, 17. He swore to Abraham (Genesis 26:3), to Isaac (Psalm 105:9; Jeremiah 11:5), and to David (Psalm 132:11; Acts 2:30). God required of the children of Israel an oath between man and man. Exodus 22:10, 11. Jesus submitted to the oath in the hour of His trial. The high priest said unto Him: "I adjure Thee by the living God, that Thou tell us whether Thou be the Christ, the Son of God." Jesus said unto him: "Thou hast said." Matthew 26:63, 64. If Jesus in His teachings to His disciples referred to the judicial oath, He would have reproved the high priest, and there enforced His teachings, for the good of His followers present. Satan has been pleased that some have viewed oath taking in a wrong light; for it has given him the opportunity to oppress them and take from them their Lord's money. The stewards of God must be more wise, lay their plans, and prepare themselves to withstand Satan's devices; for he is to make greater efforts than ever before.

Some, I saw, have a prejudice against our rulers and laws; but if it were not for law, this world would be in an awful condition. God restrains our rulers; for the hearts of all are in His hands. Bounds are set, beyond which they cannot go. Many of the rulers are those whom Satan controls; but I saw that God has His agents, even among the rulers. And some of them will yet be converted to the truth. They are now acting the part that God would have them. When Satan works through his agents, propositions are made, that, if carried out, would impede the work of God and produce great evil. The good angels move upon these agents of God to oppose such propositions with strong reasons, which Satan's agents cannot resist. A few of God's agents will have power to bear down a great mass of evil. Thus the work will go on until the third message has done its work, and at the loud cry of the third angel, these agents will have an opportunity to receive the truth, and some of them will be converted, and endure with the saints through the time of trouble. When Jesus leaves the most holy, His restraining Spirit is withdrawn from rulers and people. They are left to the control of evil angels. Then such laws will be made by the counsel and direction of Satan, that unless time should be very short, no flesh could be saved.

Duty to Children

I HAVE been shown that parents generally have not taken a proper course with their children. They have not restrained them as they should, but have left them to indulge in pride, and follow their own inclinations. Anciently, parental authority was regarded; children were then in subjection to their parents, and feared and reverenced them; but in these last days the order is reversed. Some parents are in subjection to their children. They fear to cross the will of their children, and therefore yield to them. But just as long as children are under the roof of the parents, dependent upon them, they should be subject to their control. Parents should move with decision, requiring that their views of right be followed out.

Eli might have restrained his wicked sons, but he feared their displeasure. He suffered them to go on in their rebellion, until they became a curse to Israel. Parents are required to restrain their children. The salvation of children depends very much upon the course pursued by the parents. In their mistaken love and fondness for their children, many parents indulge them to their hurt, nourish their pride, and put upon them trimmings and ornaments which make them vain, and lead them to think that dress makes the lady or gentleman. But a short acquaintance convinces those with whom they associate that an outside appearance is not sufficient to hide the deformity of a heart void of the Christian graces, but filled with self-love, haughtiness, and uncontrolled passions. Those who love meekness, humility, and virtue, should shun such society, even if it be Sabbathkeepers' children. Their company is poisonous; their influence leads to death. Par-

1861, vol. 1, pp. 216-220.

ents realize not the destructive influence of the seed which they are sowing. It will spring up and bear fruit which will make their children despise parental authority.

Even after they are of age, children are required to respect their parents, and to look after their comfort. They should listen to the counsel of godly parents, and not feel that because a few more years are added to their life, they have grown out of their duty to them. There is a commandment with promise to those who honor their father and their mother. In these last days children are so noted for their disobedience and disrespect that God has especially noticed it, and it constitutes a sign that the end is near. It shows that Satan has almost complete control of the minds of the young. By many, age is no more respected. It is considered too old-fashioned to respect the aged; it dates back as far as the days of Abraham. Says God: "I know him, that he will command his children and his household after him." Genesis 18:19.

Anciently, children were not permitted to marry without the consent of their parents. Parents chose for their children. It was considered a crime for children to contract marriage upon their own responsibility. The matter was first laid before the parents, and they were to consider whether the person to be brought into a close relation to them was worthy, and whether the parties could provide for a family. It was considered by them of the greatest importance that they, the worshipers of the true God, should not intermarry with an idolatrous people, lest their families be led away from God. Even after children were married, they were under the most solemn obligation to their parents. Their judgment was not then considered sufficient without the counsel of the parents, and they were required to respect and obey their wishes unless these should conflict with the requirements of God.

Again I was directed to the condition of the young in these last days. Children are not controlled. Parents, you should commence your first lesson of discipline when your children are babes in your arms. Teach them to yield their will to yours. This can be done by bearing an even hand, and manifesting firmness. Parents should have perfect control over their own spirits, and with mildness and yet firmness bend the will of the child until it shall expect nothing else but to yield to their wishes.

RESULT OF PARENTAL NEGLECT

Parents do not commence in season. The first manifestation of temper is not subdued, and the children grow stubborn, which increases with their growth and strengthens with their strength. Some children, as they grow older, think it a matter of course that they must have their own way, and that their parents must submit to their wishes. They expect their parents to wait upon them. They are impatient of restraint, and when old enough to be a help to their parents, they do not bear the burdens they should. They have been released from responsibilities, and grow up worthless at home and worthless abroad. They have no power of endurance. The parents have borne the burden, and have suffered them to grow up in idleness, without habits of order, industry, or economy. They have not been taught habits of self-denial, but have been petted and indulged, their appetites gratified, and they come up with enfeebled health. Their manners and deportment are not agreeable. They are unhappy themselves, and make those around them unhappy. And while the children are but children still, while they need to be disciplined, they are allowed to go out in company and mingle with the society of the young, and one has a corrupting influence over another.

The curse of God will surely rest upon unfaithful parents. Not only are they planting thorns which will wound them here, but they must meet their own unfaithfulness when the judgment shall sit. Many children will rise up in judgment and condemn their parents for not restraining them, and charge upon them their destruction. The false sympathy and blind love of parents causes them to excuse the faults of their children and pass them by without correction, and their children are lost in consequence, and the blood of their souls will rest upon the unfaithful parents.

Children who are thus brought up undisciplined, have everything to learn when they profess to be Christ's followers. Their whole religious experience is affected by their bringing up in childhood. The same self-will often appears; there is the same lack of self-denial, the same impatience under reproof, the same love of self and unwillingness to seek counsel of others, or to be influenced by others' judgment, the same indolence, shunning of burdens, lack of bearing responsibilities. All this is seen in their relation to the church. It is possible for such to overcome; but how hard the battle! how severe the conflict! How hard to pass through the course of thorough discipline which is necessary for them to reach the elevation of Christian character! Yet if they overcome at last, they will be permitted to see, before they are translated, how near the precipice of eternal destruction they came, because of the lack of right training in youth, the failure to learn submission in childhood.

Our Denominational Name

I WAS shown in regard to the remnant people of God taking a name. Two classes were presented before me. One class embraced the great bodies of professed Christians. They were trampling upon God's law and bowing to a papal institution. They were keeping the first day of the week as the Sabbath of the Lord. The other class, who were but a few in number, were bowing to the great Lawgiver. They were keeping the fourth commandment. The peculiar and prominent features of their faith were the observance of the seventh day, and waiting for the appearing of our Lord from heaven.

The conflict is between the requirements of God and the requirements of the beast. The first day, a papal institution which directly contradicts the fourth commandment, is yet to be made a test by the two-horned beast. And then the fearful warning from God declares the penalty of bowing to the beast and his image. They shall drink the wine of the wrath of God, which is poured out without mixture into the cup of His indignation.

No name which we can take will be appropriate but that which accords with our profession and expresses our faith and marks us a peculiar people. The name Seventh-day Adventist is a standing rebuke to the Protestant world. Here is the line of distinction between the worshipers of God and those who worship the beast and receive his mark. The great conflict is between the commandments of God and the requirements of the beast. It is because the saints are keeping all ten of the commandments that the dragon makes war upon them. If they will lower the standard and yield

1861, vol. 1, pp. 223, 224.

the peculiarities of their faith, the dragon will be at peace; but they excite his ire because they have dared to raise the standard and unfurl their banner in opposition to the Protestant world, who are worshiping the institution of papacy.

The name Seventh-day Adventist carries the true features of our faith in front, and will convict the inquiring mind. Like an arrow from the Lord's quiver, it will wound the transgressors of God's law, and will lead to repentance toward God and faith in our Lord Jesus Christ.

I was shown that almost every fanatic who has arisen, who wishes to hide his sentiments that he may lead away others, claims to belong to the church of God. Such a name would at once excite suspicion; for it is employed to conceal the most absurd errors. This name is too indefinite for the remnant people of God. It would lead to the supposition that we had a faith which we wished to cover up.

Entire Consecration

Dear Brother and Sister K: In my last vision I was shown some things in regard to your family. The Lord has thoughts of mercy concerning you and will not forsake you unless you forsake Him. L and M are in a lukewarm condition. They must arouse and make efforts for salvation, or they will fail of everlasting life. They must feel an individual responsibility and have an experience for themselves. They need a work wrought in their hearts by the Holy Spirit of God, which will lead them to love and choose the society of God's people above any other, and to be separate from those who have no love for spiritual things. Jesus demands a whole sacrifice, an entire consecration.

L and M, you have not realized that God requires your undivided affections. You have made a holy profession, yet have sunk down to the dead level of ordinary professors. You love the society of the young who have no regard for the sacred truths which you profess. You have appeared like your associates, and have been contented with as much religion as would render you agreeable to all, without incurring the censure of any.

Christ demands all. If He required less, His sacrifice was too dear, too great to make to bring us up to such a level. Our holy faith cries out, Separation. We should not be conformed to the world, or to dead, heartless professors. "Be ye transformed by the renewing of your mind." Romans 12:2. This is a self-denying way. And when you think that the way is too strait, that there is too much self-denial in this narrow path; when you say, How hard to give up all, ask yourselves

1861, vol. 1, pp. 240-243.

the question, What did Christ give up for me? This question puts anything that we may call self-denial in the shade.

Behold Him in the garden, sweating great drops of blood. A solitary angel is sent from heaven to strengthen the Son of God. Follow Him on His way to the judgment hall, while He is derided, mocked, and insulted by that infuriated mob. Behold Him clothed in that old purple kingly robe. Hear the coarse jest and cruel mocking. See them place upon that noble brow the crown of thorns, and then smite Him with a reed, causing the thorns to penetrate His temples, and the blood to flow from that holy brow. Hear that murderous throng eagerly crying for the blood of the Son of God. He is delivered into their hands, and they lead the noble sufferer away, pale, weak, and fainting, to His crucifixion. He is stretched upon the wooden cross, and the nails are driven through His tender hands and feet. Behold Him hanging upon the cross those dreadful hours of agony until the angels veil their faces from the horrid scene, and the sun hides its light, refusing to behold. Think of these things, and then ask, Is the way too strait? No, no.

DIVIDED INTERESTS

In a divided, halfhearted life, you will find doubt and darkness. You cannot enjoy the consolations of religion, neither the peace which the world gives. Do not sit down in Satan's easy chair of do-little, but arise, and aim at the elevated standard which it is your privilege to attain. It is a blessed privilege to give up all for Christ. Look not at the lives of others and imitate them and rise no higher. You have only one true, unerring Pattern. It is safe to follow Jesus only. Determine that if others act on the principle of the spiritual sluggard you will leave them and march forward toward the elevation of Christian character. Form a character for heaven. Sleep not at your post. Deal faithfully and truly with your own soul.

You are indulging an evil which threatens to destroy your spirituality. It will eclipse all the beauty and interest of the sacred pages. It is love for storybooks, tales, and other reading which does not have an influence for good upon the mind that is in any way dedicated to the service of God. It produces a false, unhealthy excitement, fevers the imagination, unfits the mind for usefulness, and disqualifies it for any spiritual exercise. It weans the soul from prayer and love of spiritual things. Reading that will throw light upon the Sacred Volume, and quicken your desire and diligence to study it, is not dangerous, but beneficial.

You were represented to me with your eyes turned from the Sacred Book and intently fixed upon exciting books, which are death to religion. The oftener and more diligently you peruse the Scriptures, the more beautiful will they appear, and the less relish will you have for light reading. The daily study of the Scriptures will have a sanctifying influence upon the mind. You will breathe a heavenly atmosphere. Bind this precious volume to your hearts. It will prove to you a friend and guide in perplexity.

You have had objects in view in your life, and how steadily and perseveringly have you labored to attain those objects! You have calculated and planned until your anticipations were realized. There is an object before you now worthy of a persevering, untiring, lifelong effort. It is the salvation of your soul—everlasting life. And this demands self-denial, sacrifice, and close study. You must be purified and refined. You lack the saving influence of the Spirit of God. You mingle with your associates and forget that you have named the name of Christ. You act and dress like them.

COME OUT AND BE SEPARATE

Sister K, I saw that you have a work to do. You must die to pride and let your whole interest be in the truth. Your eternal interest depends upon the course you now pursue. If you obtain eternal life, you must live for it and deny self. Come out from the world, and be separate. Your life must be marked with sobriety, watchfulness, and prayer. Angels are watching the development of character and weighing moral worth. All our words and acts are passing in review before God. It is a fearful, solemn time. The hope of eternal life is not to be taken up upon slight grounds; it must be settled between God and your own soul. Some will lean upon others' judgment and experience rather than be at the trouble of a close examination of their own hearts, and will pass along for months and years with no witness of the Spirit of God, or evidence of their acceptance. They deceive themselves. They have a supposed hope, but lack the essential qualifications of a Christian. First there must be a thorough heart work, then their manners will take that elevated, noble character which marks the true followers of Christ. It requires effort and moral courage to live out our faith.

God's people are peculiar. Their spirit cannot mingle with the spirit and influence of the world. You do not wish to bear the Christian name and yet be unworthy of it. You do not desire to meet Jesus with a profession only. You do not wish to be deceived in so important a matter. Thoroughly examine the grounds of your hope. Deal truly with your own soul. A supposed hope will never save you. Have you counted the cost? I fear not. Now decide whether you will follow Christ, cost what it will. You cannot do this and yet enjoy the society of those who pay no heed to divine things. Your spirits cannot mingle any more than oil and water.

It is a great thing to be a child of God, and a joint-heir with Christ. If this is your privilege, you will know the fellowship of Christ's sufferings. God looketh upon the heart. I saw that you must seek Him earnestly, and raise your standard of piety higher, or you will certainly fail of everlasting life. You may ask the question: Did Sister White see this? Yes; and I have tried to place it before you and give you the impressions which were given me. May the Lord help you to take heed.

Dear brother and sister, watch your children with jealous care. The spirit and influence of the world are destroying all desire in them to be true Christians. Let your influence be to draw them from young companions who have no interest in divine things. They must make a sacrifice if they win heaven at last.

Which will you choose, says Christ, Me or the world? God calls for an unconditional surrender of the heart and affections to Him. If you love friends, brothers or sisters, father or mother, houses or lands, more than Me, says Christ, you are not worthy of Me. Religion lays the soul under the greatest obligation to her claims, to walk by her principles. As the mysterious magnet points to the north, so do the claims of religion point to the glory of God. You are bound by your baptismal vows to honor your Creator and to resolutely deny self and crucify your affections and lusts, and bring even your thoughts into obedience to the will of Christ.—1872, vol. 3, p. 45.

Your worldliness does not incline you to throw wide open the door of your hard hearts at the knock of Jesus, who is seeking an entrance there. The Lord of glory, who has redeemed you by His own blood, waited at your doors for admittance; but you did not throw them open wide and welcome Him in. Some opened the door slightly and permitted a little light from His presence to enter, but did not welcome the heavenly Visitor. There was not room for Jesus. The place which should have been reserved for Him was occupied with other things. Jesus entreated you: "If any man hear My voice, and open the door, I will come in to him, and will sup with him, and he with Me." Revelation 3:20. There was a work for you to do to open the door. For a time you felt inclined to hear and open the door; but even this inclination departed, and you failed to secure the communion with the heavenly Guest which it was your privilege to have. Some, however, opened the door and heartily welcomed their Saviour.—1869, vol. 2, pp. 216, 217.

Great Distress Coming

I SAW greater distress in the land than we have yet witnessed. I heard groans and cries of distress, and saw large companies in active battle. I heard the booming of the cannon, the clash of arms, the hand-to-hand fight, and the groans and prayers of the dying. The ground was covered with the wounded and the dead. I saw desolate, despairing families, and pinching want in many dwellings. Even now many families are suffering want, but this will increase. The faces of many looked haggard, pale, and pinched with hunger.

I was shown that the people of God should be closely united in the bonds of Christian fellowship and love. God alone can be our shield and strength in this time of our national calamities. The people of God should awake. Their opportunities to spread the truth should be improved, for they will not last long. I was shown distress and perplexity and famine in the land. Satan is now seeking to hold God's people in a state of inactivity, to keep them from acting their part in spreading the truth, that they may at last be weighed in the balance and found wanting.

God's people must take warning and discern the signs of the times. The signs of Christ's coming are too plain to be doubted, and in view of these things everyone who professes the truth should be a living preacher. God calls upon all, both preachers and people, to awake. All heaven is astir. The scenes of earth's history are fast closing. We are amid the perils of the last days. Greater perils are before us, and yet we are not awake. This lack of activity and earnestness in the cause of God is dreadful. This death stupor is from

1862, vol. 1, pp. 260-264.

Satan. He controls the minds of unconsecrated Sabbathkeepers, and leads them to be jealous of one another, faultfinding, and censorious. It is his special work to divide hearts that the influence, strength, and labor of God's servants may be kept among unconsecrated Sabbathkeepers and their precious time be occupied in settling little differences when it should be spent in proclaiming the truth to unbelievers.

TIME TO ACT

I was shown God's people waiting for some change to take place—a compelling power to take hold of them. But they will be disappointed, for they are wrong. They must act, they must take hold of the work themselves and earnestly cry to God for a true knowledge of themselves. The scenes which are passing before us are of sufficient magnitude to cause us to arouse and urge the truth home to the hearts of all who will listen. The harvest of the earth is nearly ripe.

I was shown how important it is that the ministers who engage in the solemn, responsible work of proclaiming the third angel's message be right. The Lord is not straitened for means or instruments with which to do His own work. He can speak at any time, by whom He will, and His word is powerful and will accomplish the thing whereunto it is sent. But if the truth has not sanctified, made pure and clean, the hands and heart of him who ministers in holy things, he is liable to speak according to his own imperfect experience; and when he speaks of himself, according to the decisions of his own unsanctified judgment, his counsel is not then of God, but of himself. As he that is called of God is called to be holy, so he that is approved and set apart of men must give evidence of his holy calling and show forth in his heavenly conversation and conduct that he is faithful to Him who hath called him.

There are fearful woes for those who preach the truth,

but are not sanctified by it, and also for those who consent to receive and maintain the unsanctified to minister to them in word and doctrine. I am alarmed for the people of God who profess to believe solemn, important truth, for I know that many of them are not converted nor sanctified through it. Men can hear and acknowledge the whole truth, and yet know nothing of the power of godliness. All who preach the truth will not themselves be saved by it. Said the angel: "Be ye clean, that bear the vessels of the Lord." Isaiah 52:11.

The time has come when those who choose the Lord for their present and future portion must trust in Him alone. Everyone professing godliness must have an experience of his own. The recording angel is making a faithful record of the words and acts of God's people. Angels are watching the development of character and weighing moral worth. Those who profess to believe the truth should be right themselves and exert all their influence to enlighten and win others to the truth. Their words and works are the channel through which the pure principles of truth and holiness are conveyed to the world. They are the salt of the earth and the light thereof.

I saw that in looking heavenward we shall see light and peace, but in looking to the world we shall see that every refuge must soon fail us and every good soon pass away. There is no help for us but in God; in this state of earth's confusion we can be composed, strong, or safe, only in the strength of living faith; nor can we be at peace, only as we rest in God and wait for His salvation. Greater light shines upon us than shone upon our fathers. We cannot be accepted or honored of God in rendering the same service, or doing the same works, that our fathers did. In order to be accepted and blessed of God as they were, we must imitate their faithfulness and zeal,—improve our light as they improved theirs,—and do as they would have done had they lived in our day.

We must walk in the light which shines upon us, otherwise

that light will become darkness. God requires of us to exhibit to the world, in our character and works, that measure of the spirit of union and oneness which is in accordance with the sacred truths we profess and with the spirit of those prophecies that are fulfilling in these last days. The truth which has reached our understanding, and the light which has shone on the soul, will judge and condemn us, if we turn away and refuse to be led by them.

DREADFUL SCENES BEFORE US

What shall I say to arouse the remnant people of God? I was shown that dreadful scenes are before us; Satan and his angels are bringing all their powers to bear upon God's people. He knows that if they sleep a little longer he is sure of them, for their destruction is certain. I warn all who profess the name of Christ to closely examine themselves and make full and thorough confession of all their wrongs, that they may go beforehand to judgment, and that the recording angel may write pardon opposite their names. My brother, my sister, if these precious moments of mercy are not improved, you will be left without excuse. If you make no special effort to arouse, if you will not manifest zeal in repenting, these golden moments will soon pass, and you will be weighed in the balance and found wanting. Then your agonizing cries will be of no avail. Then will apply the words of the Lord: "Because I have called, and ye refused; I have stretched out My hand, and no man regarded; but ye have set at nought all My counsel, and would none of My reproof: I also will laugh at your calamity; I will mock when your fear cometh; when your fear cometh as desolation, and your destruction cometh as a whirlwind; when distress and anguish cometh upon you. Then shall they call upon Me, but I will not answer; they shall seek Me early, but they shall not find Me: for that they hated knowledge, and did not choose the fear of the Lord: they would none of My counsel:

they despised all My reproof. Therefore shall they eat of the fruit of their own way, and be filled with their own devices. For the turning away of the simple shall slay them, and the prosperity of fools shall destroy them. But whoso hearkeneth unto Me shall dwell safely, and shall be quiet from fear of evil." Proverbs 1:24-33.

Duty to the Poor

Inquiries are often made in regard to our duty to the poor who embrace the third message; and we ourselves have long been anxious to know how to manage with discretion the cases of poor families who embrace the Sabbath. But while at Roosevelt, New York, August 3, 1861, I was shown some things in regard to the poor.

God does not require our brethren to take charge of every poor family that shall embrace this message. If they should do this, the ministers must cease to enter new fields, for the funds would be exhausted. Many are poor from their own lack of diligence and economy; they know not how to use means aright. If they should be helped, it would hurt them. Some will always be poor. If they should have the very best advantages, their cases would not be helped. They have not good calculation and would use all the means they could obtain, were it much or little.

Some know nothing of denying self and economizing to keep out of debt and to get a little ahead for a time of need. If the church should help such individuals instead of leaving them to rely upon their own resources, it would injure them in the end, for they look to the church and expect to receive help from them and do not practice self-denial and economy when they are well provided for. And if they do not receive help every time, Satan tempts them, and they become jealous and very conscientious for their brethren, fearing they will fail to do all their duty to them. The mistake is on their own part. They are deceived. They are not the Lord's poor.

The instructions given in the word of God in regard to

1862, vol. 1, pp. 272-274.

helping the poor do not touch such cases, but are for the unfortunate and afflicted. God in His providence has afflicted individuals to test and prove others. Widows and invalids are in the church to prove a blessing to the church. They are a part of the means which God has chosen to develop the true character of Christ's professed followers and to call into exercise the precious traits of character manifested by our compassionate Redeemer.

WIDOWS, ORPHANS, AND INVALIDS

Many who can but barely live when they are single, choose to marry and raise a family when they know they have nothing with which to support them. And worse than this, they have no family government. Their whole course in their family is marked with their loose, slack habits. They have but little control over themselves, and are passionate, impatient, and fretful. When such embrace the message, they feel that they are entitled to assistance from their more wealthy brethren; and if their expectations are not met, they complain of the church and accuse them of not living out their faith. Who must be the sufferers in this case? Must the cause of God be sapped, and the treasury in different places exhausted, to take care of these large families of poor? No. The parents must be the sufferers. They will not, as a general thing, suffer any greater lack after they embrace the Sabbath than they did before.

There is an evil among some of the poor which will certainly prove their ruin unless they overcome it. They have embraced the truth with their coarse, rough, uncultivated habits, and it takes some time for them to see and realize their coarseness, and that it is not in accordance with the character of Christ. They look upon others who are more orderly and refined as being proud, and you may hear them say: "The truth brings us all down upon a level." But it is an entire mistake to think that the truth brings the receiver down. It brings him up, refines his taste, sanctifies his judgment, and, if lived out, is continually fitting him for the society of holy angels in the city of God. The truth is designed to bring us all up upon a level.

The more able should ever act a noble, generous part in their deal with their poorer brethren, and should also give them good advice, and then leave them to fight life's battles through. But I was shown that a most solemn duty rests upon the church to have an especial care for the destitute widows, orphans, and invalids.

Many of those who profess the truth are not sanctified by it, and may not have a heart to make even a trifling variation in the prices of produce when dealing with a poor brother, sooner than they would with an able worldling. They do not love their neighbors as themselves. It would be more pleasing to God were there less selfishness and more disinterested benevolence.—1868, vol. 2, p. 51.

Modern Spiritualism

I WAS directed to this scripture as especially applying to modern spiritualism: Colossians 2:8: "Beware lest any man spoil you through philosophy and vain deceit, after the tradition of men, after the rudiments of the world, and not after Christ." Thousands, I was shown, have been spoiled through the philosophy of phrenology and animal magnetism, and have been driven into infidelity. If the mind commences to run in this channel, it is almost sure to lose its balance and be controlled by a demon. "Vain deceit" fills the minds of poor mortals. They think there is such power in themselves to accomplish great works that they realize no necessity of a higher power. Their principles and faith are "after the tradition of men, after the rudiments of the world, and not after Christ."

Jesus has not taught them this philosophy. Nothing of the kind can be found in His teachings. He did not direct the minds of poor mortals to themselves, to a power which they possessed. He was ever directing their minds to God, the Creator of the universe, as the source of their strength and wisdom. Special warning is given in verse 18: "Let no man beguile you of your reward in a voluntary humility and worshiping of angels, intruding into those things which he hath not seen, vainly puffed up by his fleshly mind."

The teachers of spiritualism come in a pleasing, bewitching manner to deceive you, and if you listen to their fables you are beguiled by the enemy of righteousness and will surely lose your reward. When once the fascinating influence of the archdeceiver overcomes you, you are poisoned,

1862, vol. 1, pp. 297-302 (Philosophy and Vain Deceit).

and its deadly influence adulterates and destroys your faith in Christ's being the Son of God, and you cease to rely on the merits of His blood. Those deceived by this philosophy are beguiled of their reward through the deceptions of Satan. They rely upon their own merits, exercise voluntary humility, are even willing to make sacrifices, and debase themselves, and yield their minds to the belief of supreme nonsense, receiving the most absurd ideas through those whom they believe to be their dead friends. Satan has so blinded their eyes and perverted their judgment that they perceive not the evil; and they follow out the instructions purporting to be from their dead friends now angels in a higher sphere.

Satan has chosen a most certain, fascinating delusion, one that is calculated to take hold of the sympathies of those who have laid their loved ones in the grave. Evil angels assume the form of these loved ones and relate incidents connected with their lives and perform acts which their friends performed while living. In this way they deceive and lead the relatives of the dead to believe that their deceased friends are angels hovering about them and communing with them. These they regard with a certain idolatry, and what they may say has greater influence over them than the word of God. These evil angels, who assume to be dead friends, will either utterly reject God's word as idle tales, or, if it suit their purpose best, will select the vital portions which testify of Christ and point out the way to heaven, and change the plain statements of the word of God to suit their own corrupt nature and ruin souls. With due attention to the word of God, all may be convinced if they will of this soul-destroying delusion. The word of God declares in positive terms that "the dead know not anything." Ecclesiastes 9:5, 6: "For the living know that they shall die: but the dead know not anything, neither have they any more a reward; for the memory of them is forgotten. Also their love, and their hatred, and their envy, is now perished;

neither have they any more a portion forever in anything that is done under the sun."

VENTURING ON SATAN'S GROUND

Deceived mortals are worshiping evil angels, believing them to be the spirits of their dead friends. The word of God expressly declares that the dead have no more a portion in anything done under the sun. Spiritualists say that the dead know everything that is done under the sun, that they communicate to their friends on earth, give valuable information, and perform wonders. "The dead praise not the Lord, neither any that go down into silence." Psalm 115:17. Satan, transformed into an angel of light, works with all deceivableness of unrighteousness. He who could take up the Son of God, who was made a little lower than the angels, and place Him upon a pinnacle of the temple, and take Him up into an exceeding high mountain to present before Him the kingdoms of the world, can exercise his power upon the human family, who are far inferior in strength and wisdom to the Son of God, even after He had taken upon Himself man's nature.

In this degenerate age, Satan holds control over those who depart from the right and venture upon his ground. He exercises his power upon such in an alarming manner. I was directed to these words: "Intruding into those things which he hath not seen, vainly puffed up by his fleshly mind." Colossians 2:18. Some, I was shown, gratify their curiosity and tamper with the devil. They have no real faith in spiritualism and would start back with horror at the idea of being mediums. Yet they venture and place themselves in a position where Satan can exercise his power upon them. Such do not mean to enter deep into this work, but they know not what they are doing. They are venturing on the devil's ground and are tempting him to control them. This powerful destroyer considers them his lawful prey and exercises his power upon them, and that against their will. When they wish to control themselves they cannot. They yielded their minds to Satan, and he will not release his claims, but holds them captive. No power can deliver the ensnared soul but the power of God in answer to the earnest prayers of His faithful followers.

OUR ONLY SAFETY

The only safety now is to search for the truth as revealed in the word of God, as for hid treasure. The subjects of the Sabbath, the nature of man, and the testimony of Jesus are the great and important truths to be understood; these will prove as an anchor to hold God's people in these perilous times. But the mass of mankind despise the truths of God's word and prefer fables. 2 Thessalonians 2:10, 11: "Because they received not the love of the truth, that they might be saved. And for this cause God shall send them strong delusion, that they should believe a lie."

The most licentious and corrupt are highly flattered by these satanic spirits, which they believe to be the spirits of their dead friends, and they are vainly puffed up in their fleshly minds. Colossians 2:19: "And not holding the Head, from which all the body by joints and bands having nourishment ministered, and knit together, increaseth with the increase of God," they deny Him who ministers strength to the body, that every member may increase with the increase of God.

Vain philosophy. The members of the body are controlled by the head. Spiritualists lay aside the Head and believe that all the members of the body must act themselves and that fixed laws will lead them on in a state of progression to perfection without a head. John 15:1, 2, 4-6: "I am the True Vine, and My Father is the Husbandman. Every branch in Me that beareth not fruit, He taketh away: and every branch that beareth fruit, He purgeth it, that it may bring forth more fruit." "Abide in Me, and I in you. As the branch cannot bear fruit of itself, except it abide in the vine; no more can ye, except ye abide in Me. I am the Vine, ye are the branches: He that abideth in Me, and I in him, the same bringeth forth much fruit: for without Me ye can do nothing. If a man abide not in Me, he is cast forth as a branch, and is withered; and men gather them, and cast them into the fire, and they are burned."

Christ is the source of our strength. He is the Vine, we are the branches. We must receive nourishment from the living Vine. Deprived of the strength and nourishment of that Vine, we are as members of the body without a head and are in the very position which Satan wishes us to be in, that he may control us as pleases himself. He works "with all deceivableness of unrighteousness in them that perish; because they received not the love of the truth, that they might be saved. And for this cause God shall send them strong delusion, that they should believe a lie." 2 Thessalonians 2:10, 11. Spiritualism is a lie. It is founded upon the great original lie, "Ye shall *not* surely die." Genesis 3:4. Thousands cut off the Head, and the result is the members act without Jesus for their head, and another guides the body. Satan controls them.

I was shown that Satan cannot control minds unless they are yielded to his control. Those who depart from the right are in serious danger now. They separate themselves from God and from the watchcare of His angels, and Satan, ever upon the watch to destroy souls, begins to present to them his deceptions. Such are in the utmost peril; and if they see and try to resist the powers of darkness and to free themselves from Satan's snare, it is not an easy matter. They have ventured on Satan's ground, and he claims them. He will not hesitate to engage all his energies and call to his aid all his evil host to wrest a single human being from the hand of Christ.

Those who have tempted the devil to tempt them will have to make desperate efforts to free themselves from his power. But when they begin to work for themselves, then angels of

God whom they have grieved will come to their rescue. Satan and his angels are unwilling to lose their prey. They contend and battle with the holy angels, and the conflict is severe. But if those who have erred continue to plead, and in deep humility confess their wrongs, angels who excel in strength will prevail and wrench them from the power of the evil angels.

As the curtain was lifted and I was shown the corruption of this age, my heart sickened, my spirit nearly fainted within me. I saw that the inhabitants of the earth were filling up the measure of the cup of their iniquity. God's anger is kindled and will be no more appeased until the sinners are destroyed out of the earth. Satan is Christ's personal enemy. He is the originator and leader of every species of rebellion in heaven and earth. His rage increases; we do not realize his power. If our eyes could be opened to discern the fallen angels at work with those who feel at ease and consider themselves safe, we would not feel so secure. Evil angels are upon our track every moment. We expect a readiness on the part of bad men to act as Satan suggests; but while our minds are unguarded against his invisible agents, they assume new ground and work marvels and miracles in our sight. Are we prepared to resist them by the word of God, the only weapon we can use successfully?

Some will be tempted to receive these wonders as from God. The sick will be healed before us. Miracles will be performed in our sight. Are we prepared for the trial which awaits us when the lying wonders of Satan shall be more fully exhibited? Will not many souls be ensnared and taken? By departing from the plain precepts and commandments of God, and giving heed to fables, the minds of many are preparing to receive these lying wonders. We must all now seek to arm ourselves for the contest in which we must soon engage. Faith in God's word, prayerfully studied and practically applied, will be our shield from Satan's power and will bring us off conquerors through the blood of Christ.

Family Religion

I HAVE been shown the high and responsible position which God's people should occupy. They are the salt of the earth and the light of the world, and they must walk even as Christ walked. They will come up through great tribulation. The present is a time of warfare and trial. Our Saviour says in Revelation 3:21: "To him that overcometh will I grant to sit with Me in My throne, even as I also overcame, and am set down with My Father in His throne." The reward is not given to all who profess to be followers of Christ, but to those who overcome even as He overcame. We must study the life of Christ and learn what it is to confess Him before the world.

In order to confess Christ, we must have Him to confess. No one can truly confess Christ unless the mind and spirit of Christ are in him. If a form of godliness, or an acknowledgment of the truth, were always a confession of Christ, we might say: Broad is the way that leadeth unto life, and many there be that find it. We must understand what it is to confess Christ and wherein we deny Him. It is possible with our lips to confess Christ yet in our works deny Him. The fruits of the Spirit manifested in the life are a confession of Him. If we have forsaken all for Christ, our lives will be humble, our conversation heavenly, our conduct blameless. The powerful, purifying influence of truth in the soul, and the character of Christ exemplified in the life, are a confession of Him. If the words of eternal life are sown in our hearts, the fruit is righteousness and peace.

We may deny Christ in our life by indulging love of ease or

1862, vol. 1, pp. 303-310.

love of self, by jesting and joking, and by seeking the honor of the world. We may deny Him in our outward appearance by conformity to the world, by a proud look or costly apparel. Only by constant watchfulness and persevering and almost unceasing prayer shall we be able to exhibit in our life the character of Christ or the sanctifying influence of the truth. Many drive Christ from their families by an impatient, passionate spirit. Such have something to overcome in this respect.

The present enfeebled condition of the human family was presented before me. Every generation has been growing weaker, and disease of every form afflicts the race. Thousands of poor mortals with deformed, sickly bodies, shattered nerves, and gloomy minds are dragging out a miserable existence. Satan's power upon the human family increases. If the Lord should not soon come and destroy his power, the earth would erelong be depopulated.

I was shown that Satan's power is especially exercised upon the people of God. Many were presented before me in a doubting, despairing condition. The infirmities of the body affect the mind. A cunning and powerful enemy attends our steps and employs his strength and skill in trying to turn us out of the right way. And it is too often the case that the people of God are not on their watch, therefore are ignorant of his devices. He works by means which will best conceal himself from view, and he often gains his object.

Brethren have invested means in patent rights and other enterprises, and have induced others to interest themselves, who could not bear the perplexity and care of such business. Their anxious, overtaxed minds seriously affect their already diseased bodies, and they then yield to despondency, which increases to despair. They lose all confidence in themselves and think that God has forsaken them, and they dare not believe that He will be merciful to them. These poor souls will not be left to the control of Satan. They will make their way through the gloom and again fasten their trembling faith upon the promises of God; He will deliver them and turn their sorrow and mourning into peace and gladness. But such, I was shown, must learn by the things they suffer to let patent rights and these various enterprises alone. They should not allow even their brethren to flatter them to entangle themselves in such enterprises, for their anticipations will not be realized, and then they will be thrown upon the enemy's battlefield unarmed for the conflict.

Means which should be put into the treasury of God to advance His cause is worse than lost by being invested in some of these modern improvements. If any who profess the truth feel at liberty to engage, and capable of engaging, in these patent rights and inventions, they should not go among their brethren and make that their field of operation, but go among unbelievers. Let not your name and profession as an Adventist decoy your brethren who wish to consecrate their means to God. But go out into the world, and let that class invest their means who care not for the advancement of the cause of God.

I was shown the necessity of opening the doors of our houses and hearts to the Lord. When we begin to work in earnest for ourselves and for our families, then we shall have help from God. I was shown that merely observing the Sabbath and praying morning and evening are not positive evidences that we are Christians. These outward forms may all be strictly observed, and yet true godliness be lacking. Titus 2:14: "Who gave Himself for us, that He might redeem us from all iniquity, and purify unto Himself a peculiar people, *zealous of good works.*" All who profess to be Christ's followers should have command of their own spirit, not allowing themselves to speak fretfully or impatiently. The husband and father should check that impatient word he is about to utter. He should study the effect of his words, lest they leave sadness and a blight.

Infirmities and disease especially affect women. The

happiness of the family depends much upon the wife and mother. If she is weak and nervous, and is suffered to be overtaxed with labor, the mind becomes depressed, for it sympathizes with the weariness of the body; and then she too often meets with cold reserve from the husband. If everything does not move off just as pleasantly as he could wish, he blames the wife and mother. He is almost wholly unacquainted with her cares and burdens, and does not always know how to sympathize with her. He does not realize that he is aiding the great enemy in his work of tearing down.

THE CONSIDERATE HUSBAND

He should by faith in God lift up a standard against Satan; but he seems blinded to his own interest and hers. He treats her with indifference. He knows not what he is doing. He is working directly against his own happiness and is destroying the happiness of his family. The wife becomes desponding and discouraged. Hope and cheerfulness are gone. She goes her daily rounds mechanically because she sees that her work must be done. Her lack of cheerfulness and courage is felt throughout the family circle. There are many such miserable families all through the ranks of Sabbathkeepers. Angels bear the shameful tidings to heaven, and the recording angel makes a record of it all.

The husband should manifest great interest in his family. Especially should he be very tender of the feelings of a feeble wife. He can shut the door against much disease. Kind, cheerful, and encouraging words will prove more effective than the most healing medicines. These will bring courage to the heart of the desponding and discouraged, and the happiness and sunshine brought into the family by kind acts and encouraging words will repay the effort tenfold.

The husband should remember that much of the burden of training his children rests upon the mother, that she has much to do with molding their minds. This should call into exercise his tenderest feelings, and with care should he lighten her burdens. He should encourage her to lean upon his large affections, and direct her mind to heaven, where there is strength and peace, and a final rest for the weary. He should not come to his home with a clouded brow, but should with his presence bring sunlight into the family, and should encourage his wife to look up and believe in God. Unitedly they can claim the promises of God and bring His rich blessing into the family. Unkindness, complaining, and anger shut Jesus from the dwelling. I saw that angels of God will flee from a house where there are unpleasant words, fretfulness, and strife.

THE CHEERFUL WIFE

I have also been shown that there is often a great failure on the part of the wife. She does not put forth strong efforts to control her own spirit and make home happy. There is often fretfulness and unnecessary complaining on her part. The husband comes home from his labor weary and perplexed, and meets a clouded brow instead of cheerful, encouraging words. He is but human, and his affections become weaned from his wife, he loses the love of his home, his pathway is darkened, and his courage destroyed. He yields his self-respect and that dignity which God requires him to maintain. The husband is the head of the family, as Christ is the head of the church; and any course which the wife may pursue to lessen his influence and lead him to come down from that dignified, responsible position is displeasing to God. It is the duty of the wife to yield her wishes and will to her husband. Both should be yielding, but the word of God gives preference to the judgment of the husband. And it will not detract from the dignity of the wife to yield to him whom she has chosen to be her counselor, adviser, and protector.

The husband should maintain his position in his family with all meekness, yet with decision. Some have asked the question, Must I be on my guard and feel a restraint upon me continually? I have been shown that we have a great work before us to search our own hearts, and watch ourselves with jealous care. We should learn wherein we fail, and then guard ourselves upon that point. We must have perfect control over our own spirit. "If any man offend not in word, the same is a perfect man, and able also to bridle the whole body." James 3:2.

The light that shines upon our path, the truth that commends itself to our consciences, will condemn and destroy the soul, or sanctify and transform it. We are living too near the close of probation to be content with a superficial work. The same grace which we have hitherto considered sufficient will not sustain us now. Our faith must be increased, and we must become more like Christ in conduct and disposition in order to endure, and successfully resist, the temptations of Satan. The grace of God is sufficient for every follower of Christ.

SATAN'S ATTACK IN THE HOME

Our efforts to resist the attacks of Satan must be earnest and persevering. He employs his strength and skill in trying to turn us out of the right way. He watches our going out and our coming in, that he may find opportunity to hurt or destroy us. He works most successfully in darkness, injuring those who are ignorant of his devices. He could not gain advantage if his method of attack were understood. The instruments he employs to effect his purposes, and transmit his fiery darts, are often the members of our own families.

Those we love may speak or act unguardedly, which may wound us deeply. It was not their intention to do this; but Satan magnifies their words and acts before the mind, and thus hurls a dart from his quiver to pierce us. We brace ourselves to resist the one whom we think has injured us, and by so doing we encourage Satan's temptations. Instead of praying to God for strength to resist Satan, we suffer our happiness to be marred by trying to stand for what we term "our rights." Thus we allow Satan a double advantage. We act out our aggrieved feelings, and Satan uses us as his agents to wound and distress those who did not intend to injure us. The requirements of the husband may sometimes seem unreasonable to the wife, when if she should calmly, candidly take the second view of the matter, in as favorable a light for him as possible, she would see that to yield her own way and submit to his judgment, even if it conflicted with her feelings, would save them both from unhappiness and would give them great victory over the temptations of Satan.

I saw that the enemy will contend either for the usefulness or the life of the godly, and will try to mar their peace as long as they live in this world. But his power is limited. He may cause the furnace to be heated, but Jesus and angels will watch the trusting Christian, that nothing may be consumed but the dross. The fire kindled by Satan can have no power to destroy or hurt the true metal. It is important to close every door possible, against the entrance of Satan. It is the privilege of every family so to live that Satan can take no advantage of anything they may say or do, to tear one another down. Every member of the family should bear in mind that all have just as much as they can do to resist our wily foe, and with earnest prayers and unyielding faith each must rely upon the merits of the blood of Christ and claim His saving strength.

WALKING BY FAITH

The powers of darkness gather about the soul and shut Jesus from our sight, and at times we can only wait in sorrow and amazement until the cloud passes over. These seasons are sometimes terrible. Hope seems to fail, and despair seizes upon us. In these dreadful hours we must learn to trust, to depend solely upon the merits of the atonement, and in all our helpless unworthiness cast ourselves upon the merits of the crucified and risen Saviour. We shall never perish while we do this—*never!* When light shines on our pathway, it is no great thing to be strong in the strength of grace. But to wait patiently in hope when clouds envelop us and all is dark, requires faith and submission which causes our will to be swallowed up in the will of God. We are too quickly discouraged, and earnestly cry for the trial to be removed from us, when we should plead for patience to endure and grace to overcome.

Without faith it is impossible to please God. We can have the salvation of God in our families, but we must believe for it, live for it, and have a continual, abiding faith and trust in God. We must subdue a hasty temper and control our words, and in this we shall gain great victories. Unless we control our words and temper, we are slaves to Satan. We are in subjection to him. He leads us captive. All jangling and unpleasant, impatient, fretful words are an offering presented to his satanic majesty. And it is a costly offering, more costly than any sacrifice we can make for God, for it destroys the peace and happiness of whole families, destroys health, and is eventually the cause of forfeiting an eternal life of happiness.

The restraint which God's word imposes upon us is for our own interest. It increases the happiness of our families and of all around us. It refines our taste, sanctifies our judgment, and brings peace of mind, and, in the end, everlasting life. Under this holy restraint we shall increase in grace and humility, and it will become easy to speak right. The natural, passionate temper will be held in subjection. An indwelling Saviour will strengthen us every hour. Ministering angels will linger in our dwellings and with joy carry heavenward the tidings of our advance in the divine life, and the recording angel will make a cheerful, happy record.

False Ideas of Sanctification

God is now testing and proving His people. Character is being developed. Angels are weighing moral worth, and keeping a faithful record of all the acts of the children of men. Among God's professed people are corrupt hearts; but they will be tested and proved. That God who reads the hearts of everyone, will bring to light hidden things of darkness where they are often least suspected, that stumbling blocks which have hindered the progress of truth may be removed, and God have a clean and holy people to declare His statutes and judgments.

The Captain of our salvation leads His people on step by step, purifying and fitting them for translation, and leaving in the rear those who are disposed to draw off from the body, who are not willing to be led, and are satisfied with their own righteousness. "If therefore the light that is in thee be darkness, how great is that darkness!" Matthew 6:23. No greater delusion can deceive the human mind than that which leads men to indulge a self-confident spirit, to believe that they are right and in the light, when they are drawing away from God's people, and their cherished light is darkness. . . .

Brother J received from Elder K a false theory of sanctification, which is outside of the third angel's message, and wherever received destroys the love for the message. I was shown that Elder K was upon dangerous ground. He is not in union with the third angel. He once enjoyed the blessing of God, but does not now, for he has not prized and cherished the light of truth which has shone upon his pathway. He has brought along with him a theory of Methodist sanctification, and presents that in front, making it of the highest im-

1862, vol. 1, pp. 332-340 (Northern Wisconsin).

portance. And the sacred truths applicable to this time are by him made of little consequence. He has followed his own light, and been growing darker and darker, and going further and further from the truth, until it has but little influence upon him. Satan has controlled his mind, and he has done great injury to the cause of truth in northern Wisconsin.

ITS FRUITAGE

It was this theory of sanctification which Sister G received of Elder K, and which she tried to follow out, that carried her into that dreadful fanaticism. Elder K has bewildered and confused many minds with this theory of sanctification. All who embrace it lose to a great extent their interest in and love for the third angel's message. This view of sanctification is a very pretty-looking theory. It whitewashes over poor souls who are in darkness, error, and pride. It gives them an appearance of being good Christians, and of possessing holiness, when their hearts are corrupt. It is a peace-and-safety theory, which does not bring to light evil and reprove and rebuke wrong. It heals the hurt of the daughter of God's people slightly, crying: Peace, peace, when there is no peace. Men and women of corrupt hearts throw around them the garb of sanctification, and are looked upon as examples to the flock, when they are Satan's agents, used by him to allure and deceive honest souls into a bypath, that they may not feel the force and importance of the solemn truths proclaimed by the third angel.

Elder K has been looked up to as an example, while he has been an injury to the cause of God. His life has not been blameless. His ways have not been in accordance with the holy law of God, or with the spotless life of Christ. His corrupt nature is not subdued; and yet he dwells much upon sanctification, and thereby deceives many. I was directed to his past labors. He has failed to bring out souls into the truth, and to establish them upon the third angel's message. He presents a theory of sanctification as a matter of the utmost importance, while he makes of but little importance the channel through which God's blessing comes. "Sanctify them through Thy truth: Thy word is truth." John 17:17. The present truth, which is the channel, is not regarded, but is trampled underfoot. Men may cry, Holiness! holiness! sanctification! sanctification! consecration! consecration! and yet know no more by experience of what they talk than the sinner with his corrupt propensities. God will soon tear off this whitewashed garb of professed sanctification which some who are carnally minded have thrown around them to hide the deformity of the soul.

A faithful record is kept of the acts of the children of men. Nothing can be concealed from the eye of the high and holy One. Some take a course directly opposed to the law of God, and then, to cover up their sinful course, they profess to be consecrated to God. This profession of holiness does not make itself manifest in their daily lives. It does not have a tendency to elevate their minds, and lead them to "abstain from all appearance of evil." 1 Thessalonians 5:22. We are made a spectacle unto the world, to angels, and to men. Our faith is blasphemed in consequence of the crooked course of the carnally minded. They profess a part of the truth, which gives them influence, while they have no union with those who believe and are united upon the whole truth. What has been Elder K's influence? What have been the fruits of his labors? How many have been brought out and established upon present truth? . . .

I was shown the case of Mr. L. He has much to say upon sanctification, but he is deceived in himself, and others are deceived in him. His sanctification may last him while he is in meeting, but it cannot bear the test. Bible holiness purifies the life; but L's heart is not cleansed. Evil exists in the heart, and is carried out in the life, and the enemies of our faith have had occasion to reproach Sabbathkeepers. They judge of the tree by its fruits.

"But have renounced the hidden things of dishonesty, not walking in craftiness, nor handling the word of God deceitfully; but by manifestation of the truth commending ourselves to every man's conscience in the sight of God." 2 Corinthians 4:2.

Many go directly contrary to the above scripture. They do walk in craftiness, and handle the word of God deceitfully. They do not exemplify the truth in their lives. They have special exercises upon sanctification, yet cast the word of God behind them. They pray sanctification, sing sanctification, and shout sanctification. Men with corrupt hearts put on the air of innocence, and profess to be consecrated; but this is no evidence that they are right. Their deeds testify of them. Their consciences are seared, but the day of God's visitation is coming, and every man's work shall be manifest, of what sort it is. And every man shall receive according to his deeds.

Said the angel, as he pointed to L: "What hast thou to do to declare My statutes, or that thou shouldest take My covenant in thy mouth? seeing thou hatest instruction, and castest My words behind thee. When thou sawest a thief, then thou consentedst with him, and hast been partaker with adulterers. Thou givest thy mouth to evil, and thy tongue frameth deceit." Psalm 50:16-19. God will scatter and shake off these dividing influences, and will free His people, if those professing the whole truth will come up to the help of the Lord.

NO SANCTIFICATION TO THE DISOBEDIENT

There is no Bible sanctification for those who cast a part of the truth behind them. There is light enough given in the word of God, so that none need err. The truth is so elevated as to be admired by the greatest minds, and yet it is so simple that the humblest, feeblest child of God can comprehend it, and be instructed by it. Those who see not the beauty that there is in the truth, who attach no importance to the third angel's message, will be without excuse; for the truth is plain.

"But if our gospel be hid, it is hid to them that are lost: in whom the god of this world hath blinded the minds of them which believe not, lest the light of the glorious gospel of Christ, who is the image of God, should shine unto them." 2 Corinthians 4:3, 4.

"Sanctify them through Thy truth: Thy word is truth." "And for their sakes I sanctify Myself, that they also might be sanctified through the truth." John 17:17, 19.

"Seeing ye have purified your souls in obeying the truth through the Spirit unto unfeigned love of the brethren, see that ye love one another with a pure heart fervently." 1 Peter 1:22.

"Having therefore these promises, dearly beloved, let us cleanse ourselves from all filthiness of the flesh and spirit, perfecting holiness in the fear of God." 2 Corinthians 7:1.

"Wherefore, my beloved, as ye have always obeyed, not as in my presence only, but now much more in my absence, work out your own salvation with fear and trembling. For it is God which worketh in you both to will and to do of His good pleasure. Do all things without murmurings and disputings: that ye may be blameless and harmless, the sons of God, without rebuke, in the midst of a crooked and perverse nation, among whom ye shine as lights in the world." Philippians 2:12-15.

"Now ye are clean through the word which I have spoken unto you." John 15:3.

"Husbands, love your wives, even as Christ also loved the church, and gave Himself for it; that He might sanctify and cleanse it with the washing of water by the word, that He might present it to Himself a glorious church, not having spot, or wrinkle, or any such thing; but that it should be holy and without blemish." Ephesians 5:25-27.

Here is Bible sanctification. It is not merely a show or

outside work. It is sanctification received through the channel of truth. It is truth received in the heart, and practically carried out in the life.

Jesus, considered as a man, was perfect, yet He grew in grace. "And Jesus increased in wisdom and stature, and in favor with God and man." Luke 2:52. Even the most perfect Christian may increase continually in the knowledge and love of God.

"Wherefore, beloved, seeing that ye look for such things, be diligent that ye may be found of Him in peace, without spot, and blameless." "But grow in grace, and in the knowledge of our Lord and Saviour Jesus Christ. To Him be glory both now and forever. Amen." 2 Peter 3:14, 18.

A CONTINUAL GROWTH

Sanctification is not the work of a moment, an hour, or a day. It is a continual growth in grace. We know not one day how strong will be our conflict the next. Satan lives, and is active, and every day we need to cry earnestly to God for help and strength to resist him. As long as Satan reigns we shall have self to subdue, besetments to overcome, and there is no stopping place, there is no point to which we can come and say we have fully attained.

"Not as though I had already attained, either were already perfect: but I follow after, if that I may apprehend that for which also I am apprehended of Christ Jesus." Philippians 3:12.

The Christian life is constantly an onward march. Jesus sits as a refiner and purifier of His people; and when His image is perfectly reflected in them, they are perfect and holy, and prepared for translation. A great work is required of the Christian. We are exhorted to cleanse ourselves from all filthiness of the flesh and spirit, perfecting holiness in the fear of God. Here we see where the great labor rests. There is a constant work for the Christian. Every branch in the parent vine must derive life and strength from that vine, in order to yield fruit.

It will cost us an effort to secure eternal life. It is only by long and persevering effort, sore discipline, and stern conflict that we shall be overcomers. But if we patiently and determinedly, in the name of the Conqueror who overcame in our behalf in the wilderness of temptation, overcome as He overcame, we shall have the eternal reward. Our efforts, our self-denial, our perseverance, must be proportionate to the infinite value of the object of which we are in pursuit.—1873, vol. 3, pp. 324, 325.

The Power of Satan

Fallen man is Satan's lawful captive. The mission of Christ was to rescue him from the power of his great adversary. Man is naturally inclined to follow Satan's suggestions, and he cannot successfully resist so terrible a foe unless Christ, the mighty Conqueror, dwells in him, guiding his desires, and giving him strength. God alone can limit the power of Satan. He is going to and fro in the earth, and walking up and down in it. He is not off his watch for a single moment, through fear of losing an opportunity to destroy souls. It is important that God's people understand this, that they may escape his snares.

Satan is preparing his deceptions, that in his last campaign against the people of God they may not understand that it is he. "And no marvel; for Satan himself is transformed into an angel of light." 2 Corinthians 11:14. While some deceived souls are advocating that he does not exist, he is taking them captive, and is working through them to a great extent. Satan knows better than God's people the power that they can have over him when their strength is in Christ. When they humbly entreat the mighty Conqueror for help, the weakest believer in the truth, relying firmly upon Christ, can successfully repulse Satan and all his host. He is too cunning to come openly, boldly, with his temptations; for then the drowsy energies of the Christian would arouse, and he would rely upon the strong and mighty Deliverer. But he comes in unperceived, and works in disguise through the children of disobedience who profess godliness.

Satan will go to the extent of his power to harass, tempt, and mislead God's people. He who dared to face, and tempt,

1862, vol. 1, pp. 341-347.

and taunt our Lord, and who had power to take Him in his arms and carry Him to a pinnacle of the temple, and up into an exceedingly high mountain, will exercise his power to a wonderful degree upon the present generation, who are far inferior in wisdom to their Lord, and who are almost wholly ignorant of Satan's subtlety and strength. In a marvelous manner will he affect the bodies of those who are naturally inclined to do his bidding. Satan exults that he is regarded as a fiction. When he is made light of, and represented by some childish illustration, or as some animal, it suits him well. He is thought so inferior that the minds of men are wholly unprepared for his wisely laid plans, and he almost always succeeds well. If his power and subtlety were understood, many would be prepared to successfully resist him.

All should understand that Satan was once an exalted angel. His rebellion shut him out of heaven, but did not destroy his powers and make him a beast. Since his fall he has turned his mighty strength against the government of heaven. He has been growing more artful, and has learned the most successful manner in which to come to the children of men with his temptations.

SATAN'S DECEPTION

Satan has originated fables with which to deceive. He commenced in heaven to war against the foundation of God's government, and since his fall he has carried on his rebellion against the law of God, and has brought the mass of professed Christians to trample under their feet the fourth commandment, which brings to view the living God. He has torn down the original Sabbath of the Decalogue, and substituted in its place one of the laboring days of the week.

The great original lie which he told to Eve in Eden, "Ye shall not surely die" (Genesis 3:4), was the first sermon ever preached on the immortality of the soul. That sermon was crowned with success, and terrible results followed. He has brought minds to receive that sermon as truth, and ministers preach it, sing it, and pray it.

No literal devil, and probation after the coming of Christ, are fast becoming popular fables. The Scriptures plainly declare that every person's destiny is forever fixed at the coming of the Lord. Revelation 22:11, 12: "He that is unjust, let him be unjust still: and he which is filthy, let him be filthy still: and he that is righteous, let him be righteous still: and he that is holy, let him be holy still. And, behold, I come quickly; and My reward is with Me, to give every man according as his work shall be."

Satan has taken advantage of these popular fables to hide himself. He comes to poor, deceived mortals through modern spiritualism, which places no bounds to the carnally minded, and, if carried out, separates families, creates jealousy and hatred, and gives liberty to the most degrading propensities. The world knows but little as yet of the corrupting influence of spiritualism. The curtain was lifted, and much of its dreadful work was revealed to me. I was shown some who have had an experience in spiritualism, and have since renounced it, who shudder as they reflect upon how near they came to utter ruin. They had lost control of themselves, and Satan made them do that which they detested. But even they have but a faint idea of spiritualism as it is. Ministers inspired of Satan can eloquently dress up this hideous monster, hide its deformity, and make it appear beautiful to many. But it comes so direct from his satanic majesty, that he claims the right to control all who have to do with it, for they have ventured upon forbidden ground, and have forfeited the protection of their Maker.

Some poor souls who have been fascinated with the eloquent words of the teachers of spiritualism, and have yielded to its influence, afterward find out its deadly character, and would renounce and flee from it, but cannot. Satan holds them by his power, and is not willing to let them go free.

He knows that they are surely his while he has them under his special control, but that if they once free themselves from his power, he can never bring them again to believe in spiritualism, and to place themselves so directly under his control.

The only way for such poor souls to overcome Satan, is to discern between pure Bible truths and fables. As they acknowledge the claims of truth, they place themselves where they can be helped. They should entreat those who have had a religious experience, and who have faith in the promises of God, to plead with the mighty Deliverer in their behalf. It will be a close conflict. Satan will reinforce his evil angels who have controlled these persons; but if the saints of God with deep humility fast and pray, their prayers will prevail. Jesus will commission holy angels to resist Satan, and he will be driven back and his power broken from off the afflicted ones. Mark 9:29: "And He said unto them, This kind can come forth by nothing, but by prayer and fasting."

The popular ministry cannot successfully resist spiritualism. They have nothing wherewith to shield their flocks from its baleful influence. Much of the sad result of spiritualism will rest upon ministers of this age; for they have trampled the truth under their feet, and in its stead have preferred fables. The sermon which Satan preached to Eve upon the immortality of the soul—"Ye shall not surely die"—they have reiterated from the pulpit; and the people receive it as pure Bible truth. It is the foundation of spiritualism. The word of God nowhere teaches that the soul of man is immortal. Immortality is an attribute of God only. 1 Timothy 6:16: "Who only hath immortality, dwelling in the light which no man can approach unto; whom no man hath seen, nor can see: to whom be honor and power everlasting. Amen."

God's word, rightly understood and applied, is a safeguard against spiritualism. An eternally burning hell preached from the pulpit, and kept before the people, does injustice to the benevolent character of God. It presents Him as the veriest tyrant in the universe. This widespread dogma has turned thousands to universalism, infidelity, and atheism. The word of God is plain. It is a straight chain of truth, and will prove an anchor to those who are willing to receive it, even if they have to sacrifice their cherished fables. It will save them from the terrible delusions of these perilous times. Satan has led the minds of the ministers of different churches to cling tenaciously to their popular errors, as he led the Jews in their blindness to cling to their sacrifices, and crucify Christ. The rejection of light and truth leaves men captives, the subjects of Satan's deception. The greater the light they reject, the greater will be the power of deception and darkness which will come upon them.

I was shown that God's true people are the salt of the earth and the light of the world. God requires of them continual advancement in the knowledge of the truth, and in the way of holiness. Then will they understand the coming in of Satan, and in the strength of Jesus will resist him. Satan will call to his aid legions of his angels to oppose the advance of even one soul, and, if possible, wrest it from the hand of Christ.

THE CONTEST FOR SOULS

I saw evil angels contending for souls, and angels of God resisting them. The conflict was severe. Evil angels were corrupting the atmosphere with their poisonous influence, and crowding about these souls to stupefy their sensibilities. Holy angels were anxiously watching and waiting to drive back Satan's host. But it is not the work of good angels to control the minds of men against their will. If they yield to the enemy, and make no effort to resist him, then the angels of God can do but little more than hold in check the host of Satan, that they shall not destroy, until further light be given to those in peril, to move them to arouse and look to heaven for help. Jesus will not commission holy angels to extricate those who make no effort to help themselves.

If Satan sees that he is in danger of losing one soul, he will exert himself to the utmost to keep that one. And when the individual is aroused to his danger, and, with distress and fervor, looks to Jesus for strength, Satan fears that he will lose a captive, and he calls a reinforcement of his angels to hedge in the poor soul, and form a wall of darkness around him, that heaven's light may not reach him. But if the one in danger perseveres, and in his helplessness casts himself upon the merits of the blood of Christ, our Saviour listens to the earnest prayer of faith, and sends a reinforcement of those angels that excel in strength to deliver him.

Satan cannot endure to have his powerful rival appealed to, for he fears and trembles before His strength and majesty. At the sound of fervent prayer, Satan's whole host trembles. He continues to call legions of evil angels to accomplish his object. And when angels, all-powerful, clothed with the armory of heaven, come to the help of the fainting, pursued soul, Satan and his host fall back, well knowing that their battle is lost. The willing subjects of Satan are faithful, active, and united in one object. And although they hate and war with one another, yet they improve every opportunity to advance their common interest. But the great Commander in heaven and earth has limited Satan's power.

My experience has been singular, and for years I have suffered peculiar trials of mind. The condition of God's people, and my connection with the work of God, have often brought upon me a weight of sadness and discouragement which cannot be expressed. For years I have looked to the grave as a sweet resting place. In my last vision I inquired of my attending angel why I was left to suffer such perplexity of mind, and was so often thrown upon Satan's battleground. I entreated that if I must be so closely connected with the cause of truth, I might be delivered from these severe trials. There is power and strength with the angels of God, and I pleaded that I might be shielded.

Then our past life was presented before me, and I was shown that Satan had sought in various ways to destroy our usefulness; that many times he had laid his plans to remove us from the work of God; he had come in different ways, and through different agencies, to accomplish his purposes; but through the ministration of holy angels he had been defeated. I saw that in our journeying from place to place, he had frequently placed his evil angels in our path to cause accident which would destroy our lives; but holy angels were sent upon the ground to deliver. Several accidents have placed my husband and myself in great peril, and our preservation has been wonderful. I saw that we had been the special objects of Satan's attacks, because of our interest in and connection with the work of God. As I saw the great care which God has every moment for those who love and fear Him, I was inspired with confidence and trust in God, and felt reproved for my lack of faith.

It was by the display of supernatural power, in making the serpent his medium, that Satan caused the fall of Adam and Eve in Eden. Before the close of time he will work still greater wonders. So far as his power extends, he will perform actual miracles. Says the Scripture: "He . . . deceiveth them that dwell on the earth by the means of those miracles which he had power to do" (Revelation 13:13, 14), not merely those which he pretends to do. Something more than mere impostures is brought to view in this scripture. But there is a limit beyond which Satan cannot go, and here he calls deception to his aid and counterfeits the work which he has not power actually to perform. In the last days he will appear in such a manner as to make men believe him to be Christ come the second time into the world. He will indeed transform himself into an angel of light. But while he will bear the appearance of Christ in every particular, so far as mere appearance goes, it will deceive none but those who, like Pharaoh, are seeking to resist the truth.—1889, vol. 5, p. 698.

The Two Crowns

In the vision given me at Battle Creek, Michigan, October 25, 1861, I was shown this earth, dark and gloomy. Said the angel: "Look carefully!" Then I was shown the people upon the earth. Some were surrounded by angels of God, others were in total darkness, surrounded by evil angels. I saw an arm reached down from heaven, holding a golden scepter. On the top of the scepter was a crown studded with diamonds. Every diamond emitted light, bright, clear, and beautiful. Inscribed upon the crown were these words: "All who win me are happy, and shall have everlasting life."

Below this crown was another scepter, and upon this also was placed a crown, in the center of which were jewels, gold, and silver, reflecting some light. The inscription upon the crown was: "Earthly treasure. Riches is power. All who win me have honor and fame." I saw a vast multitude rushing forward to obtain this crown. They were clamorous. Some in their eagerness seemed bereft of reason. They would thrust one another, crowding back those who were weaker than they, and trampling upon those who in their haste fell. Many eagerly seized hold of the treasures within the crown, and held them fast. The heads of some were as white as silver, and their faces were furrowed with care and anxiety. Their own relatives, bone of their bone, and flesh of their flesh, they regarded not; but, as appealing looks were turned to them, they held their treasures more firmly, as though fearful that in an unguarded moment they should lose a little, or be induced to divide with them. Their eager eyes would often fasten upon the earthly crown, and count and recount

1862, vol. 1, pp. 347-353.

its treasures. Images of want and wretchedness appeared in that multitude, and looked wishfully at the treasures there, and turned hopelessly away as the stronger overpowered and drove back the weaker. Yet they could not give it up thus, but with a multitude of deformed, sickly, and aged, they sought to press their way to the earthly crown. Some died in seeking to reach it. Others fell just in the act of taking hold of it. Many had but just laid hold of it when they fell. Dead bodies strewed the ground, yet on rushed the multitude, trampling over the fallen and dead bodies of their companions. Everyone who reached the crown possessed a share in it, and was loudly applauded by an interested company standing around it.

SATANIC DECEPTION

A large company of evil angels were very busy. Satan was in the midst of them, and all looked with the most exulting satisfaction upon the company struggling for the crown. He seemed to throw a peculiar charm upon those who eagerly sought it. Many who sought this earthly crown were professed Christians. Some of them seemed to have a little light. They would look wishfully upon the heavenly crown, and would often seem charmed with its beauty, yet they had no true sense of its value and glory. While with one hand they were reaching forth languidly for the heavenly, with the other they reached eagerly for the earthly, determined to possess that; and in their earnest pursuit for the earthly, they lost sight of the heavenly. They were left in darkness, yet were anxiously groping about to secure the earthly crown. Some became disgusted with the company who sought it so eagerly; they seemed to have a sense of their danger, and turned from it, and earnestly sought for the heavenly crown. The countenances of such soon changed from dark to light, from gloom to cheerfulness and holy joy.

I then saw a company pressing through the crowd with their eyes intently fixed upon the heavenly crown. As they earnestly urged their way through the disorderly crowd, angels attended them, and made room for them to advance. As they neared the heavenly crown, the light emanating from it shone upon them and around them, dispelling their darkness, and growing clearer and brighter, until they seemed to be transformed, and resembled the angels. They cast not one lingering look upon the earthly crown. Those who were in pursuit of the earthly, mocked them, and threw black balls after them. These did them no injury while their eyes were fixed upon the heavenly crown, but those who turned their attention to the black balls were stained with them. The following scripture was presented before me:

Matthew 6:19-24: "Lay not up for yourselves treasures upon earth, where moth and rust doth corrupt, and where thieves break through and steal: but lay up for yourselves treasures in heaven, where neither moth nor rust doth corrupt, and where thieves do not break through nor steal: for where your treasure is, there will your heart be also. The light of the body is the eye: if therefore thine eye be single, thy whole body shall be full of light. But if thine eye be evil, thy whole body shall be full of darkness. If therefore the light that is in thee be darkness, how great is that darkness! No man can serve two masters: for either he will hate the one, and love the other; or else he will hold to the one, and despise the other. Ye cannot serve God and mammon."

Then that which I had seen was explained to me as follows: The multitude who were so eagerly striving for the earthly crown, were those who love this world's treasure, and are deceived and flattered with its short-lived attractions. Some, I saw, who profess to be the followers of Jesus, are so ambitious to obtain earthly treasures that they lose their love for heaven, act like the world, and are accounted of God as of the world. They profess to be seeking an immortal crown, a treasure in the heavens; but their interest and principal study is to acquire earthly treasures. Those who have their treasures in this world, and love their riches, cannot love Jesus. They may think that they are right, and, although they cling to their possessions with a miser's grasp, they cannot be made to see it, or to feel that they love money more than the cause of truth or the heavenly treasure.

TRUE AND FALSE RICHES

"If therefore the light that is in thee be darkness, how great is that darkness!" Verse 23. There was a point of time in the experience of such, when the light given them was not cherished, and it became darkness. Said the angel: "Ye cannot love and worship the treasures of earth, and have the true riches." When the young man came to Jesus and said to Him, "Good Master, what good thing shall I do, that I may have eternal life?"(Matthew 19:16)Jesus gave him his choice, to part with his possessions and have eternal life, or retain them and lose it. His riches were of greater value to him than the heavenly treasure. The condition that he must part with his treasures and give to the poor in order to become a follower of Christ and have eternal life, chilled his desire; and he went away sorrowful.

Those who were shown me as clamorous for the earthly crown, were those who will resort to any means to acquire property. They become insane upon that point. All their thoughts and energies are directed to the acquirement of earthly riches. They trample upon the rights of others, and oppress the poor, and the hireling in his wages. If they can take advantage of those who are poorer and less shrewd than they, and thus manage to increase their riches, they will not hesitate a moment to oppress them, and even see them brought to beggary.

The men whose heads were white with age, and whose faces were furrowed with care, yet who were eagerly grasping the treasures within the crown, were the aged, who have but a few years before them. Yet they were eager to secure their earthly treasures. The nearer they came to the grave, the more anxious they were to cling to them. Their own relatives were not benefited. The members of their own families were permitted to labor beyond their strength to save a little money. They did not use it for others' good, or for their own. It was enough for them to know that they had it. When their duty to relieve the wants of the poor, and to sustain God's cause are presented before them, they are sorrowful. They would gladly accept the gift of everlasting life, but are not willing that it should cost them anything. The conditions are too hard. But Abraham would not withhold his only son. In obedience to God he could sacrifice this child of promise more easily than many would sacrifice some of their earthly possessions.

It was painful to see those who should have been ripening for glory, and daily fitting for immortality, exerting all their strength to keep their earthly treasures. Such, I saw, could not value the heavenly treasure. Their strong affections for the earthly cause them to show by their works that they do not esteem the heavenly inheritance enough to make any sacrifice for it. The "young man" manifested a willingness to keep the commandments, yet our Lord told him that he lacked one thing. He desired eternal life, but loved his possessions more. Many are self-deceived. They have not sought for truth as for hid treasures. Their powers are not put to the best account. Their minds, which might be illuminated with heaven's light, are perplexed and troubled. "The cares of this world, and the deceitfulness of riches, and the lusts of other things entering in, choke the word, and it becometh unfruitful." Mark 4:19. "Such," said the angel, "are without excuse." I saw the light waning away from them. They did not desire to understand the solemn, important truths for this time, and thought they were well off without understanding them. Their light went out, and they were groping in darkness.

AGENTS OF SATAN

The multitude of deformed and sickly pressing for the earthly crown are those whose interests and treasures are in this world. Although they are disappointed on every side, they will not place their affections on heaven, and secure to themselves a treasure and home there. They fail of the earthly, yet while in pursuit of it, lose the heavenly. Notwithstanding the disappointment and unhappy life and death of those who were wholly bent upon obtaining earthly riches, others follow the same course. They rush madly on, disregarding the miserable end of those whose example they are following.

Those who reached the crown, and possessed a share in it, and were applauded, are those who obtain that which is the whole aim of their life—riches. They receive that honor which the world bestows upon those who are rich. They have influence in the world. Satan and his evil angels are satisfied. They know that such are surely theirs, that while they are living in rebellion against God, they are Satan's powerful agents.

The ones who became disgusted with the company clamoring for the earthly crown are those who have marked the life and end of all who strive for earthly riches. They see that such are never satisfied, but are unhappy, and they become alarmed, and separate themselves from that unhappy class, and seek the true and durable riches.

Those who are urging their way through the crowd for the heavenly crown, attended by holy angels, were shown me to be

God's faithful people. Angels lead them on, and they are inspired with zeal to press forward for the heavenly treasure.

The black balls which were thrown after the saints were the reproachful falsehoods put in circulation concerning God's people by those who love and make a lie. We should take the greatest care to live a blameless life, and abstain from all appearance of evil, and then it is our duty to move boldly forward, and pay no regard to the reproachful falsehoods of the wicked. While the eyes of the righteous are fixed upon the heavenly priceless treasure, they will become more and more like Christ, and thus they will be transformed and fitted for translation.

The Future

At the transfiguration, Jesus was glorified by His Father. We hear Him say: "Now is the Son of man glorified, and God is glorified in Him." John 13:31. Thus before His betrayal and crucifixion He was strengthened for His last dreadful sufferings. As the members of the body of Christ approach the period of their last conflict, "the time of Jacob's trouble," they will grow up into Christ, and will partake largely of His spirit. As the third message swells to a loud cry, and as great power and glory attend the closing work, the faithful people of God will partake of that glory. It is the latter rain which revives and strengthens them to pass through the time of trouble. Their faces will shine with the glory of that light which attends the third angel.

I saw that God will in a wonderful manner preserve His people through the time of trouble. As Jesus poured out His soul in agony in the garden, they will earnestly cry and agonize day and night for deliverance. The decree will go forth that they must disregard the Sabbath of the fourth commandment, and honor the first day, or lose their lives; but they will not yield, and trample under their feet the Sabbath of the Lord, and honor an institution of papacy. Satan's host and wicked men will surround them, and exult over them, because there will seem to be no way of escape for them. But in the midst of their revelry and triumph, there is heard peal upon peal of the loudest thunder. The heavens have gathered blackness, and are only illuminated by the blazing light and terrible glory from heaven, as God utters His voice from His holy habitation.

1862, vol. 1, pp. 353, 354.

The foundations of the earth shake; buildings totter and fall with a terrible crash. The sea boils like a pot, and the whole earth is in terrible commotion. The captivity of the righteous is turned, and with sweet and solemn whisperings they say to one another: "We are delivered. It is the voice of God." With solemn awe they listen to the words of the voice. The wicked hear, but understand not the words of the voice of God. They fear and tremble, while the saints rejoice. Satan and his angels, and wicked men, who had been exulting that the people of God were in their power, that they might destroy them from off the earth, witness the glory conferred upon those who have honored the holy law of God. They behold the faces of the righteous lighted up and reflecting the image of Jesus. Those who were so eager to destroy the saints cannot endure the glory resting upon the delivered ones, and they fall like dead men to the earth. Satan and evil angels flee from the presence of the saints glorified. Their power to annoy them is gone forever.

Parents and Children

I HAVE been shown that while parents who have the fear of God before them restrain their children, they should study their dispositions and temperaments, and seek to meet their wants. Some parents attend carefully to the temporal wants of their children; they kindly and faithfully nurse them in sickness, and then think their duty done. Here they mistake. Their work has but just begun. The wants of the mind should be cared for. It requires skill to apply the proper remedies to cure a wounded mind.

Children have trials just as hard to bear, just as grievous in character, as those of older persons. Parents themselves do not feel the same at all times. Their minds are often perplexed. They labor under mistaken views and feelings. Satan buffets them, and they yield to his temptations. They speak irritably, and in a manner to excite wrath in their children, and are sometimes exacting and fretful. The poor children partake of the same spirit, and the parents are not prepared to help them, for they were the cause of the trouble. Sometimes everything seems to go wrong. There is fretfulness all around, and all have a very miserable, unhappy time. The parents lay the blame upon their poor children and think them very disobedient and unruly, the worst children in the world, when the cause of the disturbance is in themselves.

Some parents raise many a storm by their lack of self-control. Instead of kindly asking the children to do this or that, they order them in a scolding tone, and at the same time a censure or reproof is on their lips which the children have not merited. Parents, this course pursued toward your children

1863, vol. 1, pp. 384-389.

destroys their cheerfulness and ambition. They do your bidding, not from love, but because they dare not do otherwise. Their heart is not in the matter. It is a drudgery, instead of a pleasure, and this often leads them to forget to follow out all your directions, which increases your irritation, and makes it still worse for the children. The faultfinding is repeated, their bad conduct arrayed before them in glowing colors, until discouragement comes over them, and they are not particular whether they please or not. A spirit of "I don't care" seizes them, and they seek that pleasure and enjoyment away from home, away from their parents, which they do not find at home. They mingle with street company and are soon as corrupt as the worst.

WHAT PARENTS MAY DO

Upon whom rests this great sin? If home had been made attractive, if the parents had manifested affection for their children, and with kindness found employment for them, and in love instructed them how to obey their wishes, they would have touched an answering chord in their hearts, and willing feet and hands and hearts would all have readily obeyed them. By controlling themselves, and speaking kindly, and praising the children when they try to do right, parents may encourage their efforts, make them very happy, and throw over the family circle a charm which will chase away every dark shadow and bring cheerful sunlight in.

Parents sometimes excuse their own wrong course because they do not feel well. They are nervous, and think they cannot be patient and calm, and speak pleasantly. In this they deceive themselves and please Satan, who exults that the grace of God is not regarded by them as sufficient to overcome natural infirmities. They can and should at all times control themselves. God requires it of them. They should realize that when they yield to impatience and fretfulness they cause others to suffer. Those around them are affected by the spirit they manifest, and if they in their turn act out the same spirit, the evil is increased and everything goes wrong.

Parents, when you feel fretful, you should not commit so great a sin as to poison the whole family with this dangerous irritability. At such times set a double watch over yourselves, and resolve in your heart not to offend with your lips, that you will utter only pleasant, cheerful words. Say to yourselves: "I will not mar the happiness of my children by a fretful word." By thus controlling yourselves, you will grow stronger. Your nervous system will not be so sensitive. You will be strengthened by the principles of right. The consciousness that you are faithfully discharging your duty will strengthen you. Angels of God will smile upon your efforts and help you.

When you feel impatient, you too often think the cause is in your children, and you blame them when they do not deserve it. At another time they might do the very same things and all would be acceptable and right. Children know, and mark, and feel these irregularities, and *they* are not always the same. At times they are somewhat prepared to meet changeable moods, and at other times they are nervous and fretful, and cannot bear censure. Their spirit rises up in rebellion against it. Parents want all due allowance made for their state of mind, yet do not always see the necessity of making the same allowance for their poor children. They excuse in themselves that which, if seen in their children who have not their years of experience and discipline, they would highly censure.

Some parents are of a nervous temperament, and when fatigued with labor or oppressed with care, they do not preserve a calm state of mind, but manifest to those who should be dearest to them on earth, a fretfulness and lack of forbearance which displeases God and brings a cloud over the family. Children, in their troubles, should often be soothed with tender sympathy. Mutual kindness and forbearance will make home a paradise and attract holy angels into the family circle.

The mother can and should do much toward controlling her nerves and mind when depressed; even when she is sick, she can, if she only schools herself, be pleasant and cheerful, and can bear more noise than she would once have thought possible. She should not make the children feel her infirmities and cloud their young, sensitive minds by her depression of spirits, causing them to feel that the house is a tomb and the mother's room the most dismal place in the world. The mind and nerves gain tone and strength by the exercise of the will. The power of the will in many cases will prove a potent soother of the nerves.

A CRITICAL TIME FOR CHILDREN

Do not let your children see you with a clouded brow. If they yield to temptation, and afterward see and repent of their error, forgive them just as freely as you hope to be forgiven by your Father in heaven. Kindly instruct them, and bind them to your hearts. It is a critical time for children. Influences will be thrown around them to wean them from you, which you must counteract. Teach them to make you their confidant. Let them whisper in your ear their trials and joys. By encouraging this, you will save them from many a snare that Satan has prepared for their inexperienced feet. Do not treat your children only with sternness, forgetting your own childhood, and forgetting that they are but children. Do not expect them to be perfect or try to make them men and women in their acts at once. By so doing, you will close the door of access which you might otherwise have to them, and will drive them to open a door for injurious influences, for others to poison their young minds before you awake to their danger.

Satan and his host are making most powerful efforts to sway the minds of the children, and they must be treated with candor, Christian tenderness, and love. This will give you a strong influence over them, and they will feel that they can repose unlimited confidence in you. Throw around your children the charms of home and of your society. If you do this, they will not have so much desire for the society of young associates. Satan works through these, leading them to influence and corrupt the minds of one another. It is the most effectual way in which he can work. The young have a powerful influence over one another. Their conversation is not always choice and elevated. Evil communications are breathed into the ear, which, if not decidedly resisted, find a lodgment in the heart, take root, and spring up to bear fruit and corrupt good manners. Because of the evils now in the world, and the restriction necessary to be placed upon the children, parents should have double care to bind them to their hearts and let them see that they wish to make them happy.

UNDERSTANDING PARENTS

Parents should not forget their childhood years, how much they yearned for sympathy and love, and how unhappy they felt when censured and fretfully chided. They should be young again in their feelings and bring their minds down to understand the wants of their children. Yet with firmness, mixed with love, they should require obedience from their children. The parents' word should be implicitly obeyed.

Angels of God are watching the children with the deepest interest to see what characters they develop. If Christ dealt with us as we often deal with one another and with our children, we would stumble and fall through utter discouragement. I saw that Jesus knows our infirmities, and has Himself shared our experience in all things but in sin; therefore He has prepared for us a path suited to our strength and capacity, and, like Jacob, has marched softly and in evenness with the children as they were able to endure, that He might entertain us by the comfort of His company, and be to us a perpetual guide. He does not despise, neglect, or leave behind the children of the flock. He has not bidden us move forward and leave them. He has not traveled so hastily as to leave us with our children behind. Oh, no; but He has evened the path to life, even for children. And parents are required in His name to lead them along the narrow way. God has appointed us a path suited to the strength and capacity of children.

It will pay to manifest affection in your association with your children. Do not repel them by lack of sympathy in their childish sports, joys, and griefs. Never let a frown gather upon your brow or a harsh word escape your lips. God writes all these words in His book of records. Harsh words sour the temper and wound the hearts of children, and in some cases these wounds are difficult to heal. Children are sensitive to the least injustice, and some become discouraged under it and will neither heed the loud, angry voice of command nor care for threatenings of punishment. Rebellion is too frequently established in the hearts of children through the wrong discipline of the parents, when if a proper course had been taken, the children would have formed good and harmonious characters. A mother who does not have perfect control of herself is unfit to have the management of children.—1875, vol. 3, pp. 532, 533.

Conquer your disposition to be exacting with your son, lest too frequent reproof make your presence disagreeable to him and your counsels hateful. Bind him to your heart, not by foolish indulgence, but by the silken cords of love. You can be firm yet kind. Christ must be your helper. Love will be the means of drawing other hearts to yours, and your influence may establish them in the good and right way.

I have warned you against a spirit of censure, and I would again caution you in regard to that fault. Christ sometimes reproved with severity, and in some cases it may be necessary for us to do so; but we should consider that while Christ knew the exact condition of the ones He rebuked, and just the amount of reproof they could bear, and what was necessary to correct their course of wrong, He also knew just how to pity the erring, comfort the unfortunate, and encourage the weak. He knew just how to keep souls from despondency and to inspire them with hope, because He was acquainted with the exact motives and peculiar trials of every mind. He could not make a mistake.—1876, vol. 4, p. 66.

Dangers of the Young

June 6, 1863, I was shown some of the dangers of the young. Satan is controlling the minds of the youth and leading their inexperienced feet astray. They are ignorant of his devices, and in these perilous times parents should be awake and work with perseverance and industry to shut out the first approach of the foe. They should instruct their children when they go out and when they come in, when they rise up, and when they sit down, giving line upon line, precept upon precept, here a little and there a little.

The mother's work commences with the infant. She should subdue the will and temper of her child, and bring it into subjection, teach it to obey. As the child grows older, relax not the hand. Every mother should take time to reason with her children, to correct their errors, and patiently teach them the right way. Christian parents should know that they are instructing and fitting their children to become children of God. The entire religious experience of the children is influenced by the instructions given, and the character formed, in childhood. If the will is not then subdued and made to yield to the will of the parents, it will be a difficult task to learn the lesson in afteryears. What a severe struggle, what a conflict, to yield that will which never was subdued, to the requirements of God! Parents who neglect this important work commit a great error, and sin against their poor children and against God.

Children who are under strict discipline will at times have dissatisfied feelings. They will become impatient under restraint, and will wish to have their own way, and go and come

1863, vol. 1, pp. 390-405.

as they please. Especially from the age of ten to eighteen, they will often feel that there would be no harm in going to picnics and other gatherings of young associates; yet their experienced parents can see danger. They are acquainted with the peculiar temperaments of their children and know the influence of these things upon their minds, and from a desire for their salvation keep them back from these exciting amusements.

When these children decide for themselves to leave the pleasures of the world and become Christ's disciples, what a burden is lifted from the hearts of careful, faithful parents! Yet even then the labor of the parents must not cease. The children should not be left to take their own course and always choose for themselves. They have but just commenced in earnest the warfare against sin, pride, passion, envy, jealousy, hatred, and all the evils of the natural heart. And parents need to watch and counsel their children, and decide for them, and show them that if they do not yield cheerful, willing obedience to their parents, they cannot yield willing obedience to God, and it is impossible for them to be Christians.

Parents should encourage their children to confide in *them,* and unburden to them their heart griefs, their little daily annoyances and trials. Thus the parents can learn to sympathize with their children, and can pray with and for them that God would shield and guide them. They should point them to their never-failing Friend and Counselor, who will be touched with the feeling of their infirmities, who was tempted in all points like as we are, yet without sin.

Satan tempts children to be reserved with their parents and to choose as their confidants their young and inexperienced companions, such as cannot help them, but will give them bad advice. Girls and boys get together and chat, and laugh, and joke, and drive Christ out of their hearts, and angels from their presence, by their foolish nonsense. Unprofitable conversation upon the acts of others, small talk about this young man or that girl, withers noble, devotional thoughts and feelings, and drives good and holy desires from the heart, leaving it cold and destitute of true love for God and His truth.

Children would be saved from many evils if they would be more familiar with their parents. Parents should encourage in their children a disposition to be open and frank with them, to come to them with their difficulties, and when they are perplexed as to what course is right, to lay the matter just as they view it before the parents and ask their advice. Who are so well calculated to see and point out their dangers as godly parents? Who can understand the peculiar temperaments of their own children as well as they? The mother who has watched every turn of the mind from infancy, and is thus acquainted with the natural disposition, is best prepared to counsel her children. Who can tell as well what traits of character to check and restrain, as the mother, aided by the father?

Children who are Christians will prefer the love and approbation of their God-fearing parents above every earthly blessing. They will love and honor their parents. It should be one of the principal studies of their lives, how to make their parents happy. In this rebellious age, children who have not received right instruction and discipline have but little sense of their obligations to their parents. It is often the case that the more their parents do for them, the more ungrateful they are, and the less they respect them. Children who have been petted and waited upon, always expect it; and if their expectations are not met, they are disappointed and discouraged. This same disposition will be seen through their whole lives; they will be helpless, leaning upon others for aid, expecting others to favor them and yield to them. And if they are opposed, even after they have grown to manhood and womanhood, they think themselves abused; and thus they worry their way through the world, hardly able to bear their own weight, often murmuring and fretting because everything does not suit them.

INDULGED CHILDREN

Mistaken parents are teaching their children lessons which will prove ruinous to them, and are also planting thorns for their own feet. They think that by gratifying the wishes of their children, and letting them follow their own inclinations, they can gain their love. What an error! Children thus indulged grow up unrestrained in their desires, unyielding in their dispositions, selfish, exacting, and overbearing, a curse to themselves and to all around them. To a great extent, parents hold in their own hands the future happiness of their children. Upon them rests the important work of forming the character of these children. The instructions given in childhood will follow them all through life. Parents sow the seed which will spring up and bear fruit either for good or evil. They can fit their sons and daughters for happiness or for misery.

Children should be taught very young to be useful, to help themselves, and to help others. Many daughters of this age can, without remorse of conscience, see their mothers toiling, cooking, washing, or ironing, while they sit in the parlor and read stories, knit edging, crochet, or embroider. Their hearts are as unfeeling as a stone. But where does this wrong originate? Who are the ones usually most to blame in this matter? The poor, deceived parents. They overlook the future good of their children, and in their mistaken fondness, let them sit in idleness, or do that which is of but little account, which requires no exercise of the mind or muscles, and then excuse their indolent daughters because they are weakly. What has made them weakly? In many cases it has been the wrong course of the parents. A proper amount of exercise about the house would improve both mind and body. But children are deprived of this through false ideas, until they are averse to work. It is disagreeable and does not accord with their ideas of gentility. It is thought to be unladylike and even coarse to wash dishes, iron, or stand over the washtub. This is the fashionable instruction which is given children in this unfortunate age.

God's people should be governed by higher principles than worldlings, who seek to gauge all their course of action according to fashion. God-fearing parents should train their children for a life of usefulness. They should not permit their principles of government to be tainted with the extravagant notions prevailing in this age, that they must conform to the fashions and be governed by the opinions of worldlings. They should not permit their children to choose their own associates. Teach them that it is your duty to choose for them. Prepare them to bear burdens while young.

If your children have been unaccustomed to labor, they will soon become weary. They will complain of side ache, pain in the shoulders, and tired limbs; and you will be in danger, through sympathy, of doing the work yourselves, rather than have them suffer a little. Let the burden upon the children be very light at first, and then increase it a little every day, until they can do a proper amount of labor without becoming so weary. Inactivity is the greatest cause of side ache and shoulder ache among children.

There is a class of young ladies in this age who are merely useless creatures, only good to breathe, eat, wear, chat, and talk nonsense, while they hold in their fingers a bit of embroidery or crochet. But few of the youth show real sound judgment and good common sense. They lead a butterfly life with no special object in view. When this class of worldly associates get together, about all you can hear is a few silly remarks about dress, or some frivolous matter, and then they laugh at their own remarks which they consider very bright.

This is frequently done in the presence of older persons, who can but feel saddened at such lack of reverence for their years. These youth seem to have lost all sense of modesty and good manners. Yet the manner in which they have been instructed leads them to think it the height of gentility.

This spirit is like a contagious disease. God's people should choose the society for their children and teach them to avoid the company of these vain worldlings. Mothers should take their daughters with them into the kitchen and patiently educate them. Their constitution will be better for such labor, their muscles will gain tone and strength, and their meditations will be more healthy and elevated at the close of the day. They may be weary, but how sweet is rest after a proper amount of labor. Sleep, nature's sweet restorer, invigorates the weary body, and prepares it for the next day's duties. Do not intimate to your children that it is no matter whether they labor or not. Teach them that their help is needed, that their time is of value, and that you depend on their labor.

THE SIN OF IDLENESS

I have been shown that much sin has resulted from idleness. Active hands and minds do not find time to heed every temptation which the enemy suggests, but idle hands and brains are all ready for Satan to control. The mind, when not properly occupied, dwells upon improper things. Parents should teach their children that idleness is sin. I was referred to Ezekiel 16:49: "Behold, this was the iniquity of thy sister Sodom, pride, fullness of bread, and abundance of idleness was in her and in her daughters, neither did she strengthen the hand of the poor and needy."

Children should feel that they are indebted to their parents, who have watched over them in infancy and nursed them in sickness. They should realize that their parents have suffered much anxiety on their account. Especially have conscientious, godly parents felt the deepest interest that their children should take a right course. As they have seen faults in their children, how heavy have been their hearts. If the children who caused those hearts to ache could see the effect of their course, they would certainly relent. If they could see their mother's tears and hear her prayers to God in their behalf, if they could listen to her suppressed and broken sighs, their hearts would feel, and they would speedily confess their wrongs and ask to be forgiven. There is a work to be accomplished for old and young. Parents should better qualify themselves to discharge their duty to their children. Some parents do not understand their children and are not really acquainted with them. There is often a great distance between parents and children. If the parents would enter more fully into the feelings of their children and draw out what is in their hearts, it would have a beneficial influence upon them.

CONVERSION OF CHILDREN

Parents should deal faithfully with the souls committed to their trust. They should not encourage in their children pride, extravagance, or love of show. They should not teach them, or suffer them to learn, little pranks which appear cunning in small children, but which they will have to unlearn, and for which they must be corrected, when they are older. The habits first formed are not easily forgotten. Parents, you should commence to discipline the minds of your children while very young, to the end that they may be Christians. Let all your efforts be for their salvation. Act as though they were placed in your care to be fitted as precious jewels to shine in the kingdom of God. Beware how you lull them to sleep over the pit of destruction with the mistaken thought that they are not old enough to be accountable, not old enough to repent of their sins and profess Christ.

I was referred to the many precious promises on record for those who seek their Saviour early. "Remember now thy Creator in the days of thy youth, while the evil days come not, nor the years draw nigh, when thou shalt say, I have no pleasure in them." Ecclesiastes 12:1. "I love them that love Me; and those that seek Me early shall find Me." Proverbs 8:17. The Great Shepherd of Israel is still saying: "Suffer little children to come unto Me, and forbid them not: for of such is the kingdom of God." Luke 18:16. Teach your children that youth is the best time to seek the Lord. Then the burdens of life are not heavy upon them, and their young minds are not harassed with care, and while so free they should devote the best of their strength to God.

We are living in an unfortunate age for children. A heavy current is setting downward to perdition, and more than childhood's experience and strength is needed to press against this current and not be borne down by it. The youth generally seem to be Satan's captives, and he and his angels are leading them to certain destruction. Satan and his hosts are warring against the government of God, and all who have a desire to yield their hearts to Him and obey His requirements, Satan will try to perplex and overcome with his temptations, that they may become discouraged and give up the warfare.

Parents, help your children. Arouse from the lethargy which has been upon you. Watch continually to cut off the current and roll back the weight of evil which Satan is pressing in upon your children. The children cannot do this of themselves, but parents can do much. By earnest prayer and living faith great victories will be gained. Some parents have not realized the responsibilities resting upon them and have neglected the religious education of their children. In the morning the Christian's first thoughts should be upon God. Worldly labor and self-interest should be secondary. Children should be taught to respect and reverence the hour of prayer.

Before leaving the house for labor, all the family should be called together, and the father, or the mother in the father's absence, should plead fervently with God to keep them through the day. Come in humility with a heart full of tenderness and with a sense of the temptations and dangers before yourselves and your children; by faith bind them upon the altar, entreating for them the care of the Lord. Ministering angels will guard children who are thus dedicated to God. It is the duty of Christian parents, morning and evening, by earnest prayer and persevering faith, to make a hedge about their children. They should patiently instruct them, kindly and untiringly teach them how to live in order to please God.

PROPER DISCIPLINE AND EDUCATION

Impatience in the parents excites impatience in the children. Passion manifested by the parents creates passion in the children and stirs up the evils of their nature. Some parents correct their children severely in a spirit of impatience, and often in passion. Such corrections produce no good result. In seeking to correct one evil, they create two. Continual censuring and whipping hardens children and weans them from their parents.

Parents should first learn to control themselves, then they can more successfully control their children. Every time they lose self-control, and speak and act impatiently, they sin against God. They should first reason with their children, clearly point out their wrongs, show them their sin, and impress upon them that they have not only sinned against their parents, but against God. With your own heart subdued and full of pity and sorrow for your erring children, pray with them before correcting them. Then your correction will not cause your children to hate you. They will love you. They will see that you do not punish them because they have put you to inconvenience, or because you wish to vent your displeasure upon them; but from a sense of duty, for their good, that they may not be left to grow up in sin.

Some parents have failed to give their children a religious education and have also neglected their school education. Neither should have been neglected. Children's minds will be active, and if not engaged in physical labor, or occupied with study, they will be exposed to evil influences. It is a sin for parents to allow their children to grow up in ignorance. They should supply them with useful and interesting books, and should teach them to work, to have hours for physical labor, and hours to devote to study and reading. Parents should seek to elevate the minds of their children and to improve their mental faculties. The mind left to itself, uncultivated, is generally low, sensual, and corrupt. Satan improves his opportunity and educates idle minds.

Parents, the recording angel writes every impatient, fretful word you utter to your children. Every failure on your part to give them proper instruction, and show them the exceeding sinfulness of sin, and the final result of a sinful course, is marked against your name. Every unguarded word spoken before them, carelessly or in jest, every word that is not chaste and elevated, the recording angel marks as a spot against your Christian character. All your acts are recorded, whether they are good or bad.

Parents cannot succeed well in the government of their children until they first have perfect control of themselves. They must first learn to subdue themselves, to control their words, and the very expression of the countenance. They should not suffer the tones of their voice to be disturbed or agitated with excitement and passion. Then they can have a decided influence over their children. Children may wish to do right, they may purpose in their hearts to be obedient and kind to their parents or guardians; but they need help and encouragement from them. They may make good resolutions; but unless their principles are strengthened by religion and their lives influenced by the renewing grace of God, they will fail to come up to the mark.

Parents should redouble their efforts for the salvation of their children. They should faithfully instruct them, not leaving them to gather up their education as best they can. The young should not be suffered to learn good and evil indiscriminately, with the idea that at some future time the good will predominate and the evil lose its influence. The evil will increase faster than the good. It is possible that the evil they have learned may be eradicated after many years; but who will venture this? Time is short. It is easier and much safer to sow clean and good seed in the hearts of your children than to pluck up the weeds afterward. It is the duty of parents to watch lest surrounding influences have an injurious effect upon their children. It is their duty to select the society for them and not suffer them to choose for themselves. Who will attend to this work if the parents do not? Can others have that interest for your children which you should have? Can they have that constant care and deep love that parents have?

Sabbathkeeping children may become impatient of restraint, and think their parents too strict; hard feelings may even arise in their hearts, and discontented, unhappy thoughts may be cherished by them against those who are working for their present and their future and eternal good. But if life shall be spared a few years, they will bless their parents for that strict care and faithful watchfulness over them in their years of inexperience.

Parents should explain and simplify the plan of salvation to their children that their young minds may comprehend it. Children of eight, ten, or twelve years are old enough to be addressed on the subject of personal religion. Do not teach your children with reference to some future period when they shall be old enough to repent and believe the truth. If properly instructed, very young children may have correct views of their state as sinners and of the way of salvation through Christ. Ministers are generally too indifferent to the salvation of children and are not as personal as they should be. Golden opportunities to impress the minds of children frequently pass unimproved.

HOME INFLUENCE

The evil influence around our children is almost overpowering; it is corrupting their minds and leading them down to perdition. The minds of youth are naturally given to folly; and at an early age, before their characters are formed, and their judgment matured, they frequently manifest a preference for associates who will have an injurious influence over them. Some form attachments for the other sex, contrary to the wishes and entreaties of their parents, and break the fifth commandment by thus dishonoring them. It is the duty of parents to watch the going out and the coming in of their children. They should encourage them, and present inducements before them which will attract them at home, and lead them to see that their parents are interested for them. They should make home pleasant and cheerful.

Fathers and mothers, speak kindly to your children; remember how sensitive you are, how little you can bear to be blamed; reflect, and know that your children are like you. That which you cannot bear, do not lay upon them. If you cannot bear censure and blame, neither can your children, who are weaker than you and cannot endure as much. Let your pleasant, cheerful words ever be like sunbeams in your family. The fruits of self-control, thoughtfulness, and painstaking on your part will be a hundredfold.

Parents have no right to bring a gloomy cloud over the happiness of their children by faultfinding or severe censure for trifling mistakes. Actual wrong and sin should be made to appear just as sinful as it is, and a firm, decided course should be pursued to prevent its recurrence. Children should be impressed with a sense of their wrongs, yet they should not be left in a hopeless state of mind, but with a degree of courage that they can improve and gain your confidence and approval.

TOO MUCH LENIENCY

Some parents mistake in giving their children too much liberty. They sometimes have so much confidence in them that they do not see their faults. It is wrong to allow children, at some expense, to visit at a distance, unaccompanied by their parents or guardians. It has a wrong influence upon the children. They come to feel that they are of considerable consequence and that certain privileges belong to them, and if these are not granted, they think themselves abused. They refer to children who go and come, and have many privileges, while they have so few.

And the mother, fearing that her children will think her unjust, gratifies their wishes, which in the end proves a great injury to them. Young visitors, who have not a parent's watchful eye over them to see and correct their faults, often receive impressions which it will take months to remove. I was referred to cases of parents who had good, obedient children, and who, having the utmost confidence in certain families, trusted their children to go from them at a distance to visit these friends. From that time there was an entire change in the deportment and character of their children. Formerly they were contented and happy at home, and had no great desire to be much in the company of other young persons. When they return to their parents, restraint seems unjust, and home is like a prison to them. Such unwise movements of parents decide the character of their children.

By thus visiting, some children form attachments which prove their ruin in the end. Parents, keep your children with you if you can, and watch them with the deepest solicitude. When you let them visit at a distance from you, they feel that they are old enough to take care of and choose for themselves. When the young are thus left to themselves, their conversation is often upon subjects which will not refine or elevate them, or increase their love for the things of religion. The more they are permitted to visit, the greater will be their desire to go, and the less attractive will home seem to them.

Children, God has seen fit to entrust you to the care of your parents for them to instruct and discipline, and thus act their part in forming your character for heaven. And yet it rests with you to say whether you will develop a good Christian character by making the best of the advantages you have had from godly, faithful, praying parents. Notwithstanding all the anxiety and faithfulness of parents in behalf of their children, they alone cannot save them. There is a work for the children to do. Every child has an individual case to attend to. Believing parents, you have a responsible work before you to guide the footsteps of your children, even in their religious experience. When they truly love God, they will bless and reverence you for the care which you have manifested for them, and for your faithfulness in restraining their desires and subduing their wills.

The prevailing influence in the world is to suffer the youth to follow the natural turn of their own minds. And if very wild in youth, parents say they will come right after a while, and when sixteen or eighteen years of age, will reason for themselves, and leave off their wrong habits, and become at last useful men and women. What a mistake! For years they permit an enemy to sow the garden of the heart; they suffer wrong principles to grow, and in many cases all the labor afterward bestowed on that soil will avail nothing.

Satan is an artful, persevering workman, a deadly foe. Whenever an incautious word is spoken to the injury of youth, whether in flattery or to cause them to look upon some sin with less abhorrence, Satan takes advantage of it and nourishes the evil seed that it may take root and yield a bountiful harvest. Some parents have suffered their children to form wrong habits, the marks of which may be seen all through life. Upon the parents lies this sin. These children may profess to be Christians, yet without a special work of grace upon the heart and a thorough reform in life their past habits will be seen in all their experience, and they will exhibit just the character which their parents allowed them to form.

WITH THE WORLD IN ITS PLEASURES

The standard of piety is so low among professed Christians generally that those who wish to follow Christ in sincerity find the work much more laborious and trying than they otherwise would. The influence of worldly professors is injurious to the young. The mass of professed Christians have removed the line of distinction between Christians and the world, and while they profess to be living for Christ, they are living for the world. Their faith has but little restraining influence upon their pleasures; while they profess to be children of the light, they walk in darkness and are children of the night and of darkness.

Those who walk in darkness cannot love God and sincerely desire to glorify Him. They are not enlightened to discern the excellence of heavenly things, and therefore cannot truly love them. They profess to be Christians because it is considered honorable, and there is no cross for them to bear. Their motives are often selfish. Some such professors can enter the ballroom and unite in all the amusements which it affords. Others cannot go to such a length as this, yet they can attend parties of pleasure, picnics, donation parties, and exhibitions. And the most discerning eye would fail to detect in such professed Christians one mark of Christianity. One would fail to see in their appearance any difference between them and the greatest unbeliever. The professed Christian, the profligate, the open scoffer at religion, and the openly profane all mingle together as one. And God regards them as one in spirit and practice.

A profession of Christianity without corresponding faith and works will avail nothing. No man can serve two masters. The children of the wicked one are their own master's servants; to whom they yield themselves servants to obey, his servants they are, and they cannot be the servants of God until they renounce the devil and all his works. It cannot be harmless for servants of the heavenly King to engage in the pleasures and amusements which Satan's servants engage in, even though they often repeat that such amusements are harmless. God has revealed sacred and holy truths to separate His people from the ungodly and purify them unto Himself. Seventh-day Adventists should live out their faith. Those who obey the Ten Commandments view the state of the world and religious things from a standpoint altogether different from that of professors who are lovers of pleasure, who shun the cross, and live in violation of the fourth commandment. In the present state of things in society it is no easy task for parents to restrain their children and instruct them according to the Bible rule of right. Professors of religion have so departed from the word of God that when His people return to His sacred word, and would train their children according to its precepts, and like Abraham of old command their households after them, the poor children with such an influence around them think their parents unnecessarily exacting and overcareful in regard to their associates. They naturally desire to follow the example of worldly, pleasure-loving professors.

In these days, persecution and reproach for Christ's sake are scarcely known. Very little self-denial and sacrifice is necessary in order to put on a form of godliness and have the name upon the church book; but to live in such a manner that our ways will be pleasing to God, and our names registered in the book of life, will require watchfulness and prayer, self-denial and sacrifice on our part. Professed Christians are no example for the youth, only as far as they follow Christ. Right actions are unmistakable fruits of true godliness. The Judge of all the earth will give everyone according to his works. Children who follow Christ have a warfare before them; they have a daily cross to bear in coming out from the world and being separate, and imitating the life of Christ.

Walk in the Light

I WAS shown that God's people dwell too much under a cloud. It is not His will that they should live in unbelief. Jesus is light, and in Him is no darkness at all. His children are the children of light. They are renewed in His image, and called out of darkness into His marvelous light. He is the light of the world, and so also are they that follow Him. They shall not walk in darkness, but shall have the light of life. The more closely the people of God strive to imitate Christ, the more perseveringly will they be pursued by the enemy; but their nearness to Christ strengthens them to resist the efforts of our wily foe to draw them from Christ.

I was shown that there was too much comparing ourselves among ourselves, taking fallible mortals for a pattern, when we have a sure, unerring pattern. We should not measure ourselves by the world, nor by the opinions of men, nor by what we were before we embraced the truth. But our faith and position in the world, as they now are, must be compared with what they would have been if our course had been continually onward and upward since we professed to be followers of Christ. This is the only safe comparison that can be made. In every other there will be self-deception. If the moral character and spiritual state of God's people do not correspond with the blessings, privileges, and light which have been conferred upon them, they are weighed in the balance, and angels make the report, WANTING.

With some the knowledge of their true state seems to be hidden from them. They see the truth, but perceive not its

1863, vol. 1, pp. 405-409.

importance or its claims. They hear the truth, but do not fully understand it, because they do not conform their lives to it, and therefore are not sanctified through obeying it. And yet they rest as unconcerned and well satisfied as though the cloud by day and the pillar of fire by night, as token of God's favor, went before them. They profess to know God, but in works deny Him. They reckon themselves His chosen, peculiar people, yet His presence and power to save to the uttermost are seldom manifested among them. How great is the darkness of such! yet they know it not. The light shines, but they do not comprehend it. No stronger delusion can deceive the human mind than that which makes them believe that they are right, and that God accepts their works, when they are sinning against Him. They mistake the form of godliness for the spirit and power thereof. They suppose that they are rich, and have need of nothing, when they are poor, wretched, blind, and naked, and need all things.

There are some who profess to be Christ's followers, yet put forth no effort in spiritual things. In any worldly enterprise they put forth effort, and manifest ambition to accomplish their object, and bring about the desired end; but in the enterprise of everlasting life, where all is at stake, and their eternal happiness depends upon their success, they act as indifferent as though they were not moral agents, as though another were playing the game of life for them, and they had nothing to do but wait the result. Oh, what folly! what madness! If all will only manifest that degree of ambition, zeal, and earnestness for everlasting life that they manifest in their worldly pursuits, they will be victorious overcomers. Everyone, I saw, must obtain an experience for himself, each must act well and faithfully his part in the game of life. Satan watches his opportunity to seize the precious graces when we are unguarded, and we shall have a severe conflict with the powers of darkness to retain them, or to regain a heavenly grace if through lack of watchfulness we lose it.

TO BE AWARE OF THE CONFLICT

But I was shown that it is the privilege of Christians to obtain strength from God to hold every precious gift. Fervent and effectual prayer will be regarded in heaven. When the servants of Christ take the shield of faith for their defense, and the sword of the Spirit for war, there is danger in the enemy's camp, and something must be done. Persecution and reproach only wait for those who are endowed with power from on high to call them into action. When the truth in its simplicity and strength prevails among believers, and is brought to bear against the spirit of the world, it will be evident that there is no concord between Christ and Belial. The disciples of Christ must be living examples of the life and spirit of their Master.

Young and old have a conflict, a warfare, before them. They should not sleep for a moment. A wily foe is constantly on the alert to lead them astray and overcome them. Believers in present truth must be as watchful as their enemy and manifest wisdom in resisting Satan. Will they do this? Will they persevere in this warfare? Will they be careful to depart from all iniquity? Christ is denied in many ways. We may deny Him by speaking contrary to truth, by speaking evil of others, by foolish talking or jesting, or by words that are idle. In these things we manifest but little shrewdness or wisdom. We make ourselves weak; our efforts are feeble to resist our great enemy, and we are conquered. "Out of the abundance of the heart the mouth speaketh" (Matthew 12:34), and through lack of watchfulness we confess that Christ is not in us.

Those who hesitate to devote themselves unreservedly to God make poor work of following Christ. They follow Him at so great a distance that half the time they do not really know whether they are following His footprints or the footsteps of their great enemy. Why are we so slow to give up our interest in the things of this world and take Christ for our only portion? Why should we wish to keep the friendship of our Lord's enemies, and follow their customs, and be led by their opinions? There must be an entire, unreserved surrender to God, a forsaking and turning away from the love of the world and earthly things, or we cannot be Christ's disciples.

The life and spirit of Christ is the only standard of excellence and perfection, and our only safe course is to follow His example. If we do this He will guide us by His counsel and afterward receive us to glory. We must strive diligently and be willing to suffer much in order to walk in the footsteps of our Redeemer. God is willing to work for us, to give us of His free Spirit, if we will strive for it, live for it, believe for it; and then we can walk in the light as He is in the light. We can feast upon His love and drink in of His rich fullness.

When secret prayer and reading of the Scriptures are neglected today, tomorrow they can be omitted with less remonstrance of conscience. There will be a long list of omissions, all for a single grain sown in the soil of the heart. On the other hand, every ray of light cherished will yield a harvest of light. Temptation once resisted will give power to more firmly resist the second time; every new victory gained over self will smooth the way for higher and nobler triumphs. Every victory is a seed sown to eternal life.—1882, vol. 5, p. 120.

Counterfeit Gifts of the Spirit

A SPIRIT of fanaticism has ruled a certain class of Sabbath-keepers there [in the East]; they have sipped but lightly at the fountain of truth and are unacquainted with the spirit of the message of the third angel. Nothing can be done for this class until their fanatical views are corrected. . . .

Some of these persons have exercises which they call gifts and say that the Lord has placed them in the church. They have an unmeaning gibberish which they call the unknown tongue, which is unknown not only by man but by the Lord and all heaven. Such gifts are manufactured by men and women, aided by the great deceiver. Fanaticism, false excitement, false talking in tongues, and noisy exercises have been considered gifts which God has placed in the church. Some have been deceived here. The fruits of all this have not been good. "Ye shall know them by their fruits." Matthew 7:16. Fanaticism and noise have been considered special evidences of faith.

Some are not satisfied with a meeting unless they have a powerful and happy time. They work for this and get up an excitement of feeling. But the influence of such meetings is not beneficial. When the happy flight of feeling is gone, they sink lower than before the meeting because their happiness did not come from the right source. The most profitable meetings for spiritual advancement are those which are characterized with solemnity and deep searching of heart; each seeking to know himself, and earnestly, and in deep humility, seeking to learn of Christ. . . .

There are many restless spirits who will not submit to disci-

1863, vol. 1, pp. 411-420 (The Cause in the East).

pline, system, and order. They think that their liberties would be abridged were they to lay aside their own judgment and submit to the judgment of those of experience. The work of God will not progress unless there is a disposition to submit to order and expel the reckless, disorderly spirit of fanaticism from their meetings. Impressions and feelings are no sure evidence that a person is led by the Lord. Satan will, if he is unsuspected, give feelings and impressions. These are not safe guides.

All should thoroughly acquaint themselves with the evidences of our faith, and the great study should be how they can adorn their profession and bear fruit to the glory of God. None should take a course to make themselves disgusting to unbelievers. We should be chaste, modest, and elevated in conversation, and blameless in life. A trifling, joking, reckless spirit should be rebuked. It is no evidence of the grace of God upon the heart for persons to talk and pray with talent in meeting, and then give up to a rough, careless manner of talking and acting when out of meeting. Such are miserable representatives of our faith; they are a reproach to the cause of God.

There is a strange mixture of views among professed Sabbathkeepers in ——. Some are not in harmony with the body, and while they continue to occupy the position they now do, they will be subject to the temptations of Satan and will be affected with fanaticism and the spirit of error. Some have fanciful views which blind their eyes to important, vital points of truth, leading them to place their own fanciful inferences upon a level with vital truth. The appearance of such, and the spirit which attends them, makes the Sabbath which they profess very objectionable to the sensible unbeliever. It would be far better for the progress and success of the third angel's message if such persons would leave the truth. . . .

Ministers who labor in word and doctrine should be thorough workmen, and should present the truth in its purity, yet with simplicity. They should feed the flock with clean provender, thoroughly winnowed.

There are wandering stars professing to be ministers sent of God who are preaching the Sabbath from place to place, but who have truth mixed up with error and are throwing out their mass of discordant views to the people. Satan has pushed them in to disgust intelligent and sensible unbelievers. Some of these have much to say upon the gifts and are often especially exercised. They give themselves up to wild, excitable feelings and make unintelligible sounds which they call the gift of tongues, and a certain class seem to be charmed with these strange manifestations. A strange spirit rules with this class, which would bear down and run over anyone who would reprove them. God's Spirit is not in the work and does not attend such workmen. They have another spirit. Still, such preachers have success among a certain class. But this will greatly increase the labor of those servants whom God shall send, who are qualified to present before the people the Sabbath and the gifts in their proper light, and whose influence and example are worthy of imitation.

The truth should be presented in a manner which will make it attractive to the intelligent mind. We are not understood as a people, but are looked upon as poor, weak-minded, low, and degraded. Then how important for all who teach, and all who believe the truth, to be so affected by its sanctifying influence that their consistent, elevated lives shall show unbelievers that they have been deceived in this people. How important that the cause of truth be stripped of everything like a false and fanatical excitement, that the truth may stand upon its own merits, revealing its native purity and exalted character.

I saw that it is highly important for those who preach the truth to be refined in their manners, to shun oddities and eccentricities, and present the truth in its purity and clearness. I was referred to Titus 1:9: "Holding fast the faithful word as he hath been taught, that he may be able by sound doctrine both to exhort and to convince the gainsayers." In verse 16 Paul speaks of a class who profess that they know God, but in works deny Him, being "unto every good work reprobate." He then exhorts Titus: "But speak thou the things which become sound doctrine: that the aged men be sober, grave, temperate, sound in faith, in charity, in patience. . . . Young men likewise exhort to be sober-minded. In all things showing thyself a pattern of good works: in doctrine showing uncorruptness, gravity, sincerity, sound speech, that cannot be condemned; that he that is of the contrary part may be ashamed, having no evil thing to say of you." Titus 2:1-8. This instruction is written for the benefit of all whom God has called to preach the word, and also for the benefit of His people who hear the word.

THE TRUTH ELEVATES

The truth of God will never degrade, but will elevate the receiver, refine his taste, sanctify his judgment, and perfect him for the company of the pure and holy angels in the kingdom of God. There are some whom the truth finds coarse, rough, odd, boastful, who take advantage of their neighbors if they can, in order to benefit themselves; they err in many ways, yet when the truth is believed by them from the heart, it will work an entire change in their lives. They will immediately commence the work of reformation.

The pure influence of truth will elevate the whole man. In his business deal with his fellow men he will have the fear of God before him, and will love his neighbor as himself, and will deal just as he would wish to be dealt by. His conversation will be truthful, chaste, and of so elevating a character that unbelievers cannot take advantage of it, or say evil of him justly, and are not disgusted with his uncourteous ways and unbecoming speech. He will carry the sanctifying influence of the truth into his family and let his light so shine before them that they by seeing his good works may glorify God. He will in all the walks of life exemplify the life of Christ.

The law of God will be satisfied with nothing short of perfection, of perfect and entire obedience to all its claims. To come halfway to its requirements, and not render perfect and thorough obedience, will avail nothing. The worldling and the infidel admire consistency and have ever been powerfully convicted that God was of a truth with His people when their works correspond with their faith. "By their fruits ye shall know them." Matthew 7:20. Every tree is known by its own fruits. Our words, our actions, are the fruit we bear.

There are many who hear the sayings of Christ, but do them not. They make a profession, but their fruits are such as to disgust unbelievers. They are boastful, and pray and talk in a self-righteous manner, exalting themselves, recounting their good deeds, and, like the Pharisee, virtually thanking God that they are not as other men. Yet these very ones are crafty, and overreach in business deal. Their fruits are not good. Their words and acts are wrong, and yet they seem to be blinded to their destitute, wretched condition.

I was shown that the following scripture is applicable to those who are under such a deception: "Not everyone that saith unto Me, Lord, Lord, shall enter into the kingdom of heaven; but he that doeth the will of My Father which is in heaven. Many will say to Me in that day, Lord, Lord, have not we prophesied in Thy name? and in Thy name have cast out devils? and in Thy name done many wonderful works? And then will I profess unto them, I never knew you: depart from Me, ye that work iniquity." Matthew 7:21-23.

Here is the greatest deception that can affect the human mind; these persons believe that they are right when they are wrong. They think that they are doing a great work in their religious life, but Jesus finally tears off their self-righteous covering and vividly presents before them the true picture of themselves in all their wrongs and deformity of religious character. They are found wanting when it is forever too late to have their wants supplied. God has provided means to correct the erring: yet if those who err, choose to follow their own judgment, and despise the means which He has ordained to correct them and unite them upon the truth, they will be brought into the position described by the words of our Lord quoted above.

God is bringing out a people and preparing them to stand as one, united, to speak the same things, and thus carry out the prayer of Christ for His disciples. "Neither pray I for these alone, but for them also which shall believe on Me through their word; that they all may be one; as Thou, Father, art in Me, and I in Thee, that they also may be one in Us: that the world may believe that Thou hast sent Me." John 17:20, 21.

LITTLE COMPANIES OF RESTLESS SOULS

There are little companies continually rising who believe that God is only with the very few, the very scattered, and their influence is to tear down and scatter that which God's servants build up. Restless minds who want to be seeing and believing something new continually are constantly rising, some in one place and some in another, all doing a special work for the enemy, yet claiming to have the truth. They stand separate from the people whom God is leading out and prospering, and through whom He is to do His great work. They are continually expressing their fears that the body of Sabbathkeepers are becoming like the world, but there are scarcely two of these whose views are in harmony. They are scattered and confused, and yet deceive themselves so much as to think that God is especially with them. Some of these profess to have the gifts among them; but are led by the influence and teachings of these gifts to hold in doubt those upon whom God has laid the special burden of His work, and to lead off a class from the body. The people, who, in accordance with God's word, are putting forth every effort to be one, who are established in the message of the third angel, are looked upon with suspicion for the reason that they are extending their labor and are gathering souls into the truth. They are considered worldly because they have an influence in the world, and their acts testify that they expect God yet to do a special and great work upon the earth, to bring out a people and fit them for Christ's appearing.

This class do not know what they really believe, or the reasons for their belief. They are ever learning, and never able to come to the knowledge of the truth. One man arises with wild, erroneous views, and claims that God has sent him with new and glorious light, and all must believe what he brings. Some who have no established faith, who are not subject to the body, but are drifting about without an anchor to hold them, receive that wind of doctrine. His light shines in such a manner as to cause the world to turn from him in disgust and to hate him. Then he blasphemously places himself by the side of Christ and claims that the world hate him for the same reason that they hated Christ.

Another rises, claiming to be led of God, and advocates the heresy of the nonresurrection of the wicked, which is one of Satan's great masterpieces of error. Another cherishes erroneous views in regard to the future age. Another zealously urges the American costume. They all want full religious liberty, and each acts independent of the others, and yet they claim that God is especially at work among them.

PRESUMPTUOUS LEADERS

Some rejoice and exult that they have the gifts, which others have not. May God deliver His people from such gifts. What do these gifts do for them? Are they through the exercise of these gifts, brought into the unity of the faith? And do they convince the unbeliever that God is with them of a truth? When these discordant ones, holding their different views, come together and there is considerable excitement and the unknown tongue, they let their light so shine that unbelievers would say: These people are not sane; they are carried away with a false excitement, and we know that they do not have the truth. Such stand directly in the way of sinners; their influence is effectual to keep others from accepting the Sabbath. Such will be rewarded according to their works. Would to God they would be reformed or give up the Sabbath! They would not then stand in the way of unbelievers.

God has led out men who have toiled for years, who have been willing to make any sacrifice, who have suffered privation, and endured trials to bring the truth before the world, and by their consistent course remove the reproach that fanatics have brought upon the cause of God. They have met opposition in every form. They have toiled night and day in searching the evidences of our faith that they might bring out the truth in its clearness, in a connected form, that it might withstand all opposition. Incessant labor and mental trials in connection with this great work have worn down more than one constitution and prematurely sprinkled heads with gray hairs. They have not worn out in vain. God has marked their earnest, tearful, agonizing prayers that they might have light and truth, and that the truth might shine in its clearness to others. He has marked their self-sacrificing efforts, and He will reward them as their works have been.

On the other hand, those who have not toiled to bring out these precious truths have come up and received some points, like the Sabbath truth, which are all prepared to their hand, and then all the gratitude they manifest for that which cost them nothing, but others so much, is to rise up like Korah, Dathan, and Abiram, and reproach those upon whom God has laid the burden of His work. They would say: "Ye take too much upon you, seeing all the congregation are holy, every one of them, and the Lord is among them." Numbers 16:3. They are strangers to gratitude. They possess a strong spirit which will not yield to reason and which will lead them on to their own destruction.

God has blessed His people who have moved forward following His opening providence. He has brought out a people from every class upon the great platform of truth. Infidels have been convinced that God was with His people and have humbled their hearts to obey the truth. The work of God moves steadily on. Yet notwithstanding all the evidences that God has been leading the body, there are, and will continue to be, those who profess the Sabbath, who will move independent of the body, and believe and act as they choose. Their views are confused. Their scattered state is a standing testimony that God is not with them. By the world the Sabbath and their errors are placed upon a level and thrown away together.

God is angry with those who pursue a course to make the world hate them. If a Christian is hated because of his good works and for following Christ, he will have a reward; but if he is hated because he does not take a course to be loved, hated because of his uncultivated manners and because he makes the truth a matter of quarrel with his neighbors, and takes a course to make the Sabbath as annoying as possible to them, he is a stumbling block to sinners, a reproach to the sacred truth, and unless he repents it were better for him that a millstone were hung about his neck and he were cast into the sea.

No occasion should be given to unbelievers to reproach our faith. We are considered odd and singular, and should not take a course to lead unbelievers to think us more so than our faith requires us to be.

There is in human nature a tendency to run to extremes and from one extreme to another entirely opposite. Many are fanatics. They are consumed by a fiery zeal which is mistaken for religion, but character is the true test of discipleship. Have they the meekness of Christ? have they His humility and sweet benevolence? Is the soul-temple emptied of pride, arrogance, selfishness, and censoriousness? If not, they know not what manner of spirit they are of. They do not realize that true Christianity consists in bearing much fruit to the glory of God.

Others go to an extreme in their conformity to the world. There is no clear, distinct line of separation between them and the worldling. If in one case men are driven away from the truth by a harsh, censorious, condemnatory spirit, in this they are led to conclude that the professed Christian is destitute of principle and knows nothing of a change of heart or character. "Let your light so shine before men, that they may see your good works, and glorify your Father which is in heaven" (Matthew 5:16), are the words of Christ.—1885, vol. 5, pp. 305, 306.

The Lord requires His people to use their reason, and not lay it aside for impressions. His work will be intelligible to all His children. His teaching will be such as will commend itself to the understanding of intelligent minds. It is calculated to elevate the mind. God's power is not manifested upon every occasion. Man's necessity is God's opportunity.—1861, vol. 1, p. 230.

When those who have witnessed and experienced false exercises are convinced of their mistake, then Satan takes advantage of their error, and holds it constantly before them, to make them afraid of any spiritual exercise, and in this way he seeks to destroy their faith in true godliness. Because they were once deceived, they fear to make any effort by earnest, fervent prayer to God for special aid and victory. Such must not let Satan gain his object, and drive them to cold formality and unbelief. They must remember that the foundation of God standeth sure. Let God be true, and every man a liar. Their only safety is to plant their feet upon the firm platform, to see and understand the third angel's message, to prize, love, and obey the truth.—1862, vol. 1, pp. 323, 324.

The Prayer of David

I WAS shown David entreating the Lord not to forsake him when he should be old, and what it was that called forth his earnest prayer. He saw that most of the aged around him were unhappy and that unhappy traits of character increased especially with age. If persons were naturally close and covetous, they were most disagreeably so in their old age. If they were jealous, fretful, and impatient, they were especially so when aged.

David was distressed as he saw that kings and nobles who seemed to have the fear of God before them while in the strength of manhood, became jealous of their best friends and relatives when aged. They were in continual fear that it was selfish motives which led their friends to manifest an interest for them. They would listen to the hints and the deceptive advice of strangers in regard to those in whom they should confide. Their unrestrained jealousy sometimes burned into a flame because all did not agree with their failing judgment. Their covetousness was dreadful. They often thought that their own children and relatives were wishing them to die in order to take their place and possess their wealth, and receive the homage which had been bestowed upon them. And some were so controlled by their jealous, covetous feelings as to destroy their own children.

David marked that although the lives of some while in the strength of manhood had been righteous, as old age came upon them they seemed to lose their self-control. Satan stepped in and guided their minds, making them restless and dissatisfied. He saw that many of the aged seemed forsaken of God and exposed themselves to the ridicule and reproaches of

1863, vol. 1, pp. 422-424.

his enemies. David was deeply moved; he was distressed as he looked forward to the time when he should be aged. He feared that God would leave him and that he would be as unhappy as other aged persons whose course he had noticed, and would be left to the reproach of the enemies of the Lord. With this burden upon him he earnestly prays: "Cast me not off in the time of old age; forsake me not when my strength faileth." "O God, Thou hast taught me from my youth: and hitherto have I declared Thy wondrous works. Now also when I am old and gray-headed, O God, forsake me not; until I have showed Thy strength unto this generation, and Thy power to everyone that is to come." Psalm 71:9, 17, 18. David felt the necessity of guarding against the evils which attend old age.

It is frequently the case that aged persons are unwilling to realize and acknowledge that their mental strength is failing. They shorten their days by taking care which belongs to their children. Satan often plays upon their imagination and leads them to feel a continual anxiety in regard to their money. It is their idol, and they hoard it with miserly care. They will sometimes deprive themselves of many of the comforts of life, and labor beyond their strength, rather than use the means which they have. In this way they place themselves in continual want, through fear that sometime in the future they shall want. All these fears originate with Satan. He excites the organs which lead to slavish fears and jealousies which corrupt nobleness of soul and destroy elevated thoughts and feelings. Such persons are insane upon the subject of money. If they would take the position which God would have them, their last days might be their best and happiest. Those who have children in whose honesty and judicious management they have reason to confide, should let their children make them happy. Unless they do this, Satan will take advantage of their lack of mental strength and will manage for them. They should lay aside anxiety and burdens, and occupy their time as happily as they can, and be ripening up for heaven.

Proper Observance of the Sabbath

December 25, 1865, I was shown that there has been too much slackness in regard to the observance of the Sabbath. There has not been promptness to fulfill the secular duties within the six working days which God has given to man and carefulness not to infringe upon one hour of the holy, sacred time which He has reserved to Himself. There is no business of man's that should be considered of sufficient importance to cause him to transgress the fourth precept of Jehovah.

There are cases in which Christ has given permission to labor even on the Sabbath in saving the life of men or of animals. But if we violate the letter of the fourth commandment for our own advantage from a pecuniary point of view we become Sabbathbreakers and are guilty of transgressing all the commandments, for if we offend in one point we are guilty of all.

If in order to save property we break over the express command of Jehovah, where is the stopping place? Where shall we set the bounds? Transgress in a small matter, and look upon it as no particular sin on our part, and the conscience becomes hardened, the sensibilities blunted, until we can go still further and perform quite an amount of labor and still flatter ourselves that we are Sabbathkeepers, when, according to Christ's standard, we are breaking every one of God's holy precepts. There is a fault with Sabbathkeepers in this respect; but God is very particular, and all who think that they are saving a little time, or advantaging themselves by infringing a little on the Lord's time, will meet with loss sooner or later. He cannot bless them as it would be His pleasure to do, for

1867, vol. 1, pp. 531-533.

His name is dishonored by them, His precepts lightly esteemed. God's curse will rest upon them, and they will lose tenfold or twentyfold more than they gain. "Will a man rob God? Yet ye have robbed Me, . . . even this whole nation."

God has given man six days in which to work for himself, but He has reserved one day in which He is to be specially honored. He is to be glorified, His authority respected. And yet man will rob God by stealing a little of the time which the Creator has reserved for Himself. God reserved the seventh day as a period of rest for man, for the good of man as well as for His own glory. He saw that the wants of man required a day of rest from toil and care, that his health and life would be endangered without a period of relaxation from the labor and anxiety of the six days.

The Sabbath was made for the benefit of man; and to knowingly transgress the holy commandment forbidding labor upon the seventh day is a crime in the sight of heaven which was of such magnitude under the Mosaic law as to require the death of the offender. But this was not all that the offender was to suffer, for God would not take a transgressor of His law to heaven. He must suffer the second death, which is the full and final penalty for the transgressor of the law of God.

Life Insurance

I WAS shown that Sabbathkeeping Adventists should not engage in life insurance. This is a commerce with the world which God does not approve. Those who engage in this enterprise are uniting with the world, while God calls His people to come out from among them and to be separate. Said the angel: "Christ has purchased you by the sacrifice of His life. 'What? know ye not that your body is the temple of the Holy Ghost which is in you, which ye have of God, and ye are not your own? For ye are bought with a price: therefore glorify God in your body, and in your spirit, which are God's.' 'For ye are dead, and your life is hid with Christ in God. When Christ, who is your life, shall appear, then shall ye also appear with Him in glory.' " Here is the only life insurance which heaven sanctions.

Life insurance is a worldly policy which leads our brethren who engage in it to depart from the simplicity and purity of the gospel. Every such departure weakens our faith and lessens our spirituality. Said the angel: "But ye are a chosen generation, a royal priesthood, an holy nation, a peculiar people; that ye should show forth the praises of Him who hath called you out of darkness into His marvelous light." As a people we are in a special sense the Lord's. Christ has bought us. Angels that excel in strength surround us. Not a sparrow falls to the ground without the notice of our heavenly Father. Even the hairs of our head are numbered. God has made provision for His people. He has a special care for them, and they should not distrust His providence by engaging in a policy with the world.

God designs that we should preserve in simplicity and holiness our peculiarity as a people. Those who engage in this

1867, vol. 1, pp. 549-551.

worldly policy invest means which belong to God, which He has entrusted to them to use in His cause, to advance His work. But few will realize any returns from life insurance, and without God's blessing even these will prove an injury instead of a benefit. Those whom God has made His stewards have no right to place in the enemy's ranks the means which He has entrusted to them to use in His cause.

Satan is constantly presenting inducements to God's chosen people to attract their minds from the solemn work of preparation for the scenes just in the future. He is in every sense of the word a deceiver, a skillful charmer. He clothes his plans and snares with coverings of light borrowed from heaven. He tempted Eve to eat of the forbidden fruit by making her believe that she would be greatly advantaged thereby. Satan leads his agents to introduce various inventions and patent rights, and other enterprises, that Sabbathkeeping Adventists who are in haste to be rich may fall into temptation, become ensnared, and pierce themselves through with many sorrows. He is wide awake, busily engaged in leading the world captive, and through the agency of worldlings he keeps up a continual pleasing excitement to draw the unwary who profess to believe the truth to unite with worldlings. The lust of the eye, the desire for excitement and pleasing entertainment, is a temptation and snare to God's people. Satan has many finely woven, dangerous nets which are made to appear innocent, but with which he is skillfully preparing to infatuate God's people. There are pleasing shows, entertainments, phrenological lectures, and an endless variety of enterprises constantly arising calculated to lead the people of God to love the world and the things that are in the world. Through this union with the world, faith becomes weakened, and means which should be invested in the cause of present truth are transferred to the enemy's ranks. Through these different channels Satan is skillfully draining the purses of God's people, and for it the displeasure of the Lord is upon them.

Health and Religion

There are persons with a diseased imagination to whom religion is a tyrant, ruling them as with a rod of iron. Such are constantly mourning over their depravity and groaning over supposed evil. Love does not exist in their hearts; a frown is ever upon their countenances. They are chilled by the innocent laugh from the youth or from anyone. They consider all recreation or amusement a sin and think that the mind must be constantly wrought up to just such a stern, severe pitch. This is one extreme. Others think that the mind must be ever on the stretch to invent new amusements and diversions in order to gain health. They learn to depend on excitement, and are uneasy without it. Such are not true Christians. They go to another extreme.

The true principles of Christianity open before all a source of happiness, the height and depth, the length and breadth of which are immeasurable. It is Christ in us a well of water springing up into everlasting life. It is a continual wellspring from which the Christian can drink at will and never exhaust the fountain.

That which brings sickness of body and mind to nearly all is dissatisfied feelings and discontented repinings. They have not God, they have not the hope which reaches to that within the veil, which is as an anchor to the soul both sure and steadfast. All who possess this hope will purify themselves even as He is pure. Such are free from restless longings, repinings, and discontent; they are not continually looking for evil and brooding over borrowed trouble. But we see many who are having a time of trouble beforehand; anxiety is stamped upon

1867, vol. 1, pp. 565, 566.

every feature; they seem to find no consolation, but have a continual fearful looking for of some dreadful evil.

Such dishonor God, and bring the religion of Christ into disrepute. They have not true love for God, nor for their companions and children. Their affections have become morbid. But vain amusements will never correct the minds of such. They need the transforming influence of the Spirit of God in order to be happy.

The sympathy which exists between the mind and the body is very great. When one is affected, the other responds. The condition of the mind has much to do with the health of the physical system. If the mind is free and happy, under a consciousness of rightdoing and a sense of satisfaction in causing happiness to others, it will create a cheerfulness that will react upon the whole system, causing a freer circulation of the blood and a toning up of the entire body. The blessing of God is a healer, and those who are abundant in benefiting others will realize that wondrous blessing in their hearts and lives.—1876, vol. 4, pp. 60, 61.

The religion of the Bible is not detrimental to the health of the body or of the mind. The influence of the Spirit of God is the very best medicine that can be received by a sick man or woman. Heaven is all health, and the more deeply the heavenly influences are realized the more sure will be the recovery of the believing invalid.—1872, vol. 3, p. 172.

Satan is the originator of disease; and the physician is warring against his work and power. Sickness of the mind prevails everywhere. Nine tenths of the diseases from which men suffer have their foundation here. Perhaps some living home trouble is, like a canker, eating to the very soul and weakening the life forces. Remorse for sin sometimes undermines the constitution and unbalances the mind. There are erroneous doctrines also, as that of an eternally burning hell and the endless torment of the wicked, that, by giving exaggerated and distorted views of the character of God, have produced the same result upon sensitive minds. Infidels have made the most of these unfortunate cases, attributing insanity to religion; but this is a gross libel and one which they will not be pleased to meet by and by. The religion of Christ, so far from being the cause of insanity, is one of its most effectual remedies; for it is a potent soother of the nerves.—1885, vol. 5, p. 444.

The burden of sin, with its unrest and unsatisfied desires, lies at the very foundation of a large share of the maladies the sinner suffers. Christ is the mighty healer of the sin-sick soul. These poor afflicted ones need to have a clearer knowledge of Him whom to know aright is life eternal. They need to be patiently and kindly yet earnestly taught how to throw open the windows of the soul and let the sunlight of God's love come in to illuminate the darkened chambers of the mind. —1881, vol. 4, p. 579.

Christian Temperance*

"Know ye not that your body is the temple of the Holy Ghost which is in you, which ye have of God, and ye are not your own? For ye are bought with a price: therefore glorify God in your body, and in your spirit, which are God's." 1 Corinthians 6:19, 20.

We are not our own. We have been purchased with a dear price, even the sufferings and death of the Son of God. If we could understand this, and fully realize it, we would feel a great responsibility resting upon us to keep ourselves in the very best condition of health, that we might render to God perfect service. But when we take any course which expends our vitality, decreases our strength, or beclouds the intellect we sin against God. In pursuing this course we are not glorifying Him in our bodies and spirits which are His, but are committing a great wrong in His sight.

Has Jesus given Himself for us? Has a dear price been paid to redeem us? And is it so, that we are not our own? Is it true that all the powers of our being, our bodies, our spirits, all that we have, and all we are, belong to God? It certainly is. And when we realize this, what obligation does it lay us under to God to preserve ourselves in that condition that we may honor Him upon the earth in our bodies and in our spirits which are His.

THE CLOSING HOURS OF PROBATION

We believe without a doubt that Christ is soon coming. This is not a fable to us; it is a reality. We have no doubt, neither have we had a doubt for years, that the doctrines we

* Address delivered in Battle Creek, March 6, 1869.
1870, vol. 2, pp. 354-376.

hold today are present truth, and that we are nearing the judgment. We are preparing to meet Him who, escorted by a retinue of holy angels, is to appear in the clouds of heaven to give the faithful and the just the finishing touch of immortality. When He comes He is not to cleanse us of our sins, to remove from us the defects in our characters, or to cure us of the infirmities of our tempers and dispositions. If wrought for us at all, this work will all be accomplished before that time.

When the Lord comes, those who are holy will be holy still. Those who have preserved their bodies and spirits in holiness, in sanctification and honor, will then receive the finishing touch of immortality. But those who are unjust, unsanctified, and filthy will remain so forever. No work will then be done for them to remove their defects and give them holy characters. The Refiner does not then sit to pursue His refining process and remove their sins and their corruption. This is all to be done in these hours of probation. It is *now* that this work is to be accomplished for us.

We embrace the truth of God with our different faculties, and as we come under the influence of that truth, it will accomplish the work for us which is necessary to give us a moral fitness for the kingdom of glory and for the society of the heavenly angels. We are now in God's workshop. Many of us are rough stones from the quarry. But as we lay hold upon the truth of God, its influence affects us. It elevates us and removes from us every imperfection and sin, of whatever nature. Thus we are prepared to see the King in His beauty and finally to unite with the pure and heavenly angels in the kingdom of glory. It is here that this work is to be accomplished for us, here that our bodies and spirits are to be fitted for immortality.

We are in a world that is opposed to righteousness and purity of character, and to a growth in grace. Wherever we look we see corruption and defilement, deformity and sin.

And what is the work that we are to undertake here just previous to receiving immortality? It is to preserve our bodies holy, our spirits pure, that we may stand forth unstained amid the corruptions teeming around us in these last days. And if this work is accomplished we need to engage in it at once, heartily and understandingly. Selfishness should not come in here to influence us. The Spirit of God should have perfect control of us, influencing us in all our actions. If we have a right hold on Heaven, a right hold of the power that is from above, we shall feel the sanctifying influence of the Spirit of God upon our hearts.

CAUSING OTHERS TO SUFFER

When we have tried to present the health reform to our brethren and sisters, and have spoken to them of the importance of eating and drinking and doing all that they do to the glory of God, many by their actions have said: "It is nobody's business whether I eat this or that. Whatever we do we are to bear the consequences ourselves."

Dear friends, you are greatly mistaken. You are not the only sufferers from a wrong course. The society you are in bears the consequences of your wrongs, in a great degree, as well as yourselves. If you suffer from your intemperance in eating or drinking, we that are around you or associated with you are also affected by your infirmities. We have to suffer on account of your wrong course. If it has an influence to lessen your powers of mind or body, we feel it when in your society, and are affected by it. If, instead of having a buoyancy of spirit, you are gloomy, you cast a shadow upon the spirits of all around you. If we are sad and depressed, and in trouble, you could, if in a right condition of health, have a clear brain to show us the way out and speak a comforting word to us. But if your brain is so benumbed by your wrong course of living that you cannot give us the right counsel, do we not meet with a loss? Does not your influence seriously affect us? We may have a good degree of confidence in our own judgment, yet we want to have counselors; for "in the multitude of counselors there is safety." Proverbs 11:14. We desire that our course should look consistent to those we love, and we wish to seek their counsel and have them able to give it with a clear brain. But what care we for your judgment, if your brain nerve power has been taxed to the utmost, and the vitality withdrawn from the brain to take care of the improper food placed in your stomachs, or of an enormous quantity of even healthful food? What care we for the judgment of such persons? They see through a mass of undigested food. Therefore your course of living affects us. It is impossible for you to pursue any wrong course without causing others to suffer.

RUNNING THE HEAVENLY RACE

"Know ye not that they which run in a race run all, but one receiveth the prize? So run, that ye may obtain. And every man that striveth for the mastery is temperate in all things. Now they do it to obtain a corruptible crown; but we an incorruptible. I therefore so run, not as uncertainly; so fight I, not as one that beateth the air: but I keep under my body, and bring it into subjection: lest that by any means, when I have preached to others, I myself should be a castaway." 1 Corinthians 9:24-27. Those who engaged in running the race to obtain that laurel which was considered a special honor were temperate in all things so that their muscles, their brains, and every part of them might be in the very best condition to run. If they were not temperate in all things they would not have that elasticity that they would have if they were. If temperate, they could run that race more successfully; they were more sure of receiving the crown.

But notwithstanding all their temperance,—all their efforts to subject themselves to a careful diet in order to be in the best condition,—those who ran the earthly race only ran at a venture. They might do the very best they could, and yet after all not receive the token of honor; for another might be a little in advance of them, and take the prize. Only one received the prize. But in the heavenly race we can all run and all receive the prize. There is no uncertainty, no risk, in the matter. We must put on the heavenly graces, and, with the eye directed upward to the crown of immortality, keep the Pattern ever before us. He was a man of sorrows and acquainted with grief. The humble, self-denying life of our divine Lord we are to keep constantly in view. And then as we seek to imitate Him, keeping our eye upon the mark of the prize, we can run this race with certainty, knowing that if we do the very best we can, we shall certainly secure the prize.

Men would subject themselves to self-denial and discipline in order to run and obtain a corruptible crown, one that would perish in a day, and which was only a token of honor from mortals here. But we are to run the race, at the end of which is a crown of immortality and everlasting life. Yes, a far more exceeding and eternal weight of glory will be awarded to us as the prize when the race is run. "We," says the apostle, "an incorruptible." And if those who engaged in this race here upon the earth for a temporal crown could be temperate in all things, cannot we, who have in view an incorruptible crown, an eternal weight of glory, and a life which measures with the life of God? When we have this great inducement before us, cannot we "run with patience the race that is set before us, looking unto Jesus the Author and Finisher of our faith"? Hebrews 12:1, 2. He has pointed out the way for us, and marked it all along by His own footsteps. It is the path that He traveled, and we may, with Him, experience the self-denial and the suffering, and walk in this pathway imprinted by His own blood.

"I therefore so run, not as uncertainly; so fight I, not as one that beateth the air: but I keep under my body, and bring it into subjection." There is work here for every man, woman, and child to do. Satan is constantly seeking to gain control of your bodies and spirits. But Christ has bought you, and you are His property. And now it is for you to work in union with Christ, in union with the holy angels that minister unto you. It is for you to keep the body under and bring it into subjection. Unless you do this you will certainly lose everlasting life and the crown of immortality. And yet some will say: "What business is it to anybody what I eat or what I drink?" I have shown you what relation your course has to others. You have seen that it has much to do with the influence you exert in your families. It has much to do with molding the characters of your children.

PARENTAL RESPONSIBILITY

As I said before, we live in a corrupt age. It is a time when Satan seems to have almost perfect control over minds that are not fully consecrated to God. Therefore there is a very great responsibility resting upon parents and guardians who have children to bring up. Parents have taken the responsibility of bringing these children into existence; and now what is their duty? Is it to let them come up just as they may, and just as they will? Let me tell you, a weighty responsibility rests upon these parents. "Whether therefore ye eat, or drink, or whatsoever ye do, do all to the glory of God." 1 Corinthians 10:31. Do you do this when you prepare food for your tables and call your family to partake of it? Are you placing before your children only the food that you know will make the very best blood? Is it that food that will preserve their systems in the least feverish condition? Is it that which will place them in the very best relation to life and health? Is this the food that you are studying to place before your children? Or do you, regardless of their future good, provide for them unhealthful, stimulating, irritating food?

Let me tell you that children are born to evil. Satan seems to have control of them. He takes possession of their young minds, and they are corrupted. Why do fathers and mothers act as though a lethargy were upon them? They do not mistrust that Satan is sowing evil seed in their families. They are as blind and careless and reckless in regard to these things as it is possible for them to be. Why do they not awake, and read and study upon these subjects? Says the apostle: "Add to your faith virtue; and to virtue knowledge; and to knowledge temperance; and to temperance patience," etc. 2 Peter 1:5, 6. Here is a work which rests upon every one who professes to follow Christ; it is to live upon the plan of addition. . . .

EATING TO EXCESS

Many who have adopted the health reform have left off everything hurtful, but does it follow that because they have left off these things they can eat just as much as they please? They sit down to the table, and instead of considering how much they should eat, they give themselves up to appetite and eat to great excess. And the stomach has all it can do, or all it should do, the rest of that day, to worry away with the burden imposed upon it. All the food that is put into the stomach, from which the system cannot derive benefit, is a burden to nature in her work. It hinders the living machine. The system is clogged and cannot successfully carry on its work. The vital organs are unnecessarily taxed, and the brain nerve power is called to the stomach to help the digestive organs carry on their work of disposing of an amount of food which does the system no good.

Thus the power of the brain is lessened by drawing so heavily upon it to help the stomach get along with its heavy burden. And after it has accomplished the task, what are the sensations experienced as the result of this unnecessary expenditure of vital force? A feeling of goneness, a faintness, as though you must eat more. Perhaps this feeling comes just before mealtime. What is the cause of this? Nature has worried along with her work and is so thoroughly exhausted in consequence that you have this sensation of goneness. And you think that the stomach says, "More food," when, in its faintness, it is distinctly saying, "Give me rest."

The stomach needs rest to gather up its exhausted energies for another work. But, instead of allowing it any period of rest, you think it needs more food, and so heap another load upon nature, and refuse it the needed rest. It is like a man laboring in the field all through the early part of the day until he is weary. He comes in at noon and says that he is weary and exhausted, but you tell him to go to work again and he will obtain relief. This is the way you treat the stomach. It is thoroughly exhausted. But instead of letting it rest, you give it more food, and then call the vitality from other parts of the system to the stomach to assist in the work of digestion. . . .

THE MOTHER'S FIRST WORK

I have seen mothers of large families, who could not see the work that lay right in their pathway, just before them in their own families. They wanted to be missionaries and do some great work. They were looking out for themselves some high position, but neglecting to take care of the very work at home which the Lord had left for them to do. How important that the brain be clear! How important that the body be as free as possible from disease, in order that we may do the work which Heaven has left for us to do, and perform it in such a manner that the Master can say: "Well done, thou good and faithful servant: thou hast been faithful over a few things, I will make thee ruler over many things: enter thou into the joy of thy Lord." Matthew 25:21. My sisters, do not despise the few things which the Lord has left for you to do. Let each day's actions be such that in the day of final settlement of accounts you will not be ashamed to meet the record made by the recording angel.

AN IMPOVERISHED DIET

But what about an impoverished diet? I have spoken of the importance of the quantity and quality of food being in strict accordance with the laws of health. But we would not recommend an impoverished diet. I have been shown that many take a wrong view of the health reform and adopt too poor a diet. They subsist upon a cheap, poor quality of food, prepared without care or reference to the nourishment of the system. It is important that the food should be prepared with care, that the appetite, when not perverted, can relish it. Because we from principle discard the use of meat, butter, mince pies, spices, lard, and that which irritates the stomach and destroys health, the idea should never be given that it is of but little consequence what we eat.

There are some who go to extremes. They must eat just such an amount and just such a quality, and confine themselves to two or three things. They allow only a few things to be placed before them or their families to eat. In eating a small amount of food, and that not of the best quality, they do not take into the stomach that which will suitably nourish the system. Poor food cannot be converted into good blood. An impoverished diet will impoverish the blood. . . .

Some cannot be impressed with the necessity of eating and drinking to the glory of God. The indulgence of appetite affects them in all the relations of life. It is seen in their family, in their church, in the prayer meeting, and in the conduct of their children. It has been the curse of their lives. You cannot make them understand the truths for these last days. God has bountifully provided for the sustenance and happiness of all His creatures; and if His laws were never violated, and all acted in harmony with the divine will, health, peace, and happiness, instead of misery and continual evil, would be experienced. . . .

FLESH MEATS, MILK, AND SUGAR

Flesh meats will depreciate the blood. Cook meat with spices, and eat it with rich cakes and pies, and you have a bad quality of blood. The system is too heavily taxed in disposing of this kind of food. The mince pies and the pickles, which should never find a place in any human stomach, will give a miserable quality of blood. And a poor quality of food, cooked in an improper manner, and insufficient in quantity, cannot make good blood. Flesh meats and rich food, and an impoverished diet, will produce the same results.

Now in regard to milk and sugar: I know of persons who have become frightened at the health reform, and said they would have nothing to do with it, because it has spoken against a free use of these things. Changes should be made with great care, and we should move cautiously and wisely. We want to take that course which will recommend itself to the intelligent men and women of the land. Large quantities of milk and sugar eaten together are injurious. They impart impurities to the system. Animals from which milk is obtained are not always healthy. They may be diseased. A cow may be apparently well in the morning, and die before night. Then she was diseased in the morning, and her milk was diseased; but you did not know it. The animal creation is diseased. Flesh meats are diseased. Could we know that animals were in perfect health, I would recommend that people eat flesh meats sooner than large quantities of milk and sugar. It would not do the injury that milk and sugar do. Sugar clogs the system. It hinders the working of the living machine. . . .

I frequently sit down to the tables of the brethren and sisters, and see that they use a great amount of milk and sugar. These clog the system, irritate the digestive organs, and affect the brain. Anything that hinders the active motion of the living machinery affects the brain very directly. And from the light given me, sugar, when largely used, is more injurious than meat. These changes should be made cautiously, and the subject should be treated in a manner not calculated to disgust and prejudice those whom we would teach and help.

MOTHERS AND DAUGHTERS

Our sisters often do not know how to cook. To such I would say: I would go to the very best cook that could be found in the country, and remain there if necessary for weeks, until I had become mistress of the art, an intelligent, skillful cook. I would pursue this course if I were forty years old. It is your duty to know how to cook, and it is your duty to teach your daughters to cook. When you are teaching them the art of cookery you are building around them a barrier that will preserve them from the folly and vice which they may otherwise be tempted to engage in. I prize my seamstress, I value my copyist; but my cook, who knows well how to prepare the food to sustain life and nourish brain, bone, and muscle, fills the most important place among the helpers in my family. . . .

RELIGION IN GOOD COOKING

We can have a variety of good, wholesome food, cooked in a healthful manner, so that it can be made palatable to all. And if you, my sisters, do not know how to cook, I advise you to learn. It is of vital importance to you to know how to cook. There are more souls lost from poor cooking than you have any idea of. It produces sickness, disease, and bad tempers; the system becomes deranged, and heavenly things cannot be discerned. There is more religion in a loaf of good bread than many of you think. There is more religion in good cooking than you have any idea of. We want you to learn what good religion is, and to carry it out in your families. When I have been from home sometimes, I have known that the bread upon the table, and the food generally, would hurt me; but I would be obliged to eat a little to sustain life. It is a sin in the sight of Heaven to have such food. I have suffered for want of proper food. For a dyspeptic stomach, you may place upon your tables fruits of different kinds, but not too many at one meal. In this way you may have a variety, and it will taste good, and after you have eaten your meals you will feel well. . . .

Some of you feel as though you would like to have somebody tell you how much to eat. This is not the way it should be. We are to act from a moral and religious standpoint. We are to be temperate in all things, because an incorruptible crown, a heavenly treasure, is before us. And now I wish to say to my brethren and sisters, I would have moral courage to take my position and to govern myself. I would not want to put that on someone else. You eat too much, and then you are sorry, and so you keep thinking upon what you eat and drink. Just eat that which is for the best, and go right away, feeling clear in the sight of Heaven, and not having remorse of conscience. We do not believe in removing temptations entirely away from either children or grown persons. We all have a warfare before us and must stand in a position to resist the temptations of Satan, and we want to know that we possess the power in ourselves to do this.

A PROTEST AGAINST NOVICES

And while we would caution you not to overeat, even of the best quality of food, we would also caution those that are extremists not to raise a false standard and then endeavor to bring everybody to it. There are some who are starting out as health reformers who are not fit to engage in any other enterprise, and who have not sense enough to take care of their own families, or keep their proper place in the church. And what do they do? Why, they fall back as health reform physicians, as though they could make that a success. They assume the responsibilities of their practice, and take the lives of men and women into their hands, when they really know nothing about the business.

My voice shall be raised against novices undertaking to treat disease professedly according to the principles of health reform. God forbid that we should be the subjects for them to experiment upon! We are too few. It is altogether too inglorious a warfare for us to die in. God deliver us from such danger! We do not need such teachers and physicians. Let those try to treat disease who know something about the human system. The heavenly Physician was full of compassion. This spirit is needed by those who deal with the sick. Some who undertake to become physicians are bigoted, selfish, and mulish. You cannot teach them anything. It may be they have never done anything worth doing. They may not have made life a success. They know nothing really worth knowing, and yet they have started up to practice the health reform. We cannot afford to let such persons kill off this one and that one. No; we cannot afford it!

We want to be just right every time. We want to bring our people up to the right position on the health reform. "Let us," says the apostle, "cleanse ourselves from all filthiness of the flesh and spirit, perfecting holiness in the fear of God." 2 Corinthians 7:1. We must be right in order to stand in the last days. We need clear brains and sound minds in sound bodies. We should begin to work in earnest for our children, for every member of our families. Shall we take hold and work from the right standpoint? Jesus is coming; and if we pursue a course to blind ourselves to the soul-elevating truths of these last days, how can we be sanctified through the truth? How can we be prepared for immortality? May the Lord help us that we may commence to work here as never before.

Flesh Meats and Stimulants

DEAR BROTHER AND SISTER H: I recollected your countenances as being among several that I had seen who need a work accomplished for them before they can be sanctified through the truth. You embraced the truth because you saw it to be truth, but it has not yet taken hold of you. You have not realized its sanctifying influence upon the life. The light has been shining upon your pathway in regard to health reform and the duty resting upon God's people in these last days to exercise temperance in all things. You, I saw, were among the number who would be backward to see the light and correct your manner of eating, drinking, and working. As the light of truth is received and followed out, it will work an entire reformation in the life and character of all those who are sanctified through it. . . .

Sister H is a woman whose blood is corrupt. Her system is full of scrofulous humors from the eating of flesh meats. The use of swine's flesh in your family has imparted a bad quality of blood. Sister H needs to confine herself strictly to a diet of grains, fruits, and vegetables, cooked without flesh or grease of any kind. It will take quite a length of time of strictly healthful diet to place you in better conditions of health, where you will be rightly related to life. It is impossible for those who make free use of flesh meats to have an unclouded brain and an active intellect.

We advise you to change your habits of living; but while you do this we caution you to move understandingly. I am acquainted with families who have changed from a meat diet to one that is impoverished. Their food is so poorly prepared

1868, vol. 2, pp. 60-66.

that the stomach loathes it; and such have told me that the health reform did not agree with them, that they were decreasing in physical strength. Here is one reason why some have not been successful in their efforts to simplify their food. They have a poverty-stricken diet. Food is prepared without painstaking, and there is a continual sameness. There should not be many kinds at any one meal, but all meals should not be composed of the same kinds of food without variation. Food should be prepared with simplicity, yet with a nicety which will invite the appetite. You should keep grease out of your food. It defiles any preparation of food you may make. Eat largely of fruits and vegetables.

LIABILITY TO DISEASE INCREASED

After they have reduced their physical strength by a reduced quantity and a poor quality of food, some conclude that their former way of living is the best. The system must be nourished. Yet we do not hesitate to say that flesh meat is not necessary for health or strength. If used it is because a depraved appetite craves it. Its use excites the animal propensities to increased activity and strengthens the animal passions. When the animal propensities are increased, the intellectual and moral powers are decreased. The use of the flesh of animals tends to cause a grossness of body and benumbs the fine sensibilities of the mind.

Will the people who are preparing to become holy, pure, and refined, that they may be introduced into the society of heavenly angels, continue to take the life of God's creatures and subsist on their flesh and enjoy it as a luxury? From what the Lord has shown me, this order of things will be changed, and God's peculiar people will exercise temperance in all things. Those who subsist largely upon flesh cannot avoid eating the meat of animals which are to a greater or less degree diseased. The process of fitting animals for market produces in them disease; and fitted in as healthful manner as they can be, they become heated and diseased by driving before they reach the market. The fluids and flesh of these diseased animals are received directly into the blood, and pass into the circulation of the human body, becoming fluids and flesh of the same. Thus humors are introduced into the system. And if the person already has impure blood, it is greatly aggravated by the eating of the flesh of these animals. The liability to take disease is increased tenfold by meat eating. The intellectual, the moral, and the physical powers are depreciated by the habitual use of flesh meats. Meat eating deranges the system, beclouds the intellect, and blunts the moral sensibilities. We say to you, dear brother and sister, your safest course is to let meat alone.

TEA AND COFFEE

The use of tea and coffee is also injurious to the system. To a certain extent, tea produces intoxication. It enters into the circulation and gradually impairs the energy of body and mind. It stimulates, excites, and quickens the motion of the living machinery, forcing it to unnatural action, and thus gives the tea drinker the impression that it is doing him great service, imparting to him strength. This is a mistake. Tea draws upon the strength of the nerves and leaves them greatly weakened. When its influence is gone and the increased action caused by its use is abated, then what is the result? Languor and debility corresponding to the artificial vivacity the tea imparted. When the system is already overtaxed and needs rest, the use of tea spurs up nature by stimulation to perform unwonted, unnatural action, and thereby lessens her power to perform and her ability to endure; and her powers give out long before Heaven designed they should. Tea is poisonous to the system. Christians should let it alone. The influence of coffee is in a degree the same as tea, but the effect upon the system is still worse. Its influence is exciting, and just in the degree that it elevates above par it will exhaust and bring prostration below par. Tea and coffee drinkers carry the marks upon their faces. The skin becomes sallow and assumes a lifeless appearance. The glow of health is not seen upon the countenance.

Tea and coffee do not nourish the system. The relief obtained from them is sudden, before the stomach has time to digest them. This shows that what the users of these stimulants call strength is only received by exciting the nerves of the stomach, which convey the irritation to the brain, and this in turn is aroused to impart increased action to the heart and short-lived energy to the entire system. All this is false strength that we are the worse for having. They do not give a particle of natural strength.

The second effect of tea drinking is headache, wakefulness, palpitation of the heart, indigestion, trembling of the nerves, with many other evils. . . .

You need clear, energetic minds, in order to appreciate the exalted character of the truth, to value the atonement, and to place the right estimate upon eternal things. If you pursue a wrong course, and indulge in wrong habits of eating, and thereby weaken the intellectual powers, you will not place that high estimate upon salvation and eternal life which will inspire you to conform your life to the life of Christ; you will not make those earnest, self-sacrificing efforts for entire conformity to the will of God, which His word requires, and which are necessary to give you a moral fitness for the finishing touch of immortality.

A Violated Conscience

Dear Brother N: I feel compelled by a sense of duty to address you a few lines. I have been shown some things in regard to your case which I dare not withhold. I was shown that Satan took advantage of you because your wife did not embrace the truth. You were thrown into the society of a corrupt woman, one whose steps take hold on hell. She professed great sympathy for you because of the opposition you received from your wife. Like the serpent in Eden, she made her manners fascinating. She cast the impression on your mind that you were an abused man; that your wife did not appreciate your feelings and reciprocate your affections; that a mistake had been made in your marriage relation; until you imagined the marriage vows of lifelong constancy to her whom you had taken as your wife, to be as galling chains. You went for sympathy to this apparent angel in speech. You poured into her ears that which should have been entrusted alone to your wife whom you had vowed to love, honor, and cherish as long as you both should live. You forgot to watch and pray always lest you should *enter into* temptation. Your soul was marred by a crime. You stamped your life record in heaven with a fearful blot. Yet deep humiliation and repentance before God will be acceptable to Him. The blood of Christ can avail to wash these sins away.

You have fallen, terribly fallen. Satan lured you on into his net, and then left you to disentangle yourself as best you could. You have been harassed and perplexed, and fearfully tempted. A guilty conscience troubles you. You distrust yourself and imagine that everyone else distrusts you. You

1868, vol. 2, pp. 89-93.

are jealous of yourself and imagine that jealousy exists in other hearts toward you. You have not confidence in yourself and imagine that your brethren have not confidence in you. Satan often presents the past before you and tells you that it is of no use for you to try to live out the truth, the way is too strait for you. You have been overcome; now Satan takes advantage of your sinful course to make you believe that you are past redemption.

You are on Satan's battlefield engaged in a severe conflict. The barrier which is thrown around every family circle, and which makes it sacred, you have broken down. And now Satan harasses you almost constantly. You are not at rest. You are not at peace, and you seek to make your brethren responsible for your conflicting feelings and doubts and jealousies; you feel that they are at fault, that they do not give you attention. The trouble is with yourself. You want your own way, and do not rend your heart before God, and with brokenness and contrition cast yourself all broken, sinful, and polluted, upon His mercy. Your efforts to save yourself, if persisted in, will result in your certain ruin.

Cease your jealousies and your faultfinding. Turn your attention to your own case and by humble repentance, relying alone upon the blood of Christ, save your own soul. Make thorough work for eternity. If you turn from the truth you are a ruined man, your family is ruined. After the fortifications preserving sacred the privacy and privileges of the family relation have been once broken down, it is difficult to build them up; but in the strength of God, and in His strength alone, you can do this. Truth, sacred truth, is your anchor, which will save you from drifting in the downward current to crime and destruction.

A conscience once violated is greatly weakened. It needs the strength of constant watchfulness and unceasing prayer. You are standing in a slippery place. You need all the strength that the truth can give to fortify you and save you from making entire shipwreck. Life and death are before you; which will you choose? Had you seen the necessity of being firmly settled upon principle, not moving from impulse, and not being easily discouraged, but prepared to endure hardness, you would not have been overcome as you have been. You have moved from impulse. You have not, like our faultless Pattern, been willing to endure the contradiction of sinners against yourself. We are exhorted to remember Him who endured this, lest we become weary and faint in our minds. You have been weak as a child, having no power of endurance. You have not felt the necessity of being established, strengthened, settled, grounded, and built up in the faith.

HAPPINESS OR MISERY

You have felt that it might be your duty to teach the truth to others instead of being taught yourself. But you must be willing to be a learner, to receive the truth from others, and must cease your faultfinding, your jealousies, your complaining, and in meekness receive the engrafted word which is able to save your soul. It rests with you whether you will have happiness or misery. You have once yielded to temptation and cannot now trust your own strength. Satan has great power over your mind, and you will have nothing to hold you when you break from the restraining influence of the truth. This has been as a safeguard to you to restrain you from crime and iniquity. Your only hope is to seek for thorough conversion and redeem the past by your well-ordered life and godly conversation.

You have moved from impulse. Excitement has been agreeable to your organization. Your only hope now is to sincerely repent of your past transgressions of God's law and purify your soul by obeying the truth. Cultivate purity of thought and purity of life. The grace of God will be your strength to restrain your passions and curb your appetites. Earnest prayer and watching thereunto will bring the Holy

Spirit to your aid to perfect the work and make you like your unerring Pattern.

If you choose to throw off the sacred, restraining influence of the truth, Satan will lead you captive at his will. You will be in danger of giving scope to your appetites and passions, giving loose rein to lusts, to evil and abominable desires. Instead of bearing in your countenance a calm serenity under trial and affliction, like faithful Enoch, having your face radiant with hope and that peace which passeth understanding, you will stamp your countenance with carnal thoughts, with lustful desires. You will bear the impress of the satanic instead of the divine.

"Whereby are given unto us exceeding great and precious promises: that by these ye might be partakers of the *divine nature,* having escaped the corruption that is in the world through lust." 2 Peter 1:4. It is now your privilege, by humble confession and sincere repentance, to take words and return unto the Lord. The precious blood of Christ can cleanse you from all impurity, remove all your defilement, and make you perfect in Him. The mercies of Christ are still within your reach if you will accept them. For the sake of your wronged wife, and your children, the fruit of your own body, cease to do evil, and learn to do well. That which you sow, you shall also reap. If you sow to the flesh you shall of the flesh reap corruption. If you sow to the Spirit you shall of the Spirit reap life everlasting.

You must overcome your sensitiveness and faultfinding. You are jealous that others do not give you all the attention you think you should have. The experience founded in feeling, and savoring of fanaticism, you must not adhere to. It is unsafe. Move from principle, from thorough understanding. Search the Scriptures, and be able to give to every man that asketh you the reasons of the hope which is in you, with meekness and fear. Let self-exaltation die. "Cleanse your hands, ye sinners; and purify your hearts, ye double-minded.

Be afflicted, and mourn, and weep: let your laughter be turned to mourning, and your joy to heaviness." James 4:8, 9. When harassed with temptations and evil thoughts, there is but One to whom you can flee for relief and succor. Flee to Him in your weakness. When near Him, Satan's arrows are broken and cannot harm you. Your trials and temptations borne in God will purify and humble, but will not destroy or endanger you.

Separation From the World

We are commanded, whether we eat, or drink, or whatsoever we do, to do all to the glory of God. How many have conscientiously moved from principle rather than from impulse, and obeyed this command to the letter? How many of the youthful disciples in —— have made God their trust and portion, and have earnestly sought to know and do His will? There are many who are servants of Christ in name, but who are not so in deed.

Where religious principle governs, the danger of committing great errors is small; for selfishness, which always blinds and deceives, is subordinate. The sincere desire to do others good so predominates that self is forgotten. To have firm religious principles is an inestimable treasure. It is the purest, highest, and most elevated influence mortals can possess. Such have an anchor. Every act is well considered, lest its effect be injurious to another and lead away from Christ. The constant inquiry of the mind is: Lord, how shall I best serve Thee, and glorify Thy name in the earth? How shall I conduct my life to make Thy name a praise in the earth, and lead others to love, serve, and honor Thee? Let me only desire and choose Thy will. Let the words and example of my Redeemer be the light and strength of my heart. While I follow and trust in Him, He will not leave me to perish. He will be my crown of rejoicing.

If we mistake the wisdom of man for the wisdom of God we are led astray by the foolishness of man's wisdom. Here is the great danger of many in ——. They have not an experience for themselves. They have not been in the habit of

1868, vol. 2, pp. 129-133.

prayerfully considering for themselves, with unprejudiced, unbiased judgment, questions and subjects that are new and that are ever liable to arise. They wait to see what others will think. If these dissent, that is all that is needed to convince them that the subject under consideration is of no account whatever. Although this class is large, it does not change the fact that they are inexperienced and weak-minded through long yielding to the enemy, and will always be as sickly as babes, walking by others' light, living on others' experience, feeling as others feel, and acting as others act. They act as though they had not an individuality. Their identity is submerged in others; they are merely shadows of those whom they think about right.

Unless these become sensible of their wavering character and correct it, they will all fail of everlasting life; they will be unable to cope with the perils of the last days. They will possess no stamina to resist the devil, for they do not know that it is he. Someone must be at their side to inform them whether a foe or a friend is approaching. They are not spiritual, therefore spiritual things are not discerned. They are not wise in those things which relate to the kingdom of God. Neither young nor old are excusable in trusting to another to have an experience for them. Said the angel: "Cursed be the man that trusteth in man, and maketh flesh his arm." A noble self-reliance is needed in the Christian experience and warfare.

ASKING IN FAITH

Men, women, and youth, God requires you to possess moral courage, steadiness of purpose, fortitude and perseverance, minds that cannot take the assertions of another, but which will investigate for themselves before receiving or rejecting, that will study and weigh evidence, and take it to the Lord in prayer. "If any of you lack wisdom, let him ask of God, that giveth to all men liberally, and upbraideth not; and it shall be given him." Now the condition: "But let him ask in *faith,* nothing wavering. For he that wavereth is like a wave of the sea driven with the wind and tossed. For let not that man think that he shall receive anything of the Lord." James 1:5-7. This petition for wisdom is not to be a meaningless prayer, out of mind as soon as finished. It is a prayer that expresses the strong, earnest desire of the heart, arising from a conscious lack of wisdom to determine the will of God.

After the prayer is made, if the answer is not realized immediately, do not weary of waiting and become unstable. Waver not. Cling to the promise, "Faithful is He that calleth you, who also will do it." 1 Thessalonians 5:24. Like the importunate widow, urge your case, being firm in your purpose. Is the object important and of great consequence to you? It certainly is. Then waver not, for your faith may be tried. If the thing you desire is valuable, it is worthy of a strong, earnest effort. You have the promise; watch and pray. Be steadfast and the prayer will be answered; for is it not God who has promised? If it costs you something to obtain it you will prize it the more when obtained. You are plainly told that if you waver you need not think that you shall receive anything of the Lord. A caution is here given not to become weary, but to rest firmly upon the promise. If you ask, He will give you liberally and upbraid not.

Here is where many make a mistake. They waver from their purpose, and their faith fails. This is the reason they receive nothing of the Lord, who is our Source of strength. None need go in darkness, stumbling along like a blind man; for the Lord has provided light if they will accept it in His appointed way, and not choose their own way. He requires of all a diligent performance of everyday duties. Especially is this required of all who are engaged in the solemn, important work in the office of publication, both of those upon whom rest the more weighty responsibilities of the work, and of those who bear the least responsibilities. This can be done only by looking to God for ability to enable them faithfully to perform what is right in the sight of Heaven, doing all things as though governed by unselfish motives, as if the eye of God were visible to all, looking upon all, and investigating the acts of all.

THE BLIGHT OF SELFISHNESS

The sin which is indulged to the greatest extent, and which separates us from God and produces so many contagious spiritual disorders, is selfishness. There can be no returning to the Lord except by self-denial. Of ourselves we can do nothing; but, through God strengthening us, we can live to do good to others, and in this way shun the evil of selfishness. We need not go to heathen lands to manifest our desire to devote all to God in a useful, unselfish life. We should do this in the home circle, in the church, among those with whom we associate and with whom we do business. Right in the common walks of life is where self is to be denied and kept in subordination. Paul could say: "I die daily." It is the daily dying to self in the little transactions of life that makes us overcomers. We should forget self in the desire to do good to others. With many there is a decided lack of love for others. Instead of faithfully performing their duty, they seek rather their own pleasure.

God positively enjoins upon all His followers a duty to bless others with their influence and means, and to seek that wisdom of Him which will enable them to do all in their power to elevate the thoughts and affections of those who come within their influence. In doing for others, a sweet satisfaction will be experienced, an inward peace which will be a sufficient reward. When actuated by a high and noble desire to do others good, they will find true happiness in a faithful discharge of life's manifold duties. This will bring more than an earthly reward; for every faithful, unselfish performance of duty is noticed by the angels and shines in the life record.

In heaven none will think of self, nor seek their own pleasure; but all, from pure, genuine love, will seek the happiness of the heavenly beings around them. If we wish to enjoy heavenly society in the earth made new, we must be governed by heavenly principles here.

Every act of our lives affects others for good or evil. Our influence is tending upward or downward; it is felt, acted upon, and to a greater or less degree reproduced by others. If by our example we aid others in the development of good principles, we give them power to do good. In their turn they exert the same beneficial influence upon others, and thus hundreds and thousands are affected by our unconscious influence. If we by acts strengthen or force into activity the evil powers possessed by those around us, we share their sin, and will have to render an account for the good we might have done them and did not do, because we made not God our strength, our guide, our counselor.

True Love

True love is not a strong, fiery, impetuous passion. On the contrary, it is calm and deep in its nature. It looks beyond mere externals and is attracted by qualities alone. It is wise and discriminating, and its devotion is real and abiding. God tests and proves us by the common occurrences of life. It is the little things which reveal the chapters of the heart. It is the little attentions, the numerous small incidents and simple courtesies of life, that make up the sum of life's happiness; and it is the neglect of kindly, encouraging, affectionate words, and the little courtesies of life, which helps compose the sum of life's wretchedness. It will be found at last that the denial of self for the good and happiness of those around us constitutes a large share of the life record in heaven. And the fact will also be revealed that the care of self, irrespective of the good and happiness of others, is not beneath the notice of our heavenly Father.

Brother B, the Lord is working for you, and will bless and strengthen you in the course of right. You understand the theory of truth, and should be obtaining all the knowledge you can of God's will and work, that you may be prepared to fill a more responsible position if He, seeing you can glorify His name best in so doing, should require it of you. But you have yet an experience to gain. You are too impulsive, too easily affected by circumstances. God is willing to strengthen, stablish, settle you, if you will earnestly and humbly seek wisdom of Him who is unerring, and who has promised that you shall not seek in vain.

In teaching the truth to others, you are in danger of talking

1868, vol. 2, pp. 133-136.

too strong, in a manner not in keeping with your short experience. You take in things at a glance, and can see the bearing of subjects readily. All are not organized as you are, and cannot do this. You will not be prepared to patiently, calmly wait for those to weigh evidence who cannot see as readily as you do. You will be in danger of urging others too much to see at once as you see and feel all that zeal and necessity of action that you feel. If your expectations are not realized, you will be in danger of becoming discouraged and restless, and wishing a change.

You must shun a disposition to censure, to bear down. Keep clear of everything that savors of a denunciatory spirit. It is not pleasing to God for this spirit to be found in any of His servants of long experience. It is proper for a youth, if graced with humility and the inward adorning, to manifest ardor and zeal; but when a rash zeal and a denunciatory spirit are manifested by a youth who has but a few years of experience, it is most unbecoming and positively disgusting. Nothing can destroy his influence as soon as this. Mildness, gentleness, forbearance, long-suffering, being not easily provoked, bearing all things, hoping all things, enduring all things—these are the fruit growing upon the precious tree of love, which is of heavenly growth. This tree, if nourished, will prove to be an evergreen. Its branches will not decay, its leaves will not wither. It is immortal, eternal, watered continually by the dews of heaven.

THE POWER OF LOVE

Love is power. Intellectual and moral strength are involved in this principle, and cannot be separated from it. The power of wealth has a tendency to corrupt and destroy; the power of force is strong to do hurt; but the excellence and value of pure love consist in its efficiency to do good, and to do nothing else than good. Whatsoever is done out of pure love, be it ever so little or contemptible in the sight of men, is wholly fruitful;

for God regards more with how much love one worketh than the amount he doeth. Love is of God. The unconverted heart cannot originate nor produce this plant of heavenly growth, which lives and flourishes only where Christ reigns.

Love cannot live without action, and every act increases, strengthens, and extends it. Love will gain the victory when argument and authority are powerless. Love works not for profit nor reward; yet God has ordained that great gain shall be the certain result of every labor of love. It is diffusive in its nature and quiet in its operation, yet strong and mighty in its purpose to overcome great evils. It is melting and transforming in its influence, and will take hold of the lives of the sinful and affect their hearts when every other means has proved unsuccessful. Wherever the power of intellect, of authority, or of force is employed, and love is not manifestly present, the affections and will of those whom we seek to reach assume a defensive, repelling position, and their strength of resistance is increased. Jesus was the Prince of Peace. He came into the world to bring resistance and authority into subjection to Himself. Wisdom and strength He could command, but the means He employed with which to overcome evil were the wisdom and strength of love. Suffer nothing to divide your interest from your present work until God shall see fit to give you another piece of work in the same field. Seek not for happiness, for it is never to be found by seeking for it. Go about your duty. Let faithfulness mark all your doings, and be clothed with humility.

"Whatsoever ye would that men should do to you, do ye even so to them." Matthew 7:12. Blessed results would appear as the fruit of such a course. "With what measure ye mete, it shall be measured to you again." Verse 2. Here are strong motives which should constrain us to love one another with a pure heart, fervently. Christ is our example. He went about doing good. He lived to bless others. Love beautified and ennobled all His actions. We are not commanded to do to *ourselves* what we wish others to do unto us; we are to *do unto others* what we wish them to do to us under like circumstances. The measure we mete is always measured to us again. Pure love is simple in its operations, and is distinct from any other principle of action. The love of influence and the desire for the esteem of others may produce a well-ordered life and frequently a blameless conversation. Self-respect may lead us to avoid the appearance of evil. A selfish heart may perform generous actions, acknowledge the present truth, and express humility and affection in an outward manner, yet the motives may be deceptive and impure; the actions that flow from such a heart may be destitute of the savor of life and the fruits of true holiness, being destitute of the principles of pure love. Love should be cherished and cultivated, for its influence is divine.

Heaven is to begin on this earth. When the Lord's people are filled with meekness and tenderness, they will realize that His banner over them is love, and His fruit will be sweet to their taste. They will make a heaven below in which to prepare for heaven above.—1902, vol. 7, p. 131.

Prayer for the Sick

In the case of Sister F, there needed to be a great work accomplished. Those who united in praying for her needed a work done for them. Had God answered their prayers, it would have proved their ruin. In such cases of affliction, where Satan has control of the mind, before engaging in prayer there should be the closest self-examination to discover if there are not sins which need to be repented of, confessed, and forsaken. Deep humility of soul before God is necessary, and firm, humble reliance upon the merits of the blood of Christ alone.

Fasting and prayer will accomplish nothing while the heart is estranged from God by a wrong course of action. "Is not this the fast that I have chosen? to loose the bands of wickedness, to undo the heavy burdens, and to let the oppressed go free, and that ye break every yoke? Is it not to deal thy bread to the hungry, and that thou bring the poor that are cast out to thy house? when thou seest the naked, that thou cover him; and that thou hide not thyself from thine own flesh?" "Then shalt thou call, and the Lord shall answer; thou shalt cry, and He shall say, Here I am. If thou take away from the midst of thee the yoke, the putting forth of the finger, and speaking vanity; and if thou draw out thy soul to the hungry, and satisfy the afflicted soul; then shall thy light rise in obscurity, and thy darkness be as the noonday: and the Lord shall guide thee continually, and satisfy thy soul in drought, and make fat thy bones: and thou shalt be like a watered garden, and like a spring of water, whose waters fail not." Isaiah 58:6, 7, 9-11.

1868, vol. 2, pp. 145-149.

It is heartwork that the Lord requires, good works springing from a heart filled with love. All should carefully and prayerfully consider the above scriptures, and investigate their motives and actions. The promise of God to us is on condition of obedience, compliance with all His requirements. "Cry aloud," saith the prophet Isaiah, "spare not, lift up thy voice like a trumpet, and show My people their transgression, and the house of Jacob their sins. Yet they seek Me daily, and delight to know My ways, as a nation that did righteousness, and forsook not the ordinance of their God: they ask of Me the ordinances of justice; they take delight in approaching to God. Wherefore have we fasted, say they, and Thou seest not? wherefore have we afflicted our soul, and Thou takest no knowledge?" Verses 1-3.

A people are here addressed who make high profession, who are in the habit of praying, and who delight in religious exercises; yet there is a lack. They realize that their prayers are not answered; their zealous, earnest efforts are not observed in heaven, and they earnestly inquire why the Lord makes them no returns. It is not because there is any neglect on the part of God. The difficulty is with the people. While professing godliness, they do not bear fruit to the glory of God; their works are not what they should be. They are living in neglect of positive duties. Unless these are performed, God cannot answer their prayers according to His glory.

In the case of offering prayer for Sister F, there was confusion of sentiment. Some were fanatical and moved from impulse. They possessed a zeal, but not according to knowledge. Some looked at the great thing to be accomplished in this case and began to triumph before the victory was gained. There was much of the Jehu spirit manifested: "Come with me, and see my zeal for the Lord." 2 Kings 10:16. In place of this self-confident assurance, the case should have been presented to God with a spirit of humbleness and distrustfulness of self, and with a broken and a contrite heart.

HOW TO PRAY

I was shown that in case of sickness, where the way is clear for the offering up of prayer for the sick, the case should be committed to the Lord in calm faith, not with a storm of excitement. He alone is acquainted with the past life of the individual and knows what his future will be. He who is acquainted with the hearts of all men knows whether the person, if raised up, would glorify His name or dishonor Him by backsliding and apostasy. All that we are required to do is to ask God to raise the sick up if in accordance with His will, believing that He hears the reasons which we present and the fervent prayers offered. If the Lord sees it will best honor Him, He will answer our prayers. But to urge recovery without submission to His will is not right.

What God promises He is able at any time to perform, and the work which He gives His people to do He is able to accomplish by them. If they will live according to every word He has spoken, every good word and promise will be fulfilled unto them. But if they come short of perfect obedience, the great and precious promises are afar off, and they cannot reach the fulfillment.

All that can be done in praying for the sick is to earnestly importune God in their behalf, and in perfect confidence rest the matter in His hands. If we regard iniquity in our hearts the Lord will not hear us. He can do what He will with His own. He will glorify Himself by working in and through them who wholly follow Him, so that it shall be known that it is the Lord and that their works are wrought in God. Said Christ: "If any man serve Me, him will My Father honor." John 12:26. When we come to Him we should pray that we may enter into and accomplish His purpose, and that our desires and interests may be lost in His. We should acknowledge our acceptance of His will, not praying Him to concede to ours. It is better for us that God does not always answer our prayers just when we desire, and in just the manner we wish. He will do more and better for us than to accomplish all our wishes, for our wisdom is folly.

We have united in earnest prayer around the sickbed of men, women, and children, and have felt that they were given back to us from the dead in answer to our earnest prayers. In these prayers we thought we must be positive and, if we exercised faith, that we must ask for nothing less than life. We dared not say, "If it will glorify God," fearing it would admit a semblance of doubt. We have anxiously watched those who have been given back, as it were, from the dead. We have seen some of these, especially youth, raised to health, and they have forgotten God, become dissolute in life, causing sorrow and anguish to parents and friends, and have become a shame to those who feared to pray. They lived not to honor and glorify God, but to curse Him with their lives of vice.

We no longer mark out a way nor seek to bring the Lord to our wishes. If the life of the sick can glorify Him, we pray that they may live; nevertheless, not as we will but as He will. Our faith can be just as firm, and more reliable, by committing the desire to the all-wise God, and, without feverish anxiety, in perfect confidence, trusting all to Him. We have the promise. We know that He hears us if we ask according to His will. Our petitions must not take the form of a command, but of intercession for Him to do the things we desire of Him.

When the church are united, they will have strength and power; but when part of them are united to the world, and many are given to covetousness, which God abhors, He can do but little for them. Unbelief and sin shut them away from God. We are so weak that we cannot bear much spiritual prosperity, lest we take the glory, and accredit goodness and righteousness to ourselves as the reason of the signal blessing of God, when it was all because of the great mercy and loving-kindness of our compassionate heavenly Father, and not because any good was found in us.

I saw that the reason why God did not hear the prayers of His servants for the sick among us more fully was that He could not be glorified in so doing while they were violating the laws of health. And I also saw that He designed the health reform and Health Institute to prepare the way for the prayer of faith to be fully answered. Faith and good works should go hand in hand in relieving the afflicted among us, and in fitting them to glorify God here and to be saved at the coming of Christ. God forbid that these afflicted ones should ever be disappointed and grieved in finding the managers of the Institute working only from a worldly standpoint instead of adding to the hygienic practice the blessings and virtues of nursing fathers and mothers in Israel.

Let no one obtain the idea that the Institute is the place for them to come to be raised up by the prayer of faith. That is the place to find relief from disease by treatment and right habits of living, and to learn how to avoid sickness. But if there is one place under the heavens more than another where soothing, sympathizing prayer should be offered by men and women of devotion and faith it is at such an institute. Those who treat the sick should move forward in their important work with strong reliance upon God for His blessing to attend the means which He has graciously provided, and to which He has in mercy called our attention as a people, such as pure air, cleanliness, healthful diet, proper periods of labor and repose, and the use of water.—1867, vol. 1, p. 561.

Wiles of Satan

SATAN has great advantages. He possessed the wonderful intellectual power of an angel, of which few form any just idea. Satan was conscious of his power, or he would not have engaged in a conflict with the mighty God, the everlasting Father, and the Prince of Peace. Satan closely watches events, and when he finds one who has a specially strong spirit of opposition to the truth of God he will even reveal to him unfulfilled events, that he may more firmly secure himself a seat in his heart. He who did not hesitate to brave a conflict with Him who holds creation as in His hand, has malignity to persecute and deceive. He holds mortals in his snare at the present time. During his experience of nearly six thousand years he has lost none of his skill and shrewdness. All this time he has been a close observer of all that concerns our race.

Those who have bitterly opposed the truth of God, Satan uses as his mediums. To such he will appear in the assumed person and garb of another, it may be a friend of the medium. He will increase their faith by using the words of this friend and relating circumstances which are about to take place or which really have taken place and of which the medium knew nothing. Sometimes previous to a death or an accident he gives a dream or, personating another, converses with the medium, even imparting knowledge by means of his suggestions. But it is wisdom from beneath and not from above. The wisdom taught by Satan is opposed to the truth, unless, to serve his purpose, he apparently clothes himself with the light which enshrouds angels. To a certain class of minds he will come sanctioning a part of what Christ's followers

1868, vol. 2, pp. 171-173 (Burden Bearers in the Church).

believe to be truth, while he warns them to reject the other part as dangerous and fatal error.

Satan is a master workman. His infernal wisdom he employs with good success. He is ready and able to teach those who reject the counsel of God against their own souls. The bait which he has found will avail in bringing souls into his net, that he may fasten his hellish grasp upon them, he will clothe with every possible good and make as attractive as possible. All who are thus ensnared will learn at a dreadful expense the folly of selling heaven and immortality for a deception that is fatal in its consequences.

Our adversary, the devil, is not void of wisdom or strength. He goeth about like a roaring lion, seeking whom he may devour. He will work "with all power and signs and lying wonders, and with all deceivableness of unrighteousness in them that perish; because they received not the love of the truth, that they might be saved." Because they rejected the truth, "God shall send them strong delusion, that they should believe a lie: that they all might be damned who believed not the truth, but had pleasure in unrighteousness." 2 Thessalonians 2:9-12. We have a powerful, deceptive foe with whom to contend, and our only safety is in Him who is to come who will consume this archdeceiver with the spirit of His mouth, and destroy with the brightness of His coming.

The Sufferings of Christ

In order to fully realize the value of salvation, it is necessary to understand what it cost. In consequence of limited ideas of the sufferings of Christ, many place a low estimate upon the great work of the atonement. The glorious plan of man's salvation was brought about through the infinite love of God the Father. In this divine plan is seen the most marvelous manifestation of the love of God to the fallen race. Such love as is manifested in the gift of God's beloved Son amazed the holy angels. "God so loved the world, that He gave His only-begotten Son, that whosoever believeth in Him should not perish, but have everlasting life." John 3:16. This Saviour was the brightness of His Father's glory and the express image of His person. He possessed divine majesty, perfection, and excellence. He was equal with God. "It pleased the Father that in Him should all fullness dwell." Colossians 1:19. "Who, being in the form of God, thought it not robbery to be equal with God: but made Himself of no reputation, and took upon Him the form of a servant, and was made in the likeness of men: and being found in fashion as a man, He humbled Himself, and became obedient unto death, even the death of the cross." Philippians 2:6-8.

Christ consented to die in the sinner's stead, that man, by a life of obedience, might escape the penalty of the law of God. His death did not make the law of none effect; it did not slay the law, lessen its holy claims, nor detract from its sacred dignity. The death of Christ proclaimed the justice of His Father's law in punishing the transgressor, in that He consented to suffer the penalty of the law Himself in order to

1869, vol. 2, pp. 200-215.

save fallen man from its curse. The death of God's beloved Son on the cross shows the immutability of the law of God. His death magnifies the law and makes it honorable, and gives evidence to man of its changeless character. From His own divine lips are heard the words: "Think not that I am come to destroy the law, or the prophets: I am not come to destroy, but to fulfill." Matthew 5:17. The death of Christ justified the claims of the law.

THE DIVINE-HUMAN SAVIOUR

In Christ were united the human and the divine. His mission was to reconcile God and man, to unite the finite with the infinite. This was the only way in which fallen men could be exalted through the merits of the blood of Christ to be partakers of the divine nature. Taking human nature fitted Christ to understand man's trials and sorrows, and all the temptations wherewith he is beset. Angels who were unacquainted with sin could not sympathize with man in his peculiar trials. Christ condescended to take man's nature and was tempted in all points like as we, that He might know how to succor all who should be tempted.

As the human was upon Him, He felt His need of strength from His Father. He had select places of prayer. He loved to hold communion with His Father in the solitude of the mountain. In this exercise His holy, human soul was strengthened for the duties and trials of the day. Our Saviour identifies Himself with our needs and weaknesses, in that He became a suppliant, a nightly petitioner, seeking from His Father fresh supplies of strength, to come forth invigorated and refreshed, braced for duty and trial. He is our example in all things. He is a brother in our infirmities, but not in possessing like passions. As the sinless One, His nature recoiled from evil. He endured struggles and torture of soul in a world of sin. His humanity made prayer a necessity and privilege. He required all the stronger divine support and comfort which His Father was ready to impart to Him, to Him who had, for the benefit of man, left the joys of heaven and chosen His home in a cold and thankless world. Christ found comfort and joy in communion with His Father. Here He could unburden His heart of the sorrows that were crushing Him. He was a man of sorrows and acquainted with grief.

OUR EXAMPLE

Through the day He labored earnestly to do good to others, to save men from destruction. He healed the sick, comforted the mourning, and brought cheerfulness and hope to the despairing. He brought the dead to life. After His work was finished for the day, He went forth, evening after evening, away from the confusion of the city, and His form was bowed in some retired grove in supplication to His Father. At times the bright beams of the moon shone upon His bowed form. And then again the clouds and darkness shut away all light. The dew and frost of night rested upon His head and beard while in the attitude of a suppliant. He frequently continued His petitions through the entire night. He is our example. If we could remember this, and imitate Him, we would be much stronger in God.

If the Saviour of men, with His divine strength, felt the need of prayer, how much more should feeble, sinful mortals feel the necessity of prayer—fervent, constant prayer! When Christ was the most fiercely beset by temptation, He ate nothing. He committed Himself to God and, through earnest prayer and perfect submission to the will of His Father, came off conqueror. Those who profess the truth for these last days, above every other class of professed Christians, should imitate the great Exemplar in prayer.

"It is enough for the disciple that he be as his master, and the servant as his lord." Matthew 10:25. Our tables are frequently spread with luxuries neither healthful nor necessary, because we love these things more than we love self-denial, freedom from disease, and soundness of mind. Jesus sought earnestly for strength from His Father. This the divine Son of God considered of more value, even for Himself, than to sit at the most luxurious table. He has given us evidence that prayer is essential in order to receive strength to contend with the powers of darkness, and to do the work allotted us. Our own strength is weakness, but that which God gives is mighty and will make everyone who obtains it more than conqueror.

IN GETHSEMANE

As the Son of God bowed in the attitude of prayer in the Garden of Gethsemane, the agony of His spirit forced from His pores sweat like great drops of blood. It was here that the horror of great darkness surrounded Him. The sins of the world were upon Him. He was suffering in man's stead as a transgressor of His Father's law. Here was the scene of temptation. The divine light of God was receding from His vision, and He was passing into the hands of the powers of darkness. In His soul anguish He lay prostrate on the cold earth. He was realizing His Father's frown. He had taken the cup of suffering from the lips of guilty man, and proposed to drink it Himself, and in its place give to man the cup of blessing. The wrath that would have fallen upon man was now falling upon Christ. It was here that the mysterious cup trembled in His hand.

Jesus had often resorted to Gethsemane with His disciples for meditation and prayer. They were all well acquainted with this sacred retreat. Even Judas knew where to lead the murderous throng, that he might betray Jesus into their hands. Never before had the Saviour visited the spot with a heart so full of sorrow. It was not bodily suffering from which the Son of God shrank, and which wrung from His lips, in the presence of His disciples, these mournful words: "My soul is exceeding sorrowful, even unto death." "Tarry ye here," said He, "and watch with Me." Matthew 26:38.

Leaving His disciples within hearing of His voice, He went a little distance from them and fell on His face and prayed. His soul was agonized, and He pleaded: "O My Father, if it be possible, let this cup pass from Me: nevertheless not as I will, but as Thou wilt." Verse 39. The sins of a lost world were upon Him and overwhelming Him. It was a sense of His Father's frown, in consequence of sin, which rent His heart with such piercing agony and forced from His brow great drops of blood, which, rolling down His pale cheeks, fell to the ground, moistening the earth.

"WATCH AND PRAY"

Rising from His prostrate position, He came to His disciples and found them sleeping. He said unto Peter: "What, could ye not watch with Me one hour? Watch and pray, that ye enter not into temptation: the spirit indeed is willing, but the flesh is weak." Verses 40, 41. At the most important time—the time when Jesus had made a special request for them to watch with Him—the disciples were found sleeping. He knew that severe conflicts and terrible temptations were before them. He had taken them with Him that they might be a strength to Him, and that the events they should witness that night, and the lessons of instruction they should receive, might be indelibly printed upon their memories. This was necessary that their faith might not fail, but be strengthened for the test just before them.

But instead of watching with Christ, they were burdened with sorrow, and fell asleep. Even the ardent Peter, who, only a few hours before, had declared that he would suffer and, if need be, die for his Lord, was asleep. At the most critical moment, when the Son of God was in need of their sympathy and heartfelt prayers, they were found asleep. They lost much by thus sleeping. Our Saviour designed to fortify them for the severe test of their faith to which they would soon be subjected. If they had spent that mournful period in watching with the dear Saviour, and in prayer to God, Peter would not have been left to his own feeble strength to deny his Lord in the time of trial.

The Son of God went away the second time, and prayed, saying: "O My Father, if this cup may not pass away from Me, except I drink it, Thy will be done." Matthew 26:42. And again He came to His disciples and found them sleeping. Their eyes were heavy. By these sleeping disciples is represented a sleeping church, when the day of God's visitation is nigh. It is a time of clouds and thick darkness, when to be found asleep is most perilous.

Jesus has left us this warning: "Watch ye therefore: for ye know not when the Master of the house cometh, at even, or at midnight, or at the cockcrowing, or in the morning: lest coming suddenly He find you sleeping." Mark 13:35, 36. The church of God is required to fulfill her night watch, however perilous, whether long or short. Sorrow is no excuse for her to be less watchful. Tribulation should not lead to carelessness, but to double vigilance. Christ has directed the church by His own example to the Source of their strength in times of need, distress, and peril. The attitude of watching is to designate the church as God's people indeed. By this sign the waiting ones are distinguished from the world and show that they are pilgrims and strangers upon the earth.

Again the Saviour turned sadly from His sleeping disciples, and prayed the third time, saying the same words. Then He came to them and said: "Sleep on now, and take your rest: behold, the hour is at hand, and the Son of man is betrayed into the hands of sinners." Matthew 26:45. How cruel for the disciples to permit sleep to close their eyes, and slumber to chain their senses, while their divine Lord was enduring such inexpressible mental anguish! If they had remained watching they would not have lost their faith as they beheld the Son of God dying upon the cross.

This important night watch should have been signalized by noble mental struggles and prayers, which would have brought them strength to witness the unspeakable agony of the Son of God. It would have prepared them, as they should behold His sufferings upon the cross, to understand something of the nature of the overpowering anguish which He endured in the Garden of Gethsemane. And they would have been better able to recall the words He had spoken to them in reference to His sufferings, death, and resurrection; and, amid the gloom of that terrible, trying hour, some rays of hope would have lighted up the darkness and sustained their faith.

Christ had told them before that these things would take place, but they did not understand Him. The scene of His sufferings was to be a fiery ordeal to His disciples, hence the necessity of watchfulness and prayer. Their faith needed to be sustained by an unseen strength as they should experience the triumph of the powers of darkness.

INEXPRESSIBLE ANGUISH

We can have but faint conceptions of the inexpressible anguish of God's dear Son in Gethsemane, as He realized His separation from His Father in consequence of bearing man's sin. He became sin for the fallen race. The sense of the withdrawal of His Father's love pressed from His anguished soul these mournful words: "My soul is exceeding sorrowful, even unto death." "If it be possible, let this cup pass from Me." Then with entire submission to His Father's will, He adds: "Nevertheless not as I will, but as Thou wilt." Matthew 26:38, 39.

The divine Son of God was fainting, dying. The Father sent a messenger from His presence to strengthen the divine Sufferer and brace Him to tread His bloodstained path. Could mortals have viewed the amazement and the sorrow of the angelic host as they watched in silent grief the Father separating His beams of light, love, and glory from the beloved Son of His bosom, they would better understand how offensive sin is in His sight. The sword of justice was now to awake against His dear Son. He was betrayed by a kiss into the hands of His enemies, and hurried to the judgment hall of an earthly court, there to be derided and condemned to death by sinful mortals. There the glorious Son of God was "wounded for our transgressions, He was bruised for our iniquities." He bore insult, mockery, and shameful abuse, until "His visage was so marred more than any man, and His form more than the sons of men." Isaiah 53:5; 52:14.

INCOMPREHENSIBLE LOVE

Who can comprehend the love here displayed! The angelic host beheld with wonder and with grief Him who had been the Majesty of heaven, and who had worn the crown of glory, now wearing the crown of thorns, a bleeding victim to the rage of an infuriated mob, fired to insane madness by the wrath of Satan. Behold the patient Sufferer! Upon His head is the thorny crown. His lifeblood flows from every lacerated vein. All this in consequence of sin! Nothing could have induced Christ to leave His honor and majesty in heaven, and come to a sinful world, to be neglected, despised, and rejected by those He came to save, and finally to suffer upon the cross, but eternal, redeeming love, which will ever remain a mystery.

Wonder, O heavens, and be astonished, O earth! Behold the oppressor and the oppressed! A vast multitude enclose the Saviour of the world. Mockings and jeerings are mingled with the coarse oaths of blasphemy. His lowly birth and humble life are commented upon by unfeeling wretches. His claim to be the Son of God is ridiculed by the chief priests and elders, and vulgar jests and insulting derision are passed from lip to lip. Satan was having full control of the minds of his servants. In order to do this effectually, he commences with the chief priests and elders, and imbues them with religious frenzy. They are actuated by the same satanic spirit which moves the most vile and hardened wretches. There is a corrupt harmony in the feelings of all, from the hypocritical priests and elders down to the most debased. Christ, the precious Son of God, was led forth, and the cross was laid upon His shoulders. At every step was left blood which flowed from His wounds. Thronged by an immense crowd of bitter enemies and unfeeling spectators, He is led away to the crucifixion. "He was oppressed, and He was afflicted, yet He opened not His mouth: He is brought as a lamb to the slaughter, and as a sheep before her shearers is dumb, so He openeth not His mouth." Isaiah 53:7.

ON THE CROSS

His sorrowing disciples follow Him at a distance, behind the murderous throng. He is nailed to the cross, and hangs suspended between the heavens and the earth. Their hearts are bursting with anguish as their beloved Teacher is suffering as a criminal. Close to the cross are the blind, bigoted, faithless priests and elders, taunting, mocking, and jeering: "Thou that destroyest the temple, and buildest it in three days, save Thyself. If Thou be the Son of God, come down from the cross. Likewise also the chief priests mocking Him, with the scribes and elders, said, He saved others; Himself He cannot save. If He be the King of Israel, let Him now come down from the cross, and we will believe Him. He trusted in God; let Him deliver Him now, if He will have Him: for He said, I am the Son of God." Matthew 27:40-43.

Not one word did Jesus answer to all this. While the nails were being driven through His hands, and the sweat drops of agony were forced from His pores, from the pale, quivering lips of the innocent Sufferer a prayer of pardoning love was breathed for His murderers: "Father, forgive them; for they know not what they do." Luke 23:34. All heaven was gazing with profound interest upon the scene. The glorious Redeemer of a lost world was suffering the penalty of man's transgression of the Father's law. He was about to ransom His people with His own blood. He was paying the just claims of God's holy law. This was the means through which an end was to be finally made of sin and Satan, and his host to be vanquished.

Oh, was there ever suffering and sorrow like that endured by the dying Saviour! It was the sense of His Father's displeasure which made His cup so bitter. It was not bodily suffering which so quickly ended the life of Christ upon the cross. It was the crushing weight of the sins of the world, and a sense of His Father's wrath. The Father's glory and sustaining presence had left Him, and despair pressed its crushing weight of darkness upon Him and forced from His pale and quivering lips the anguished cry: "My God, My God, why hast Thou forsaken Me?" Matthew 27:46.

Jesus had united with the Father in making the world. Amid the agonizing sufferings of the Son of God, blind and deluded men alone remain unfeeling. The chief priests and elders revile God's dear Son while in His expiring agonies. Yet inanimate nature groans in sympathy with her bleeding, dying Author. The earth trembles. The sun refuses to behold the scene. The heavens gather blackness. Angels have witnessed the scene of suffering until they can look no longer, and hide their faces from the horrid sight. Christ is dying! He is in despair! His Father's approving smile is removed, and angels are not permitted to lighten the gloom of the terrible hour. They can only behold in amazement their loved Commander, the Majesty of heaven, suffering the penalty of man's transgression of the Father's law.

INTO THE DEPTHS

Even doubts assailed the dying Son of God. He could not see through the portals of the tomb. Bright hope did not present to Him His coming forth from the tomb a conqueror and His Father's acceptance of His sacrifice. The sin of the world, with all its terribleness, was felt to the utmost by the Son of God. The displeasure of the Father for sin, and its penalty, which is death, were all that He could realize through this amazing darkness. He was tempted to fear that sin was so offensive in the sight of His Father that He could not be reconciled to His Son. The fierce temptation that His own Father had forever left Him caused that piercing cry from the cross: "My God, My God, why hast Thou forsaken Me?" Matthew 27:46.

Christ felt much as sinners will feel when the vials of God's wrath shall be poured out upon them. Black despair, like the pall of death, will gather about their guilty souls, and then they will realize to the fullest extent the sinfulness of sin. Salvation has been purchased for them by the suffering and death of the Son of God. It might be theirs, if they would accept of it willingly, gladly; but none are compelled to yield obedience to the law of God. If they refuse the heavenly benefit and choose the pleasures and deceitfulness of sin, they have their choice, and at the end receive their wages, which is the wrath of God and eternal death. They will be forever separated from the presence of Jesus, whose sacrifice they had despised. They will have lost a life of happiness and sacrificed eternal glory for the pleasures of sin for a season.

Faith and hope trembled in the expiring agonies of Christ because God had removed the assurance He had heretofore given His beloved Son of His approbation and acceptance. The Redeemer of the world then relied upon the evidences which had hitherto strengthened Him, that His Father accepted His labors and was pleased with His work. In His dying agony, as He yields up His precious life, He has by faith alone to trust in Him whom it has ever been His joy to obey. He is not cheered with clear, bright rays of hope on the right hand nor on the left. All is enshrouded in oppressive gloom. Amid the awful darkness which is felt by sympathizing nature, the Redeemer drains the mysterious cup even to its dregs. Denied even bright hope and confidence in the triumph which will be His in the future, He cries with a loud voice: "Father, into Thy hands I commend My spirit." Luke 23:46. He is acquainted with the character of His Father, with His justice, His mercy, and His great love, and in submission He drops into His hands. Amid the convulsions of nature are heard by the amazed spectators the dying words of the Man of Calvary.

Nature sympathized with the suffering of its Author. The heaving earth, the rent rocks, proclaimed that it was the Son of God who died. There was a mighty earthquake. The veil of the temple was rent in twain. Terror seized the executioners and spectators as they beheld the sun veiled in darkness and felt the earth shake beneath them, and saw and heard the rending of the rocks. The mocking and jeering of the chief priests and elders were hushed as Christ commended His spirit into the hands of His Father. The astonished throng began to withdraw and grope their way in the darkness to the city. They smote upon their breasts as they went and in terror, speaking scarcely above a whisper, said among themselves: "It is an innocent person that has been murdered. What if, indeed, He is, as He asserted, the Son of God?"

"IT IS FINISHED"

Jesus did not yield up His life till He had accomplished the work which He came to do, and exclaimed with His departing breath: "It is finished." John 19:30. Satan was then defeated. He knew that his kingdom was lost. Angels rejoiced as the words were uttered: "It is finished." The great plan of redemption, which was dependent on the death of Christ, had been thus far carried out. And there was joy in heaven that the sons of Adam could, through a life of obedience, be finally exalted to the throne of God. Oh, what love! What amazing love! that brought the Son of God to earth to be made sin for us, that we might be reconciled to God, and elevated to a life with Him in His mansions in glory. Oh, what is man, that such a price should be paid for his redemption!

When men and women can more fully comprehend the magnitude of the great sacrifice which was made by the Majesty of heaven in dying in man's stead, then will the plan of salvation be magnified, and reflections of Calvary will awaken tender, sacred, and lively emotions in the Christian's heart. Praises to God and the Lamb will be in their hearts and upon their lips. Pride and self-esteem cannot flourish in the hearts that keep fresh in memory the scenes of Calvary. This world will appear of but little value to those who appreciate the great price of man's redemption, the precious blood of God's dear Son. All the riches of the world are not of sufficient value to redeem one perishing soul. Who can measure the love Christ felt for a lost world as He hung upon the cross, suffering for the sins of guilty men? This love was immeasurable, infinite.

LOVE STRONGER THAN DEATH

Christ has shown that His love was stronger than death. He was accomplishing man's salvation; and although He had the most fearful conflict with the powers of darkness, yet, amid it all, His love grew stronger and stronger. He endured the hiding of His Father's countenance, until He was led to exclaim in the bitterness of His soul: "My God, My God, why hast Thou forsaken Me?" Matthew 27:46. His arm brought salvation. The price was paid to purchase the redemption of man, when, in the last soul struggle, the blessed words were uttered which seemed to resound through creation: "It is finished."

Many who profess to be Christians become excited over worldly enterprises, and their interest is awakened for new and exciting amusements, while they are coldhearted, and appear as if frozen, in the cause of God. Here is a theme, poor formalist, which is of sufficient importance to excite you. Eternal interests are here involved. Upon this theme it is sin to be calm and unimpassioned. The scenes of Calvary call for the deepest emotion. Upon this subject you will be excusable if you manifest enthusiasm. That Christ, so excellent, so innocent, should suffer such a painful death, bearing the weight of the sins of the world, our thoughts and imaginations can never fully comprehend. The length, the breadth, the height, the depth, of such amazing love we cannot fathom. The contemplation of the matchless depths of a Saviour's love should fill the mind, touch and melt the soul, refine and elevate the affections, and completely transform the whole character. The language of the apostle is: "I determined not to know anything among you, save Jesus Christ, and Him crucified." 1 Corinthians 2:2. We also may look toward Calvary and exclaim: "God forbid that I should glory, save in the cross of our Lord Jesus Christ, by whom the world is crucified unto me, and I unto the world." Galatians 6:14.

Considering at what an immense cost our salvation has been purchased, what will be the fate of those who neglect so great salvation? What will be the punishment of those who profess to be followers of Christ, yet fail to bow in humble obedience to the claims of their Redeemer, and who do not take the cross as humble disciples of Christ and follow Him from the manger to Calvary? "He that gathereth not with Me," says Christ, "scattereth abroad." Matthew 12:30.

LIMITED VIEWS OF THE ATONEMENT

Some have limited views of the atonement. They think that Christ suffered only a small portion of the penalty of the law of God; they suppose that, while the wrath of God was felt by His dear Son, He had, through all His painful sufferings, the evidence of His Father's love and acceptance; that the portals of the tomb before Him were illuminated with bright hope, and that He had the abiding evidence of

His future glory. Here is a great mistake. Christ's keenest anguish was a sense of His Father's displeasure. His mental agony because of this was of such intensity that man can have but faint conception of it.

With many the story of the condescension, humiliation, and sacrifice of our divine Lord awakens no deeper interest, and stirs the soul and affects the life no more, than does the history of the death of the martyrs of Jesus. Many have suffered death by slow tortures; others have suffered death by crucifixion. In what does the death of God's dear Son differ from these? It is true He died upon the cross a most cruel death; yet others, for His dear sake, have suffered equally, so far as bodily torture is concerned. Why, then, was the suffering of Christ more dreadful than that of other persons who have yielded their lives for His sake? If the sufferings of Christ consisted in physical pain alone, then His death was no more painful than that of some of the martyrs.

But bodily pain was but a small part of the agony of God's dear Son. The sins of the world were upon Him, also the sense of His Father's wrath as He suffered the penalty of the law transgressed. It was these that crushed His divine soul. It was the hiding of His Father's face—a sense that His own dear Father had forsaken Him—which brought despair. The separation that sin makes between God and man was fully realized and keenly felt by the innocent, suffering Man of Calvary. He was oppressed by the powers of darkness. He had not one ray of light to brighten the future. And He was struggling with the power of Satan, who was declaring that he had Christ in his power, that he was superior in strength to the Son of God, that the Father had disowned His Son, and that He was no longer in the favor of God any more than himself. If He was indeed still in favor with God, why need He die? God could save Him from death.

Christ yielded not in the least degree to the torturing foe, even in His bitterest anguish. Legions of evil angels were all about the Son of God, yet the holy angels were bidden not to break their ranks and engage in conflict with the taunting, reviling foe. Heavenly angels were not permitted to minister unto the anguished spirit of the Son of God. It was in this terrible hour of darkness, the face of His Father hidden, legions of evil angels enshrouding Him, the sins of the world upon Him, that the words were wrenched from His lips: "My God, My God, why hast Thou forsaken Me?" Matthew 27:46.

A MEASURE OF THE SOUL'S VALUE

The death of the martyrs can bear no comparison with the agony endured by the Son of God. We should take broader and deeper views of the life, sufferings, and death of God's dear Son. When the atonement is viewed correctly, the salvation of souls will be felt to be of infinite value. In comparison with the enterprise of everlasting life, every other sinks into insignificance. But how have the counsels of this loving Saviour been despised! The heart has been devoted to the world, and selfish interests have closed the door against the Son of God. Hollow hypocrisy and pride, selfishness and gain, envy, malice, and passion, have so filled the hearts of many that Christ can have no room.

He was eternally rich, yet for our sakes He became poor, that we through His poverty might be made rich. He was clothed with light and glory, and was surrounded with hosts of heavenly angels waiting to execute His commands. Yet He put on our nature and came to sojourn among sinful mortals. Here is love that no language can express. It passes knowledge. Great is the mystery of godliness. Our souls should be enlivened, elevated, and enraptured with the theme of the love of the Father and the Son to man. The followers of Christ should here learn to reflect in some degree that mysterious love preparatory to joining all the redeemed in ascribing "blessing, and honor, and glory, and power, . . . unto Him that sitteth upon the throne, and unto the Lamb for ever and ever." Revelation 5:13.

Christ gave Himself, an atoning sacrifice, for the saving of a lost world. He was treated as we deserve, in order that we might be treated as He deserves. He was condemned for our sins, in which He had no share, that we might be justified by His righteousness, in which we had no share. He suffered the death which was ours, that we might receive the life which was His. "With His stripes we are healed." Isaiah 53:5.—1904, vol. 8, pp. 208, 209.

Christ's favorite theme was the paternal character and abundant love of God. This knowledge of God was Christ's own gift to men, and this gift He has committed to His people to be communicated by them to the world.—1900, vol. 6, p. 55.

Christian Zeal

There is a noisy zeal, without aim or purpose, which is not according to knowledge, which is blind in its operations and destructive in its results. This is not Christian zeal. Christian zeal is controlled by principle and is not spasmodic. It is earnest, deep, and strong, engaging the whole soul and arousing to exercise the moral sensibilities. The salvation of souls and the interests of the kingdom of God are matters of the highest importance. What object is there that calls for greater earnestness than the salvation of souls and the glory of God? There are considerations here which cannot be lightly regarded. They are as weighty as eternity. Eternal destinies are at stake. Men and women are deciding for weal or woe. Christian zeal will not exhaust itself in talk, but will feel and act with vigor and efficiency. Yet Christian zeal will not act for the sake of being seen. Humility will characterize every effort and be seen in every work. Christian zeal will lead to earnest prayer and humiliation, and to faithfulness in home duties. In the family circle will be seen the gentleness and love, benevolence and compassion, which are ever the fruits of Christian zeal. . . .

Oh, how few feel the worth of souls! How few are willing to sacrifice to bring souls to the knowledge of Christ! There is much talking, much professed love for perishing souls; but talk is cheap stuff. It is earnest Christian zeal that is wanted —a zeal that will be manifested by doing something. All must now work for themselves, and when they have Jesus in their hearts they will confess Him to others. No more could a soul who possesses Christ be hindered from confessing Him than could the waters of Niagara be stopped from flowing over the falls.

1869, vol. 2, pp. 232, 233 (Warnings to the Church).

Responsibilities of the Young

If the youth could only see how much good it is in their power to accomplish, if they would make God their strength and wisdom, they would no longer pursue a course of careless indifference toward Him; they would no longer be swayed by the influence of those who are unconsecrated. Instead of feeling that an individual responsibility rests upon them to put forth efforts to do others good, and lead others to righteousness, they give themselves up to seek their own amusement. They are useless members of society, and live as aimless lives as do the butterflies. The young may have a knowledge of the truth, and believe it, but not live it. Such possess a dead faith. Their hearts are not reached so as to affect their conduct and character in the sight of God, and they are no nearer doing His will than are unbelievers. Their hearts do not conform to the will of God; they are at enmity with Him. Those who are devoted to amusements, and who love the society of pleasure seekers, have an aversion to religious exercises. Will the Master say to these youth who profess His name, Well done, good and faithful servants, unless they are good and faithful?

The young are in great danger. Great evil results from their light reading. Much time is lost which should be spent in useful employment. Some would even deprive themselves of sleep to finish some ridiculous love story. The world is flooded with novels of every description. Some are not of as dangerous a character as others. Some are immoral, low, and vulgar; others are clothed with more refinement; but all are pernicious in their influence. Oh, that the young would reflect upon the influence which exciting stories have upon the mind!

1869, vol. 2, pp. 235-237 (Warnings to the Church).

Can you, after such reading, open the word of God and read the words of life with interest? Do you not find the book of God uninteresting? The charm of that love story is upon the mind, destroying its healthy tone, and making it impossible for you to fix your mind upon the important, solemn truths which concern your eternal interest. You sin against your parents in devoting to such a poor purpose the time which belongs to them, and you sin against God in thus using the time which should be spent in devotion to Him.

It is the duty of the youth to encourage sobriety. Lightness, jesting, and joking will result in barrenness of soul and the loss of the favor of God. Many of you think you do not exert a bad influence upon others, and thus feel in a measure satisfied; but do you exert an influence for good? Do you seek in your conversation and acts to lead others to the Saviour, or, if they profess Christ, to lead them to a closer walk with Him?

The young should cultivate a spirit of devotion and piety. They cannot glorify God unless they constantly aim to attain unto the fullness of the stature of Christ—perfection in Christ Jesus. Let the Christian graces be and abound in you. Give to your Saviour your best and holiest affections. Render entire obedience to His will. He will accept nothing short of this. Be not moved from your steadfastness by the jeers and scoffs of those whose minds are given to vanity. Follow your Saviour through evil as well as good report; count it all joy, and a sacred honor, to bear the cross of Christ. Jesus loves you. He died for you. Unless you seek to serve Him with your undivided affections, you will fail to perfect holiness in His fear, and you will be compelled to hear at last the fearful word, *Depart*.

A Birthday Letter

My dear Son: I write this for your nineteenth birthday. It has been a pleasure to have you with us a few weeks in the past. You are about to leave us, yet our prayers shall follow you.

Another year of your life closes today. How can you look back upon it? Have you made advancement in the divine life? Have you increased in spirituality? Have you crucified self, with the affections and lusts? Have you an increased interest in the study of God's word? Have you gained decided victories over your own feelings and waywardness? Oh, what has been the record of your life for the year which has now passed into eternity, never to be recalled?

As you enter upon a new year, let it be with an earnest resolve to have your course onward and upward. Let your life be more elevated and exalted than it has hitherto been. Make it your aim not to seek your own interest and pleasure, but to advance the cause of your Redeemer. Remain not in a position where you ever need help yourself, and where others have to guard you to keep you in the narrow way. You may be strong to exert a sanctifying influence upon others. You may be where your soul's interest will be awakened to do good to others, to comfort the sorrowful, strengthen the weak, and to bear your testimony for Christ whenever opportunity offers. Aim to honor God in everything, always and everywhere. Carry your religion into everything. Be thorough in whatever you undertake.

You have not experienced the saving power of God as it is your privilege, because you have not made it the great aim of your life to glorify Christ. Let every purpose you form, every

1869, vol. 2, pp. 261-268.

work in which you engage, and every pleasure you enjoy, be to the glory of God. Let this be the language of your heart: I am thine, O God, to live for Thee, to work for Thee, and to suffer for Thee.

Many profess to be on the Lord's side, but they are not; the weight of all their actions is on Satan's side. By what means shall we determine whose side we are on? Who has the heart? With whom are our thoughts? Upon whom do we love to converse? Who has our warmest affections and our best energies? If we are on the Lord's side, our thoughts are with Him, and our sweetest thoughts are of Him. We have no friendship with the world; we have consecrated all that we have and are to Him. We long to bear His image, breathe His Spirit, do His will, and please Him in all things.

A POSITIVE INFLUENCE

You should pursue so decided a course that none need to be mistaken in you. You cannot exert an influence upon the world without decision. Your resolutions may be good and sincere, but they will prove a failure unless you make God your strength and move forward with a firm determination of purpose. You should throw your whole heart into the cause and work of God. You should be in earnest to obtain an experience in the Christian life. You should exemplify Christ in your life.

You cannot serve God and mammon. You are either wholly on the Lord's side or on the side of the enemy. "He that is not with Me is against Me; and he that gathereth not with Me scattereth abroad." Matthew 12:30. Some persons make their religious life a failure because they are always wavering and do not have determination. They are frequently convicted and come almost up to the point of surrendering all for God; but, failing to meet the point, they fall back again. While in this state the conscience is hardening and becoming less and less susceptible to the impressions of the Spirit of God. His Spirit has warned, has convicted, and has been disregarded, until it is nearly grieved away. God will not be trifled with. He shows duty clearly, and if there is a neglect to follow the light, it becomes darkness.

God bids you become a worker with Him in His vineyard. Commence just where you are. Come to the cross and there renounce self, the world, and every idol. Take Jesus into your heart fully. You are in a hard place to preserve consecration and to exert an influence which shall lead others from sin and pleasure and folly to the narrow way, cast up for the ransomed of the Lord to walk in.

Make an entire surrender to God; yield up everything unreservedly, and thus seek for that peace which passes understanding. You cannot draw nourishment from Christ unless you are in Him. If not in Him, you are a branch that is withered. You do not feel your want of purity and true holiness. You should feel an earnest desire for the Holy Spirit and should pray earnestly to obtain it. You cannot expect the blessing of God without seeking for it. If you used the means within your reach you would experience a growth in grace and would rise to a higher life.

It is not natural for you to love spiritual things; but you can acquire that love by exercising your mind, the strength of your being, in that direction. The power of doing is what you need. True education is the power of using our faculties so as to achieve beneficial results. Why is it that religion occupies so little of our attention, while the world has the strength of brain, bone, and muscle? It is because the whole force of our being is bent in that direction. We have trained ourselves to engage with earnestness and power in worldly business, until it is easy for the mind to take that turn. This is why Christians find a religious life so hard and a worldly life so easy. The faculties have been trained to exert their force in that direction. In religious life there has been an assent to the truths of God's word, but not a practical illustration of them in the life.

To cultivate religious thoughts and devotional feelings is not made a part of education. These should influence and control the entire being. The *habit* of doing right is wanting. There is spasmodic action under favorable influences, but to think naturally and readily upon divine things is not the ruling principle of the mind.

SPIRITUAL DWARFS

There is no need of being spiritual dwarfs if the mind is continually exercised in spiritual things. But merely praying for this, and about this, will not meet the necessities of the case. You must habituate the mind to concentration upon spiritual things. Exercise will bring strength. Many professed Christians are in a fair way to lose both worlds. To be half a Christian and half a worldly man makes you about one-hundredth part a Christian and all the rest worldly.

Spiritual living is what God requires, yet thousands are crying out: "I don't know what is the matter; I have no spiritual strength, I do not enjoy the Spirit of God." Yet the same ones will become active and talkative, and even eloquent, when talking upon worldly matters. Listen to such ones in meeting. About a dozen words are spoken in hardly an audible voice. They are men and women of the world. They have cultivated worldly propensities until their faculties have become strong in that direction. Yet they are as weak as babes in regard to spiritual things, when they should be strong and intelligent. They do not love to dwell upon the mystery of godliness. They know not the language of heaven and are not educating their minds so as to be prepared to sing the songs of heaven or to delight in the spiritual exercises which will there engage the attention of all.

Professed Christians, worldly Christians, are unacquainted with heavenly things. They will never be brought to the gates of the New Jerusalem to engage in exercises which have not hitherto specially interested them. They have not trained their minds to delight in devotion and in meditation upon things of God and heaven. How, then, can they engage in the services of heaven? how delight in the spiritual, the pure, the holy in heaven, when it was not a special delight to them upon earth? The very atmosphere there will be purity itself. But they are unacquainted with it all. When in the world, pursuing their worldly vocations, they knew just where to take hold and just what to do. The lower order of faculties being in so constant exercise, grew, while the higher, nobler powers of the mind, not being strengthened by use, are incapable of awaking at once to spiritual exercises. Spiritual things are not discerned, because they are viewed with world-loving eyes, which cannot estimate the value and glory of the divine above the temporal.

The mind must be educated and disciplined to love purity. A love for spiritual things should be encouraged; yea, must be encouraged, if you would grow in grace and in the knowledge of the truth. Desires for goodness and true holiness are right so far as they go; but if you stop here, they will avail nothing. Good purposes are right, but will prove of no avail unless resolutely carried out. Many will be lost while hoping and desiring to be Christians; but they made no earnest effort, therefore they will be weighed in the balances and found wanting. The will must be exercised in the right direction. I *will* be a wholehearted Christian. I *will* know the length and breadth, the height and depth, of perfect love. Listen to the words of Jesus: "Blessed are they which do hunger and thirst after righteousness: for they shall be filled." Matthew 5:6. Ample provisions are made by Christ to satisfy the soul that hungers and thirsts for righteousness.

HIGHER SPIRITUAL ATTAINMENTS

The pure element of love will expand the soul for higher attainments, for increased knowledge of divine things, so that it will not be satisfied short of the fullness. Most professed Christians have no sense of the spiritual strength they might obtain were they as ambitious, zealous, and persevering to gain a knowledge of divine things as they are to obtain the paltry, perishable things of this life. The masses professing to be Christians have been satisfied to be spiritual dwarfs. They have no disposition to make it their object to seek first the kingdom of God and His righteousness; hence godliness is a hidden mystery to them, they cannot understand it. They know not Christ by experimental knowledge.

Let those men and women who are satisfied with their dwarfed, crippled condition in divine things be suddenly transported to heaven and for an instant witness the high, the holy state of perfection that ever abides there,—every soul filled with love; every countenance beaming with joy; enchanting music in melodious strains rising in honor of God and the Lamb; and ceaseless streams of light flowing upon the saints from the face of Him who sitteth upon the throne, and from the Lamb; and let them realize that there is higher and greater joy yet to experience, for the more they receive of the enjoyment of God, the more is their capacity increased to rise higher in eternal enjoyment, and thus continue to receive new and greater supplies from the ceaseless sources of glory and bliss inexpressible,—could such persons, I ask, mingle with the heavenly throng, participate in their songs, and endure the pure, exalted, transporting glory that emanates from God and the Lamb? Oh, no! their probation was lengthened for years that they might learn the language of heaven, that they might become "partakers of the divine nature, having escaped the corruption that is in the world through lust." 2 Peter 1:4.

But they had a selfish business of their own to engage the powers of their minds and the energies of their beings. They could not afford to serve God unreservedly and make this a business. Worldly enterprises must come first and take the best of their powers, and a transient thought is devoted to God. Are such to be transformed after the final decision: "He that is holy, let him be holy still," "he which is filthy, let him be filthy still"? Such a time is coming.

Those who have trained the mind to delight in spiritual exercises are the ones who can be translated and not be overwhelmed with the purity and transcendent glory of heaven. You may have a good knowledge of the arts, you may have an acquaintance with the sciences, you may excel in music and in penmanship, your manners may please your associates, but what have these things to do with a preparation for heaven? What have they to do to prepare you to stand before the tribunal of God?

Be not deceived. God is not mocked. Nothing but holiness will prepare you for heaven. It is sincere, experimental piety alone that can give you a pure, elevated character and enable you to enter into the presence of God, who dwelleth in light unapproachable. The heavenly character must be acquired on earth, or it can never be acquired at all. Then begin at once. Flatter not yourself that a time will come when you can make an earnest effort easier than now. Every day increases your distance from God. Prepare for eternity with such zeal as you have not yet manifested. Educate your mind to love the Bible, to love the prayer meeting, to love the hour of meditation, and, above all, the hour when the soul communes with God. Become heavenly-minded if you would unite with the heavenly choir in the mansions above.

A new year of your life now commences. A new page is turned in the book of the recording angel. What will be the record upon its pages? Shall it be blotted with neglect of God, with unfulfilled duties? God forbid. Let a record be stamped there which you will not be ashamed to have revealed to the gaze of men and angels.

Greenville, Michigan, July 27, 1868.

Deceitfulness of Riches

Dear Sister M: When the Lord showed me your case, I was pointed back many years in the past, when you became a believer in the near coming of Christ. You looked for, and loved, His appearing. . . .

I saw you struggling with poverty, seeking to support yourself and your children. Many times you knew not what to do; the future looked dark and uncertain. In your distress you cried unto the Lord, and He comforted and helped you, and hopeful rays of light shone around you. How precious was God to you at such times! how sweet His comforting love! You felt that you had a precious treasure laid up in heaven. As you viewed the reward of the afflicted children of God, what a consolation to feel that you could claim Him as your Father! . . .

My attention was called to your desire to possess means. The sentiment of your heart was: "Oh, if I only had means, I would not squander it! I would set an example to those who are close and penurious. I would show them the great blessing there is to be received in doing good." Your soul abhorred covetousness. As you have seen those who possessed abundance of this world's goods shut their hearts to the cry of the needy you have said: "God will visit them; He will reward them according to their works." As you have seen the wealthy walking in their pride, their hearts girt about with selfishness, as with iron bands, you have felt that they were poorer than yourself, although you were in want and suffering. When you have seen these purse-proud men bearing themselves loftily because money has power, you have felt pity for them, and in no case would you have been induced

1869, vol. 2, pp. 268-288.

to change places with them. Yet you desired means that you might so use it as to be a rebuke to the covetous.

TESTED BY PROSPERITY

The Lord said to His angel who had hitherto ministered unto you: "I have proved her in poverty and affliction, and she has not separated herself from Me, nor rebelled against Me. I will now prove her with prosperity. I will reveal to her a page of the human heart with which she is unacquainted. I will show her that money is the most dangerous foe she has ever met. I will reveal to her the deceitfulness of riches; that they are a snare, even to those who feel that they are secure from selfishness, and proof against exaltation, extravagance, pride, and love of the praise of men."

I was then shown that a way was opened for you to improve your condition in life and at length to obtain the means which you had thought you would use with wisdom and to the glory of God. How anxiously did your ministering angel watch the new trial to see how you would stand the test. As means came into your hands, I saw you gradually and almost imperceptibly separating from God. The means entrusted to you were expended for your own convenience, to surround yourself with the good things of this life. I saw the angels looking upon you with yearning sadness, their faces half averted, loath to leave you. Yet their presence was not perceived by you, and your course was pursued without reference to your angel guard. . . .

In your prosperity you did not carry out the resolves you had made in adversity. The deceitfulness of riches turned you from your purposes. Cares increased upon you. Your influence became extended. As the afflicted realized relief from suffering, they glorified you, and you learned to love praise from the lips of poor mortals. You were in a popular city, and thought it necessary for the success of your business, as well as to retain your influence, for your surroundings to be somewhat in accordance with your business. But you carried things too far. You were swayed too much by the opinions and judgment of others. You expended means needlessly, only to gratify the lust of the eye and the pride of life. You forgot that you were handling your Lord's money. When means were expended by you which would only encourage vanity, you did not consider that the recording angel was making a record which you would blush to meet again. Said the angel, pointing to you: "You glorified yourself, but did not magnify God." You even gloried in the fact that it was in your power to purchase these things. . . .

A TIME OF PERIL

Your faith and simple trust in God began to wane as soon as means flowed in upon you. You did not depart from God all at once. Your backsliding was gradual. You ceased the morning and evening devotions because it was not always convenient. Your son's wife caused you trials of a peculiar, aggravating character, which had considerable to do in discouraging you from continuing family devotions. Your house became a prayerless house. Your business was made primary, and the Lord and His truth were made secondary. Look back to the days of your earlier experience; would these trials then have driven you from family prayer?

Here, in the neglect of vocal prayer, you lost an influence in your house which you could have retained. It was your duty to acknowledge God in your family, irrespective of consequences. Your petitions should have been offered to God morning and evening. You should have been as priest of the household, confessing your sins and the sins of your children. Had you been faithful, God, who had been your guide, would not have left you to your own wisdom.

Means were expended needlessly for show. Over this sin in

others you had felt deeply grieved. And while thus using means, you were robbing God. Then the Lord said: "I will scatter. I will permit her for a time to walk in the way of her own choosing. I will blind judgment, and remove wisdom. I will show her that her strength is weakness, and her wisdom foolishness. I will humble her, and open her eyes to see how far she has departed from Me. If she will not then turn unto Me with her whole heart, and in all her ways acknowledge Me, My hand shall scatter, and the pride of the mother and of the children shall be brought down, and poverty shall again be their lot. My name shall be exalted. The loftiness of man shall be brought down, and the pride of man shall be laid low." . . .

In your earlier experience the Lord imparted to you talents of influence, but did not give you talents of means, and therefore did not expect you in your poverty to bestow that which you had not to give. Like the widow, you did give what you could, although, had you considered your own circumstances, you would have felt excused from doing even as much as you did. In your sickness, God did not require from you that active energy of which disease had deprived you. Though you were restricted in your influence and in your means, yet God accepted your efforts to do good and to advance His cause according to what you had, not according to what you had not. The Lord does not despise the humblest offering bestowed with readiness and sincerity.

You possess an ardent temperament. Earnestness in a good cause is praiseworthy. In your former trials and perplexity, you were obtaining an experience which was to be of advantage to others. You were zealous in the service of God. You loved to present the evidences of our position to those who did not believe present truth. You could speak with assurance, for these things were a reality to you. The truth was a part of your being; and those who listened to your earnest appeals had not a doubt of your honesty, but were convinced that these things were so.

In the providence of God your influence has been extended; in addition to this, God has seen fit to prove you by giving you talents of means. You are thereby laid under double responsibility. When your condition in life began to improve, you said: "As soon as I can get me a home, I will then donate to the cause of God." But when you had a home you saw so many improvements to make to have everything about you convenient and pleasant that you forgot the Lord and His claims upon you, and were less inclined to help the cause of God than in the days of your poverty and affliction.

You were seeking friendship with the world, and separating further and further from God. You forgot the exhortation of Christ: "Take heed to yourselves, lest at any time your hearts be overcharged with surfeiting, and drunkenness, and cares of this life, and so that day come upon you unawares." Luke 21:34. "Let him that thinketh he standeth take heed lest he fall." 1 Corinthians 10:12.

There are three watchwords in the Christian life, which must be heeded if we would not have Satan steal a march upon us; namely, Watch, pray, work. Prayer and watching thereunto are necessary for advancement in the divine life. Never was there a time in your history more important than the present. Your only safety is to live like a watchman. Watch and pray always. Oh, what a preventive against yielding to temptation and falling into the snares of the world! How earnestly should you have been at work the past few years, when your influence was extensive.

Dear sister, the praise of men and the flattery current in the world have had greater influence upon you than you have been aware of. You have not been improving your talents—putting them out to the exchangers. You are naturally affectionate and generous. These traits of character have been exercised to a degree, but not as much as God requires. Merely possessing these excellent gifts is not enough; God requires them to be kept in constant exercise; for through them He blesses those who need to be helped, and carries forward His work for the salvation of man. . . .

OPPORTUNITY TO RETURN

To you, my sister, are committed talents of influence and talents of money; and your responsibility is great. You should move cautiously and in the fear of God. Your wisdom is weakness, but the wisdom from above is strong. The Lord designs to enlighten your darkness and again give you a glimpse of the heavenly treasure, that you may have some sense of the comparative value of both worlds, and then leave you to choose between this world and the eternal inheritance. I saw that there was yet opportunity to return to the fold. Jesus has redeemed you by His own blood, and He requires you to employ your talents in His service. You have not become hardened to the influence of the Holy Spirit. When the truth of God is presented, it meets a response in your heart. . . .

My dear sister, the Lord has been very merciful to you and your family. You are laid under obligation to your heavenly Father to praise and glorify His holy name upon the earth. In order to continue in His love, you should labor constantly for humbleness of mind and that meek and quiet spirit which is in the sight of God of great price. Your strength in God will increase while you consecrate all to Him; so that you can say with confidence: "Who shall separate us from the love of Christ? shall tribulation, or distress, or persecution, or famine, or nakedness, or peril, or sword?" "For I am persuaded, that neither death, nor life, nor angels, nor principalities, nor powers, nor things present, nor things to come, nor height, nor depth, nor any other creature, shall be able to separate us from the love of God, which is in Christ Jesus our Lord." Romans 8:35, 38, 39.

True Conversion

Conversion is a work that most do not appreciate. It is not a small matter to transform an earthly, sin-loving mind and bring it to understand the unspeakable love of Christ, the charms of His grace, and the excellency of God, so that the soul shall be imbued with divine love and captivated with the heavenly mysteries. When he understands these things, his former life appears disgusting and hateful. He hates sin, and, breaking his heart before God, he embraces Christ as the life and joy of the soul. He renounces his former pleasures. He has a new mind, new affections, new interest, new will; his sorrows, and desires, and love are all new. The lust of the flesh, the lust of the eye, and the pride of life, which have heretofore been preferred before Christ, are now turned from, and Christ is the charm of his life, the crown of his rejoicing. Heaven, which once possessed no charms, is now viewed in its riches and glory; and he contemplates it as his future home, where he shall see, love, and praise the One who hath redeemed him by His precious blood.

The works of holiness, which appeared wearisome, are now his delight. The word of God, which was dull and uninteresting, is now chosen as his study, the man of his counsel. It is as a letter written to him from God, bearing the inscription of the Eternal. His thoughts, his words, and his deeds are brought to this rule and tested. He trembles at the commands and threatenings which it contains, while he firmly grasps its promises and strengthens his soul by appropriating them to himself. The society of the most godly is now chosen by him, and the wicked, whose company he once loved, he no longer

1869, vol. 2, pp. 294-296.

delights in. He weeps over those sins in them at which he once laughed. Self-love and vanity are renounced, and he lives unto God, and is rich in good works. This is the sanctification which God requires. Nothing short of this will He accept.

A PERSONAL APPEAL

I beg of you, my brother, to search your heart diligently and inquire: "What road am I traveling, and where will it end?" You have reason to rejoice that your life has not been cut off while you have no certain hope of eternal life. God forbid that you should longer neglect this work, and so perish in your sins. Do not flatter your soul with false hopes. You see no way to get hold again but one so humble that you cannot consent to accept it. Christ presents to you, even to you, my erring brother, a message of mercy: "Come; for all things are now ready." Luke 14:17. God is ready to accept you and to pardon all your transgressions, if you will but come. Though you have been a prodigal, and have separated from God and stayed away from Him so long, He will meet you even now. Yes; the Majesty of heaven invites you to come to Him, that you may have life. Christ is ready to cleanse you from sin when you lay hold upon Him. What profit have you found in serving sin? what profit in serving the flesh and the devil? Is it not poor wages you receive? Oh! turn ye, turn ye; for why will ye die?

You have had many convictions, many pangs of conscience. You have had so many purposes and made so many promises, and yet you linger and will not come to Christ that you may have life. Oh, that your heart may be impressed with a sense of this time, that you may now turn and live! Cannot you hear the voice of the True Shepherd in this message? How can you disobey? Trifle not with God, lest He leave you to your own crooked ways. It is life or death with you. Which will you choose? It is a fearful thing to contend with God and resist His pleadings. You may have the love of God burning upon the altar of your heart as you once felt it. You may commune with God as you have done in times past. If you will make a clean track behind you you may again experience the riches of His grace, and your countenance again express His love.

It is not required of you to confess to those who know not your sin and errors. It is not your duty to publish a confession which will lead unbelievers to triumph; but to those to whom it is proper, who will take no advantage of your wrong, confess according to the word of God, and let them pray for you, and God will accept your work, and will heal you. For your soul's sake, be entreated to make thorough work for eternity. Lay aside your pride, your vanity, and make straight work. Come back again to the fold. The Shepherd is waiting to receive you. Repent, and do your first works, and again come into favor with God.

Moral Pollution

I HAVE been shown that we live amid the perils of the last days. Because iniquity abounds, the love of many waxes cold. The word "many" refers to the professed followers of Christ. They are affected by the prevailing iniquity and backslide from God, but it is not necessary that they should be thus affected. The cause of this declension is that they do not stand clear from this iniquity. The fact that their love to God is waxing cold because iniquity abounds shows that they are, in some sense, partakers in this iniquity, or it would not affect their love for God and their zeal and fervor in His cause.

A terrible picture of the condition of the world has been presented before me. Immorality abounds everywhere. Licentiousness is the special sin of this age. Never did vice lift its deformed head with such boldness as now. The people seem to be benumbed, and the lovers of virtue and true goodness are nearly discouraged by its boldness, strength, and prevalence. The iniquity which abounds is not merely confined to the unbeliever and the scoffer. Would that this were the case, but it is not. Many men and women who profess the religion of Christ are guilty. Even some who profess to be looking for His appearing are no more prepared for that event than Satan himself. They are not cleansing themselves from all pollution. They have so long served their lust that it is natural for their thoughts to be impure and their imaginations corrupt. It is as impossible to cause their minds to dwell upon pure and holy things as it would be to turn the course of Niagara and send its waters pouring up the falls.

Youth and children of both sexes engage in moral pollu-

1869, vol. 2, pp. 346-353.

tion, and practice this disgusting, soul-and-body-destroying vice. Many professed Christians are so benumbed by the same practice that their moral sensibilities cannot be aroused to understand that it is sin, and that if continued its sure results will be utter shipwreck of body and mind. Man, the noblest being upon the earth, formed in the image of God, transforms himself into a beast! He makes himself gross and corrupt. Every Christian will have to learn to restrain his passions and be controlled by principle. Unless he does this he is unworthy of the Christian name.

Some who make a high profession do not understand the sin of self-abuse and its sure results. Long-established habit has blinded their understanding. They do not realize the exceeding sinfulness of this degrading sin, which is enervating the system and destroying their brain nerve power. Moral principle is exceedingly weak when it conflicts with established habit. Solemn messages from heaven cannot forcibly impress the heart that is not fortified against the indulgence of this degrading vice. The sensitive nerves of the brain have lost their healthy tone by morbid excitation to gratify an unnatural desire for sensual indulgence. The brain nerves which communicate with the entire system are the only medium through which Heaven can communicate to man and affect his inmost life. Whatever disturbs the circulation of the electric currents in the nervous system lessens the strength of the vital powers, and the result is a deadening of the sensibilities of the mind. In consideration of these facts, how important that ministers and people who profess godliness should stand forth clear and untainted from this soul-debasing vice!

My soul has been bowed down with anguish as I have been shown the weak condition of God's professed people. Iniquity abounds, and the love of many waxes cold. There are but few professed Christians who regard this matter in the right light and who hold proper government over themselves when public opinion and custom do not condemn them. How few restrain their passions because they feel under moral obligation to do so and because the fear of God is before their eyes! The higher faculties of man are enslaved by appetite and corrupt passions.

DEPART FROM INIQUITY

Some will acknowledge the evil of sinful indulgences, yet will excuse themselves by saying that they cannot overcome their passions. This is a terrible admission for any person to make who names Christ. "Let everyone that nameth the name of Christ depart from iniquity." 2 Timothy 2:19. Why is this weakness? It is because the animal propensities have been strengthened by exercise until they have gained the ascendancy over the higher powers. Men and women lack principle. They are dying spiritually because they have so long pampered their natural appetites that their power of self-government seems gone. The lower passions of their nature have taken the reins, and that which should be the governing power has become the servant of corrupt passion. The soul is held in lowest bondage. Sensuality has quenched the desire for holiness and withered spiritual prosperity.

My soul mourns for the youth who are forming characters in this degenerate age. I tremble for their parents also; for I have been shown that as a general thing they do not understand their obligations to train up their children in the way they should go. Custom and fashion are consulted, and the children soon learn to be swayed by these and are corrupted; while their indulgent parents are themselves benumbed and asleep to their danger. But very few of the youth are free from corrupt habits. They are excused from physical exercise to a great degree for fear they will overwork. The parents bear burdens themselves which their children should bear.

Overwork is bad, but the result of indolence is more to be dreaded. Idleness leads to the indulgence of corrupt habits. Industry does not weary and exhaust one-fifth part as much as the pernicious habit of self-abuse. If simple, well-regulated labor exhausts your children, be assured, parents, there is something, aside from their labor, which is enervating their systems and producing a sense of constant weariness. Give your children physical labor, which will call into exercise the nerves and muscles. The weariness attending such labor will lessen their inclination to indulge in vicious habits. Idleness is a curse. It produces licentious habits.

Many cases have been presented before me, and as I have had a view of their inner lives, my soul has been sick and disgusted with the rotten-heartedness of human beings who profess godliness and talk of translation to heaven. I have frequently asked myself: Whom can I trust? Who is free from iniquity?

ASKING FOR PRAYER

My husband and I once attended a meeting where our sympathies were enlisted for a brother who was a great sufferer with the phthisic. He was pale and emaciated. He requested the prayers of the people of God. He said that his family were sick and that he had lost a child. He spoke with feeling of his bereavement. He said that he had been waiting for some time to see Brother and Sister White. He had believed that if they would pray for him he would be healed. After the meeting closed, the brethren called our attention to the case. They said that the church was assisting them; that his wife was sick, and his child had died. The brethren had met at his house, and united in praying for the afflicted family. We were much worn, and had the burden of labor upon us during the meeting, and wished to be excused.

I had resolved not to engage in prayer for anyone unless

the Spirit of the Lord should dictate in the matter. I had been shown that there was so much iniquity abounding, even among professed Sabbathkeepers, that I did not wish to unite in prayer for those of whose history I had no knowledge. I stated my reason. I was assured by the brethren that, as far as they knew, he was a worthy brother. I conversed a few words with the one who had solicited our prayers that he might be healed, but I could not feel free. He wept, and said that he had waited for us to come, and he felt assured that if we would pray for him he would be restored to health. We told him that we were unacquainted with his life, that we would rather those who knew him would pray for him. He importuned us so earnestly that we decided to consider his case and present it before the Lord that night; and if the way seemed clear, we would comply with his request.

That night we bowed in prayer and presented his case before the Lord. We entreated that we might know the will of God concerning him. All we desired was that God might be glorified. Would the Lord have us pray for this afflicted man? We left the burden with the Lord and retired to rest. In a dream the case of that man was clearly presented. His course from his childhood up was shown, and that if we should pray the Lord would not hear us; for he regarded iniquity in his heart. The next morning the man came for us to pray for him. We took him aside and told him we were sorry to be compelled to refuse his request. I related my dream, which he acknowledged was true. He had practiced self-abuse from his boyhood up, and he had continued the practice during his married life, but said he would try to break himself of it.

This man had a long-established habit to overcome. He was in the middle age of life. His moral principles were so weak that when brought in conflict with long-established indulgence they were overcome. The baser passions had gained the ascendancy over the higher nature. I asked him in regard to health reform. He said he could not live it. His wife would throw graham flour out of doors if it were brought into the house. This family had been helped by the church. Prayer had also been offered in their behalf. Their child had died, the wife was sick, and the husband and father would leave his case upon us for us to bring before a pure and holy God, that He might work a miracle and make him well. The moral sensibilities of this man were benumbed.

When the young adopt vile practices while the spirit is tender, they will never obtain force to fully and correctly develop physical, intellectual, and moral character. Here was a man debasing himself daily, and yet daring to venture into the presence of God and ask an increase of strength which he had vilely squandered, and which, if granted, he would consume upon his lust. What forbearance has God! If He should deal with man according to his corrupt ways, who could live in His sight? What if we had been less cautious and carried the case of this man before God while he was practicing iniquity, would the Lord have heard? would He have answered? "For Thou art not a God that hath pleasure in wickedness: neither shall evil dwell with Thee. The foolish shall not stand in Thy sight: Thou hatest all workers of iniquity." "If I regard iniquity in my heart, the Lord will not hear me." Psalms 5:4, 5; 66:18.

This is not a solitary case. Even the marriage relation was not sufficient to preserve this man from the corrupt habits of his youth. I wish I could be convinced that such cases as the one I have presented are rare, but I know they are frequent. Children born to parents who are controlled by corrupt passions are worthless. What can be expected of such children but that they will sink lower in the scale than their parents? What can be expected of the rising generation? Thousands are devoid of principle. These very ones are transmitting to their offspring their own miserable, corrupt passions. What a legacy! Thousands drag out their unprincipled lives, tainting their associates, and perpetuating their debased passions by transmitting them to their children. They take the responsibility of giving to them the stamp of their own characters.

RELATION OF DIET TO MORALS

I come again to Christians. If all who profess to obey the law of God were free from iniquity, my soul would be relieved; but they are not. Even some who profess to keep all the commandments of God are guilty of the sin of adultery. What can I say to arouse their benumbed sensibilities? Moral principle, strictly carried out, becomes the only safeguard of the soul. If ever there was a time when the diet should be of the most simple kind, it is now. Meat should not be placed before our children. Its influence is to excite and strengthen the lower passions, and has a tendency to deaden the moral powers. Grains and fruits prepared free from grease, and in as natural a condition as possible, should be the food for the tables of all who claim to be preparing for translation to heaven. The less feverish the diet, the more easily can the passions be controlled. Gratification of taste should not be consulted irrespective of physical, intellectual, or moral health.

Indulgence of the baser passions will lead very many to shut their eyes to the light, for they fear that they will see sins which they are unwilling to forsake. All may see if they will. If they choose darkness rather than light, their criminality will be none the less. Why do not men and women read, and become intelligent upon these things which so decidedly affect their physical, intellectual, and moral strength? God has given you a habitation to care for and preserve in the best condition for His service and glory. Your bodies are not your own. "What? know ye not that your body is the temple of the Holy Ghost which is in you, which ye have of

God, and ye are not your own? For ye are bought with a price: therefore glorify God in your body, and in your spirit, which are God's." 1 Corinthians 6:19, 20. "Know ye not that ye are the temple of God, and that the Spirit of God dwelleth in you? If any man defile the temple of God, him shall God destroy; for the temple of God is holy, which temple ye are." 1 Corinthians 3:16, 17.

Why God Reproves His Own People

Seventh-day Adventists, above all other people in the world, should be patterns of piety, holy in heart and in conversation. I related in the presence of —— that the people whom God had chosen as His peculiar treasure were required to be elevated, refined, sanctified, partakers of the divine nature, having escaped the corruption that is in the world through lust. Should they who make so high a profession indulge in sin and iniquity, their guilt would be very great. The Lord reproves the sins of one, that others may take warning and fear.

Warnings and reproofs are not given to the erring among Seventh-day Adventists because their lives are more blameworthy than are the lives of professed Christians of the nominal churches, nor because their example or their acts are worse than those of the Adventists who will not yield obedience to the claims of God's law, but because they have great light, and have by their profession taken their position as God's special, chosen people, having the law of God written in their hearts. They signify their loyalty to the God of heaven by yielding obedience to the laws of His government. They are God's representatives upon the earth. Any sin in them separates them from God and, in a special manner, dishonors His name by giving the enemies of His holy law occasion to reproach His cause and His people, whom He has called "a chosen generation, a royal priesthood, an holy nation, a peculiar people," (1 Peter 2:9), that they should show forth the praises of Him that hath called them out of darkness into His marvelous light.

1870, vol. 2, pp. 451-453 (An Appeal to the Church).

The people who are at war with the law of the great Jehovah, who consider it a special virtue to talk, write, and act the most bitter and hateful things to show their contempt of that law, may make exalted profession of love to God, and apparently have much religious zeal, as did the Jewish chief priests and elders; yet, in the day of God, "Found wanting" will be said of them by the Majesty of heaven. "By the law is the knowledge of sin." Romans 3:20. The mirror which would discover to them the defects in their characters, they are infuriated against, because it points out their sins. Leading Adventists who have rejected the light are fired with madness against God's holy law, as the Jewish nation were against the Son of God. They are in a terrible deception, deceiving others and being deceived themselves. They will not come to the light, lest their deeds should be reproved. Such will not be taught. But the Lord reproves and corrects the people who profess to keep His law. He points out their sins and lays open their iniquity because He wishes to separate all sin and wickedness from them, that they may perfect holiness in His fear and be prepared to die in the Lord or to be translated to heaven. God rebukes, reproves, and corrects them, that they may be refined, sanctified, elevated, and finally exalted to His own throne.

An Appeal for Self-Control

THE exhortation of Peter is of the highest value to all who are striving for immortality. He addresses those of like precious faith:

"Simon Peter, a servant and an apostle of Jesus Christ, to them that have obtained like precious faith with us through the righteousness of God and our Saviour Jesus Christ: Grace and peace be multiplied unto you through the knowledge of God, and of Jesus our Lord, according as His divine power hath given unto us all things that pertain unto life and godliness, through the knowledge of Him that hath called us to glory and virtue: whereby are given unto us exceeding great and precious promises: that by these ye might be partakers of the divine nature, having escaped the corruption that is in the world through lust. And beside this, giving all diligence, add to your faith virtue; and to virtue knowledge; and to knowledge temperance; and to temperance patience; and to patience godliness; and to godliness brotherly kindness; and to brotherly kindness charity. For if these things be in you, and abound, they make you that ye shall neither be barren nor unfruitful in the knowledge of our Lord Jesus Christ. But he that lacketh these things is blind, and cannot see afar off, and hath forgotten that he was purged from his old sins. Wherefore the rather, brethren, give diligence to make your calling and election sure: for if ye do these things, ye shall never fall: for so an entrance shall be ministered unto you abundantly into the everlasting kingdom of our Lord and Saviour Jesus Christ." 2 Peter 1:1-11.

We are in a world where light and knowledge abound, yet

1870, vol. 2, pp. 471-478 (An Appeal to the Church).

many claiming to be of like precious faith are willingly ignorant. Light is all around them, yet they do not appropriate it to themselves. Parents do not see the necessity of informing themselves, obtaining knowledge, and putting it to a practical use in their married life. If they followed out the exhortation of the apostle, and lived upon the plan of addition, they would not be unfruitful in the knowledge of our Lord Jesus Christ. But many do not understand the work of sanctification. They seem to think they have attained to it, when they have learned only the first lessons in addition. Sanctification is a progressive work; it is not attained to in an hour or a day, and then maintained without any special effort on our part.

Many parents do not obtain the knowledge that they should in the married life. They are not guarded lest Satan take advantage of them and control their minds and their lives. They do not see that God requires them to control their married lives from any excesses. But very few feel it to be a religious duty to govern their passions. They have united themselves in marriage to the object of their choice, and therefore reason that marriage sanctifies the indulgence of the baser passions. Even men and women professing godliness give loose rein to their lustful passions, and have no thought that God holds them accountable for the expenditure of vital energy, which weakens their hold on life and enervates the entire system.

The marriage covenant covers sins of the darkest hue. Men and women professing godliness debase their own bodies through the indulgence of the corrupt passions, and thus lower themselves beneath the brute creation. They abuse the powers which God has given them to be preserved in sanctification and honor. Health and life are sacrificed upon the altar of base passion. The higher, nobler powers are brought into subjection to the animal propensities. Those who thus sin are not acquainted with the result of their course. Could all see the amount of suffering which they bring upon themselves by their own sinful indulgence, they would be alarmed, and some, at least, would shun the course of sin which brings such dreaded wages. So miserable an existence is entailed upon a large class that death would to them be preferable to life; and many do die prematurely, their lives sacrificed in the inglorious work of excessive indulgence of the animal passions. Yet because they are married they think they commit no sin.

A FALSE CONCEPTION OF LOVE

Men and women, you will one day learn what is lust and the result of its gratification. Passion of just as base a quality may be found in the marriage relation as outside of it. The apostle Paul exhorts husbands to love their wives "even as Christ also loved the church, and gave Himself for it." "So ought men to love their wives as their own bodies. He that loveth his wife loveth himself. For no man ever yet hated his own flesh; but nourisheth and cherisheth it, even as the Lord the church." Ephesians 5:25, 28, 29. It is not pure love which actuates a man to make his wife an instrument to minister to his lust. It is the animal passions which clamor for indulgence.

How few men show their love in the manner specified by the apostle: "Even as Christ also loved the church, and gave Himself for it; that He might [not pollute it, but] sanctify and cleanse it; . . . that it should be holy and without blemish." Verses 25-27. This is the quality of love in the marriage relation which God recognizes as holy. Love is a pure and holy principle; but lustful passion will not admit of restraint, and will not be dictated to or controlled by reason. It is blind to consequences; it will not reason from cause to effect. Many women are suffering from great debility and settled disease because the laws of their being have been disregarded; nature's laws have been trampled upon. The brain nerve power is squandered by men and women, being called into unnatural action to gratify base passions; and this hideous monster, base, low passion, assumes the delicate name of love.

Many professed Christians who passed before me seemed destitute of moral restraint. They were more animal than divine. In fact, they were about all animal. Men of this type degrade the wife whom they have promised to nourish and cherish. She is made an instrument to minister to the gratification of low, lustful propensities. And very many women submit to become slaves to lustful passion; they do not possess their bodies in sanctification and honor. The wife does not retain the dignity and self-respect which she possessed previous to marriage. This holy institution should have preserved and increased her womanly respect and holy dignity; but her chaste, dignified, godlike womanhood has been consumed upon the altar of base passion; it has been sacrificed to please her husband. She soon loses respect for the husband, who does not regard the laws to which the brute creation yield obedience. The married life becomes a galling yoke; for love dies out, and frequently distrust, jealousy, and hate take its place.

THE FRUITAGE OF EXCESSES

No man can truly love his wife when she will patiently submit to become his slave and minister to his depraved passions. In her passive submission, she loses the value she once possessed in his eyes. He sees her dragged down from everything elevating, to a low level; and soon he suspects that she will as tamely submit to be degraded by another as by himself. He doubts her constancy and purity, tires of her, and seeks new objects to arouse and intensify his hellish passions. The law of God is not regarded. These men are worse than brutes; they are demons in human form. They are unacquainted with the elevating, ennobling principles of true, sanctified love.

The wife also becomes jealous of the husband and suspects that if opportunity should offer he would just as readily pay his addresses to another as to her. She sees that he is not controlled by conscience or the fear of God; all these sanctified barriers are broken down by lustful passions; all that is godlike in the husband is made the servant of low, brutish lust.

The world is filled with men and women of this order; and neat, tasty, yea, expensive houses contain a hell within. Imagine, if you can, what must be the offspring of such parents. Will not the children sink still lower in the scale? The parents give the stamp of character to their children. Therefore children that are born of these parents inherit from them qualities of mind which are of a low, base order. And Satan nourishes anything tending to corruption. The matter now to be settled is: Shall the wife feel bound to yield implicitly to the demands of her husband, when she sees that nothing but base passions control him, and when her reason and judgment are convinced that she does it to the injury of her body, which God has enjoined upon her to possess in sanctification and honor, to preserve as a living sacrifice to God?

It is not pure, holy love which leads the wife to gratify the animal propensities of her husband at the expense of health and life. If she possesses true love and wisdom, she will seek to divert his mind from the gratification of lustful passions to high and spiritual themes by dwelling upon interesting spiritual subjects. It may be necessary to humbly and affectionately urge, even at the risk of his displeasure, that she cannot debase her body by yielding to sexual excess. She should, in a tender, kind manner, remind him that God has the first and highest claim upon her entire being, and that she cannot disregard this claim, for she will be held accountable in the great day of God. "What? know ye not that your body is the temple of the Holy Ghost which is in you, which ye have of God, and ye are not your own? For ye are bought with a price: therefore glorify God in your body, and in your spirit, which are

God's." 1 Corinthians 6:19, 20. "Ye are bought with a price; be not ye the servants of men." 1 Corinthians 7:23.

If she will elevate her affections, and in sanctification and honor preserve her refined, womanly dignity, woman can do much by her judicious influence to sanctify her husband, and thus fulfill her high mission. In so doing, she can save both her husband and herself, thus performing a double work. In this matter, so delicate and so difficult to manage, much wisdom and patience are necessary, as well as moral courage and fortitude. Strength and grace can be found in prayer. Sincere love is to be the ruling principle of the heart. Love to God and love to the husband can alone be the right ground of action.

Let the wife decide that it is the husband's prerogative to have full control of her body, and to mold her mind to suit his in every respect, to run in the same channel as his own, and she yields her individuality; her identity is lost, merged in that of her husband. She is a mere machine for his will to move and control, a creature of his pleasure. He thinks for her, decides for her, and acts for her. She dishonors God in occupying this passive position. She has a responsibility before God which it is her duty to preserve.

When the wife yields her body and mind to the control of her husband, being passive to his will in all things, sacrificing her conscience, her dignity, and even her identity, she loses the opportunity of exerting that mighty influence for good which she should possess to elevate her husband. She could soften his stern nature, and her sanctifying influence could be exerted in a manner to refine and purify, leading him to strive earnestly to govern his passions and be more spiritually minded, that they might be partakers together of the divine nature, having escaped the corruption that is in the world through lust.

SELF-DENIAL AND TEMPERANCE

The power of influence can be great to lead the mind to high and noble themes, above the low, sensual indulgences for which the heart unrenewed by grace naturally seeks. If the wife feels that in order to please her husband she must come down to his standard, when animal passion is the principal basis of his love and controls his actions, she displeases God; for she fails to exert a sanctifying influence upon her husband. If she feels that she must submit to his animal passions without a word of remonstrance, she does not understand her duty to him nor to her God. Sexual excess will effectually destroy a love for devotional exercises, will take from the brain the substance needed to nourish the system, and will most effectively exhaust the vitality. No woman should aid her husband in this work of self-destruction. She will not do it if she is enlightened and has true love for him.

The more the animal passions are indulged, the stronger do they become, and the more violent will be their clamors for indulgence. Let God-fearing men and women awake to their duty. Many professed Christians are suffering with paralysis of nerve and brain because of their intemperance in this direction. Rottenness is in the bones and marrow of many who are regarded as good men, who pray and weep, and who stand in high places, but whose polluted carcasses will never pass the portals of the heavenly city.

Oh, that I could make all understand their obligation to God to preserve the mental and physical organism in the best condition to render perfect service to their Maker! Let the Christian wife refrain, both in word and act, from exciting the animal passions of her husband. Many have no strength at all to waste in this direction. From their youth up they have weakened the brain and sapped the constitution by the gratification of animal passions. Self-denial and temperance should be the watchword in their married life.

Social Meetings

I RECENTLY received a letter from a brother whom I highly respect, making inquiries in regard to how meetings should be conducted. He inquires if there should be many prayers offered in succession, and then a relief of a few moments, and quite a number of prayers again.

From the light I have had upon the subject I have decided that God does not require us, as we assemble for His worship, to make these seasons tedious and wearisome by remaining bowed quite a length of time, listening to several long prayers. Those in feeble health cannot endure this taxation without extreme weariness and exhaustion. The body becomes weary by remaining bowed down so long; and what is worse still, the mind becomes so wearied by the continuous exercise of prayer that no spiritual refreshment is realized, and the meeting is to them worse than a loss. They have become wearied mentally and physically, and they have obtained no spiritual strength.

Meetings for conference and prayer should not be made tedious. If possible, all should be prompt to the hour appointed; and if there are dilatory ones, who are half an hour or even fifteen minutes behind the time, there should be no waiting. If there are but two present, they can claim the promise. The meeting should open at the appointed hour if possible, be there few or many present. Formality and cold stiffness should be laid aside, and all should be prompt to duty. Upon common occasions there should not be prayer of more than ten minutes' duration. After there has been a change of posi-

1871, vol. 2, pp. 577-582.

tion, and the exercise of singing or exhortation has relieved the sameness, then, if any feel the burden of prayer, let them pray.

SHORT, POINTED PRAYERS

All should feel it a Christian duty to pray short. Tell the Lord just what you want, without going all over the world. In private prayer all have the privilege of praying as long as they desire and of being as explicit as they please. They can pray for all their relatives and friends. The closet is the place to tell all their private difficulties, and trials, and temptations. A common meeting to worship God is not the place to open the privacies of the heart.

What is the object of assembling together? Is it to inform God, to instruct Him by telling Him all we know in prayer? We meet together to edify one another by an interchange of thoughts and feelings, to gather strength, and light, and courage by becoming acquainted with one another's hopes and aspirations; and by our earnest, heartfelt prayers, offered up in faith, we receive refreshment and vigor from the Source of our strength. These meetings should be most precious seasons and should be made interesting to all who have any relish for religious things.

There are some, I fear, who do not take their troubles to God in private prayer, but reserve them for the prayer meeting, and there do up their praying for several days. Such may be named conference and prayer meeting killers. They emit no light; they edify no one. Their cold, frozen prayers and long, backslidden testimonies cast a shadow. All are glad when they get through, and it is almost impossible to throw off the chill and darkness which their prayers and exhortations bring into the meeting. From the light which I have received, our meetings should be spiritual and social, and not too long. Reserve, pride, vanity, and fear of man should be left at home. Little differences and prejudices should not be taken with us to these meetings. As in a united family, simplicity, meekness, confidence, and love should exist in the hearts of brethren and sisters who meet to be refreshed and invigorated by bringing their lights together.

"Ye are the light of the world," says the heavenly Teacher. All have not the same experience in their religious life. But those of diverse exercises come together and with simplicity and humbleness of mind talk out their experience. All who are pursuing the onward Christian course should have, and will have, an experience that is living, that is new and interesting. A living experience is made up of daily trials, conflicts, and temptations, strong efforts and victories, and great peace and joy gained through Jesus. A simple relation of such experiences gives light, strength, and knowledge that will aid others in their advancement in the divine life. The worship of God should be both interesting and instructive to those who have any love for divine and heavenly things.

THE MEETINGS JESUS CONDUCTED

Jesus, the heavenly Teacher, did not hold Himself aloof from the children of men; but in order to benefit them He came from heaven to earth, where they were, that the purity and holiness of His life might shine upon the pathway of all and light the way to heaven. The Redeemer of the world sought to make His lessons of instruction plain and simple, that all might comprehend them. He generally chose the open air for His discourses. No walls could enclose the multitude which followed Him; but He had special reasons for resorting to the groves and the seaside to give His lessons of instruction. He could there have a commanding view of the landscape and make use of objects and scenes with which those in humble life were familiar, to illustrate the important truths He made known to them. With His lessons of instruction He associated the works of God in nature. The birds which were caroling forth their songs without a care, the flowers of the valley glowing in their beauty, the lily that reposed in its purity upon the bosom of the lake, the lofty trees, the cultivated land, the waving grain, the barren soil, the tree that bore no fruit, the everlasting hills, the bubbling stream, the setting sun, tinting and gilding the heavens—all these He employed to impress His hearers with divine truth. He connected the works of God's finger in the heavens and upon the earth with the words of life He wished to impress upon their minds, that, as they should look upon the wonderful works of God in nature, His lessons might be fresh in their memories.

In all His efforts Christ sought to make His teachings interesting. He knew that a tired, hungry throng could not receive spiritual benefit, and He did not forget their bodily needs. Upon one occasion He wrought a miracle to feed five thousand who had gathered to listen to the words of life which fell from His lips. Jesus regarded His surroundings when giving His precious truth to the multitude. The scenery was such as would attract the eye and awaken admiration in the breasts of the lovers of the beautiful. He could extol the wisdom of God in His creative works, and could bind up His sacred lessons by directing their minds through nature up to nature's God.

Thus the landscape, the trees, the birds, the flowers of the valley, the hills, the lake, and the beautiful heavens were associated in their minds with sacred truths which would make them hallowed in memory as they should look upon them after Christ's ascension to heaven.

When Christ taught the people, He did not devote the time to prayer. He did not enforce upon them, as did the Pharisees, long, tedious ceremonies and prayers. He taught His disciples how to pray: "And when thou prayest, thou shalt not be as the hypocrites are: for they love to pray standing in the synagogues and in the corners of the streets, that they may be seen of men. Verily I say unto you, They have their reward. But thou, when thou prayest, enter into thy closet, and when thou hast shut thy door, pray to thy Father which is in secret; and thy Father which seeth in secret shall reward thee openly. But when ye pray, use not vain repetitions, as the heathen do: for they think that they shall be heard for their much speaking. Be not ye therefore like unto them: for your Father knoweth what things ye have need of, before ye ask Him. After this manner therefore pray ye." Matthew 6:5-9.

PUBLIC PRAYER

Christ impressed upon His disciples the idea that their prayers should be short, expressing just what they wanted, and no more. He gives the length and substance of their prayers, expressing their desires for temporal and spiritual blessings, and their gratitude for the same. How comprehensive this sample prayer! It covers the actual need of all. One or two minutes is long enough for any ordinary prayer. There may be instances where prayer is in a special manner indited by the Spirit of God, where supplication is made in the Spirit. The yearning soul becomes agonized and groans after God. The spirit wrestles as did Jacob and will not be at rest without special manifestations of the power of God. This is as God would have it.

But many offer prayer in a dry, sermonizing manner. These pray to men, not to God. If they were praying to God, and really understood what they were doing, they would be alarmed at their audacity; for they deliver a discourse to the Lord in the mode of prayer, as though the Creator of the universe needed special information upon general questions in relation to things transpiring in the world. All such prayers are as sounding brass and a tinkling cymbal. They are made no account of in heaven. Angels of God are wearied with them, as well as mortals who are compelled to listen to them.

Jesus was often found in prayer. He resorted to the lonely groves or to the mountains to make His requests known to His Father. When the business and cares of the day were ended, and the weary were seeking rest, Jesus devoted the time to prayer. We would not discourage prayer, for there is far too little praying and watching thereunto. And there is still less praying with the Spirit and the understanding also. Fervent and effectual prayer is always in place, and will never weary. Such prayer interests and refreshes all who have a love for devotion.

Secret prayer is neglected, and this is why many offer such long, tedious, backslidden prayers when they assemble to worship God. They go over in their prayers a week of neglected duties, and pray round and round, hoping to make up for their neglect and pacify their condemned consciences, which are scourging them. They hope to pray themselves into the favor of God. But frequently these prayers result in bringing other minds down to their own low level in spiritual darkness. If Christians would take home the teachings of Christ in regard to watching and praying, they would become more intelligent in their worship of God.

We must gather about the cross. Christ and Him crucified must be the theme of contemplation, of conversation, and of our most joyful emotion. We should have these special appointments for the purpose of keeping fresh in our thoughts everything which we receive from God, and of expressing our gratitude for His great love, and our willingness to trust everything to the hand that was nailed to the cross for us. We should learn here to talk the language of Canaan, to sing the songs of Zion. By the mystery and glory of the cross we can estimate the value of man, and then we shall see and feel the importance of working for our fellow men, that they may be exalted to the throne of God.—1880, vol. 4, p. 462.

How Shall We Keep the Sabbath?

God is merciful. His requirements are reasonable, in accordance with the goodness and benevolence of His character. The object of the Sabbath was that all mankind might be benefited. Man was not made to fit the Sabbath; for the Sabbath was made after the creation of man, to meet his necessities. After God had made the world in six days, He rested and sanctified and blessed the day upon which He rested from all His work which He had created and made. He set apart that special day for man to rest from his labor, that, as he should look upon the earth beneath and the heavens above, he might reflect that God made all these in six days and rested upon the seventh; and that, as he should behold the tangible proofs of God's infinite wisdom, his heart might be filled with love and reverence for his Maker.

In order to keep the Sabbath holy, it is not necessary that we enclose ourselves in walls, shut away from the beautiful scenes of nature and from the free, invigorating air of heaven. We should in no case allow burdens and business transactions to divert our minds upon the Sabbath of the Lord, which He has sanctified. We should not allow our minds to dwell upon things of a worldly character even. But the mind cannot be refreshed, enlivened, and elevated by being confined nearly all the Sabbath hours within walls, listening to long sermons and tedious, formal prayers. The Sabbath of the Lord is put to a wrong use if thus celebrated. The object for which it was instituted is not attained. The Sabbath was made for man, to be a blessing to him by calling his mind from secular labor to contemplate the goodness and glory of God. It is necessary

1871, vol. 2, pp. 582-585.

that the people of God assemble to talk of Him, to interchange thoughts and ideas in regard to the truths contained in His word, and to devote a portion of time to appropriate prayer. But these seasons, even upon the Sabbath, should not be made tedious by their length and lack of interest.

THE BOOK OF NATURE

During a portion of the day, all should have an opportunity to be out of doors. How can children receive a more correct knowledge of God, and their minds be better impressed, than in spending a portion of their time out of doors, not in play, but in company with their parents? Let their young minds be associated with God in the beautiful scenery of nature, let their attention be called to the tokens of His love to man in His created works, and they will be attracted and interested. They will not be in danger of associating the character of God with everything that is stern and severe; but as they view the beautiful things which He has created for the happiness of man, they will be led to regard Him as a tender, loving Father. They will see that His prohibitions and injunctions are not made merely to show His power and authority, but that He has the happiness of His children in view. As the character of God puts on the aspect of love, benevolence, beauty, and attraction, they are drawn to love Him. You can direct their minds to the lovely birds making the air musical with their happy songs, to the spires of grass, and the gloriously tinted flowers in their perfection perfuming the air. All these proclaim the love and skill of the heavenly Artist, and show forth the glory of God.

Parents, why not make use of the precious lessons which God has given us in the book of nature, to give our children a correct idea of His character? Those who sacrifice simplicity to fashion, and shut themselves away from the beauties of nature, cannot be spiritually minded. They cannot understand the skill and power of God as revealed in His created works; therefore their hearts do not quicken and throb with new love and interest, and they are not filled with awe and reverence as they see God in nature.

All who love God should do what they can to make the Sabbath a delight, holy and honorable. They cannot do this by seeking their own pleasure in sinful, forbidden amusements. Yet they can do much to exalt the Sabbath in their families and make it the most interesting day of the week. We should devote time to interesting our children. A change will have a happy influence upon them. We can walk out with them in the open air; we can sit with them in the groves and in the bright sunshine, and give their restless minds something to feed upon by conversing with them upon the works of God, and can inspire them with love and reverence by calling their attention to the beautiful objects in nature.

The Sabbath should be made so interesting to our families that its weekly return will be hailed with joy. In no better way can parents exalt and honor the Sabbath than by devising means to impart proper instruction to their families and interesting them in spiritual things, giving them correct views of the character of God and what He requires of us in order to perfect Christian characters and attain to eternal life. Parents, make the Sabbath a delight, that your children may look forward to it and have a welcome in their hearts for it.

Christian Recreation*

I HAVE been thinking what a contrast would be seen between our gathering here today and such gatherings as they are generally conducted by unbelievers. Instead of prayer, and the mention of Christ and religious things, would be heard silly laughter and trifling conversation. Their object would be to have a general high time. It would commence in folly and end in vanity. We want to have these gatherings so conducted, and to so conduct ourselves, that we can return to our homes with a conscience void of offense toward God and man; a consciousness that we have not wounded nor injured in any manner those with whom we have associated, or had an injurious influence over them.

Here is where very many fail. They do not consider that they are accountable for the influence they daily exert; that they must render an account to God for the impressions they make, and the influence they cast, in all their associations in life. If this influence is such as shall have a tendency to draw the minds of others away from God and attract them into the channel of vanity and folly, leading them to seek their own pleasure in amusements and foolish indulgences, they must give an account for this. And if these persons are men and women of influence, if their position is such that their example will affect others, then a greater sin will rest upon them for neglecting to regulate their conduct by the Bible standard.

---

*Reported as spoken before a company of about two hundred who were enjoying a season of recreation at Goguac Lake, near Battle Creek, Michigan, May, 1870.

1871, vol. 2, pp. 585-587.

The occasion we are enjoying today is just according to my ideas of recreation. I have tried to give my *views* upon this subject, but they are better illustrated than expressed. I was on this ground about one year ago when there was a gathering similar to this. Nearly everything passed off very pleasantly then, but still some things were objectionable. Considerable jesting and joking were indulged in by some. All were not Sabbathkeepers, and an influence was manifest that was not as pleasant as we could wish.

But I believe that, while we are seeking to refresh our spirits and invigorate our bodies, we *are required of God* to use all our powers at all times to the best purpose. We may associate together as we do here today, and do all to the glory of God. We can and should conduct our recreations in such a manner that we shall be fitted for the more successful discharge of the duties devolving upon us, and that our influence shall be more beneficial upon those with whom we associate. Especially should it be the case upon an occasion like this, which should be of good cheer to us all. We can return to our homes improved in mind and refreshed in body, and prepared to engage in the work anew, with better hope and better courage.

We believe that it is our privilege every day of our lives to glorify God upon the earth; that we are not to live in this world merely for our own amusement, merely to please ourselves. We are here to benefit humanity, to be a blessing to society. And if we should let our minds run in that low channel in which many who are seeking only vanity and folly permit their minds to run, how could we be a blessing to society, a benefit to our race and generation? We cannot innocently indulge in any amusement which will unfit us for the more faithful discharge of ordinary life duties.

We want to seek the elevated and lovely. We want to direct the mind away from those things that are superficial and of no importance, that have no solidity. What we desire is, to be gathering new strength from all that we engage in. From all these gatherings for the purpose of recreation, from all these pleasant associations, we want to be gathering new strength to become better men and women. From every source possible we want to gather new courage, new strength, new power, that we may elevate our lives to purity and holiness, and not come down upon the low level of this world. . . .

No Probation After Christ Comes

When Jesus rises up in the most holy place, and lays off His mediatorial garments, and clothes Himself with the garments of vengeance in place of the priestly attire, the work for sinners will be done. The period of time will then have come when the mandate will go forth: "He that is unjust, let him be unjust still: . . . and he that is righteous, let him be righteous still: and he that is holy, let him be holy still. And, behold, I come quickly; and My reward is with Me, to give every man according as his work shall be." Revelation 22: 11, 12.

God has given His word for all to investigate, that they may learn the way to life. None need err if they will submit to the conditions of salvation laid down in the word of God. Probation is granted to all, that all may form characters for eternal life. An opportunity will be given to all to decide for life or death. Men will be judged according to the measure of light given them. None will be accountable for their darkness and their errors if the light has not been brought to them. They have not sinned in not accepting what has not been given them. All will be tested before Jesus leaves His position in the most holy place. The probation of all closes when the pleading for sinners is ended and the garments of vengeance are put on.

Many entertain the view that probation is granted after Jesus leaves His work as mediator in the most holy apartment. This is the sophistry of Satan. God tests and proves the world by the light which He is pleased to give them previous to the coming of Christ. Characters are then formed for life or

1871, vol. 2, pp. 691-695.

death. But the probation of those who choose to live a life of sin, and neglect the great salvation offered, closes when Christ's ministration ceases just previous to His appearing in the clouds of heaven.

Those who love the world, and whose minds are carnal and at enmity with God, will flatter themselves that a period of probation will be granted after Christ appears in the clouds of heaven. The carnal heart, which is so averse to submission and obedience, will be deceived with this pleasing view. Many will remain in carnal security and continue in rebellion against God, flattering themselves that there is then to be a period for repentance of sin and an opportunity for them to accept the truth which now is unpopular and crossing to their natural inclination and desires. When they have nothing to venture, nothing to lose, by yielding obedience to Christ and the truth, they think they will take their chance for salvation.

There are in the Scriptures some things which are hard to be understood and which, according to the language of Peter, the unlearned and unstable wrest unto their own destruction. We may not, in this life, be able to explain the meaning of every passage of Scripture; but there are no vital points of practical truth that will be clouded in mystery. When the time shall come, in the providence of God, for the world to be tested upon the truth for that time, minds will be exercised by His Spirit to search the Scriptures, even with fasting and with prayer, until link after link is searched out and united in a perfect chain. Every fact which immediately concerns the salvation of souls will be made so clear that none need err or walk in darkness.

ACCOUNTABLE FOR LIGHT

As we have followed down the chain of prophecy, revealed truth for our time has been clearly seen and explained. We are accountable for the privileges that we enjoy and for the light that shines upon our pathway. Those who lived in past generations were accountable for the light which was permitted to shine upon them. Their minds were exercised in regard to different points of Scripture which tested them. But they did not understand the truths which we do. They were not responsible for the light which they did not have. They had the Bible, as we have; but the time for the unfolding of special truth in relation to the closing scenes of this earth's history is during the last generations that shall live upon the earth.

Special truths have been adapted to the conditions of the generations as they have existed. The present truth, which is a test to the people of this generation, was not a test to the people of generations far back. If the light which now shines upon us in regard to the Sabbath of the fourth commandment had been given to the generations in the past, God would have held them accountable for that light.

When the temple of God was opened in heaven, John saw in holy vision a class of people whose attention was arrested and who were looking with reverential awe at the ark, which contained the law of God. The special test upon the fourth commandment did not come until after the temple of God was opened in heaven.

Those who died before the light was given upon the law of God and the claims of the fourth commandment were not guilty of the sin of violating the seventh-day Sabbath. The wisdom and mercy of God in dispensing light and knowledge at the proper time, as the people need it, is unsearchable. Previous to His coming to judge the world in righteousness, He sends forth a warning to arouse the people and call their attention to their neglect of the fourth commandment, that they may be enlightened, and may repent of their transgression of His law, and prove their allegiance to the great Lawgiver. He has made provision that all may be holy and happy if they choose. Sufficient light has been given to this generation, that we may learn what our duties and privileges are, and enjoy the precious and solemn truths in their simplicity and power.

We are accountable only for the light that shines upon us. The commandments of God and the testimony of Jesus are testing us. If we are faithful and obedient, God will delight in us, and bless us as His own chosen, peculiar people. When perfect faith and perfect love and obedience abound, working in the hearts of those who are Christ's followers, they will have a powerful influence. Light will emanate from them, dispelling the darkness around them, refining and elevating all who come within the sphere of their influence, and bringing to a knowledge of the truth all who are willing to be enlightened and to follow in the humble path of obedience.

NEGLECTING TRUTHS FOR THE FANCIFUL

Those who possess the carnal mind cannot comprehend the sacred force of vital truth upon which their salvation depends, because they cherish pride of heart, love of the world, love of ease, selfishness, covetousness, envy, jealousy, lust, hatred, and every evil. If they would overcome these they might be partakers of the divine nature. Many leave the plain truths of God's word and neglect to follow the light that shines clearly upon their pathway; they try to pry into secrets not plainly revealed and conjecture and talk and dispute in regard to questions which they are not required to understand, for they have no special reference to their salvation. Thousands have been beguiled in this way by Satan. They have neglected present faith and present duty which are clear and comprehensive to all who have their reasoning powers; they have dwelt upon doubtful theories and scriptures which they could not comprehend, and have erred concerning the faith; they have a mixed faith.

God would have all make a practical use of the plain teachings of His word in regard to the salvation of man. If they are doers of the word, which is plain and powerful in its simplicity, they will not fail to perfect Christian character. They will be sanctified through the truth, and through humble obedience to it will secure everlasting life. God wants servants that are true, not only in word, but in deed. Their fruits will show the genuineness of their faith.

Brother O, you will be subject to Satan's temptations if you continue to cherish your erroneous views. Your faith will be a mixed faith, and you will be in danger of confusing the minds of others. God requires His people to be a unit. Your peculiar views will prove an injury to your influence; and if you continue to cherish them and talk them, they will finally serve to separate you from your brethren. If God has light which is necessary for the salvation of His people, He will give it to them as He has given other great and important truths. Here you should let the matter rest. Let God work in His own way to accomplish His purposes in His own time and manner. May God enable you to walk in the light as He is in the light.

Sacredness of the Sabbath

When the Sabbath commences, we should place a guard upon ourselves, upon our acts and our words, lest we rob God by appropriating to our own use that time which is strictly the Lord's. We should not do ourselves, nor suffer our children to do, any manner of our own work for a livelihood, or anything which could have been done on the six working days.

Friday is the day of preparation. Time can then be devoted to making the necessary preparation for the Sabbath and to thinking and conversing about it. Nothing which will in the sight of Heaven be regarded as a violation of the holy Sabbath should be left unsaid or undone, to be said or done upon the Sabbath. God requires not only that we refrain from physical labor upon the Sabbath, but that the mind be disciplined to dwell upon sacred themes. The fourth commandment is virtually transgressed by conversing upon worldly things or by engaging in light and trifling conversation. Talking upon anything or everything which may come into the mind is speaking our own words. Every deviation from right brings us into bondage and condemnation.

Brother P, you should discipline yourself to discern the sacredness of the Sabbath of the fourth commandment and should labor to raise the standard in your family and wherever you have, by example, lowered it among God's people. You should counteract the influence you have cast in this respect, by changing your words and actions. You have frequently failed to "remember the Sabbath day, to keep it holy;"

1871, vol. 2, pp. 702-705 (Accountability for Light).

you have often forgotten, and have spoken your own words upon God's sanctified day. You have been unguarded, and have upon the Sabbath joined with the unconsecrated in conversation upon the common topics of the day, such as gains and losses, stocks, crops, and provisions. In this your example injures your influence. You should reform.

Those who are not fully converted to the truth frequently let their minds run freely upon worldly business, and, although they may rest from physical toil upon the Sabbath, their tongues speak out what is in their minds; hence these words concerning cattle, crops, losses, and gains. All this is Sabbathbreaking. If the mind is running upon worldly matters, the tongue will reveal it; for out of the abundance of the heart the mouth speaketh.

THE MINISTER'S RESPONSIBILITY

The example of ministers especially should be circumspect in this respect. Upon the Sabbath they should conscientiously restrict themselves to conversation upon religious themes—to present truth, present duty, the Christian's hopes and fears, trials, conflicts, and afflictions; to overcoming at last, and the reward to be received.

Ministers of Jesus should stand as reprovers to those who fail to remember the Sabbath to keep it holy. They should kindly and solemnly reprove those who engage in worldly conversation upon the Sabbath and at the same time claim to be Sabbathkeepers. They should encourage devotion to God upon His holy day.

CATCHING UP ON SLEEP

None should feel at liberty to spend sanctified time in an unprofitable manner. It is displeasing to God for Sabbathkeepers to sleep during much of the Sabbath. They dishonor their Creator in so doing, and, by their example, say that the six days are too precious for them to spend in resting. They must make money, although it be by robbing themselves of needed sleep, which they make up by sleeping away holy time. They then excuse themselves by saying: "The Sabbath was given for a day of rest. I will not deprive myself of rest to attend meeting, for I need rest." Such make a wrong use of the sanctified day. They should, upon that day especially, interest their families in its observance and assemble at the house of prayer with the few or with the many, as the case may be. They should devote their time and energies to spiritual exercises, that the divine influence resting upon the Sabbath may attend them through the week. Of all the days in the week, none are so favorable for devotional thoughts and feelings as the Sabbath.

All heaven was represented to me as beholding and watching upon the Sabbath those who acknowledge the claims of the fourth commandment and are observing the Sabbath. Angels were marking their interest in, and high regard for, this divine institution. Those who sanctified the Lord God in their hearts by a strictly devotional frame of mind, and who sought to improve the sacred hours in keeping the Sabbath to the best of their ability, and to honor God by calling the Sabbath a delight—these the angels were specially blessing with light and health, and special strength was given them. But, on the other hand, the angels were turning from those who failed to appreciate the sacredness of God's sanctified day, and were removing from them their light and their strength. I saw them overshadowed with a cloud, desponding, and frequently sad. They felt a lack of the Spirit of God.

Unbalanced Minds

God has committed to each of us sacred trusts, for which He holds us accountable. It is His purpose that we so educate the mind as to be able to exercise the talents He has given us in such a manner as to accomplish the greatest good and reflect the glory to the Giver. We are indebted to God for all the qualities of the mind. These powers can be cultivated, and so discreetly directed and controlled as to accomplish the purpose for which they were given. It is duty to so educate the mind as to bring out the energies of the soul and develop every faculty. When all the faculties are in exercise, the intellect will be strengthened, and the purpose for which they were given will be accomplished.

Many are not doing the greatest amount of good because they exercise the intellect in one direction and neglect to give careful attention to those things for which they think they are not adapted. Some faculties that are weak are thus allowed to lie dormant because the work that should call them into exercise, and consequently give them strength, is not pleasant. All the powers of the mind should be exercised, all the faculties cultivated. Perception, judgment, memory, and all the reasoning powers should have equal strength in order that minds may be well balanced.

If certain faculties are used to the neglect of others, the design of God is not fully carried out in us; for all the faculties have a bearing and are dependent, in a great measure, upon one another. One cannot be effectually used without the operation of all, that the balance may be carefully preserved. If all the attention and strength are given to one, while others lie dormant, the development is strong in that one and will lead to extremes, because all the powers have not been cultivated. Some minds are dwarfed and not properly balanced.

1872, vol. 3, pp. 32-36.

All minds are not naturally constituted alike. We have varied minds; some are strong upon certain points and very weak upon others. These deficiencies, so apparent, need not and should not exist. If those who possess them would strengthen the weak points in their character by cultivation and exercise they would become strong.

It is agreeable, but not most profitable, to exercise those faculties which are naturally the strongest, while we neglect those that are weak, but which need to be strengthened. The feeblest faculties should have careful attention, that all the powers of the intellect may be nicely balanced and all do their part like well-regulated machinery. We are dependent upon God for the preservation of all our faculties. Christians are under obligation to Him to so train the mind that all the faculties may be strengthened and more fully developed. If we neglect to do this, they will never accomplish the purpose for which they were designed. We have no right to neglect any one of the powers that God has given us. We see monomaniacs all over the country. They are frequently sane upon every subject but one. The reason of this is that one organ of the mind was specially exercised while the others were permitted to lie dormant. The one that was in constant use became worn and diseased, and the man became a wreck. God was not glorified by his pursuing this course. Had he exercised all the organs equally, all would have had a healthy development; all the labor would not have been thrown upon one, therefore no one would have broken down.

Ministers should be guarded, lest they thwart the purposes of God by plans of their own. They are in danger of narrowing down the work of God, and confining their labor to certain localities, and not cultivating a special interest for the work of God in all its various departments. There are some who concentrate their minds upon one subject to the exclusion of others which may be of equal importance. They are one-idea men. All the strength of their being is concentrated on the subject upon which the mind is exercised for the time. Every other consideration is lost sight of. This one favorite theme is the burden of their thoughts and the theme of their conversation. All the evidence which has a bearing upon that subject is eagerly seized and appropriated, and dwelt upon at so great length that minds are wearied in following them.

Time is frequently lost in explaining points which are really unimportant, and which would be taken for granted without producing proof; for they are self-evident. But the real, vital points should be made as plain and forcible as language and proof can make them. The power to concentrate the mind upon one subject to the exclusion of all others is well in a degree; but the constant exercise of this faculty wears upon those organs that are called into use to do this work; it throws too great a tax upon them, and the result is a failure to accomplish the greatest amount of good. The principal wear comes upon one set of organs, while the others lie dormant. The mind cannot thus be healthfully exercised, and, in consequence, life is shortened.

All the faculties should bear a part of the labor, working harmoniously, balancing one another. Those who put the whole strength of their mind into one subject are greatly deficient on other points, for the reason that the faculties are not equally cultivated. The subject before them enchains their attention, and they are led on and on, and go deeper and deeper into the matter. They see knowledge and light as they become interested and absorbed. But there are very few minds that can follow them unless they have given the subject the same depth of thought. There is danger of such men plowing, and planting the seed of truth so deep that the tender, precious blade will never find the surface.

Much hard labor is often expended that is not called for and that will never be appreciated. If those who have large concentrativeness cultivate this faculty to the neglect of others, they cannot have well-proportioned minds. They are like machinery in which only one set of wheels works at a time. While some wheels are rusting from inaction, others are wearing from constant use. Men who cultivate one or two faculties, and do not exercise all equally, cannot accomplish one half the good in the world that God designed they should. They are one-sided men; only half of the power that God has given them is put to use, while the other half is rusting with inaction.

If this class of minds have a special work, requiring thought, they should not exercise all their powers upon that one thing, to the exclusion of every other interest. While they make the subject before them their principal business, other branches of the work should have a portion of their time. This would be much better for themselves and for the cause generally. One branch of the work should not have exclusive attention to the neglect of all others.

In their writings some need to be constantly guarded, that they do not make points blind that are plain, by covering them up with many arguments which will not be of lively interest to the reader. If they linger tediously upon points, giving every particular which suggests itself to the mind, their labor is nearly lost. The interest of the reader will not be deep enough to pursue the subject to its close. The most essential points of truth may be made indistinct by giving attention to every minute point. Much ground is covered; but the work upon which so much labor is expended is not calculated to do the greatest amount of good, by awakening a general interest.

In this age, when pleasing fables are drifting upon the surface and attracting the mind, truth presented in an easy style, backed up with a few strong proofs, is better than to search and bring forth an overwhelming array of evidence; for the point then does not stand so distinct in many minds as before the objections and evidences were brought before them. With many, assertions will go further than long arguments. They take many things for granted. Proof does not help the case in the minds of such.

Faithfulness in Home Duties

Dear Sister O: I think you are not happy. In seeking for some great work to do, you overlook present duties lying directly in your path. You are not happy, because you are looking above the little everyday duties of life for some higher and greater work to do. You are restless, uneasy, and dissatisfied. You love to dictate better than you love to perform. You love better to tell others what to do than with ready cheerfulness to take hold and do yourself.

You could have made your father's home more happy had you studied your inclination less and the happiness of others more. When engaged in the common, ordinary duties of life you fail to put your heart into your labor. Your mind is reaching forward and beyond to a work more agreeable, higher, or more honorable. Somebody must do these very things that you take no pleasure in and even dislike. These plain, simple duties, if done with willingness and faithfulness, will give you an education which it is necessary for you to obtain in order to have a love for household duties. Here is an experience that is highly essential for you to gain, but you do not love it. You murmur at your lot, thus making those around you unhappy and meeting with a great loss yourself. You may never be called to do a work which will bring you before the public. But all the work we do that is necessary to be done, be it washing dishes, setting tables, waiting upon the sick, cooking, or washing, is of moral importance; and until you can cheerfully and happily take up these duties you are not fitted for greater and higher duties. The humble tasks before us are to be taken up by someone; and those who do them should feel that they are doing a necessary and honorable work, and that in their mis-

1872, vol. 3, pp. 79-81.

sion, humble though it may be, they are doing the work of God just as surely as was Gabriel when sent to the prophets. All are working in their order in their respective spheres. Woman in her home, doing the simple duties of life that must be done, can and should exhibit faithfulness, obedience, and love as sincere as angels in their sphere. Conformity to the will of God makes any work honorable that must be done.

What you need is love and affection. Your character needs to be molded. Your worrying must be laid aside, and in place of this you must cherish gentleness and love. Deny self. We were not created angels, but lower than the angels; yet our work is important. We are not in heaven, but upon the earth. When we are in heaven, then we shall be qualified to do the lofty and elevating work of heaven. It is here in this world that we must be tested and proved. We should be armed for conflict and for duty.

The highest duty that devolves upon youth is in their own homes, blessing father and mother, brothers and sisters, by affection and true interest. Here they can show self-denial and self-forgetfulness in caring and doing for others. Never will woman be degraded by this work. It is the most sacred, elevated office that she can fill. What an influence a sister may have over brothers! If she is right she may determine the character of her brothers. Her prayers, her gentleness, and her affection may do much in a household. My sister, these noble qualities can never be communicated to other minds unless they first exist in your own. That contentment of mind, that affection, gentleness, and sunniness of temper which will reach every heart, will reflect upon you what your heart gives forth to others. If Christ does not reign in the heart, there will be discontent and moral deformity. Selfishness will require of others that which we are unwilling to give them. If Christ is not in the heart, the character will be unlovely.

It is not a great work and great battles alone which try the soul and demand courage. Everyday life brings its perplexities, trials, and discouragements. It is the humble work which frequently draws upon the patience and the fortitude. Self-reliance and resolution will be necessary to meet and conquer all difficulties. Secure the Lord to stand with you, in every place to be your consolation and comfort. A meek and quiet spirit you much need, and without it you cannot have happiness. May God help you, my sister, to seek meekness and righteousness. It is the Spirit of God that you need. If you are willing to be anything or nothing, God will help and strengthen and bless you. But if you neglect the little duties you will never be entrusted with greater.

Vain Thoughts

All your* acts, however secret you may think they have been, are open to your heavenly Father. Nothing is hidden, nothing covered. All your acts and the motives which prompt them are open to His sight. He has full knowledge of all your words and thoughts. It is your duty to control your thoughts. You will have to war against a vain imagination. You may think that there can be no sin in permitting your thoughts to run as they naturally would without restraint. But this is not so. You are responsible to God for the indulgence of vain thoughts; for from vain imaginations arises the committal of sins, the actual doing of those things upon which the mind has dwelt. Govern your thoughts, and it will then be much easier to govern your actions.

Your thoughts need to be sanctified. Paul writes to the Corinthians: "Casting down imaginations, and every high thing that exalteth itself against the knowledge of God, and bringing into captivity every thought to the obedience of Christ." 2 Corinthians 10:5. When you come into this position, the work of consecration will be better understood by you both. Your thoughts will be pure, chaste, and elevated; your actions pure and sinless. Your bodies will be preserved in sanctification and honor, that you may present them "a living sacrifice, holy, acceptable unto God, which is your reasonable service." Romans 12:1. You are required to deny self in little as well as in greater things. You should make an entire surrender to God; you are not approved of Him in your present state. . . .

1872, vol. 3, pp. 82-84.

*Note: Portion of a testimony addressed to two young people.

In order to answer life's great ends you must avoid the example of those who are seeking for their own pleasure and enjoyment, and who have not the fear of God before them. God has made provisions for you that are ample. He has provided that if you comply with the conditions laid down in His word, and separate from the world, you may receive strength from Him to repress every debasing influence and to develop that which is noble, good, and elevating. Christ will be in you "a well of water springing up into everlasting life." John 4:14. The will, the intellect, and every emotion, when controlled by religion, have a transforming power.

Consideration for the Erring

If, after one has done the best he can in his judgment, another thinks he can see where he could have improved the matter, he should kindly and patiently give the brother the benefit of his judgment, but should not censure him nor question his integrity of purpose any sooner than he himself would wish to be suspected or unjustly censured. If the brother who feels the cause of God at heart sees that, in his earnest efforts to do, he has made a failure, he will feel deeply over the matter; for he will be inclined to distrust himself and to lose confidence in his own judgment. Nothing will so weaken his courage and godlike manhood as to realize his mistakes in the work that God has appointed him to do, a work which he loves better than his life. How unjust, then, for his brethren who discover his errors to keep pressing the thorn deeper and deeper into his heart, to make him feel more intensely, when with every thrust they are weakening his faith and courage, and his confidence in himself to work successfully in the upbuilding of the cause of God.

Frequently the truth and facts are to be plainly spoken to the erring, to make them see and feel their error that they may reform. But this should ever be done with pitying tenderness, not with harshness or severity, but considering one's own weakness, lest he also be tempted. When the one at fault sees and acknowledges his error, then, instead of grieving him, and seeking to make him feel more deeply, comfort should be given. In the sermon of Christ upon the mount He said: "Judge not, that ye be not judged. For with what judgment ye judge, ye shall be judged: and with what measure ye mete, it

1872, vol. 3, pp. 92-94 (The Work at Battle Creek).

shall be measured to you again." Matthew 7:1, 2. Our Saviour reproved for rash judgment. "Why beholdest thou the mote that is in thy brother's eye; . . . and, behold, a beam is in thine own eye?" Verses 3, 4. It is frequently the case that while one is quick to discern the errors of his brethren, he may be in greater faults himself, but be blind to them.

All who are followers of Christ should deal with one another exactly as we wish the Lord to deal with us in our errors and weaknesses, for we are all erring and need His pity and forgiveness. Jesus consented to take human nature, that He might know how to pity, and how to plead with His Father in behalf of sinful, erring mortals. He volunteered to become man's Advocate, and He humiliated Himself to become acquainted with the temptations wherewith man was beset, that He might succor those who should be tempted, and be a tender and faithful high priest.

Frequently there is necessity for plainly rebuking sin and reproving wrong. But ministers who are working for the salvation of their fellow men should not be pitiless toward the errors of one another, nor make prominent the defects in their organizations. They should not expose or reprove their weaknesses. They should inquire if such a course, pursued by another toward themselves, would bring about the desired effect; would it increase their love for, and confidence in, the one who thus made prominent their mistakes? Especially should the mistakes of ministers who are engaged in the work of God be kept within as small a circle as possible, for there are many weak ones who will take advantage if they are aware that those who minister in word and doctrine have weaknesses like other men. And it is a most cruel thing for the faults of a minister to be exposed to unbelievers, if that minister is counted worthy to labor in the future for the salvation of souls. No good can come of this exposure, but only harm. The Lord frowns upon this course, for it is undermining the confidence of the people in those whom He accepts to carry forward His work.

The character of every fellow laborer should be jealously guarded by brother ministers. Saith God: "Touch not Mine anointed, and do My prophets no harm." 1 Chronicles 16:22; Psalm 105:15. Love and confidence should be cherished. A lack of this love and confidence in one minister for another does not increase the happiness of the one thus deficient, but as he makes his brother unhappy he is unhappy himself. There is greater power in love than was ever found in censure. Love will melt its way through barriers, while censure will close up every avenue of the soul.

Parables of the Lost

THE LOST SHEEP

I WAS referred to the parable of the lost sheep. The ninety and nine sheep are left in the wilderness, and search is instituted for the one that has strayed. When the lost sheep is found, the shepherd elevates it to his shoulder and returns with rejoicing. He does not return murmuring and censuring the poor lost sheep for having made him so much trouble, but his return with the burden of the sheep is with rejoicing.

And a still greater demonstration of joy is demanded. Friends and neighbors are called to rejoice with the finder, "for I have found my sheep which was lost." The finding was the theme of rejoicing; the straying was not dwelt upon; for the joy of finding overbalanced the sorrow of the loss and the care, the perplexity and the peril, incurred in searching for the lost sheep and restoring it to safety. "I say unto you, that likewise joy shall be in heaven over one sinner that repenteth, more than over ninety and nine just persons, which need no repentance." Luke 15:6, 7.

THE LOST SILVER

The lost piece of silver is designed to represent the erring, straying sinner. The carefulness of the woman to find the lost silver is to teach the followers of Christ a lesson in regard to their duty to the erring ones who are straying from the path of right. The woman lighted the candle to increase her light, and then swept the house, and sought diligently till she found it.

Here is clearly defined the duty of Christians toward those who need help because of their straying from God. The erring ones are not to be left in darkness and error, but every avail-

1872, vol. 3, pp. 99-104 (The Work at Battle Creek).

able means is to be used to bring them again to the light. The candle is lighted; and, with earnest prayer for heavenly light to meet the cases of those enshrouded in darkness and unbelief, the word of God is searched for clear points of truth, that Christians may be so fortified with arguments from the word of God, with its reproofs, threatenings, and encouragements, that the erring ones may be reached. Indifference or neglect will meet the frown of God.

When the woman found the silver, she called her friends and her neighbors together, saying: "Rejoice with me; for I have found the piece which I had lost. Likewise, I say unto you, there is joy in the presence of the angels of God over one sinner that repenteth." Luke 15:9, 10. If the angels of God rejoice over the erring who see and confess their wrongs and return to the fellowship of their brethren, how much more should the followers of Christ, who are themselves erring, and who every day need the forgiveness of God and of their brethren, feel joy over the return of a brother or a sister who has been deceived by the sophistry of Satan and has taken a wrong course and suffered because of it.

Instead of holding the erring off, their brethren should meet them where they are. Instead of finding fault with them because they are in the dark, they should light their own lamp by obtaining more divine grace and a clearer knowledge of the Scriptures, that they may dispel the darkness of those in error by the light that they bring to them. And when they succeed, and the erring feel their error and submit to follow the light, they should be received gladly, and not with a spirit of murmuring or an effort to impress upon them their exceeding sinfulness, which had called forth extra exertion, anxiety, and wearisome labor. If the pure angels of God hail the event with joy, how much more should their brethren rejoice, who have themselves needed sympathy, love, and help when they have erred and in their darkness have not known how to help themselves.

THE PRODIGAL SON

My attention was called to the parable of the prodigal son. He made a request that his father should give him his portion of the estate. He desired to separate his interest from that of his father, and to manage his share as best suited his own inclination. His father complied with the request, and the son selfishly withdrew from his father, that he might not be troubled with his counsel or reproofs.

The son thought he should be happy when he could use his portion according to his own pleasure, without being annoyed by advice or restraint. He did not wish to be troubled with mutual obligation. If he shared his father's estate, his father had claims upon him as a son. But he did not feel under any obligation to his generous father, and he braced his selfish, rebellious spirit with the thought that a portion of his father's property belonged to him. He requested his share, when rightfully he could claim nothing and should have had nothing.

After his selfish heart had received the treasure, of which he was so undeserving, he went his way at a distance from his father, that he might even forget that he had a father. He despised restraint and was fully determined to have pleasure in any way and manner that he chose. After he had, by his sinful indulgences, spent all that his father had given him, the land was visited by a famine, and he felt pinching want. He then began to regret his sinful course of extravagant pleasure, for he was destitute and needed the means that he had squandered. He was obliged to come down from his life of sinful indulgence to the low business of feeding swine.

After he had come as low as he could he thought of the kindness and love of his father. He then felt the need of a father. He had brought upon himself his position of friendlessness and want. His own disobedience and sin had resulted in his separating himself from his father. He thought of the privileges and bounties that the hired servants of his father's house freely enjoyed, while he who had alienated himself from his father's house was perishing with hunger. Humiliated through adversity, he decided to return to his father by humble confession. He was a beggar, destitute of comfortable or even decent clothing. He was wretched in consequence of privation and was emaciated with hunger.

THE FATHER'S LOVE

While the son was at a distance from his home, his father saw the wanderer, and his first thought was of that rebellious son who had left him years before to follow a course of unrestrained sin. The paternal feeling was stirred. Notwithstanding all the marks of his degradation the father discerned his own image. He did not wait for his son to come all the distance to him, but hastened to meet him. He did not reproach his son, but with the tenderest pity and compassion, that, in consequence of his course of sin, he had brought upon himself so much suffering, the father hastened to give him proofs of his love and tokens of his forgiveness.

Although his son was emaciated and his countenance plainly indicated the dissolute life he had passed, although he was clothed with beggar's rags and his naked feet were soiled with the dust of travel, the father's tenderest pity was excited as the son fell prostrate in humility before him. He did not stand back upon his dignity; he was not exacting. He did not array before his son his past course of wrong and sin, to make him feel how low he had sunk. He lifted him up and kissed him. He took the rebellious son to his breast and wrapped his own rich robe about the nearly naked form. He took him to his heart with such warmth, and evinced such pity, that if the son had ever doubted the goodness and love of his father, he could do so no longer. If he had a sense of his sin when he decided to return to his father's house, he had a much deeper sense of his ungrateful course when he was thus received. His heart, before subdued, was now broken because he had grieved that father's love.

The penitent, trembling son, who had greatly feared that he would be disowned, was unprepared for such a reception. He knew he did not deserve it, and he thus acknowledged his sin in leaving his father: "I have sinned against heaven, and in thy sight, and am no more worthy to be called thy son." Luke 15:21. He begged only to be accounted as a hired servant. But the father requested his servants to pay him special tokens of respect and to clothe him as if he had ever been his own obedient son.

THE JEALOUS BROTHER

The father made the return of his son an occasion of special rejoicing. The elder son in the field knew not that his brother had returned, but he heard the general demonstrations of joy and inquired of the servants what it all meant. It was explained that his brother, whom they had thought dead, had returned, and that his father had killed the fatted calf for him because he had received him again as from the dead.

The brother was then angry and would not go in to see or receive his brother. His indignation was stirred that his unfaithful brother, who had left his father and thrown the heavy responsibility upon him of fulfilling the duties which should have been shared by both, should now be received with such honor. This brother had pursued a course of wicked profligacy, wasting the means his father had given him, until he was reduced to want, while his brother at home had been faithfully performing the duties of a son; and now this profligate comes to his father's house and is received with respect and honor beyond anything that he himself had ever received.

The father entreated his elder son to go and receive his brother with gladness because he was lost and is found; he was dead in sin and iniquity, but is alive again; he has come to his moral senses and abhors his course of sin. But his elder son pleads: "Lo, these many years do I serve thee, neither transgressed I at any time thy commandment: and yet thou never gavest me a kid, that I might make merry with my friends: but as soon as this thy son was come, which hath devoured thy living with harlots, thou hast killed for him the fatted calf." Luke 15:29-32.

He assured his son that he was ever with him, and that all he had was his, but that it was right that they should show this demonstration of joy, for "thy brother was dead, and is alive again; and was lost, and is found." The fact that the lost is found, the dead is alive again, overbears all other considerations with the father.

This parable was given by Christ to represent the manner in which our heavenly Father receives the erring and repenting. The father is the one sinned against; yet he, in the compassion of his soul, full of pity and forgiveness, meets the prodigal and shows his great joy that his son, whom he believed to be dead to all filial affection, has become sensible of his great sin and neglect, and has come back to his father, appreciating his love and acknowledging his claims. He knows that the son who has pursued a course of sin and now repents needs his pity and his love. This son has suffered; he has felt his need, and he comes to his father as the only one who can supply this great need.

The return of the prodigal son was a source of the greatest joy. The complaints of the elder brother were natural, but not right. Yet this is frequently the course that brother pursues toward brother. There is too much effort to make those in error feel where they have erred, and to keep reminding them of their mistakes. Those who have erred need pity, they need help, they need sympathy. They suffer in their feelings, and are frequently desponding and discouraged. Above everything else, they need free forgiveness.

The Wheat and Tares

In another parable which Jesus presented to His disciples, He likened the kingdom of heaven to a field wherein a man sowed good seed, but in which, while he was sleeping, the enemy sowed tares. The question was asked the householder: "Didst not thou sow good seed in thy field? from whence then hath it tares? He said unto them, An enemy hath done this. The servants said unto him, Wilt thou then that we go and gather them up? But he said, Nay; lest while ye gather up the tares, ye root up also the wheat with them. Let both grow together until the harvest: and in the time of harvest I will say to the reapers, Gather ye together first the tares, and bind them in bundles to burn them: but gather the wheat into my barn." Matthew 13:27-30. If faithfulness and vigilance had been preserved, if there had been no sleeping or negligence upon the part of any, the enemy would not have had so favorable an opportunity to sow tares among the wheat. Satan never sleeps. He is watching, and he improves every opportunity to set his agents to scatter error, which finds good soil in many unsanctified hearts.

The sincere believers of truth are made sad, and their trials and sorrows greatly increased, by the elements among them which annoy, dishearten, and discourage them in their efforts. But the Lord would teach His servants a lesson of great carefulness in all their moves. "Let both grow together." Do not forcibly pull up the tares, lest in rooting them up the precious blades will become loosened. Both ministers and church members should be very cautious, lest they get a zeal not according to knowledge. There is danger of doing too much to cure difficulties in the church, which, if let alone, will frequently work

1872, vol. 3, pp. 113-116 (Labor Among the Churches).

their own cure. It is bad policy to take hold of matters in any church prematurely. We shall have to exercise the greatest care, patience, and self-control to bear these things and not go to work in our own spirit to set them in order.

The work done in —— was premature and caused an untimely separation in that little church. If the servants of God could have felt the force of our Saviour's lesson in the parable of the wheat and tares, they would not have undertaken the work they did. Before steps are taken which will give even those who are utterly unworthy the least occasion to complain of being separated from the church, the matter should always be made a subject of the most careful consideration and earnest prayer.

Steps were taken in —— which created an opposition party. Some were wayside hearers, others were stony-ground hearers, and still others were of that class who received the truth while the heart had a growth of thorns which choked the good seed—these would never have perfected Christian characters. But there were a few who might have been nourished and strengthened, and have become settled and established in the truth. But the positions taken by Brethren R and S brought a premature crisis, and then there was a lack of wisdom and judgment in managing the faction.

If persons are as deserving of being separated from the church as Satan was of being cast out of heaven, they will have sympathizers. There is always a class who are more influenced by individuals than they are by the Spirit of God and sound principles; and, in their unconsecrated state, these are ever ready to take sides with the wrong and give their pity and sympathy to the very ones who least deserve it. These sympathizers have a powerful influence with others; things are seen in a perverted light, great harm is done, and many souls are ruined. Satan in his rebellion took a third part of the angels. They turned from the Father and from His Son, and united with the instigator of rebellion. With these facts before us we should move with the greatest caution. What can we expect but trial and perplexity in our connection with men and women of peculiar minds? We must bear this and avoid the necessity of rooting up the tares, lest the wheat be rooted up also.

THE BLESSING OF TRIALS AND ADVERSITY

"In the world ye shall have tribulation," says Christ; but in Me ye shall have peace. The trials to which Christians are subjected in sorrow, adversity, and reproach are the means appointed of God to separate the chaff from the wheat. Our pride, selfishness, evil passions, and love of worldly pleasure must all be overcome; therefore God sends us afflictions to test and prove us, and show us that these evils exist in our characters. We must overcome through His strength and grace, that we may be partakers of the divine nature, having escaped the corruption that is in the world through lust. "For our light affliction," says Paul, "which is but for a moment, worketh for us a far more exceeding and eternal weight of glory; while we look not at the things which are seen, but at the things which are not seen: for the things which are seen are temporal; but the things which are not seen are eternal." 2 Corinthians 4:17, 18. Afflictions, crosses, temptations, adversity, and our varied trials are God's workmen to refine us, sanctify us, and fit us for the heavenly garner.

The harm done to the cause of truth by premature moves can never be fully repaired. The cause of God in —— has not advanced as it might, and will not stand in as favorable a light before the people as before this work was done. There are frequently persons among us whose influence seems to be but a cipher on the right side. Their lives seem to be useless; but let them become rebellious and combative, and they become zealous workmen for Satan. This work is more in accordance with the feelings of the natural heart. There is great need of self-examination and secret prayer. God has promised wisdom to those who ask Him. Missionary labor is frequently entered upon by those unprepared for the work. Outward zeal is cultivated, while secret prayer is neglected. When this is the case, much harm is done, for these laborers seek to regulate the consciences of others by their own rule. Self-control is much needed. Hasty words stir up strife. Brother S is in danger of indulging a spirit of sharp criticism. This does not become ministers of righteousness.

Brother S, you have much to learn. You have been inclined to charge your failures and your discouragements to Brother W, but close investigation of your motives and of your course of action would reveal other causes which exist in yourself for these discouragements. Following the inclinations of your own natural heart brings you into bondage. The severe, torturing spirit in which you sometimes indulge cuts off your influence. My brother, you have a work to do for yourself which no other person can do for you. Each must give an account of himself to God. He has given us His law as a mirror into which we may look and discover the defects in our characters. We are not to look into this mirror for the purpose of seeing our neighbor's faults reflected, of watching to see if he comes up to the standard, but to see the defects in ourselves, that we may remove them. Knowledge is not all that we need; we must follow the light. We are not left to choose for ourselves and to obey that which is agreeable to us and to disobey when it best suits our convenience. Obedience is better than sacrifice.

Proper Education

It is the nicest work ever assumed by men and women to deal with youthful minds. The greatest care should be taken in the education of youth to so vary the manner of instruction as to call forth the high and noble powers of the mind. Parents and schoolteachers are certainly disqualified to properly educate children if they have not first learned the lesson of self-control, patience, forbearance, gentleness, and love. What an important position for parents, guardians, and teachers! There are very few who realize the most essential wants of the mind and how to direct the developing intellect, the growing thoughts and feelings of youth.

There is a time for training children and a time for educating youth, and it is essential that in school both of these be combined in a great degree. Children may be trained for the service of sin or for the service of righteousness. The early education of youth shapes their characters both in their secular and in their religious life. Solomon says: "Train up a child in the way he should go: and when he is old, he will not depart from it." Proverbs 22:6. This language is positive. The training which Solomon enjoins is to direct, educate, and develop. In order for parents and teachers to do this work, they must themselves understand "the way" the child should go. This embraces more than merely having a knowledge of books. It takes in everything that is good, virtuous, righteous, and holy. It comprehends the practice of temperance, godliness, brotherly kindness, and love to God and to one another. In order to attain this object, the physical, mental, moral, and religious education of children must have attention.

1872, vol. 3, pp. 131-135.

The education of children, at home or at school, should not be like the training of dumb animals; for children have an intelligent will, which should be directed to control all their powers. Dumb animals need to be trained, for they have not reason and intellect. But the human mind must be taught self-control. It must be educated to rule the human being, while animals are controlled by a master and are trained to be submissive to him. The master is mind, judgment, and will for his beast. A child may be so trained as to have, like the beast, no will of his own. Even his individuality may be merged in the one who superintends his training; his will, to all intents and purposes, is subject to the will of the teacher.

Children who are thus educated will ever be deficient in moral energy and individual responsibility. They have not been taught to move from reason and principle; their wills have been controlled by another, and the mind has not been called out, that it might expand and strengthen by exercise. They have not been directed and disciplined with respect to their peculiar constitutions and capabilities of mind, to put forth their strongest powers when required. Teachers should not stop here, but should give special attention to the cultivation of the weaker faculties, that all the powers may be brought into exercise, and carried forward from one degree of strength to another, that the mind may attain due proportions.

TEACHING SELF-RELIANCE

There are many families of children who appear to be well trained while under the training discipline; but when the system which has held them to set rules is broken up, they seem to be incapable of thinking, acting, or deciding for themselves. These children have been so long under iron rule, not allowed to think and act for themselves in those things in which it was highly proper that they should, that they have no confidence in themselves to move out upon their own judgment, having an opinion of their own. And when they go out from their parents to act for themselves, they are easily led by others' judgment in the wrong direction. They have not stability of character. They have not been thrown upon their own judgment as fast and as far as practicable, and therefore their minds have not been properly developed and strengthened. They have so long been absolutely controlled by their parents that they rely wholly upon them; their parents are mind and judgment for them.

On the other hand, the young should not be left to think and act independently of the judgment of their parents and teachers. Children should be taught to respect experienced judgment and to be guided by their parents and teachers. They should be so educated that their minds will be united with the minds of their parents and teachers, and so instructed that they can see the propriety of heeding their counsel. Then when they go forth from the guiding hand of their parents and teachers, their characters will not be like the reed trembling in the wind.

The severe training of youth, without properly directing them to think and act for themselves as their own capacity and turn of mind will allow, that by this means they may have growth of thought, feelings of self-respect, and confidence in their own ability to perform, will ever produce a class who are weak in mental and moral power. And when they stand in the world to act for themselves they will reveal the fact that they were trained like the animals, and not educated. Their wills, instead of being guided, were forced into subjection by the harsh discipline of parents and teachers.

Those parents and teachers who boast of having complete control of the minds and wills of the children under their care would cease their boastings could they trace out the future lives of the children who are thus brought into subjection by force or through fear. These are almost wholly unprepared to share in the stern responsibilities of life. When these youth are no longer under their parents and teachers, and are compelled to think and act for themselves, they are almost sure to take a wrong course and yield to the power of temptation. They do not make this life a success, and the same deficiencies are seen in their religious life. Could the instructors of children and youth have the future result of their mistaken discipline mapped out before them, they would change their plan of education. That class of teachers who are gratified that they have almost complete control of the wills of their scholars are not the most successful teachers, although the appearance for the time being may be flattering.

God never designed that one human mind should be under the complete control of another. And those who make efforts to have the individuality of their pupils merged in themselves, and to be mind, will, and conscience for them, assume fearful responsibilities. These scholars may, upon certain occasions, appear like well-drilled soldiers. But when the restraint is removed, there will be seen a want of independent action from firm principle existing in them. Those who make it their object to so educate their pupils that they may see and feel that the power lies in themselves to make men and women of firm principle, qualified for any position in life, are the most useful and permanently successful teachers. Their work may not show to the very best advantage to careless observers, and their labors may not be valued as highly as are those of the teacher who holds the minds and wills of his scholars by absolute authority; but the future lives of the pupils will show the fruits of the better plan of education.

There is danger of both parents and teachers commanding and dictating too much, while they fail to come sufficiently into social relation with their children or scholars. They often hold themselves too much reserved, and exercise their authority in a cold, unsympathizing manner which cannot win the hearts of their children and pupils. If they would gather the children close to them, and show that they love them, and would manifest an interest in all their efforts and even in their sports, sometimes even being a child among children, they would make the children very happy and would gain their love and win their confidence. And the children would sooner respect and love the authority of their parents and teachers.

The habits and principles of a teacher should be considered of even greater importance than his literary qualifications. If he is a sincere Christian he will feel the necessity of having an equal interest in the physical, mental, moral, and spiritual education of his scholars. In order to exert the right influence, he should have perfect control over himself, and his own heart should be richly imbued with love for his pupils, which will be seen in his looks, words, and acts. He should have firmness of character, and then he can mold the minds of his pupils as well as instruct them in the sciences. The early education of youth generally shapes their characters for life. Those who deal with the young should be very careful to call out the qualities of the mind, that they may better know how to direct its powers so that they may be exercised to the very best account.

The Health Reform

December 10, 1871, I was again shown that the health reform is one branch of the great work which is to fit a people for the coming of the Lord. It is as closely connected with the third angel's message as the hand is with the body. The law of Ten Commandments has been lightly regarded by man, but the Lord would not come to punish the transgressors of that law without first sending them a message of warning. The third angel proclaims that message. Had men ever been obedient to the law of Ten Commandments, carrying out in their lives the principles of those precepts, the curse of disease now flooding the world would not be.

Men and women cannot violate natural law by indulging depraved appetite and lustful passions, and not violate the law of God. Therefore He has permitted the light of health reform to shine upon us, that we may see our sin in violating the laws which He has established in our being. All our enjoyment or suffering may be traced to obedience or transgression of natural law. Our gracious heavenly Father sees the deplorable condition of men who, some knowingly but many ignorantly, are living in violation of the laws that He has established. And in love and pity to the race, He causes the light to shine upon health reform. He publishes His law and the penalty that will follow the transgression of it, that all may learn and be careful to live in harmony with natural law. He proclaims His law so distinctly and makes it so prominent that it is like a city set on a hill. All accountable beings can understand it if they will. Idiots will not be responsible. To make plain natural law, and urge the obedience of it, is the work that accompanies the third angel's message to prepare a people for the coming of the Lord.

1872, vol. 3, p. 161.

Danger of Applause

I HAVE been shown that great caution should be used, even when it is necessary to lift a burden of oppression from men and women, lest they lean to their own wisdom and fail to make God their only dependence. It is not safe to speak in praise of persons or to exalt the ability of a minister of Christ. In the day of God, very many will be weighed in the balance and found wanting because of exaltation. I would warn my brethren and sisters never to flatter persons because of their ability, for they cannot bear it. Self is easily exalted, and, in consequence, persons lose their balance.

I say again to my brethren and sisters: If you would have your souls clean from the blood of all men, never flatter, never praise the efforts of poor mortals; for it may prove their ruin. It is unsafe, by our words and actions, to exalt a brother or sister, however apparently humble may be his or her deportment. If they really possess the meek and lowly spirit which God so highly esteems, help them to retain it. This will not be done by censuring them nor by neglecting to properly appreciate their true worth. But there are few who can bear praise without being injured.

Some ministers of ability who are now preaching present truth, love approbation. Applause stimulates them, as the glass of wine does the inebriate. Place these ministers where they have a small congregation which promises no special excitement and which provokes no decided opposition, and they will lose their interest and zeal, and appear as languid in the work as the inebriate when he is deprived of his dram. These men will fail to make real, practical laborers until they learn to labor without the excitement of applause.

1872, vol. 3, pp. 185, 186.

Labor for the Erring

CHRIST identified Himself with the necessities of His people. Their needs and their sufferings were His. He says: "I was anhungered, and ye gave Me meat: I was thirsty, and ye gave Me drink: I was a stranger, and ye took Me in: naked, and ye clothed Me: I was sick, and ye visited Me: I was in prison, and ye came unto Me." Matthew 25:35, 36. God's servants should have hearts of tender affection and sincere love for the followers of Christ. They should manifest that deep interest that Christ brings to view in the care of the shepherd for the lost sheep; they should follow the example given by Christ and exercise the same compassion and gentleness, and the same tender, pitying love that He has exercised toward us.

The great moral powers of the soul are faith, hope, and love. If these are inactive, a minister may be ever so earnest and zealous, but his labor will not be accepted of God and cannot be productive of good to the church. A minister of Christ who bears the solemn message from God to the people should ever deal justly, love mercy, and walk humbly before God. The spirit of Christ in the heart will incline every power of the soul to nourish and protect the sheep of His pasture, like a faithful, true shepherd. Love is the golden chain which binds believing hearts to one another in willing bonds of friendship, tenderness, and faithful constancy, and which binds the soul to God.

There is a decided lack of love, compassion, and pitying tenderness among brethren. The ministers of Christ are too cold and heartless. Their hearts are not all aglow with tender compassion and earnest love. The purest and most elevated devotion to God is that which is manifested in the most ear-

1872, vol. 3, pp. 186-188.

nest desires and efforts to win souls to Christ. The reason ministers who preach present truth are not more successful is that they are deficient, greatly deficient, in faith, hope, and love. There are toils and conflicts, self-denials and secret heart trials, for us all to meet and bear. There will be sorrow and tears for our sins; there will be constant struggles and watchings, mingled with remorse and shame because of our deficiencies.

Let not the ministers of the cross of our dear Saviour forget their experience in these things; but let them ever bear in mind that they are but men, liable to err, and possessing like passions with their brethren, and that if they help their brethren they must be persevering in their efforts to do them good, having their hearts filled with pity and love. They must come to the hearts of their brethren and help them where they are weak and need help the most. Those who labor in word and doctrine should break their own hard, proud, unbelieving hearts if they would witness the same in their brethren.

Christ has done all for us because we were helpless; we were bound in chains of darkness, sin, and despair, and could therefore do nothing for ourselves. It is through the exercise of faith, hope, and love that we come nearer and nearer to the standard of perfect holiness. Our brethren feel the same pitying need of help that we have felt. We should not burden them with unnecessary censure, but should let the love of Christ constrain us to be very compassionate and tender, that we can weep over the erring and those who have backslidden from God. The soul is of infinite value. Its worth can be estimated only by the price paid to ransom it. Calvary! Calvary! Calvary! will explain the true value of the soul.

Mild measures, soft answers, and pleasant words are much better fitted to reform and save, than severity and harshness. A little too much unkindness may place persons beyond your reach, while a conciliatory spirit would be the means of binding them to you, and you might then establish them in the right way. You should be actuated by a forgiving spirit also, and give due credit to every good purpose and action of those around you.—1876, vol. 4, p. 65.

Love and Duty

Love has a twin sister, which is duty. Love and duty stand side by side. Love exercised while duty is neglected will make children headstrong, willful, perverse, selfish, and disobedient. If stern duty is left to stand alone without love to soften and win, it will have a similar result. Duty and love must be blended in order that children may be properly disciplined.

Anciently, directions were given to the priests: "And they shall teach My people the difference between the holy and profane, and cause them to discern between the unclean and the clean. And in controversy they shall stand in judgment; and they shall judge it according to My judgments." Ezekiel 44:23, 24. "When I say unto the wicked, O wicked man, thou shalt surely die; if thou dost not speak to warn the wicked from his way, that wicked man shall die in his iniquity; but his blood will I require at thine hand. Nevertheless, if thou warn the wicked of his way to turn from it; if he do not turn from his way, he shall die in his iniquity; but thou hast delivered thy soul." Ezekiel 33:8, 9.

Here the duty of God's servants is made plain. They cannot be excused from the faithful discharge of their duty to reprove sins and wrongs in the people of God, although it may be a disagreeable task and may not be received by the one who is at fault. But in most cases the one reproved would accept the warning and heed reproof were it not that others stand in the way. They come in as sympathizers and pity the one reproved and feel that they must stand in his defense. They do not see that the Lord is displeased with the wrongdoer, because the cause of God has been wounded and His name reproached. Souls have been turned aside from the truth and have made

1872, vol. 3, pp. 195, 196.

shipwreck of faith as the result of the wrong course pursued by the one in fault; but the servant of God whose discernment is clouded and whose judgment is swayed by wrong influences would as soon take his position with the offender whose influence has done much harm, as with the reprover of wrong and of sin, and in so doing he virtually says to the sinner: "Do not be troubled, do not be cast down; you are about right after all." These say to the sinner: "It shall be well with thee."

God requires His servants to walk in the light and not cover their eyes that they may not discern the working of Satan. They should be prepared to warn and reprove those who are in danger through his subtlety. Satan is working on the right hand and on the left to obtain vantage ground. He rests not. He is persevering. He is vigilant and crafty to take advantage of every circumstance and turn it to his account in his warfare against the truth and the interests of the kingdom of God. It is a lamentable fact that God's servants are not half as much awake to the wiles of Satan as they should be. And instead of resisting the devil that he may flee from them, many are inclined to make a compromise with the powers of darkness.

The Laodicean Church

The message to the church of the Laodiceans is a startling denunciation, and is applicable to the people of God at the present time.

"And unto the angel of the church of the Laodiceans write: These things saith the Amen, the faithful and true Witness, the beginning of the creation of God; I know thy works, that thou art neither cold nor hot: I would thou wert cold or hot. So then because thou art lukewarm, and neither cold nor hot, I will spew thee out of My mouth. Because thou sayest, I am rich, and increased with goods, and have need of nothing; and knowest not that thou art wretched, and miserable, and poor, and blind, and naked." Revelation 3:14-17.

The Lord here shows us that the message to be borne to His people by ministers whom He has called to warn the people is not a peace-and-safety message. It is not merely theoretical, but practical in every particular. The people of God are represented in the message to the Laodiceans as in a position of carnal security. They are at ease, believing themselves to be in an exalted condition of spiritual attainments. "Because thou sayest, I am rich, and increased with goods, and have need of nothing; and knowest not that thou art wretched, and miserable, and poor, and blind, and naked."

What greater deception can come upon human minds than a confidence that they are right when they are all wrong! The message of the True Witness finds the people of God in a sad deception, yet honest in that deception. They know not that their condition is deplorable in the sight of God. While those addressed are flattering themselves that they are in an exalted spiritual condition, the message of the True Witness breaks their security by the startling denunciation of their true con-

1873, vol. 3, pp. 252-258.

dition of spiritual blindness, poverty, and wretchedness. The testimony, so cutting and severe, cannot be a mistake, for it is the True Witness who speaks, and His testimony must be correct.

It is difficult for those who feel secure in their attainments, and who believe themselves to be rich in spiritual knowledge, to receive the message which declares that they are deceived and in need of every spiritual grace. The unsanctified heart is "deceitful above all things, and desperately wicked." Jeremiah 17:9. I was shown that many are flattering themselves that they are good Christians, who have not a ray of light from Jesus. They have not a living experience for themselves in the divine life. They need a deep and thorough work of self-abasement before God before they will feel their true need of earnest, persevering effort to secure the precious graces of the Spirit.

God leads His people on step by step. The Christian life is a constant battle and a march. There is no rest from the warfare. It is by constant, unceasing effort that we maintain the victory over the temptations of Satan. As a people we are triumphing in the clearness and strength of the truth. We are fully sustained in our positions by an overwhelming amount of plain Scriptural testimony. But we are very much wanting in Bible humility, patience, faith, love, self-denial, watchfulness, and the spirit of sacrifice. We need to cultivate Bible holiness. Sin prevails among the people of God. The plain message of rebuke to the Laodiceans is not received. Many cling to their doubts and their darling sins while they are in so great a deception as to talk and feel that they are in need of nothing. They think the testimony of the Spirit of God in reproof is uncalled for or that it does not mean them. Such are in the greatest need of the grace of God and spiritual discernment that they may discover their deficiency in spiritual knowledge. They lack almost every qualification necessary to perfect Christian character. They have not a practical knowledge of Bible truth, which leads to lowliness of life and a conformity of their will to the will of Christ. They are not living in obedience to all God's requirements.

It is not enough to merely profess to believe the truth. All the soldiers of the cross of Christ virtually obligate themselves to enter the crusade against the adversary of souls, to condemn wrong and sustain righteousness. But the message of the True Witness reveals the fact that a terrible deception is upon our people, which makes it necessary to come to them with warnings, to break their spiritual slumber, and arouse them to decided action.

In my last vision I was shown that even this decided message of the True Witness had not accomplished the design of God. The people slumber on in their sins. They continue to declare themselves rich and having need of nothing. Many inquire: Why are all these reproofs given? Why do the *Testimonies* continually charge us with backsliding and with grievous sins? We love the truth; we are prospering; we are in no need of these testimonies of warning and reproof. But let these murmurers see their hearts and compare their lives with the practical teachings of the Bible, let them humble their souls before God, let the grace of God illuminate the darkness, and the scales will fall from their eyes, and they will realize their true spiritual poverty and wretchedness. They will feel the necessity of buying gold, which is pure faith and love; white raiment, which is a spotless character made pure in the blood of their dear Redeemer; and eyesalve, which is the grace of God and which will give clear discernment of spiritual things and detect sin. These attainments are more precious than the gold of Ophir.

THE CAUSE OF SPIRITUAL BLINDNESS

I have been shown that the greatest reason why the people of God are now found in this state of spiritual blindness is that they will not receive correction. Many have despised the reproofs and warnings given them. The True Witness condemns the lukewarm condition of the people of God, which gives Satan great power over them in this waiting, watching time. The selfish, the proud, and the lovers of sin are ever assailed with doubts. Satan has ability to suggest doubts and to devise objections to the pointed testimony that God sends, and many think it a virtue, a mark of intelligence in them, to be unbelieving and to question and quibble. Those who desire to doubt will have plenty of room. God does not propose to remove all occasion for unbelief. He gives evidence, which must be carefully investigated with a humble mind and a teachable spirit, and all should decide from the weight of evidence.

Eternal life is of infinite value and will cost us all that we have. I was shown that we do not place a proper estimate upon eternal things. Everything worth possessing, even in this world, must be secured by effort, and sometimes by most painful sacrifice. And this is merely to obtain a perishable treasure. Shall we be less willing to endure conflict and toil, and to make earnest efforts and great sacrifices, to obtain a treasure which is of infinite value, and a life which will measure with that of the Infinite? Can heaven cost us too much?

Faith and love are golden treasures, elements that are greatly wanting among God's people. I have been shown that unbelief in the testimonies of warning, encouragement, and reproof is shutting away the light from God's people. Unbelief is closing their eyes so that they are ignorant of their true condition. The True Witness thus describes their blindness: "And knowest not that thou art wretched, and miserable, and poor, and blind, and naked." Revelation 3:17.

Faith in the soon coming of Christ is waning. "My Lord delayeth His coming" is not only said in the heart, but expressed in words and most decidedly in works. Stupidity in this watching time is sealing the senses of God's people as to the signs of the times. The terrible iniquity which abounds calls for the greatest diligence and for the living testimony, to keep sin out of the church. Faith has been decreasing to a fearful degree, and it is only by exercise that it can increase.

In the rise of the third angel's message those who engaged in the work of God had something to venture; they had sacrifices to make. They started this work in poverty and suffered the greatest deprivations and reproach. They met determined opposition, which drove them to God in their necessity and kept their faith alive. Our present plan of systematic benevolence* amply sustains our ministers, and there is no want and no call for the exercise of faith as to a support. Those who start out now to preach the truth have nothing to venture. They have no risks to run, no special sacrifices to make. The system of truth is made ready to their hand, and publications are provided for them, vindicating the truths they advance.

Some young men start out with no real sense of the exalted character of the work. They have no privations, hardships, or severe conflicts to meet, which would call for the exercise of faith. They do not cultivate practical self-denial and cherish a spirit of sacrifice. Some are becoming proud and lifted up, and have no real burden of the work upon them. The True Witness speaks to these ministers: "Be zealous therefore, and repent." Some of them are so lifted up in pride that they are really a hindrance and a curse to the precious cause of God. They do not exert a saving influence upon others. These men need to be thoroughly converted to God themselves and sanctified by the truths they present to others.

POINTED TESTIMONIES IN THE CHURCH

Very many feel impatient and jealous because they are frequently disturbed with warnings and reproofs which keep

*NOTE: The first attempts of systematic giving, which provided for a specified weekly offering for each member, and an amount equal to a percentage of property valuation, was known as Systematic Benevolence. It was the forerunner of the tithing system so well understood by Seventh-day Adventists today.

[WHITE TRUSTEES.]

their sins before them. Says the True Witness: "I know thy works." The motives, the purposes, the unbelief, the suspicions and jealousies may be hid from men, but not from Christ. The True Witness comes as a counselor: "I counsel thee to buy of Me gold tried in the fire, that thou mayest be rich; and white raiment, that thou mayest be clothed, and that the shame of thy nakedness do not appear; and anoint thine eyes with eyesalve, that thou mayest see. As many as I love, I rebuke and chasten; be zealous therefore, and repent. Behold, I stand at the door, and knock: if any man hear My voice, and open the door, I will come in to him, and will sup with him, and he with Me. To him that overcometh will I grant to sit with Me in My throne, even as I also overcame, and am set down with My Father in His throne." Revelation 3:18-21.

Those who are reproved by the Spirit of God should not rise up against the humble instrument. It is God, and not an erring mortal, who has spoken to save them from ruin. Those who despise the warning will be left in blindness to become self-deceived. But those who heed it, and zealously go about the work of separating their sins from them in order to have the needed graces, will be opening the door of their hearts that the dear Saviour may come in and dwell with them. This class you will ever find in perfect harmony with the testimony of the Spirit of God.

Ministers who are preaching present truth should not neglect the solemn message to the Laodiceans. The testimony of the True Witness is not a smooth message. The Lord does not say to them, You are about right; you have borne chastisement and reproof that you never deserved; you have been unnecessarily discouraged by severity; you are not guilty of the wrongs and sins for which you have been reproved.

The True Witness declares that when you suppose you are really in a good condition of prosperity you are in need of everything. It is not enough for ministers to present theoretical subjects; they should also present those subjects which are practical. They need to study the practical lessons that Christ gave His disciples and make a close application of the same to their own souls and to the people. Because Christ bears this rebuking testimony, shall we suppose that He is destitute of tender love to His people? Oh, no! He who died to redeem man from death, loves with a divine love, and those whom He loves He rebukes. "As many as I love, I rebuke and chasten." Revelation 3:19. But many will not receive the message that Heaven in mercy sends them. They cannot endure to be told of their neglect of duty and of their wrongs, their selfishness, their pride and love of the world.

Perils of the Last Days.—We are living in a most solemn, important time of this earth's history. We are amid the perils of the last days. Important and fearful events are before us. How necessary that all who do fear God and love His law should humble themselves before Him, and be afflicted and mourn, and confess the sins that have separated God from His people. That which should excite the greatest alarm is that we do not feel or understand our condition, our low estate, and that we are satisfied to remain as we are. We should flee to the word of God and to prayer, individually seeking the Lord earnestly, that we may find Him. We should make this our first business.—1872, vol. 3, p. 53.

Duty to Reprove Sin

I HAVE been shown that God here illustrates how He regards sin among those who profess to be His commandment-keeping people. Those whom He has specially honored with witnessing the remarkable exhibitions of His power, as did ancient Israel, and who will even then venture to disregard His express directions, will be subjects of His wrath. He would teach His people that disobedience and sin are exceedingly offensive to Him and are not to be lightly regarded. He shows us that when His people are found in sin they should at once take decided measures to put that sin from them, that His frown may not rest upon them all.

But if the sins of the people are passed over by those in responsible positions, His frown will be upon them, and the people of God, as a body, will be held responsible for those sins. In His dealings with His people in the past the Lord shows the necessity of purifying the church from wrongs. One sinner may diffuse darkness that will exclude the light of God from the entire congregation. When the people realize that darkness is settling upon them, and they do not know the cause, they should seek God earnestly, in great humility and self-abasement, until the wrongs which grieve His Spirit are searched out and put away.

The prejudice which has arisen against us because we have reproved the wrongs that God has shown me existed, and the cry that has been raised of harshness and severity, are unjust. God bids us speak, and we will not be silent. If wrongs are apparent among His people, and if the servants of God pass on indifferent to them, they virtually sustain and justify the sinner, and are alike guilty and will just as surely receive the

1873, vol. 3, pp. 265-269 (The Laodicean Church).

displeasure of God; for they will be made responsible for the sins of the guilty. In vision I have been pointed to many instances where the displeasure of God has been incurred by a neglect on the part of His servants to deal with the wrongs and sins existing among them. Those who have excused these wrongs have been thought by the people to be very amiable and lovely in disposition, simply because they shunned to discharge a plain Scriptural duty. The task was not agreeable to their feelings; therefore they avoided it.

The spirit of hatred which has existed with some because the wrongs among God's people have been reproved has brought blindness and a fearful deception upon their own souls, making it impossible for them to discriminate between right and wrong. They have put out their own spiritual eyesight. They may witness wrongs, but they do not feel as did Joshua and humble themselves because the danger of souls is felt by them.

The true people of God, who have the spirit of the work of the Lord and the salvation of souls at heart, will ever view sin in its real, sinful character. They will always be on the side of faithful and plain dealing with sins which easily beset the people of God. Especially in the closing work for the church, in the sealing time of the one hundred and forty-four thousand who are to stand without fault before the throne of God, will they feel most deeply the wrongs of God's professed people. This is forcibly set forth by the prophet's illustration of the last work under the figure of the men each having a slaughter weapon in his hand. One man among them was clothed with linen, with a writer's inkhorn by his side. "And the Lord said unto him, Go through the midst of the city, through the midst of Jerusalem, and set a mark upon the foreheads of the men that sigh and that cry for all the abominations that be done in the midst thereof." Ezekiel 9:4.

Who are standing in the counsel of God at this time? Is it those who virtually excuse wrongs among the professed people of God and who murmur in their hearts, if not openly, against those who would reprove sin? Is it those who take their stand against them and sympathize with those who commit wrong? No, indeed! Unless they repent, and leave the work of Satan in oppressing those who have the burden of the work and in holding up the hands of sinners in Zion, they will never receive the mark of God's sealing approval. They will fall in the general destruction of the wicked, represented by the work of the five men bearing slaughter weapons. Mark this point with care: Those who receive the pure mark of truth, wrought in them by the power of the Holy Ghost, represented by a mark by the man in linen, are those "that sigh and that cry for all the abominations that be done" in the church. Their love for purity and the honor and glory of God is such, and they have so clear a view of the exceeding sinfulness of sin, that they are represented as being in agony, even sighing and crying. Read the ninth chapter of Ezekiel.

But the general slaughter of all those who do not thus see the wide contrast between sin and righteousness, and do not feel as those do who stand in the counsel of God and receive the mark, is described in the order to the five men with slaughter weapons: "Go ye after him through the city, and smite: let not your eye spare, neither have ye pity: slay utterly old and young, both maids, and little children, and women: but come not near any man upon whom is the mark; and begin at My sanctuary." Verses 5, 6.

ACHAN AN OBJECT LESSON

In the case of Achan's sin God said to Joshua: "Neither will I be with you any more, except ye destroy the accursed from among you." Joshua 7:12. How does this instance compare with the course pursued by those who will not raise their voice against sin and wrong, but whose sympathies are ever found with those who trouble the camp of Israel with their sins? Said God to Joshua: "Thou canst not stand before thine enemies, until ye take away the accursed thing from among you." Verse 13. He pronounced the punishment which would follow the transgression of His covenant.

Joshua then began a diligent search to find out the guilty one. He took Israel by their tribes, then by their families, and next individually; and Achan was designated as the guilty one. But that the matter might be plain to all Israel, that there should be no occasion given them to murmur and to say that the guiltless was made to suffer, Joshua used policy. He knew Achan was the transgressor and that he had concealed his sin and provoked God against His people. Joshua discreetly induced Achan to make confession of his sin, that God's honor and justice might be vindicated before Israel. "And Joshua said unto Achan, My son, give, I pray thee, glory to the Lord God of Israel, and make confession unto Him; and tell me now what thou hast done; hide it not from me.

"And Achan answered Joshua, and said, Indeed I have sinned against the Lord God of Israel, and thus and thus have I done: When I saw among the spoils a goodly Babylonish garment, and two hundred shekels of silver, and a wedge of gold of fifty shekels weight, then I coveted them, and took them; and, behold, they are hid in the earth in the midst of my tent, and the silver under it. So Joshua sent messengers, and they ran unto the tent; and, behold, it was hid in his tent, and the silver under it. And they took them out of the midst of the tent, and brought them unto Joshua, and unto all the children of Israel, and laid them out before the Lord. And Joshua, and all Israel with him, took Achan the son of Zerah, and the silver, and the garment, and the wedge of gold, and his sons, and his daughters, and his oxen, and his asses, and his sheep, and his tent, and all that he had: and they brought them unto the Valley of Achor. And Joshua said, Why hast thou troubled us? the Lord shall trouble thee this day. And all Israel stoned him with stones, and burned them with fire, after they had stoned them with stones." Verses 19-25.

The Lord told Joshua that Achan had not only taken the things which He had positively charged them not to take, lest they be accursed, but he had stolen and had also dissembled. The Lord said that Jericho and all its spoils should be consumed, except the gold and silver, which were to be reserved for the treasury of the Lord. The victory of taking Jericho was not obtained through warfare or the exposure of the people. The Captain of the Lord's host had led the armies of heaven. The battle was the Lord's; it was He who fought the battle. The children of Israel did not strike a blow. The victory and glory were the Lord's, and the spoils were His. He directed all to be consumed except the gold and silver, which He reserved for His treasury. Achan understood well the reserve made and that the treasures of gold and silver which he coveted were the Lord's. He stole from God's treasury for his own benefit.

Confessing or Denying Christ

In our mingling in society, in families, or in whatever relations of life we are placed, either limited or extended, there are many ways wherein we may acknowledge our Lord and many ways wherein we may deny Him. We may deny Him in our words, by speaking evil of others, by foolish talking, jesting and joking, by idle or unkind words, or by prevaricating, speaking contrary to truth. In our words we may confess that Christ is not in us. In our character we may deny Him by loving our ease, by shunning the duties and burdens of life which someone must bear if we do not, and by loving sinful pleasure. We may also deny Christ by pride of dress and conformity to the world, or by uncourteous behavior. We may deny Him by loving our own opinions and by seeking to maintain and justify self. We may also deny Him in allowing the mind to run in the channel of lovesick sentimentalism and to brood over our supposed hard lot and trials.

No one can truly confess Christ before the world unless the mind and spirit of Christ live in him. It is impossible to communicate that which we have not. The conversation and the deportment should be a real and visible expression of grace and truth within. If the heart is sanctified, submissive, and humble, the fruits will be seen outwardly and will be a most effectual confession of Christ. Words and profession are not enough. You, my sister, must have something more than this. You are deceiving yourself. Your spirit, your character, and your actions do not show a spirit of meekness, self-denial, and charity. Words and profession may express much humility and love; but if the conduct is not regulated daily by the grace of God, you are not a partaker of the heavenly gift, you have

1873, vol. 3, pp. 331-335 (Daydreaming).

not forsaken all for Christ, you have not surrendered your own will and pleasure to become His disciple.

You commit sin and deny your Saviour by dwelling on gloomy things, by gathering trials to yourself, and by borrowing troubles. You bring the troubles of tomorrow into today, and embitter your own heart, and bring burdens and a cloud upon those around you, by manufacturing trials. The precious probationary time that God has given you in which to do good and become rich in good works you are very unwise to employ in thinking unhappy thoughts and in airy castle-building. You suffer your imagination to run upon subjects that will bring you no relief or happiness. Your daydreaming stands directly in the way of your obtaining a sound, healthy, intelligent experience in the things of God and a moral fitness for the better life.

The truth of God received into the heart is able to make you wise unto salvation. In believing and obeying it you will receive grace sufficient for the duties and trials of today. Grace for tomorrow you do not need. You should feel that you have only to do with today. Overcome for today; deny self for today; watch and pray for today; obtain victories in God for today. Our circumstances and surroundings, the changes daily transpiring around us, and the written word of God which discerns and proves all things—these are sufficient to teach us our duty and just what we ought to do, day by day. Instead of suffering your mind to run in a channel of thought from which you will derive no benefit, you should be searching the Scriptures daily and doing those duties in daily life which may now be irksome to you, but which must be done by someone.

LESSONS FROM NATURE

The beauties of nature have a tongue that speaks to our senses without ceasing. The open heart can be impressed with the love and glory of God as seen in the works of His hand.

The listening ear can hear and understand the communications of God through the works of nature. There is a lesson in the sunbeam and in the various objects in nature that God has presented to our view. The green fields, the lofty trees, the buds and flowers, the passing cloud, the falling rain, the babbling brook, the sun, moon, and stars in the heavens, all invite our attention and meditation, and bid us become acquainted with God, who made them all. The lessons to be learned from the various objects of the natural world are these: They are obedient to the will of their Creator; they never deny God, never refuse obedience to any intimation of His will. Fallen beings alone refuse to yield full obedience to their Maker. Their words and works are at variance with God and opposed to the principles of His government. . . .

Those professed Christians who are constantly whining and complaining, and who seem to think happiness and a cheerful countenance a sin, have not the genuine article of religion. Those who look upon nature's beautiful scenery as they would upon a dead picture, who choose to look upon dead leaves rather than to gather the beautiful living flowers, who take a mournful pleasure in all that is melancholy in the language spoken to them by the natural world, who see no beauty in valleys clothed with living green and grand mountain heights clothed with verdure, who close their senses to the joyful voice which speaks to them in nature and which is sweet and musical to the listening ear—these are not in Christ. They are not walking in the light, but are gathering to themselves darkness and gloom, when they could just as well have brightness and the blessing of the Sun of Righteousness arising in their hearts with healing in His beams.

Despisers of Reproof

The apostle Paul plainly states that the experience of the Israelites in their travels has been recorded for the benefit of those living in this age of the world, those upon whom the ends of the world are come. We do not consider that our dangers are any less than those of the Hebrews, but greater. There will be temptations to jealousies and murmurings, and there will be outspoken rebellion, as are recorded of ancient Israel. There will ever be a spirit to rise up against the reproof of sins and wrongs. But shall the voice of reproof be hushed because of this? If so, we shall be in no better situation than are the various denominations in our land who are afraid to touch the errors and prevailing sins of the people.

Those whom God has set apart as ministers of righteousness have solemn responsibilities laid upon them to reprove the sins of the people. Paul commanded Titus: "These things speak, and exhort, and rebuke with all authority. Let no man despise thee." Titus 2:15. There are ever those who will despise the one who dares to reprove sin; but there are times when reproof must be given. Paul directs Titus to rebuke a certain class sharply, that they may be sound in the faith. Men and women who, with their different organizations, are brought together in church capacity have peculiarities and faults. As these are developed, they will require reproof. If those who are placed in important positions never reproved, never rebuked, there would soon be a demoralized condition of things that would greatly dishonor God. But how shall the reproof be given? Let the apostle answer: "With all longsuffering and doctrine." 2 Timothy 4:2. Principle should be brought to bear upon the one who needs reproof, but never

1875, vol. 3, pp. 358-362 (The Great Rebellion).

should the wrongs of God's people be passed by indifferently.

There will be men and women who despise reproof and whose feelings will ever rise up against it. It is not pleasant to be told of our wrongs. In almost every case where reproof is necessary, there will be some who entirely overlook the fact that the Spirit of the Lord has been grieved and His cause reproached. These will pity those who deserved reproof, because personal feelings have been hurt. All this unsanctified sympathy places the sympathizers where they are sharers in the guilt of the one reproved. In nine cases out of ten if the one reproved had been left under a sense of his wrongs, he might have been helped to see them and thereby have been reformed. But meddlesome, unsanctified sympathizers place altogether a wrong construction upon the motives of the reprover and the nature of the reproof given, and by sympathizing with the one reproved lead him to feel that he has been really abused; and his feelings rise up in rebellion against the one who has only done his duty. Those who faithfully discharge their unpleasant duties under a sense of their accountability to God will receive His blessing. God requires His servants to be always in earnest to do His will. In the apostle's charge to Timothy he exhorts him to "preach the word; be instant in season, out of season; reprove, rebuke, exhort with all long-suffering and doctrine." Verse 2.

The Hebrews were not willing to submit to the directions and restrictions of the Lord. They simply wanted their own way, to follow the leadings of their own mind, and be controlled by their own judgment. Could they have been left free to do this, no complaints would have been made of Moses; but they were restless under restraint.

UNITY IN ACTION AND JUDGMENT

God would have His people disciplined and brought into harmony of action, that they may see eye to eye and be of the same mind and of the same judgment. In order to bring about this state of things, there is much to be done. The carnal heart must be subdued and transformed. God designs that there shall ever be a living testimony in the church. It will be necessary to reprove and exhort, and some will need to be rebuked sharply, as the case demands. We hear the plea: "Oh, I am so sensitive, I cannot bear the least reflection!" If these persons would state the case correctly, they would say: "I am so self-willed, so self-sufficient, so proud-spirited, that I will not be dictated to; I will not be reproved. I claim the right of individual judgment; I have a right to believe and talk as I please." The Lord would not have us yield up our individuality. But what man is a proper judge of how far this matter of individual independence should be carried?

Peter exhorts his brethren: "Likewise, ye younger, submit yourselves unto the elder. Yea, all of you be subject one to another, and be clothed with humility: for God resisteth the proud, and giveth grace to the humble." 1 Peter 5:5. The apostle Paul also exhorts his Philippian brethren to unity and humility: "If there be therefore any consolation in Christ, if any comfort of love, if any fellowship of the Spirit, if any bowels and mercies, fulfill ye my joy, that ye be like-minded, having the same love, being of one accord, of one mind. Let nothing be done through strife or vainglory; but in lowliness of mind let each esteem other better than themselves. Look not every man on his own things, but every man also on the things of others. Let this mind be in you, which was also in Christ Jesus." Philippians 2:1-5. Again Paul exhorts his brethren: "Let love be without dissimulation. Abhor that which is evil; cleave to that which is good. Be kindly affectioned one to another with brotherly love; in honor preferring one another." Romans 12:9, 10. In writing to the Ephesians he says: "Submitting yourselves one to another in the fear of God." Ephesians 5:21.

The history of the Israelites presents before us the great danger of deception. Many do not have a sense of the sinfulness of their own natures nor of the grace of forgiveness. They are in nature's darkness, subject to temptations and to great deception. They are far from God; yet they take great satisfaction in their lives, when their conduct is abhorred of God. This class will ever be at war with the leadings of the Spirit of God, especially with reproof. They do not wish to be disturbed. Occasionally they have selfish fears and good purposes, and sometimes anxious thoughts and convictions; but they have not a depth of experience, because they are not riveted to the eternal Rock. This class never see the necessity of the plain testimony. Sin does not appear so exceedingly sinful to them for the very reason that they are not walking in the light as Christ is in the light.

There is still another class who have had great light and special conviction, and a genuine experience in the workings of the Spirit of God; but the manifold temptations of Satan have overcome them. They do not appreciate the light that God has given them. They do not heed the warnings and reproofs from the Spirit of God. They are under condemnation. These will ever be at variance with the straight testimony because it condemns them.

God designs that His people shall be a unit, that they shall see eye to eye and be of the same mind and of the same judgment. This cannot be accomplished without a clear, pointed, living testimony in the church. The prayer of Christ was that His disciples might be one as He was one with His Father. "Neither pray I for these alone, but for them also which shall believe on Me through their word; that they all may be one; as Thou, Father, art in Me, and I in Thee, that they also may be one in Us: that the world may believe that Thou hast sent Me. And the glory which Thou gavest Me I have given them; that they may be one, even as We are one: I in them, and Thou in Me, that they may be made perfect in one; and that the world may know that Thou hast sent Me, and hast loved them, as Thou hast loved Me." John 17:20-23.

Appeal to the Young

Dear Youth: From time to time the Lord has given me testimonies of warning for you. He has given you encouragement if you would yield your hearts' best and holiest affections to Him. As these warnings revive distinctly before me, I feel a sense of your danger that I know you do not feel. The school located in Battle Creek* brings together many young people of different mental organizations. If these youth are not consecrated to God and obedient to His will, and do not walk humbly in the way of His commandments, the location of a school in Battle Creek will prove a means of great discouragement to the church. This school may be made a blessing or a curse. I entreat you who have named the name of Christ to depart from all iniquity and develop characters that God can approve.

I inquire: Do you believe that the testimonies of reproof which have been given you are of God? If you really believe that the voice of God has spoken to you, pointing out your dangers, do you heed the counsels given? Do you keep these testimonies of warning fresh in your minds by reading them often with prayerful hearts? The Lord has spoken to you, children and youth, again and again; but you have been slow to heed the warnings given. If you have not rebelliously braced your hearts against the views that God has given of your characters and your dangers, and against the course marked out for you to pursue, some of you have been inat-

1875, vol. 3, pp. 362-371.

*Note: When this statement was penned, the only Seventh-day Adventist college was located at Battle Creek, Michigan.
[White Trustees.]

tentive in regard to the things required of you that you might gain spiritual strength and be a blessing in the school, in the church, and to all with whom you associate.

Young men and women, you are accountable to God for the light that He has given you. This light and these warnings, if not heeded, will rise up in the judgment against you. Your dangers have been plainly stated; you have been cautioned and guarded on every side, hedged in with warnings. In the house of God you have listened to the most solemn, heart-searching truths presented by the servants of God in demonstration of the Spirit. What weight do these solemn appeals have upon your hearts? What influence do they have upon your characters? You will be held responsible for every one of these appeals and warnings. They will rise up in the judgment to condemn those who pursue a life of vanity, levity, and pride.

Dear young friends, that which you sow, you will also reap. Now is the sowing time for you. What will the harvest be? What are you sowing? Every word you utter, every act you perform, is a seed which will bear good or evil fruit and will result in joy or sorrow to the sower. As is the seed sown, so will be the crop. God has given you great light and many privileges. After this light has been given, after your dangers have been plainly presented before you, the responsibility becomes yours. The manner in which you treat the light that God gives you will turn the scale for happiness or woe. You are shaping your destinies for yourselves.

You all have an influence for good or for evil on the minds and characters of others. And just the influence which you exert is written in the book of records in heaven. An angel is attending you and taking record of your words and actions. When you rise in the morning, do you feel your helplessness and your need of strength from God? and do you humbly, heartily make known your wants to your heavenly Father? If so, angels mark your prayers, and if these prayers have not gone forth out of feigned lips, when you are in danger of unconsciously doing wrong and exerting an influence which will lead others to do wrong, your guardian angel will be by your side, prompting you to a better course, choosing your words for you, and influencing your actions.

If you feel in no danger, and if you offer no prayer for help and strength to resist temptations, you will be sure to go astray; your neglect of duty will be marked in the book of God in heaven, and you will be found wanting in the trying day.

There are some around you who have been religiously instructed, and some who have been indulged, petted, flattered, and praised until they have been literally spoiled for practical life. I am speaking in regard to persons that I know. Their characters are so warped by indulgence, flattery, and indolence that they are useless for this life. And if useless so far as this life is concerned, what may we hope for that life where all is purity and holiness, and where all have harmonious characters? I have prayed for these persons; I have addressed them personally. I could see the influence that they would exert over other minds in leading them to vanity, love of dress, and carelessness in regard to their eternal interests. The only hope for this class is for them to take heed to their ways, humble their proud, vain hearts before God, make confession of their sins, and be converted.

LOVE OF DISPLAY AND AMUSEMENT

Vanity in dress as well as the love of amusement is a great temptation for the youth. God has sacred claims upon us all. He claims the whole heart, the whole soul, the whole affections. The answer which is sometimes made to this statement is: "Oh, I do not profess to be a Christian!" What if you do not? Has not God the same claims upon you that He has upon the one who professes to be His child? Because you are bold in your careless disregard of sacred things, is your sin of neglect and rebellion passed over by the Lord? Every day that you disregard the claims of God, every opportunity of offered mercy that you slight, is charged to your account and will swell the list of sins against you in the day when the accounts of every soul will be investigated. I address you, young men and women, professors or nonprofessors: God calls for your affections, for your cheerful obedience and devotion to Him. You now have a short time of probation, and you may improve this opportunity to make an unconditional surrender to God.

Obedience and submission to God's requirements are the conditions given by the inspired apostle by which we become children of God, members of the royal family. Every child and youth, every man and woman, has Jesus rescued by His own blood from the abyss of ruin to which Satan was compelling them to go. Because sinners will not accept of the salvation freely offered them, are they released from their obligations? Their choosing to remain in sin and bold transgression does not lessen their guilt. Jesus paid a price for them, and they belong to Him. They are His property; and if they will not yield obedience to Him who has given His life for them, but devote their time and strength and talents to the service of Satan, they are earning their wages, which is death.

Immortal glory and eternal life is the reward that our Redeemer offers to those who will be obedient to Him. He has made it possible for them to perfect Christian character through His name and to overcome on their own account as He overcame in their behalf. He has given them an example in His own life, showing them how they may overcome. "The wages of sin is death; but the gift of God is eternal life through Jesus Christ our Lord." Romans 6:23.

The claims of God are equally binding upon all. Those who choose to neglect the great salvation offered to them freely, who choose to serve themselves and remain enemies of God, enemies of the self-sacrificing Redeemer, are earning their wages. They are sowing to the flesh and will of the flesh reap corruption.

Those who have put on Christ by baptism, by this act showing their separation from the world and that they have covenanted to walk in newness of life, should not set up idols in their hearts. Those who have once rejoiced in the evidence of sins forgiven, who have tasted a Saviour's love and who then persist in uniting with the foes of Christ, rejecting the perfect righteousness that Jesus offers them and choosing the ways that He has condemned, will be more severely judged than the heathen who have never had the light and have never known God or His law. Those who refuse to follow the light which God has given them, choosing the amusements, vanities, and follies of the world, and refusing to conform their conduct to the just and holy requirements of God's law, are guilty of the most aggravating sins in the sight of God. Their guilt and their wages will be proportionate to the light and privileges which they have had.

We see the world absorbed in their own amusements. The first and highest thoughts of the larger portion, especially of women, are of display. Love of dress and pleasure is wrecking the happiness of thousands. And some of those who profess to love and keep the commandments of God ape this class as near as they possibly can and retain the Christian name. Some of the young are so eager for display that they are even willing to give up the Christian name if they can only follow out their inclination for vanity of dress and love of pleasure.

Self-denial in dress is a part of our Christian duty. To dress plainly, abstaining from display of jewelry and ornaments of every kind, is in keeping with our faith. Are we of the number who see the folly of worldlings in indulging in extravagance of dress as well as in love of amusements? If so, we should be of that class who shun everything that gives sanction to this spirit which takes possession of the minds and hearts of those who live for this world only and who have no thought or care for the next.

Christian youth, I have seen in some of you a love for dress and display which has pained me. In some who have been well instructed, who have had religious privileges from their babyhood, and who have put on Christ by baptism, thus professing to be dead to the world, I have seen a vanity in dress and a levity in conduct that have grieved the dear Saviour and have been a reproach to the cause of God. I have marked with pain your religious declension and your disposition to trim and ornament your apparel. Some have been so unfortunate as to come into possession of gold chains or pins, or both, and have shown bad taste in exhibiting them, making them conspicuous to attract attention. I can but associate these characters with the vain peacock, that displays his gorgeous feathers for admiration. It is all this poor bird has to attract attention, for his voice and form are anything but attractive.

THE ORNAMENT OF A MEEK AND QUIET SPIRIT

The young may endeavor to excel in seeking for the ornament of a meek and quiet spirit, a jewel of inestimable value that may be worn with heavenly grace. This adorning will possess attractions for many in this world, and will be esteemed of great price by the heavenly angels, and above all by our heavenly Father, and will fit the wearers to be welcome guests in the heavenly courts.

The youth have faculties that, with proper cultivation, would qualify them for almost any position of trust. If they had made it their object in obtaining an education to so exercise and develop the powers that God has given them that they might be useful and prove a blessing to others, their minds would not be dwarfed to an inferior standard. They would show depth of thought and firmness of principle, and would command influence and respect. They might have an elevating influence upon others, which would lead souls to see and acknowledge the power of an intelligent Christian life. Those who have greater care to ornament their persons for display than to educate the mind and exercise their powers for the greatest usefulness, that they may glorify God, do not realize their accountability to God. They will be inclined to be superficial in all they undertake and will narrow their usefulness and dwarf their intellect.

I feel deeply pained at heart for the fathers and mothers of these youth, as well as for the children. There has been a lack in the training of these children, which leaves a heavy responsibility somewhere. Parents who have petted and indulged their children instead of from principle judiciously restraining them, can see the characters they have formed. As the training has been, so the character inclines.

FAITHFUL ABRAHAM

My mind goes back to faithful Abraham, who, in obedience to the divine command given him in a night vision at Beersheba, pursues his journey with Isaac by his side. He sees before him the mountain which God had told him He would signalize as the one upon which he was to sacrifice. He removes the wood from the shoulder of his servant and lays it upon Isaac, the one to be offered. He girds up his soul with firmness and agonizing sternness, ready for the work which God requires him to do. With a breaking heart and unnerved hand, he takes the fire, while Isaac inquires: Father, here is the fire and the wood; but where is the offering? But, oh, Abraham cannot tell him now!

Father and son build the altar, and the terrible moment comes for Abraham to make known to Isaac that which has agonized his soul all that long journey, that Isaac himself is the victim. Isaac is not a lad; he is a full-grown young man. He could have refused to submit to his father's design had he chosen to do so. He does not accuse his father of insanity, nor does he even seek to change his purpose. He submits. He believes in the love of his father and that he would not make this terrible sacrifice of his only son if God had not bidden him do so. Isaac is bound by the trembling, loving hands of his pitying father because God has said it. The son submits to the sacrifice because he believes in the integrity of his father. But when everything is ready, when the faith of the father and the submission of the son are fully tested, the angel of God stays the uplifted hand of Abraham that is about to slay his son and tells him that it is enough. "Now I know that thou fearest God, seeing thou hast not withheld thy son, thine only son from Me." Genesis 22:12.

This act of faith in Abraham is recorded for our benefit. It teaches us the great lesson of confidence in the requirements of God, however close and cutting they may be; and it teaches children perfect submission to their parents and to God. By Abraham's obedience we are taught that nothing is too precious for us to give to God.

A LESSON IN TYPE

Isaac was a figure of the Son of God, who was offered a sacrifice for the sins of the world. God would impress upon Abraham the gospel of salvation to man. In order to do this, and make the truth a reality to him as well as to test his faith, He required him to slay his darling Isaac. All the sorrow and agony that Abraham endured through that dark and fearful trial were for the purpose of deeply impressing upon his understanding the plan of redemption for fallen man. He was made to understand in his own experience how unutterable was the self-denial of the infinite God in giving His own Son to die to rescue man from utter ruin. To Abraham no mental torture could be equal to that which he endured in obeying the divine command to sacrifice his son.

God gave His Son to a life of humiliation, self-denial, poverty, toil, reproach, and to the agonizing death of crucifixion. But there was no angel to bear the joyful message: "It is enough; You need not die, My well-beloved Son." Legions of angels were sorrowfully waiting, hoping that, as in the case of Isaac, God would at the last moment prevent His shameful death. But angels were not permitted to bear any such message to God's dear Son. The humiliation in the judgment hall and on the way to Calvary went on. He was mocked, derided, and spit upon. He endured the jeers, taunts, and revilings of those who hated Him, until upon the cross He bowed His head and died.

Could God give us any greater proof of His love than in thus giving His Son to pass through this scene of suffering? And as the gift of God to man was a free gift, His love infinite, so His claims upon our confidence, our obedience, our whole heart, and the wealth of our affections are correspondingly infinite. He requires all that it is possible for man to give. The submission on our part must be proportionate to the gift of God; it must be complete and wanting in nothing. We are all debtors to God. He has claims upon us that we cannot meet without giving ourselves a full and willing sacrifice. He claims prompt and willing obedience, and nothing short of this will He accept. We have opportunity now to secure the love and favor of God. This year may be the last year in the lives of some who read this. Are there any among the youth who read this appeal who would choose the pleasures of the world before that peace which Christ gives the earnest seeker and the cheerful doer of His will?

CHARACTERS BEING WEIGHED

God is weighing our characters, our conduct, and our motives in the balances of the sanctuary. It will be a fearful thing to be pronounced wanting in love and obedience by our Redeemer, who died upon the cross to draw our hearts unto Him. God has bestowed upon us great and precious gifts. He has given us light and a knowledge of His will, so that we need not err or walk in darkness. To be weighed in the balance and found wanting in the day of final settlement and rewards will be a fearful thing, a terrible mistake which can never be corrected. Young friends, shall the book of God be searched in vain for your names?

God has appointed you a work to do for Him which will make you colaborers with Him. All around you there are souls to save. There are those whom you can encourage and bless by your earnest efforts. You may turn souls from sin to righteousness. When you have a sense of your accountability to God you will feel the need of faithfulness in prayer and faithfulness in watching against the temptations of Satan. You will, if you are indeed Christians, feel more like mourning over the moral darkness in the world than indulging in levity and pride of dress. You will be among those who are sighing and crying for the abominations that are done in the land. You will resist the temptations of Satan to indulge in vanity and in trimmings and ornaments for display. The mind is narrowed and the intellect dwarfed that can be gratified with these frivolous things to the neglect of high responsibilities.

The youth in our day may be workers with Christ if they will; and in working, their faith will strengthen and their knowledge of the divine will will increase. Every true purpose and every act of right doing will be recorded in the book of life. I wish I could arouse the youth to see and feel the sinfulness of living for their own gratification and dwarfing their intellects to the cheap, vain things of this life. If they would elevate their thoughts and words above the frivolous attractions of this world and make it their aim to glorify God, His peace, which passeth all understanding, would be theirs.

The Power of Prayer in Temptation

How graciously and tenderly our heavenly Father deals with His children! He preserves them from a thousand dangers to them unseen and guards them from the subtle arts of Satan, lest they should be destroyed. Because the protecting care of God through His angels is not seen by our dull vision, we do not try to contemplate and appreciate the ever-watchful interest that our kind and benevolent Creator has in the work of His hands; and we are not grateful for the multitude of mercies that He daily bestows upon us.

The young are ignorant of the many dangers to which they are daily exposed. They can never fully know them all; but if they are watchful and prayerful, God will keep their consciences sensitive and their perceptions clear, that they may discern the workings of the enemy and be fortified against his attacks. But many of the young have so long followed their own inclinations that duty is a meaningless word to them. They do not realize the high and holy duties which they may have to do for the benefit of others and for the glory of God; and they utterly neglect to perform them.

If the youth could only awake to deeply feel their need of strength from God to resist the temptations of Satan, precious victories would be theirs, and they would obtain a valuable experience in the Christian warfare. How few of the young think of the exhortation of the inspired apostle Peter: "Be sober, be vigilant; because your adversary the devil, as a roaring lion, walketh about, seeking whom he may devour: whom resist steadfast in the faith." 1 Peter 5:8, 9. In the vision given to John he saw the power of Satan over men and exclaimed: "Woe to the inhabiters of the earth and of the sea!

1875, vol. 3, pp. 373-378 (Appeal to the Young).

for the devil is come down unto you, having great wrath, because he knoweth that he hath but a short time." Revelation 12:12.

The only safety for the young is in unceasing watchfulness and humble prayer. They need not flatter themselves that they can be Christians without these. Satan conceals his temptations and his devices under a cover of light, as when he approached Christ in the wilderness. He was then in appearance as one of the heavenly angels. The adversary of our souls will approach us as a heavenly guest, and the apostle recommends sobriety and vigilance as our only safety. The young who indulge in carelessness and levity, and who neglect Christian duties, are continually falling under the temptations of the enemy, instead of overcoming as Christ overcame.

The service of Christ is not drudgery to the fully consecrated soul. Obedience to our Saviour does not detract from our happiness and true pleasure in this life, but it has a refining, elevating power upon our characters. The daily study of the precious words of life found in the Bible strengthens the intellect and furnishes a knowledge of the grand and glorious works of God in nature. Through the study of the Scriptures we obtain a correct knowledge of how to live so as to enjoy the greatest amount of unalloyed happiness. The Bible student is also furnished with Scripture arguments so that he can meet the doubts of unbelievers and remove them by the clear light of truth. Those who have searched the Scriptures may ever be fortified against the temptations of Satan; they may be thoroughly furnished to all good works and prepared to give to every man that asketh them a reason of the hope that is in them. . . .

While you pray, dear youth, that you may not be led into temptation, remember that your work does not end with the prayer. You must then answer your own prayer as far as possible by resisting temptation, and leave that which you cannot do for yourselves for Jesus to do for you. You cannot be too guarded in your words and in your deportment, lest you invite the enemy to tempt you. Many of our youth, by their careless disregard of the warnings and reproofs given them, open the door wide for Satan to enter. With God's word for our guide and Jesus as our heavenly Teacher we need not be ignorant of His requirements or of Satan's devices and be overcome by his temptations. It will be no unpleasant task to be obedient to the will of God when we yield ourselves fully to be directed by His Spirit.

Tithes and Offerings

The mission of the church of Christ is to save perishing sinners. It is to make known the love of God to men and to win them to Christ by the efficacy of that love. The truth for this time must be carried into the dark corners of the earth, and this work may begin at home. The followers of Christ should not live selfish lives; but, imbued with the Spirit of Christ, they should work in harmony with Him.

There are causes for the present coldness and unbelief. The love of the world and the cares of life separate the soul from God. The water of life must be in us, and flowing out from us, springing up into everlasting life. We must work out what God works in. If the Christian would enjoy the light of life, he must increase his efforts to bring others to the knowledge of the truth. His life must be characterized by exertion and sacrifices to do others good; and then there will be no complaints of lack of enjoyment.

Angels are ever engaged in working for the happiness of others. This is their joy. That which selfish hearts would consider humiliating service, ministering to those who are wretched and in every way inferior in character and rank, is the work of the pure, sinless angels in the royal courts of heaven. The spirit of Christ's self-sacrificing love is the spirit which pervades heaven and is the very essence of its bliss.

Those who feel no special pleasure in seeking to be a blessing to others, in working, even at a sacrifice, to do them good, cannot have the spirit of Christ or of heaven; for they have no union with the work of heavenly angels and cannot participate in the bliss that imparts elevated joy to them. Christ has said: "Joy shall be in heaven over one sinner that repent-

1875, vol. 3, pp. 381-408.

eth, more than over ninety and nine just persons, which need no repentance." Luke 15:7. If the joy of angels is to see sinners repent, will it not be the joy of sinners, saved by the blood of Christ, to see others repent and turn to Christ through their instrumentality? In working in harmony with Christ and the holy angels we shall experience a joy that cannot be realized aside from this work.

The principle of the cross of Christ brings all who believe under heavy obligations to deny self, to impart light to others, and to give of their means to extend the light. If they are in connection with heaven they will be engaged in the work in harmony with the angels.

The principle of worldlings is to get all they can of the perishable things of this life. Selfish love of gain is the ruling principle in their lives. But the purest joy is not found in riches nor where covetousness is always craving, but where contentment reigns and where self-sacrificing love is the ruling principle. There are thousands who are passing their lives in indulgence and whose hearts are filled with repining. They are victims of selfishness and discontent in the vain effort to satisfy their minds with indulgence. But unhappiness is stamped upon their very countenances, and behind them is a desert, because their course is not fruitful in good works.

In proportion as the love of Christ fills our hearts and controls our lives, covetousness, selfishness, and love of ease will be overcome, and it will be our pleasure to do the will of Christ, whose servants we claim to be. Our happiness will then be proportionate to our unselfish works, prompted by the love of Christ.

Divine wisdom has appointed, in the plan of salvation, the law of action and reaction, making the work of beneficence, in all its branches, twice blessed. He that gives to the needy blesses others, and is blessed himself in a still greater degree. God could have reached His object in saving sinners without the aid of man; but He knew that man could not be happy without acting a part in the great work in which he would be cultivating self-denial and benevolence.

That man might not lose the blessed results of benevolence, our Redeemer formed the plan of enlisting him as His co-worker. By a chain of circumstances which would call forth his charities, He bestows upon man the best means of cultivating benevolence and keeps him habitually giving to help the poor and to advance His cause. He sends His poor as the representatives of Himself. By their necessities a ruined world are drawing forth from us talents of means and of influence to present to them the truth, of which they are in perishing need. And as we heed these calls by labor and by acts of benevolence we are assimilated to the image of Him who for our sakes became poor. In bestowing we bless others, and thus accumulate true riches.

WORLDLY INTERESTS AND HEAVENLY TREASURES

There has been a great lack of Christian benevolence in the church. Those who were the best able to do for the advancement of the cause of God have done but little. God has mercifully brought a class to the knowledge of the truth, that they might appreciate its priceless value in comparison with earthly treasures. Jesus has said to these: "Follow Me." He is testing them with an invitation to the supper which He has prepared. He is watching to see what characters they will develop, whether their own selfish interests will be considered of greater value than eternal riches. Many of these dear brethren are now by their actions framing the excuses mentioned in the following parable:

"Then said He unto him, A certain man made a great supper, and bade many: and sent his servant at suppertime to say to them that were bidden, Come; for all things are now ready. And they all with one consent began to make excuse. The first said unto him, I have bought a piece of ground, and I must needs go and see it: I pray thee have me excused. And another said, I have bought five yoke of oxen, and I go to prove them: I pray thee have me excused. And another said, I have married a wife, and therefore I cannot come. So that servant came, and showed his lord these things. Then the master of the house being angry said to his servant, Go out quickly into the streets and lanes of the city, and bring in hither the poor, and the maimed, and the halt, and the blind." Luke 14:16-21.

This parable correctly represents the condition of many professing to believe the present truth. The Lord has sent them an invitation to come to the supper which He has prepared for them at great cost to Himself; but worldly interests look to them of greater importance than the heavenly treasure. They are invited to take part in things of eternal value; but their farms, their cattle, and their home interests seem of so much greater importance than obedience to the heavenly invitation that they overpower every divine attraction, and these earthly things are made the excuse for their disobedience to the heavenly command, "Come; for all things are now ready." These brethren are blindly following the example of those represented in the parable. They look at their worldly possessions, and say: No, Lord, I cannot follow Thee; "I pray Thee have me excused."

The very blessings which God has given to these men to prove them, to see if they will render "unto God the things that are God's," they use as an excuse that they cannot obey the claims of truth. They have grasped their earthly treasure in their arms and say, "I must take care of these things; I must not neglect the things of this life; these things are mine." Thus the hearts of these men have become as unimpressible as the beaten highway. They close the door of their hearts to the heavenly messenger, who says, "Come; for all things are now ready," and throw it open, inviting the entrance of the world's burden and business cares, and Jesus knocks in vain for admittance.

THE GALLING YOKE OF SELFISHNESS

Their hearts are so overgrown with thorns and with the cares of this life that heavenly things can find no place in them. Jesus invites the weary and heavy-laden with promises of rest if they will come to Him. He invites them to exchange the galling yoke of selfishness and covetousness, which makes them slaves to mammon, for His yoke, which He declares is easy, and His burden, which is light. He says: "Learn of Me; for I am meek and lowly in heart: and ye shall find rest unto your souls." Matthew 11:29. He would have them lay aside the heavy burdens of worldly care and perplexity, and take His yoke, which is self-denial and sacrifice for others. This burden will prove to be light. Those who refuse to accept the relief which Christ offers them, and continue to wear the galling yoke of selfishness, tasking their souls to the utmost in plans to accumulate money for selfish gratification, have not experienced the peace and rest found in bearing the yoke of Christ and lifting the burdens of self-denial and disinterested benevolence which Christ has borne in their behalf.

When the love of the world takes possession of the heart and becomes a ruling passion, there is no room left for adoration to God; for the higher powers of the mind submit to the slavery of mammon, and cannot retain thoughts of God and of heaven. The mind loses its remembrance of God and is narrowed and dwarfed to the accumulation of money.

Because of selfishness and love of the world, these men have been passing on with less and less sense of the magnitude of the work for these last days. They have not educated their minds to make a business of serving God. They have not an experience in that direction. Their property has absorbed their affections and eclipsed the magnitude of the plan of salvation. While they are improving and enlarging their worldly plans, they see no necessity for the enlargement and extension of the work of God. They invest their means in temporal but not in eternal things. Their hearts are ambitious for more means. God has made them depositaries of His law, that they might let the light so graciously given them shine forth to others. But they have so increased their cares and anxieties that they have no time to bless others with their influence, to converse with their neighbors, to pray with and for them, and to seek to bring them to the knowledge of the truth.

These men are responsible for the good they might do, but from which they excuse themselves because of worldly cares and burdens, which engross their minds and absorb their affections. Souls for whom Christ died might be saved by their personal effort and godly example. Precious souls are perishing for the light which God has given to men to be reflected upon the pathway of others. But the precious light is hid under a bushel, and it gives no light to those who are in the house.

THE PARABLE OF THE TALENTS

Every man is a steward of God. To each the Master has committed His means, but man claims that means as his own. Christ says: "Occupy till I come." Luke 19:13. A time is coming when Christ will require His own with usury. He will say to each of His stewards: "Give an account of thy stewardship." Luke 16:2. Those who have hid their Lord's money in a napkin in the earth, instead of putting it out to the exchangers, and those who have squandered their Lord's money by expending it for needless things, instead of putting it out to usury by investing it in His cause, will not receive approval from the Master, but decided condemnation. The unprofitable servant in the parable brought back the one talent to God, and said: "I knew thee that thou art an hard man, reaping where thou hast not sown, and gathering where thou hast not strewed: and I was afraid, and went and hid thy talent in the earth: lo, there thou hast that is thine." His Lord takes up his words: "Thou wicked and slothful servant, thou knewest that I reap where I sowed not, and gather where I have not strewed: thou oughtest therefore to have put my money to the exchangers, and then at my coming I should have received mine own with usury." Matthew 25:24-27.

This unprofitable servant was not ignorant of God's plans, but he set himself firmly to thwart the purpose of God, charging Him with unfairness in requiring improvement upon the talents entrusted to him. This very complaint and murmuring is made by a large class of wealthy men professing to believe the truth. Like the unfaithful servant they are afraid that the increase of the talent that God has lent them will be called for to advance the spread of truth; therefore they tie it up by investing it in earthly treasures and burying it in the world, thus making it so fast that they have nothing, or next to nothing, to invest in the cause of God. They have buried it, fearing that God would call for some of the principal or increase. When, at the demand of their Lord, they bring the amount given them, they come with ungrateful excuses for not having put the means lent them by God out to the exchangers, by investing it in His cause to carry on His work.

He who embezzles his Lord's goods not only loses the talent lent him of God, but loses eternal life. Of him it is said: "Cast ye the unprofitable servant into outer darkness." Matthew 25:30. The faithful servant, who invests his money in the cause of God to save souls, employs his means to the glory of God and will receive the commendation of the Master: "Well done, thou good and faithful servant: . . . enter thou into the joy of thy Lord." Verse 21. What will be this joy of our Lord? It will be the joy of seeing souls saved in the kingdom of glory. "Who for the joy that was set before Him endured the cross, despising the shame, and is set down at the right hand of the throne of God." Hebrews 12:2.

The idea of stewardship should have a practical bearing upon all the people of God. The parable of the talents, rightly understood, will bar out covetousness, which God calls idolatry. Practical benevolence will give spiritual life to thousands of nominal professors of the truth who now mourn over their darkness. It will transform them from selfish, covetous worshipers of mammon to earnest, faithful co-workers with Christ in the salvation of sinners.

SELF-DENIAL AND SACRIFICE

The foundation of the plan of salvation was laid in *sacrifice*. Jesus left the royal courts and became poor, that we through His poverty might be made rich. All who share this salvation, purchased for them at such an infinite sacrifice by the Son of God, will follow the example of the true Pattern. Christ was the chief Cornerstone, and we must build upon this Foundation. Each must have a spirit of self-denial and self-sacrifice. The life of Christ upon earth was unselfish; it was marked with humiliation and sacrifice. And shall men, partakers of the great salvation which Jesus came from heaven to bring them, refuse to follow their Lord and to share in His self-denial and sacrifice? Says Christ: "I am the Vine, ye are the branches." John 15:5. "Every branch in Me that beareth not fruit He taketh away: and every branch that beareth fruit, He purgeth it, that it may bring forth more fruit." Verse 2. The very vital principle, the sap which flows through the vine, nourishes the branches, that they may flourish and bear fruit. Is the servant greater than his Lord? Shall the world's Redeemer practice self-denial and sacrifice on our account, and the members of Christ's body practice self-indulgence? Self-denial is an essential condition of discipleship.

"Then said Jesus unto His disciples, If any man will come after Me, let him deny himself, and take up his cross, and follow Me." Matthew 16:24. I lead the way in the path of self-denial. I require nothing of you, My followers, but that of which I, your Lord, give you an example in My own life.

The Saviour of the world conquered Satan in the wilderness of temptation. He overcame to show man how he may overcome. He announced in the synagogue of Nazareth: "The Spirit of the Lord is upon Me, because He hath anointed Me to preach the gospel to the poor; He hath sent Me to heal the brokenhearted, to preach deliverance to the captives, and recovering of sight to the blind, to set at liberty them that are bruised, to preach the acceptable year of the Lord." Luke 4:18, 19.

The great work which Jesus announced that He came to do was entrusted to His followers upon the earth. Christ, as our head, leads out in the great work of salvation and bids us follow His example. He has given us a world-wide message. This truth must be extended to all nations, tongues, and people. Satan's power was to be contested, and he was to be overcome by Christ and also by His followers. An extensive war was to be maintained against the powers of darkness. And in order to do this work successfully, means were required. God does not propose to send means direct from heaven, but He gives into the hands of His followers talents of means to use for the very purpose of sustaining this warfare.

THE TITHING SYSTEM

He has given His people a plan for raising sums sufficient to make the enterprise self-sustaining. God's plan in the tithing system is beautiful in its simplicity and equality. All may take hold of it in faith and courage, for it is divine in its origin. In it are combined simplicity and utility, and it does not require depth of learning to understand and execute it. All may feel that they can act a part in carrying forward the precious work of salvation. Every man, woman, and youth may become a treasurer for the Lord and may be an agent to meet the demands upon the treasury. Says the apostle: "Let every one of you lay by him in store, as God hath prospered him." 1 Corinthians 16:2.

Great objects are accomplished by this system. If one and all would accept it, each would be made a vigilant and faithful treasurer for God, and there would be no want of means with which to carry forward the great work of sounding the last message of warning to the world. The treasury will be full if all adopt this system, and the contributors will not be left the poorer. Through every investment made they will become more wedded to the cause of present truth. They will be "laying up in store for themselves a good foundation against the time to come, that they may lay hold on eternal life." 1 Timothy 6:19.

As the persevering, systematic workers see that the tendency of their benevolent efforts is to nourish love to God and their fellow men, and that their personal efforts are extending their sphere of usefulness, they will realize that it is a great blessing to be co-workers with Christ. The Christian church, as a general thing, are disowning the claims of God upon them to give alms of the things which they possess to support the warfare against the moral darkness which is flooding the world. Never can the work of God advance as it should until the followers of Christ become active, zealous workers.

Every individual in the church should feel that the truth which he professes is a reality, and all should be disinterested workers. Some rich men feel like murmuring because the work of God is extending and there is a demand for money. They say that there is no end to the calls for means. One object after another is continually arising, demanding help. To such we would say that we hope the cause of God will so extend that there will be greater occasion, and more frequent and urgent calls, for supplies from the treasury to prosecute the work.

If the plan of systematic benevolence* were adopted by every individual and fully carried out, there would be a constant supply in the treasury. The income would flow in like a

*NOTE: See note on page 331.

steady stream constantly supplied by overflowing springs of benevolence. Almsgiving is a part of gospel religion. Does not the consideration of the infinite price paid for our redemption leave upon us solemn obligations pecuniarily, as well as lay claim upon all our powers to be devoted to the work of the Master?

We shall have a debt to settle with the Master by and by, when He shall say: "Give an account of thy stewardship." Luke 16:2. If men prefer to set aside the claims of God and to grasp and selfishly retain all that He gives them, He will hold His peace at present and continue frequently to test them by increasing His bounties and letting His blessings flow on, and these men may pass on receiving honor of men and without censure in the church; but by and by He will say: "Give an account of thy stewardship." Says Christ: "Inasmuch as ye did it not to one of the least of these, ye did it not to Me." Matthew 25:45. "Ye are not your own; for ye are bought with a price," and are under obligation to glorify God with your means as well as in your body and in your spirit, which are His. "Ye are bought with a *price,*" not "with corruptible things, as silver and gold," "but with the precious blood of Christ." He asks a return of the gifts that He has entrusted to us, to aid in the salvation of souls. He has given His blood; He asks our silver. It is through His poverty that we are made rich; and will we refuse to give back to Him His own gifts?

CO-WORKERS WITH GOD

God is not dependent upon man for the support of His cause. He could have sent means direct from heaven to supply His treasury, if His providence had seen that this was best for man. He might have devised means whereby angels would have been sent to publish the truth to the world without the agency of men. He might have written the truth upon the heavens, and let that declare to the world His requirements in living characters. God is not dependent upon any man's gold or silver. He says: "Every beast of the forest is Mine, and the cattle upon a thousand hills." "If I were hungry, I would not tell thee: for the world is Mine, and the fullness thereof." Psalm 50:10, 12. Whatever necessity there is for our agency in the advancement of the cause of God, He has purposely arranged for our good. He has honored us by making us co-workers with Him. He has ordained that there should be a necessity for the co-operation of men, that they may keep in exercise their benevolence.

God has in His wise providence placed the poor always with us, that while we should witness the various forms of want and suffering in the world, we should be tested and proved, and brought into positions to develop Christian character. He has placed the poor among us to call out from us Christian sympathy and love.

Sinners, who are perishing for lack of knowledge, must be left in ignorance and darkness unless men carry to them the light of truth. God will not send angels from heaven to do the work which He has left for man to do. He has given all a work to do, for the very reason that He might prove them and that they might reveal their true character. Christ places the poor among us as His representatives. "I was anhungered," He says, "and ye gave Me no meat: I was thirsty, and ye gave Me no drink." Matthew 25:42. Christ identifies Himself with suffering humanity in the persons of the suffering children of men. He makes their necessities His own and takes to His bosom their woes.

The moral darkness of a ruined world pleads to Christian men and women to put forth individual effort, to give of their means and of their influence, that they may be assimilated to the image of Him who, though He possessed infinite riches, yet for our sakes became poor. The Spirit of God cannot abide with those to whom He has sent the message of His truth but who need to be urged before they can have any sense of their duty to be co-workers with Christ. The apostle enforces the duty of giving from higher grounds than merely human sympathy because the feelings are moved. He enforces the principle that we should labor unselfishly with an eye single to the glory of God.

Christians are required by the Scriptures to enter upon a plan of active benevolence which will keep in constant exercise an interest in the salvation of their fellow men. The moral law enjoined the observance of the Sabbath, which was not a burden except when that law was transgressed and they were bound by the penalties involved in breaking it. The tithing system was no burden to those who did not depart from the plan. The system enjoined upon the Hebrews has not been repealed or relaxed by the One who originated it. Instead of being of no force now, it was to be more fully carried out and more extended, as salvation through Christ alone should be more fully brought to light in the Christian age.

Jesus made known to the lawyer that the condition of his having eternal life was to carry out in his life the special requirements of the law, which consisted in his loving God with all his heart, and soul, and mind, and strength, and his neighbor as himself. When the typical sacrifices ceased at the death of Christ, the original law, engraved in tables of stone, stood immutable, holding its claims upon man in all ages. And in the Christian age the duty of man was not limited, but more especially defined and simply expressed.

The gospel, extending and widening, required greater provisions to sustain the warfare after the death of Christ, and this made the law of almsgiving a more urgent necessity than under the Hebrew government. Now God requires, not less, but greater gifts than at any other period of the world. The principle laid down by Christ is that the gifts and offerings should be in proportion to the light and blessings enjoyed. He has said: "For unto whomsoever much is given, of him shall be much required." Luke 12:48.

The blessings of the Christian Age were responded to by

the first disciples in works of charity and benevolence. The outpouring of the Spirit of God, after Christ left His disciples and ascended to heaven, led to self-denial and self-sacrifice for the salvation of others. When the poor saints at Jerusalem were in distress, Paul wrote to the Gentile Christians in regard to works of benevolence, and said: "Therefore, as ye abound in everything, in faith, and utterance, and knowledge, and in all diligence, and in your love to us, see that ye abound in this grace also." 2 Corinthians 8:7. Here benevolence is placed by the side of faith, love, and Christian diligence. Those who think that they can be good Christians and close their ears and hearts to the calls of God for their liberalities, are in a fearful deception. There are those who abound in professions of great love for the truth, and, so far as words are concerned, have an interest to see the truth advance, but who do nothing for its advancement. The faith of such is dead, not being made perfect by works. The Lord never made such a mistake as to convert a soul and leave it under the power of covetousness.

FROM THE DAYS OF ADAM

The tithing system reaches back beyond the days of Moses. Men were required to offer to God gifts for religious purposes before the definite system was given to Moses, even as far back as the days of Adam. In complying with God's requirements, they were to manifest in offerings their appreciation of His mercies and blessings to them. This was continued through successive generations, and was carried out by Abraham, who gave tithes to Melchizedek, the priest of the most high God. The same principle existed in the days of Job. Jacob, when at Bethel, an exile and penniless wanderer, lay down at night, solitary and alone, with a rock for his pillow, and there promised the Lord: "Of all that Thou shalt give me I will surely give the tenth unto Thee." Genesis 28:22. God does not compel men to give. All that they give must be voluntary. He will not have His treasury replenished with unwilling offerings.

The Lord designed to bring man into close relationship with Himself and into sympathy and love with his fellow men by placing upon him responsibilities in deeds that would counteract selfishness and strengthen his love for God and man. The plan of system in benevolence God designed for the good of man, who is inclined to be selfish and to close his heart to generous deeds. The Lord requires gifts to be made at stated times, being so arranged that giving will become habit and benevolence be felt to be a Christian duty. The heart, opened by one gift, is not to have time to become selfishly cold and to close before the next is bestowed. The stream is to be continually flowing, thus keeping open the channel by acts of benevolence.

A TENTH OF THE INCREASE

As to the amount required, God has specified one tenth of the increase. This is left to the conscience and benevolence of men, whose judgment in this tithing system should have free play. And while it is left free to the conscience, a plan has been laid out definite enough for all. No compulsion is required.

God called for men in the Mosaic dispensation to give the tenth of all their increase. He committed to their trust the things of this life, talents to be improved and returned to Him. He has required a tenth, and this He claims as the very least that man should return to Him. He says: I give you nine tenths, while I require one tenth; that is Mine. When men withhold the one tenth, they rob God. Sin offerings, peace offerings, and thank offerings were also required in addition to the tenth of the increase.

All that is withheld of that which God claims, the tenth of the increase, is recorded in the books of heaven against the withholders, as robbery. Such defraud their Creator; and when this sin of neglect is brought before them, it is not enough for them to change their course and begin to work from that time upon the right principle. This will not correct the figures made in the heavenly record for embezzling the property committed to them in trust to be returned to the Lender. Repentance for unfaithful dealing with God, and for base ingratitude, is required.

"Will a man rob God? Yet ye have robbed Me. But ye say, Wherein have we robbed Thee? In tithes and offerings. Ye are cursed with a curse: for ye have robbed Me, even this whole nation. Bring ye all the tithes into the storehouse, that there may be meat in Mine house, and prove Me now herewith, saith the Lord of hosts, if I will not open you the windows of heaven, and pour you out a blessing, that there shall not be room enough to receive it." Malachi 3:8-10. A promise is here given that, if all the tithes are brought into the storehouse, a blessing from God will be poured upon the obedient.

"And I will rebuke the devourer for your sakes, and he shall not destroy the fruits of your ground; neither shall your vine cast her fruit before the time in the field, saith the Lord of hosts. And all nations shall call you blessed: for ye shall be a delightsome land, saith the Lord of hosts." Verses 11, 12. If all who profess the truth will come up to the claims of God in giving the tenth, which God says is His, the treasury will be abundantly supplied with means to carry forward the great work for the salvation of man.

God gives man nine tenths, while He claims one tenth for sacred purposes, as He has given man six days for his own work and has reserved and set apart the seventh day to Himself. For, like the Sabbath, a tenth of the increase is sacred; God has reserved it for Himself. He will carry forward His work upon the earth with the increase of the means that He has entrusted to man.

God required of His ancient people three yearly gatherings. "Three times in a year shall all thy males appear before the Lord thy God in the place which He shall choose; in the Feast of Unleavened Bread, and in the Feast of Weeks, and in the

Feast of Tabernacles: and they shall not appear before the Lord empty: every man shall give as he is able, according to the blessing of the Lord thy God which He hath given thee." Deuteronomy 16:16, 17. No less than one third of their income was devoted to sacred and religious purposes.

Whenever God's people, in any period of the world, have cheerfully and willingly carried out His plan in systematic benevolence and in gifts and offerings, they have realized the standing promise that prosperity should attend all their labors just in proportion as they obeyed His requirements. When they acknowledged the claims of God and complied with His requirements, honoring Him with their substance, their barns were filled with plenty. But when they robbed God in tithes and in offerings they were made to realize that they were not only robbing Him but themselves, for He limited His blessings to them just in proportion as they limited their offerings to Him.

NO IRKSOME BURDEN

Some will pronounce this one of the rigorous laws binding upon the Hebrews. But this was not a burden to the willing heart that loved God. It was only when their selfish natures were strengthened by withholding that men lost sight of eternal considerations and valued their earthly treasures above souls. There are even more urgent necessities upon the Israel of God in these last days than were upon ancient Israel. There is a great and important work to be accomplished in a very short time. God never designed that the law of the tithing system should be of no account among His people; but, instead of this, He designed that the spirit of sacrifice should widen and deepen for the closing work.

Systematic benevolence should not be made systematic compulsion. It is freewill offerings that are acceptable to God. True Christian benevolence springs from the principle of grateful love. Love to Christ cannot exist without corresponding love to those whom He came into the world to redeem. Love to Christ must be the ruling principle of the being, controlling all the emotions and directing all the energies. Redeeming love should awaken all the tender affection and self-sacrificing devotion that can possibly exist in the heart of man. When this is the case, no heart-stirring appeals will be needed to break through their selfishness and awaken their dormant sympathies, to call forth benevolent offerings for the precious cause of truth.

Jesus has purchased us at an infinite sacrifice. All our capabilities and our influence are indeed our Saviour's, and should be dedicated to His service. By doing this we show our gratitude that we have been ransomed from the slavery of sin by the precious blood of Christ. Our Saviour is ever working for us. He has ascended on high and pleads in behalf of the purchase of His blood. He pleads before His Father the agonies of the crucifixion. He raises His wounded hands and intercedes for His church, that they may be kept from falling under temptation.

If our perceptions could be quickened to take in this wonderful work of our Saviour for our salvation, love, deep and ardent, would burn in our hearts. Our apathy and cold indifference would then alarm us. Entire devotion and benevolence, prompted by grateful love, will impart to the smallest offering, the willing sacrifice, a divine fragrance, making the gift of priceless value. But, after willingly yielding to our Redeemer all that we can bestow, be it ever so valuable to us, if we view our debt of gratitude to God as it really is, all that we may have offered will seem to us very insufficient and meager. But angels take these offerings, which to us seem poor, and present them as a fragrant offering before the throne, and they are accepted.

We do not, as followers of Christ, realize our true position. We do not have correct views of our responsibilities as hired servants of Christ. He has advanced us the wages in His suffering life and spilled blood, to bind us in willing servitude to Himself. All the good things we have are a loan from our Saviour. He has made us stewards. Our smallest offerings, our humblest services, presented in faith and love, may be consecrated gifts to win souls to the service of the Master and to promote His glory. The interest and prosperity of Christ's kingdom should be paramount to every other consideration. Those who make their pleasure and selfish interest the chief objects of their lives are not faithful stewards.

Those who deny self to do others good, and who devote themselves and all they have to Christ's service, will realize the happiness which the selfish man seeks for in vain. Said our Saviour: "Whosoever he be of you that forsaketh not all that he hath, he cannot be My disciple." Luke 14:33. Charity "seeketh not her own." This is the fruit of that disinterested love and benevolence which characterized the life of Christ. The law of God in our hearts will bring our own interests in subordination to high and eternal considerations.

TREASURE ON EARTH

We are enjoined by Christ to seek first the kingdom of God and His righteousness. This is our first and highest duty. Our Master expressly warned His servants not to lay up treasures upon the earth; for in so doing their hearts would be upon earthly rather than heavenly things. Here is where many poor souls have made shipwreck of faith. They have gone directly contrary to the express injunction of our Lord, and have allowed the love of money to become the ruling passion of their lives. They are intemperate in their efforts to acquire means. They are as much intoxicated with their insane desire for riches as is the inebriate with his liquor.

Christians forget that they are servants of the Master; that they themselves, their time, and all that they have belong to Him. Many are tempted, and the majority are overcome, by the delusive inducements which Satan presents to invest their money where it will yield them the greatest profit in dollars and cents. There are but few who consider the binding claims that God has upon them to make it their first business to meet the necessities of His cause and let their own desires be served last. There are but few who invest in God's cause in proportion to their means. Many have fastened their money in property which they must sell before they can invest it in the cause of God and thus put it to a practical use. They make this an excuse for doing but little in their Redeemer's cause. They have as effectually buried their money in the earth as had the man in the parable. They rob God of the tenth, which He claims as His own, and in robbing Him they rob themselves of the heavenly treasure.

FOR MAN'S BENEFIT

The plan of systematic benevolence does not press heavily upon any one man. "Now concerning the collection for the saints, as I have given order to the churches of Galatia, even so do ye. Upon the first day of the week let every one of you lay by him in store, as God hath prospered him, that there be no gatherings when I come." 1 Corinthians 16:1, 2. The poor are not excluded from the privilege of giving. They, as well as the wealthy, may act a part in this work. The lesson that Christ gave in regard to the widow's two mites shows us that the smallest willing offerings of the poor, if given from a heart of love, are as acceptable as the largest donations of the rich.

In the balances of the sanctuary the gifts of the poor, made from love to Christ, are not estimated according to the amount given, but according to the love which prompts the sacrifice. The promises of Jesus will as surely be realized by the liberal poor man, who has but little to offer, but who gives that little freely, as by the wealthy man who gives of his abundance. The poor man makes a sacrifice of his little, which he really feels. He really denies himself of some things that he needs for his own comfort, while the wealthy man gives of his abundance, and feels no want, denies himself nothing that he really needs. Therefore there is a sacredness in the poor man's offering that is not found in the rich man's gift, for the rich give of their abundance. God's providence has arranged the entire plan of systematic benevolence for the benefit of man. His providence never stands still. If God's servants follow His opening providence, all will be active workers.

Those who withhold from the treasury of God and hoard their means for their children, endanger the spiritual interest of their children. They place their property, which is a stumbling block to themselves, in the pathway of their children, that they may stumble over it to perdition. Many are making a great mistake in regard to the things of this life. They economize, withholding from themselves and others the good they might receive from a right use of the means which God has lent them, and become selfish and avaricious. They neglect their spiritual interests and become dwarfs in religious growth, all for the sake of accumulating wealth which they cannot use. They leave their property to their children, and nine times out of ten it is even a greater curse to their heirs than it has been to themselves. Children, relying upon the property of their parents, often fail to make a success of this life, and generally utterly fail to secure the life to come.

The very best legacy which parents can leave their children is a knowledge of useful labor and the example of a life characterized by disinterested benevolence. By such a life they show the true value of money, that it is only to be appreciated for the good that it will accomplish in relieving their own wants and the necessities of others, and in advancing the cause of God.

ACCOUNTABILITY OF THE POOR

Some are willing to give according to what they have, and feel that God has no further claims upon them, because they have not a great amount of means. They have no income that they can spare from the necessities of their families. But there are many of this class who might ask themselves the question: Am I giving according to what I might have had? God designed that their powers of body and mind should be put to use. Some have not improved to the best account the ability that God has given them. Labor is apportioned to man. It was connected with the curse, because made necessary by sin. The physical, mental, and moral well-being of man makes a life of useful labor necessary. "Be . . . not slothful in business," is the injunction of the inspired apostle Paul.

No person, whether rich or poor, can glorify God by a life of indolence. All the capital that many poor men have is time and physical strength, and this is frequently wasted in love of ease and in careless indolence so that they have nothing to bring to their Lord in tithes and in offerings. If Christian men lack wisdom to labor to the best account and to make a judicious appropriation of their physical and mental powers, they should have meekness and lowliness of mind to receive advice and counsel of their brethren, that their better judgment may supply their own deficiencies. Many poor men who are now content to do nothing for the good of their fellow men and for the advancement of the cause of God might do much if they would. They are as accountable to God for their capital of physical strength as is the rich man for his capital of money.

Some who ought to put means into the treasury of God will be receivers from it. There are those who are now poor who might improve their condition by a judicious use of their time, by avoiding patent rights, and by restraining their inclination to engage in speculations in order to obtain means in some easier way than by patient, persevering labor. If those who have not made life a success were willing to be instructed, they could train themselves to habits of self-denial and strict economy, and have the satisfaction of being distributors, rather than receivers, of charity. There are many slothful servants. If they would do what it is in their power to do they would experience so great a blessing in helping others that they would indeed realize that "it is more blessed to give than to receive."

Rightly directed benevolence draws upon the mental and moral energies of men, and excites them to most healthful action in blessing the needy and in advancing the cause of God. If those who have means should realize that they are accountable to God for every dollar that they expend, their supposed wants would be much less. If conscience were alive, she would testify of needless appropriations to the gratification of appetite, of pride, vanity, and love of amusements, and would report the squandering of the Lord's money, which should have been devoted to His cause. Those who waste their Lord's goods will by and by have to give an account of their course to the Master.

A CAUTION TO THE WEALTHY

If professed Christians would use less of their wealth in adorning the body and in beautifying their own houses, and would consume less in extravagant, health-destroying luxuries upon their tables, they could place much larger sums in the treasury of God. They would thus imitate their Redeemer, who left heaven, His riches, and His glory, and for our sakes became poor, that we might have eternal riches. If we are too poor to faithfully render to God the tithes and offerings that He requires, we are certainly too poor to dress expensively and to eat luxuriously; for we thus waste our Lord's money in hurtful indulgences to please and glorify ourselves. We should inquire diligently of ourselves: What treasure have we secured in the kingdom of God? Are we rich toward God?

Jesus gave His disciples a lesson upon covetousness. "And He spake a parable unto them, saying, The ground of a certain rich man brought forth plentifully: and he thought within himself, saying, What shall I do, because I have no room where to bestow my fruits? And he said, This will I do: I will pull down my barns, and build greater; and there will I bestow all my fruits and my goods. And I will say to my soul, Soul, thou hast much goods laid up for many years; take thine ease, eat, drink, and be merry. But God said unto him, Thou fool, this night thy soul shall be required of thee: then whose shall those things be, which thou hast provided? So is he that layeth up treasure for himself, and is not rich toward God." Luke 12:16-21.

The length and happiness of life does not consist in the amount of our earthly possessions. This foolish rich man in his supreme selfishness had laid up for himself treasures that he could not use. He had lived only for himself. He had overreached in trade, had made sharp bargains, and had not exercised mercy or the love of God. He had robbed the fatherless and widow, and defrauded his fellow men, to add to his increasing stock of wordly possessions. He might have laid up his treasure in heaven in bags that wax not old; but through his covetousness he lost both worlds. Those who humbly use to the glory of God the means that He has entrusted to them will receive their treasure by and by from the Master's hand with the benediction: "Well done, good and faithful servant: . . . enter thou into the joy of thy Lord." Matthew 25:23.

When we consider the infinite sacrifice made for the salvation of men we are lost in amazement. When selfishness clamors for the victory in the hearts of men, and they are tempted to withhold their due proportion in any good work, they should strengthen their principles of right by the thought that He who was rich in heaven's priceless treasure turned away from it all and became poor. He had not where to lay His head. And all this sacrifice was in our behalf, that we might have eternal riches.

Christ set His own feet in the path of self-denial and sacrifice which all His disciples must travel if they would be exalted with Him at last. He took to His own heart the sorrows which man must suffer. The minds of worldly men frequently become gross. They can see only earthly things, which eclipse the glory and value of heavenly things. Men will compass land and sea for earthly gain, and endure privation and suffering to obtain their object, yet will turn away from heaven's attractions and not regard eternal riches. Men who are in comparative poverty are usually the ones who do the most to sustain the cause of God. They are generous with their little. They have strengthened their generous impulses by continual liberalities. When their expenditures pressed close upon the income, their passion for earthly riches had no room or chance to strengthen.

But many, when they begin to gather earthly riches, commence to calculate how long it will be before they can be in possession of a certain sum. In their anxiety to amass wealth for themselves they fail to become rich toward God. Their benevolence does not keep pace with their accumulation. As their passion for riches increases, their affections are bound up with their treasure. The increase of their property strengthens the eager desire for more, until some consider that their giving to the Lord a tenth is a severe and unjust tax. Inspiration has said: "If riches increase, set not your heart upon them." Psalm 62:10. Many have said: "If I were as rich as such a one, I would multiply my gifts to the treasury of God. I would do nothing else with my wealth but use it for the advancement of the cause of God." God has tested some of these by giving them riches; but with the riches came the fiercer temptation, and their benevolence was far less than in the days of their poverty. A grasping desire for greater riches absorbed their minds and hearts, and they committed idolatry.

UNDIVIDED ALLEGIANCE

He who presents to men infinite riches and an eternal life of blessedness in His kingdom as the reward of faithful obedience, will not accept a divided heart. We are living amid the perils of the last days, where there is everything to divert the mind and allure the affections from God. Our duty will only be discerned and appreciated when viewed in the light which shines from the life of Christ. As the sun rises in the east and passes toward the west, filling the world with light, so the true follower of Christ will be a light unto the world. He will go out into the world as a bright and shining light, that those who are in darkness may be lightened and warmed by the rays shining forth from him. Christ says of His followers: "Ye are the light of the world. A city that is set on an hill cannot be hid."

Our great Exemplar was self-denying, and shall the course of His professed followers be in such marked contrast to His? The Saviour gave all for a perishing world, not withholding even Himself. The church of God are asleep. They are enfeebled by inaction. Voices come to us from every part of the world, "Come over and help us;" but there is no answering movement. There is a feeble effort now and then; a few show that they would be co-workers with their Master; but such are frequently left to toil almost alone. There is but one missionary* from our people in all the wide field in foreign countries.

The truth is mighty, but it is not carried into practice. It is not sufficient to lay money alone upon the altar. God calls for men, volunteers, to carry the truth to other nations and tongues and people. It is not our numbers nor our wealth that will give us a signal victory; but it is devotion to the work, moral courage, ardent love for souls, and untiring, unflagging zeal.

THE BLESSING OF BENEVOLENCE

There are many who have looked upon the Jewish nation as a people to be pitied because they were constantly taxed for the support of their religion; but God, who created man and

*Note: These words were penned in 1875 shortly after Elder J. N. Andrews had been sent to Europe, and before foreign missions had become a topic in which every church member was interested. [White Trustees.]

provided him with all the blessings he enjoys, knew what was for his best good. And through His blessing He made their nine tenths worth more to them than the entire amount without His blessing. If any, through selfishness, robbed God or brought to Him an offering not perfect, disaster and loss were sure to follow them. God reads the motives of the heart. He is acquainted with the purposes of men and will mete out to them in His own good time as they have merited.

The special system of tithing was founded upon a principle which is as enduring as the law of God. This system of tithing was a blessing to the Jews, else God would not have given it them. So also will it be a blessing to those who carry it out to the end of time. Our heavenly Father did not originate the plan of systematic benevolence to enrich Himself, but to be a great blessing to man. He saw that this system of beneficence was just what man needed.

Those churches who are the most systematic and liberal in sustaining the cause of God are the most prosperous spiritually. True liberality in the follower of Christ identifies his interest with that of his Master. In God's dealing with the Jews and His people to the end of time, He requires systematic benevolence proportionate to their income. The plan of salvation was laid by the infinite sacrifice of the Son of God. The light of the gospel shining from the cross of Christ rebukes selfishness and encourages liberality and benevolence. It is not to be a lamented fact that there are increasing calls to give. God in His providence is calling His people out from their limited sphere of action to enter upon greater enterprises. Unlimited effort is demanded at this time when moral darkness is covering the world. Worldliness and covetousness are eating out the vitals of God's people. They should understand that it is His mercy which multiplies the demands for their means. The angel of God places benevolent acts close beside prayer. He said to Cornelius: "Thy prayers and thine alms are come up for a memorial before God." Acts 10:4.

In the teachings of Christ He said: "If therefore ye have not been faithful in the unrighteous mammon, who will commit to your trust the true riches?" Luke 16:11. The spiritual health and prosperity of the church is dependent in a great degree upon her systematic benevolence. It is like the lifeblood which must flow through the whole being, vitalizing every member of the body. It increases love for the souls of our fellow men; for by self-denial and self-sacrifice we are brought into a closer relation to Christ, who for our sakes became poor. The more we invest in the cause of God to aid in the salvation of souls, the closer to our hearts will they be brought. Were our numbers half as large, and all of these devoted workers, we should have a power that would make the world tremble. To the active workers Christ has addressed these words: "Lo, I am with you alway, even unto the end of the world." Matthew 28:20.

INTO ALL THE WORLD

We shall meet opposition arising from selfish motives and from bigotry and prejudice; yet, with undaunted courage and living faith, we should sow beside all waters. The agents of Satan are formidable; we shall meet them and must combat them. Our labors are not to be confined to our own country. The field is the world; the harvest is ripe. The command given by Christ to the disciples just before He ascended was: "Go ye into all the world, and preach the gospel to every creature." Mark 16:15.

We feel pained beyond measure to see some of our ministers hovering about the churches, apparently putting forth some little effort, but having next to nothing to show for their labors. The field is the world. Let them go out into the unbelieving world and labor to convert souls to the truth. We refer our brethren and sisters to the example of Abraham going up to Mount Moriah to offer his only son at the command of God. Here was obedience and sacrifice. Moses was in kingly courts, and a prospective crown was before him. But he turned away from the tempting bribe, and "refused to be called the son of Pharaoh's daughter; choosing rather to suffer affliction with the people of God, than to enjoy the pleasures of sin for a season; esteeming the reproach of Christ greater riches than the treasures in Egypt." Hebrews 11:24-26.

The apostles counted not their lives dear unto themselves, rejoicing that they were counted worthy to suffer shame for the name of Christ. Paul and Silas suffered the loss of all things. They suffered scourging, and were in no gentle manner thrown upon the cold floor of a dungeon in a most painful position, their feet elevated and fastened in the stocks. Did repinings and complaints then reach the ear of the jailer? Oh, no! From the inner prison, voices broke the silence of midnight with songs of joy and praise to God. These disciples were cheered by a deep and earnest love for the cause of their Redeemer, for which they suffered.

As the truth of God fills our hearts, absorbs our affections, and controls our lives, we also will count it joy to suffer for the truth's sake. No prison walls, no martyr's stake, can then daunt or hinder us in the great work.

Come, O my soul, to Calvary.

Mark the humble life of the Son of God. He was "a man of sorrows, and acquainted with grief." Isaiah 53:3. Behold His ignominy, His agony in Gethsemane, and learn what self-denial is. Are we suffering want? so was Christ, the Majesty of heaven. But His poverty was for our sakes. Are we ranked among the rich? so was He. But He consented for our sakes to become poor, that we through His poverty might be made rich. In Christ we have self-denial exemplified. His sacrifice consisted not merely in leaving the royal courts of heaven, in being tried by wicked men as a criminal and pronounced guilty, and in being delivered up to die as a malefactor, but in bearing the weight of the sins of the world. The life of

Christ rebukes our indifference and coldness. We are near the close of time, when Satan has come down, having great wrath, knowing that his time is short. He is working with all deceivableness of unrighteousness in them that perish. The warfare has been left in our hands by our great Leader for us to carry forward with vigor. We are not doing a twentieth part of what we might do if we were awake. The work is retarded by love of ease and a lack of the self-denying spirit of which our Saviour has given us an example in His life.

Co-workers with Christ, men who feel the need of extended effort, are wanted. The work of our presses should not be lessened, but doubled. Schools should be established in different places to educate our youth preparatory to their laboring to advance the truth.

Already a great deal of time has been wasted, and angels bear to heaven the record of our neglects. Our sleepy and unconsecrated condition has lost to us precious opportunities which God has sent us in the persons of those who were qualified to help us in our present need. Oh, how much we need our Hannah More* to aid us at this time in reaching other nations! Her extensive knowledge of missionary fields would give us access to those of other tongues whom we cannot now approach. God brought this gift among us to meet our present emergency; but we prized not the gift, and He took her from us. She is at rest from her labors, but her self-denying works follow her. It is to be deplored that our missionary work should be retarded for the want of knowledge how to gain access to the different nations and localities in the great harvest field.

We feel anguish of spirit because some gifts are lost to us

*NOTE: Hannah More, a missionary of experience in Africa, having become a Seventh-day Adventist while in mission service, lost the support of the mission board which had sent her out, so returned to the United States. At Battle Creek she found that her abilities and talents were not fully appreciated and utilized.

[WHITE TRUSTEES.]

that we might now have if we had only been awake. Laborers have been kept back from the whitening harvest. It becomes the people of God to humble their hearts before Him, and in the deepest humiliation to pray the Lord to pardon our apathy and selfish indulgence, and to blot out the shameful record of duties neglected and privileges unimproved. In contemplation of the cross of Calvary the true Christian will abandon the thought of restricting his offerings to that which costs him nothing and will hear in trumpet tones:

Go, labor in My vineyard;
There's resting by and by.

When Jesus was about to ascend on high, He pointed to the harvest fields and said to His followers: "Go ye into all the world, and preach the gospel." "Freely ye have received, freely give." Matthew 10:8. Shall we deny self that the wasting harvest may be gathered?

God calls for talents of influence and of means. Shall we refuse to obey? Our heavenly Father bestows gifts and solicits a portion back, that He may test us whether we are worthy to have the gift of everlasting life.

The offerings of little children may be acceptable and pleasing to God. In accordance with the spirit that prompts the gifts will be the value of the offering. The poor, by following the rule of the apostle and laying by a small sum every week, help to swell the treasury, and their gifts are wholly acceptable to God; for they make just as great, and even greater, sacrifices than their more wealthy brethren. The plan of systematic benevolence will prove a safeguard to every family against temptations to spend means for needless things, and especially will it prove a blessing to the rich by guarding them from indulging in extravagances.—1875, vol. 3, p. 412.

The Authority of the Church

THE world's Redeemer has invested great power with His church. He states the rules to be applied in cases of trial with its members. After He has given explicit directions as to the course to be pursued, He says: "Verily I say unto you, Whatsoever ye shall bind on earth shall be bound in heaven: and whatsoever [in church discipline] ye shall loose on earth shall be loosed in heaven." Matthew 18:18. Thus even the heavenly authority ratifies the discipline of the church in regard to its members when the Bible rule has been followed.

The word of God does not give license for one man to set up his judgment in opposition to the judgment of the church, neither is he allowed to urge his opinions against the opinions of the church. If there were no church discipline and government, the church would go to fragments; it could not hold together as a body. There have ever been individuals of independent minds who have claimed that they were right, that God had especially taught, impressed, and led them. Each has a theory of his own, views peculiar to himself, and each claims that his views are in accordance with the word of God. Each one has a different theory and faith, yet each claims special light from God. These draw away from the body, and each one is a separate church of himself. All these cannot be right, yet they all claim to be led of the Lord. The word of Inspiration is not Yea and Nay, but Yea and Amen in Christ Jesus.

Our Saviour follows His lessons of instruction with a promise that if two or three should be united in asking anything of God it should be given them. Christ here shows that there must be union with others, even in our desires for a

1875, vol. 3, pp. 428-433 (Individual Independence).

given object. Great importance is attached to the united prayer, the union of purpose. God hears the prayers of individuals, but on this occasion Jesus was giving especial and important lessons that were to have a special bearing upon His newly organized church on the earth. There must be an agreement in the things which they desire and for which they pray. It was not merely the thoughts and exercises of one mind, liable to deception; but the petition was to be the earnest desire of several minds centered on the same point.

In the wonderful conversion of Paul we see the miraculous power of God. A brightness above the glory of the midday sun shone round about him. Jesus, whose name of all others he most hated and despised, revealed Himself to Paul for the purpose of arresting his mad yet honest career, that He might make this most unpromising instrument a chosen vessel to bear the gospel to the Gentiles. He had conscientiously done many things contrary to the name of Jesus of Nazareth. In his zeal he was a persevering, earnest persecutor of the church of Christ. His convictions of his duty to exterminate this alarming doctrine, which was prevailing everywhere, that Jesus was the Prince of life were deep and strong.

Paul verily believed that faith in Jesus made of none effect the law of God, the religious service of sacrificial offerings, and the rite of circumcision, which had in all past ages received the full sanction of God. But the miraculous revelation of Christ brings light into the darkened chambers of his mind. The Jesus of Nazareth whom he is arrayed against is indeed the Redeemer of the world.

DIRECTED TO THE CHURCH FOR INSTRUCTION

Paul sees his mistaken zeal and cries out: "Lord, what wilt Thou have me to do?" Acts 9:6. Jesus did not then and there tell him, as He might have done, the work that He had assigned him. Paul must receive instruction in the Christian faith and move understandingly. Christ sends him to the very disciples whom he had been so bitterly persecuting, to learn of them. The light of heavenly illumination had taken away Paul's eyesight; but Jesus, the Great Healer of the blind, does not restore it. He answers the question of Paul in these words: "Arise, and go into the city, and it shall be told thee what thou must do." Jesus could not only have healed Paul of his blindness, but He could have forgiven his sins and told him his duty by marking out his future course. From Christ all power and mercies were to flow; but He did not give Paul an experience, in his conversion to truth, independent of His church recently organized upon the earth.

The marvelous light given Paul upon that occasion astonished and confounded him. He was wholly subdued. This part of the work man could not do for Paul, but there was a work still to be accomplished which the servants of Christ could do. Jesus directs him to His agents in the church for a further knowledge of duty. Thus He gives authority and sanction to His organized church. Christ had done the work of revelation and conviction, and now Paul was in a condition to learn of those whom God had ordained to teach the truth. Christ directs Paul to His chosen servants, thus placing him in connection with His church.

The very men whom Paul was purposing to destroy were to be his instructors in the very religion that he had despised and persecuted. He passed three days without food or sight, making his way to the men whom, in his blind zeal, he was purposing to destroy. Here Jesus places Paul in connection with his representatives upon the earth. The Lord gave Ananias a vision to go up to a certain house in Damascus and call for Saul of Tarsus; "for, behold, he prayeth."

After Saul was directed to go to Damascus, he was led by the men who accompanied him to help him bring the disciples bound to Jerusalem to be tried and put to death. Saul tarried with Judas at Damascus, devoting the time to fasting and prayer. Here the faith of Saul was tested. Three days he was in darkness of mind in regard to what was required of him, and three days he was without sight. He had been directed to go to Damascus, for it should there be told him what he should do. He is in uncertainty, and he cries earnestly to God.

An angel is sent to Ananias, directing him to go to a certain house where Saul is praying to be instructed in what he is to do next. Saul's pride is gone. A little before he was self-confident, thinking he was engaged in a good work for which he should receive a reward; but all is now changed. He is bowed down and humbled to the dust in penitence and shame, and his supplications are fervent for pardon. Said the Lord, through His angel, to Ananias: "Behold, he prayeth." The angel informed the servant of God that he had revealed to Saul in vision a man named Ananias coming in and putting his hand on him that he might receive his sight. Ananias can scarcely credit the words of the angel, and repeats what he has heard of Saul's bitter persecution of the saints at Jerusalem. But the command to Ananias is imperative: "Go thy way: for he is a chosen vessel unto Me, to bear My name before the Gentiles, and kings, and the children of Israel." Verse 15.

Ananias was obedient to the direction of the angel. He laid his hands upon the man who so recently was exercised with a spirit of the deepest hatred, breathing out threatenings against all who believed on the name of Christ. Ananias said to Saul: "Brother Saul, the Lord, even Jesus, that appeared unto thee in the way as thou camest, hath sent me, that thou mightest receive thy sight, and be filled with the Holy Ghost. And immediately there fell from his eyes as it had been scales: and he received sight forthwith, and arose, and was baptized." Verses 17, 18.

Jesus might have done all this work for Paul directly, but this was not His plan. Paul had something to do in the line of confession to the men whose destruction he had premeditated, and God had a responsible work for the men to do whom

He had ordained to act in His stead. Paul was to take those steps necessary in conversion. He was required to unite himself to the very people whom he had persecuted for their religion. Christ here gives all His people an example of the manner of His working for the salvation of men. The Son of God identified Himself with the office and authority of His organized church. His blessings were to come through the agencies that He has ordained, thus connecting man with the channel through which His blessings come. Paul's being strictly conscientious in his work of persecuting the saints does not make him guiltless when the knowledge of his cruel work is impressed upon him by the Spirit of God. He is to become a learner of the disciples.

He learns that Jesus, whom in his blindness he considered an impostor, is indeed the author and foundation of all the religion of God's chosen people from Adam's day, and the finisher of the faith, now so clear to his enlightened vision. He saw Christ as the vindicator of truth, the fulfiller of all prophecies. Christ had been regarded as making of none effect the law of God; but when his spiritual vision was touched by the finger of God, he learned of the disciples that Christ was the originator and the foundation of the entire Jewish system of sacrifices, that in the death of Christ type met antitype, and that Christ came into the world for the express purpose of vindicating His Father's law.

INDEPENDENCE NOT SANCTIONED

In the light of the law, Paul sees himself a sinner. That very law which he thought he had been keeping so zealously he finds he has been transgressing. He repents and dies to sin, becomes obedient to the claims of God's law, and has faith in Christ as his Saviour, is baptized, and preaches Jesus as earnestly and zealously as he once condemned Him. In the conversion of Paul are given us important principles which we should ever bear in mind. The Redeemer of the world does not sanction experience and exercise in religious matters independent of His organized and acknowledged church, where He has a church.

Many have the idea that they are responsible to Christ alone for their light and experience, independent of His acknowledged followers in the world. But this is condemned by Jesus in His teachings and in the examples, the facts, which He has given for our instruction. Here was Paul, one whom Christ was to fit for a most important work, one who was to be a chosen vessel unto Him, brought directly into the presence of Christ; yet He does not teach him the lessons of truth. He arrests his course and convicts him; and when he asks, "What wilt Thou have me to do?" the Saviour does not tell him directly, but places him in connection with His church. They will tell thee what thou must do. Jesus is the sinner's friend, His heart is ever open, ever touched with human woe; He has all power, both in heaven and upon earth; but He respects the means which He has ordained for the enlightenment and salvation of men. He directs Saul to the church, thus acknowledging the power that He has invested in it as a channel of light to the world. It is Christ's organized body upon the earth, and respect is required to be paid to His ordinances. In the case of Saul, Ananias represents Christ, and he also represents Christ's ministers upon the earth who are appointed to act in Christ's stead.

Christ gives power to the voice of the church. "Verily I say unto you, Whatsoever ye shall bind on earth shall be bound in heaven: and whatsoever ye shall loose on earth shall be loosed in heaven." Matthew 18:18. No such thing is countenanced as one man's starting out upon his own individual responsibility and advocating what views he chooses, irrespective of the judgment of the church. God has bestowed the highest power under heaven upon His church. It is the voice of God in His united people in church capacity which is to be respected.

God has given to His church men who have an experience, those who have fasted and wept and prayed, even through the entire night, for the Lord to open the Scriptures to their minds. In humility these men have given the world the benefit of their mature experience. Is this light of heaven, or of men? Is it of any value, or is it worthless?—1875, vol. 3, pp. 450, 451.

The State of the World

I WAS shown the state of the world, that it is fast filling up its cup of iniquity. Violence and crime of every description are filling our world, and Satan is using every means to make crime and debasing vice popular. The youth who walk the streets are surrounded with handbills and notices of crime and sin, presented in some novel or to be acted at some theater. Their minds are educated into familiarity with sin. The course pursued by the base and vile is kept before them in the periodicals of the day, and everything which can excite curiosity and arouse the animal passions is brought before them in thrilling and exciting stories.

The literature that proceeds from corrupted intellects poisons the minds of thousands in our world. Sin does not appear exceeding sinful. They hear and read so much of debasing crime and vileness that the once tender conscience which would have recoiled with horror becomes so blunted that it can dwell upon the low and vile sayings and actions of men with greedy interest.

"As it was in the days of Noah, so shall it be also in the days of the Son of man." Luke 17:26. God will have a people zealous of good works, standing firm amid the pollutions of this degenerate age. There will be a people who hold so fast to the divine strength that they will be proof against every temptation. Evil communications in flaming handbills may seek to speak to their senses and corrupt their minds; yet they will be so united to God and angels that they will be as those who see not and hear not. They have a work to do which no one can do for them, which is to fight the good fight of faith, and lay hold on eternal life. They will not be self-confident

1875, vol. 3, pp. 471-474.

and self-sufficient. Knowing their weakness, they will unite their ignorance to Christ's wisdom, their weakness to His strength.

AN EXAMPLE OF PURITY

The youth may have principles so firm that the most powerful temptations of Satan will not draw them away from their allegiance. Samuel was a child surrounded by the most corrupting influences. He saw and heard things that grieved his soul. The sons of Eli, who ministered in holy office, were controlled by Satan. These men polluted the whole atmosphere which surrounded them. Men and women were daily fascinated with sin and wrong, yet Samuel walked untainted. His robes of character were spotless. He did not fellowship, or have the least delight in, the sins which filled all Israel with fearful reports. Samuel loved God; he kept his soul in such close connection with heaven that an angel was sent to talk with him in reference to the sins of Eli's sons, which were corrupting Israel.

Appetite and passion are overcoming thousands of Christ's professed followers. Their senses become so blunted on account of familiarity with sin that they do not abhor it, but view it as attractive. The end of all things is at hand. God will not much longer bear with the crimes and debasing iniquity of the children of men. Their crimes have indeed reached unto the heavens and will soon be answered by the fearful plagues of God upon the earth. They will drink the cup of God's wrath unmixed with mercy.

I have seen that there is danger that even the professed children of God will be corrupted. Licentiousness is binding men and women as captives. They seem to be infatuated and powerless to resist and overcome upon the point of appetite and passion. In God there is power; in Him there is strength. If they will take hold upon it, the life-giving power of Jesus will stimulate everyone who has named the name of Christ.

Dangers and perils surround us; and we are only safe when we feel our weakness and cling with the grasp of faith to our mighty Deliverer. It is a fearful time in which we live. We cannot cease watchfulness and prayer for a moment. Our helpless souls must rely on Jesus, our compassionate Redeemer.

A TIME FOR WATCHFULNESS

I was shown the greatness and importance of the work before us. But few realize the true state of things. All who are asleep, and who cannot realize any necessity for vigilance and alarm, will be overcome. Young men are arising to engage in the work of God, some of whom have scarcely any sense of the sacredness and responsibility of the work. They have but little experience in exercising faith and in earnest soul hunger for the Spirit of God, which ever brings returns. Some men of good capabilities, who might fill important positions, do not know what spirit they are of. They run in a jovial mood as naturally as water flows downhill. They talk nonsense, and sport with young girls, while almost daily listening to the most solemn, soul-stirring truths. These men have a religion of the head, but their hearts are not sanctified by the truths they hear. Such can never lead others to the Fountain of living waters until they have drunk of the stream themselves.

It is no time now for lightness, vanity, or trifling. The scenes of this earth's history are soon to close. Minds that have been left to loose thought need change. Says the apostle Peter: "Gird up the loins of your mind, be sober, and hope to the end for the grace that is to be brought unto you at the revelation of Jesus Christ; as obedient children, not fashioning yourselves according to the former lusts in your ignorance: but as He which hath called you is holy, so be ye holy in all manner of conversation; because it is written, Be ye holy; for I am holy." 1 Peter 1:13-16.

Loose thoughts must be gathered up and centered on God. The very thoughts should be in obedience to the will of God. Praise should not be given or expected; for this will have a tendency to foster self-confidence rather than to increase humility, to corrupt rather than to purify. Men who are really qualified and who feel that they have a part to act in connection with the work of God will feel pressed beneath the sense of the sacredness of the work, as a cart beneath sheaves. Now is the time to make the most earnest efforts to overcome the natural feelings of the carnal heart.

The State of the Church

There is great necessity for a reformation among the people of God. The present state of the church leads to the inquiry: Is this a correct representation of Him who gave His life for us? Are these the followers of Christ and the brethren of those who counted not their lives dear unto themselves? Those who come up to the Bible standard, the Bible description of Christ's followers, will be found rare indeed. Having forsaken God, the Fountain of living waters, they have hewn them out cisterns, "broken cisterns, that can hold no water." Said the angel: "Lack of love and faith are the great sins of which God's people are now guilty." Lack of faith leads to carelessness and to love of self and the world. Those who separate themselves from God and fall under temptation indulge in gross vices, for the carnal heart leads to great wickedness. And this state of things is found among many of God's professed people. While they are professedly serving God they are to all intents and purposes corrupting their ways before Him. Appetite and passion are indulged by many, notwithstanding the clear light of truth points out the danger and lifts its warning voice: Beware, restrain, deny. "The wages of sin is death." Romans 6:23. Although the example of those who have made shipwreck of faith stands as a beacon to warn others from pursuing the same course, yet many rush madly on. Satan has control of their minds and seems to have power over their bodies.

Oh, how many flatter themselves that they have goodness and righteousness, when the true light of God reveals that all their lives they have only lived to please themselves! Their whole conduct is abhorred of God. How many are alive with-

1875, vol. 3, pp. 474-477.

out the law! In their gross darkness they view themselves with complacency; but let the law of God be revealed to their consciences, as it was to Paul, and they would see that they are sold under sin and must die to the carnal mind. Self must be slain.

How sad and fearful the mistakes that many are making! They are building on the sand, but flatter themselves that they are riveted to the eternal Rock. Many who profess godliness are rushing on as recklessly, and are as insensible of their danger, as though there were no future judgment. A fearful retribution awaits them, and yet they are controlled by impulse and gross passion; they are filling out a dark life record for the judgment. I lift my voice of warning to all who name the name of Christ to depart from all iniquity. Purify your souls by obeying the truth. Cleanse yourselves from all filthiness of the flesh and spirit, perfecting holiness in the fear of God. You to whom this applies know what I mean. Even you who have corrupted your ways before the Lord, partaken of the iniquity that abounds, and blackened your souls with sin, Jesus still invites you to turn from your course, take hold of His strength, and find in Him that peace, power, and grace that will make you more than conquerors in His name.

The corruptions of this degenerate age have stained many souls who have been professedly serving God. But even now it is not too late for wrongs to be righted and for the blood of a crucified and risen Saviour to atone in your behalf if you repent and feel your need of pardon. We need now to watch and pray as never before, lest we fall under the power of temptation and leave the example of a life that is a miserable wreck. We must not, as a people, become careless and look upon sin with indifference. The camp needs purging. All who name the name of Christ need to watch and pray and guard the avenues of the soul; for Satan is at work to corrupt and destroy if the least advantage is given him.

WALK IN THE LIGHT

My brethren, God calls upon you as His followers to walk in the light. You need to be alarmed. Sin is among us, and it is not seen to be exceedingly sinful. The senses of many are benumbed by the indulgence of appetite and by familiarity with sin. We need to advance nearer heaven. We may grow in grace and in the knowledge of the truth. Walking in the light, running in the way of God's commandments, does not give the idea that we can stand still and do nothing. We must be advancing.

In self-love, self-exaltation, and pride there is great weakness; but in humility there is great strength. Our true dignity is not maintained when we think most of ourselves, but when God is in all our thoughts and our hearts are all aglow with love to our Redeemer and love to our fellow men. Simplicity of character and lowliness of heart will give happiness, while self-conceit will bring discontent, repining, and continual disappointment. It is learning to think less of ourselves and more of making others happy that will bring to us divine strength.

In our separation from God, in our pride and darkness, we are constantly seeking to elevate ourselves, and we forget that lowliness of mind is power. Our Saviour's power was not in a strong array of sharp words that would pierce through the very soul; it was His gentleness and His plain, unassuming manners that made Him a conqueror of hearts. Pride and self-importance, when compared with lowliness and humility, are indeed weakness. We are invited to learn of Him who was meek and lowly of heart; then we shall experience that rest and peace so much to be desired.

Love of the World

The temptation that was presented by Satan to our Saviour upon the exceeding high mountain is one of the leading temptations which humanity must meet. The kingdoms of the world in their glory were offered to Christ by Satan as a gift upon condition that Christ would yield to him the honor due to a superior. Our Saviour felt the strength of this temptation, but He met it in our behalf and conquered. He would not have been tested upon this point if man were not to be tried with the same temptation. In His resistance, He gave us an example of the course that we should pursue when Satan should come to us individually to lead us from our integrity.

No man can be a follower of Christ and yet place his affections upon the things of the world. John in his first epistle writes: "Love not the world, neither the things that are in the world. If any man love the world, the love of the Father is not in him." 1 John 2:15. Our Redeemer, who met this temptation of Satan in its fullest power, is acquainted with man's danger of yielding to the temptation to love the world.

Christ identified Himself with humanity by bearing the test upon this point and overcoming in man's behalf. He has guarded with warnings those very points where Satan would best succeed in his temptations to man. He knew that Satan would gain the victory over man unless he was especially guarded upon the points of appetite and the love of worldly riches and honor. He says: "Lay not up for yourselves treasures upon earth, where moth and rust doth corrupt, and where thieves break through and steal: but lay up for yourselves treasures in heaven, where neither moth nor rust doth corrupt, and where thieves do not break through nor steal:

1875, vol. 3, pp. 477-482.

for where your treasure is, there will your heart be also." "No man can serve two masters: for either he will hate the one, and love the other; or else he will hold to the one, and despise the other. Ye cannot serve God and mammon." Matthew 6:19-21, 24.

Here Christ has brought before us two masters, God and the world, and has plainly presented the fact that it is simply impossible for us to serve both. If our interest in, and love for, this world predominate, we shall not appreciate the things, which, above all others, are worthy of our attention. The love of the world will exclude the love of God and make our highest interests subordinate to worldly considerations. Thus God will not hold so exalted a place in our affections and devotions as do the things of the world.

Our works will show the exact extent to which earthly treasures have our affections. The greatest care, anxiety, and labor are devoted to worldly interests, while eternal considerations are made secondary. Here Satan receives of man that homage which he claimed of Christ but failed to obtain. It is the selfish love of the world which corrupts the faith of the professed followers of Christ and makes them weak in moral power. The more they love their earthly riches, the further they depart from God, and the less do they partake of His divine nature that would give them a sense of the corrupting influences in the world and the dangers to which they are exposed.

In Satan's temptations it is his purpose to make the world very attractive. Through love of riches and worldly honor he has a bewitching power to gain the affections of even the professed Christian world. A large class of professedly Christian men will make any sacrifice to gain riches, and the better they succeed in their object the less love they have for precious truth and the less interest for its advancement. They lose their love for God and act like insane men. The more they are prospered in securing riches the poorer they feel because they have no more, and the less will they invest in the cause of God.

The works of those men who have an insane love for riches show that it is not possible for them to serve two masters, God and mammon. Money is their god. They yield homage to its power. They serve the world to all intents and purposes. Their honor, which is their birthright, is sacrificed for worldly gain. This ruling power controls their minds, and they will violate the law of God to serve personal interests, to increase their earthly treasure.

SERVANTS OF MAMMON

Many may profess the religion of Christ who love not and heed not the letter or principles of Christ's teachings. They give the best of their strength to worldly pursuits and bow down to mammon. It is alarming that so many are deceived by Satan and their imaginations excited by their brilliant prospects of worldly gain. They become infatuated with the prospect of perfect happiness if they can gain their object in acquiring honor and wealth in the world. Satan tempts them with the alluring bribe, "All this will I give thee," all this power, all this wealth, with which you may do a great amount of good. But when the object for which they have labored is gained, they do not have that connection with the self-denying Redeemer which would make them partakers of the divine nature. They hold to their earthly treasures and despise the self-denial and self-sacrifice required for Christ. They have no desire to part with the dear earthly treasures upon which their hearts are set. They have exchanged masters; they have accepted mammon in the place of Christ. Mammon is their god, and mammon they serve.

Satan has secured to himself the worship of these deceived souls through their love of riches. The change has been so imperceptibly made, and Satan's power is so deceptive, so wily, that they are conformed to the world and perceive not that they have parted with Christ and are no longer His servants except in name.

Satan deals with men more guardedly than he dealt with Christ in the wilderness of temptation, for he is admonished that he there lost his case. He is a conquered foe. He does not come to man directly and demand homage by outward worship. He simply asks men to place their affections upon the good things of this world. If he succeeds in engaging the mind and affections, the heavenly attractions are eclipsed. All he wants of man is for him to fall under the deceitful power of his temptations, to love the world, to love rank and position, to love money, and to place his affections upon earthly treasures. If he secures this, he gains all that he asked of Christ.

DELIVERANCE THROUGH CHRIST

The example of Christ shows us that our only hope of victory is in continual resistance of Satan's attacks. He who triumphed over the adversary of souls in the conflict of temptation understands Satan's power over the race and has conquered him in our behalf. As an overcomer He has given us the advantage of His victory, that in our efforts to resist the temptations of Satan we may unite our weakness to His strength, our worthlessness to His merits. And, sustained by His enduring might under strong temptation, we may resist in His all-powerful name and overcome as He overcame.

It was through inexpressible suffering that our Redeemer placed redemption within our reach. In this world He was unhonored and unknown, that through His wonderful condescension and humiliation He might exalt man to receive heavenly honors and immortal joys in His kingly courts. Will fallen man murmur because heaven can be obtained only by conflict, self-abasement, and toil?

The inquiry of many a proud heart is: Why need I go in humiliation and penitence before I can have the assurance of my acceptance with God, and attain the immortal reward?

Why is not the path to heaven less difficult and more pleasant and attractive? We refer all these doubting, murmuring ones to our great Exemplar while suffering under the load of man's guilt and enduring the keenest pangs of hunger. He was sinless, and more than this, He was the Prince of heaven; but in man's behalf He became sin for the race. "He was wounded for our transgressions, He was bruised for our iniquities: the chastisement of our peace was upon Him; and with His stripes we are healed." Isaiah 53:5.

Christ sacrificed everything for man in order to make it possible for him to gain heaven. Now it is for fallen man to show what he will sacrifice on his own account for Christ's sake, that he may win immortal glory. Those who have any just sense of the magnitude of salvation and of its cost will never murmur that their sowing must be in tears and that conflict and self-denial are the Christian's portion in this life. The conditions of salvation for man are ordained of God. Self-abasement and cross bearing are the provisions made by which the repenting sinner is to find comfort and peace. The thought that Jesus submitted to humiliation and sacrifice that man will never be called to endure, should hush every murmuring voice. The sweetest joy comes to man through his sincere repentance toward God because of the transgression of His law, and faith in Christ as the sinner's Redeemer and Advocate.

Men labor at great cost to secure the treasures of this life. They suffer toil and endure hardships and privations to gain some worldly advantage. Why should the sinner be less willing to endure, to suffer, and to sacrifice in order to secure an imperishable treasure, a life that runs parallel with the life of God, a crown of immortal glory that fadeth not away? The infinite treasures of heaven, the inheritance which passes all estimate in value, which is an eternal weight of glory, must be obtained by us at any cost. We should not murmur at self-denial, for the Lord of life and glory endured it before us. Suffering and deprivation we should not avoid, for the Majesty of heaven accepted these in behalf of sinners. Sacrifice of ease and convenience should not cause one thought of repining, because the world's Redeemer accepted all these in our behalf. Making the largest estimate of all our self-denials, privations, and sacrifices, it costs us far less in every respect than it did the Prince of life. Any sacrifice that we may make sinks into insignificance when compared with that which Christ made in our behalf.

Presumption

There are those who have a reckless spirit, which they term courage and bravery. They needlessly place themselves in scenes of danger and peril, thus exposing themselves to temptations out of which it would require a miracle of God to bring them unharmed and untainted. Satan's temptation to the Saviour of the world to cast Himself from the pinnacle of the temple was firmly met and resisted. Satan quoted a promise of God as security that Christ might with safety do this on the strength of the promise. Christ met the temptation with scripture: "It is written, . . . Thou shalt not tempt the Lord thy God." Matthew 4:7. The only safe course for Christians is to repulse the enemy with God's word. Satan urges men into places where God does not require them to go, and presents scripture to justify his suggestions.

God's precious promises are not given to strengthen man in a presumptuous course or for him to rely upon when he rushes needlessly into danger. The Lord requires us to move with a humble dependence upon His providence. "It is not in man that walketh to direct his steps." Jeremiah 10:23. In God is our prosperity and our life. Nothing can be done prosperously without the permission and blessing of God. He can set His hand to prosper and bless, or He can turn His hand against us. "Commit thy way unto the Lord; trust also in Him; and He shall bring it to pass." Psalm 37:5. We are required, as children of God, to maintain a consistent Christian character. We should exercise prudence, caution, and humility, and walk circumspectly toward them that are without. Yet we are not in any case to surrender principle.

Our only safety is in giving no place to the devil, for his

1875, vol. 3, pp. 482-485.

suggestions and purposes are ever to injure us and hinder us from relying upon God. He transforms himself into an angel of purity that he may, through his specious temptations, introduce his devices in such a manner that we may not discern his wiles. The more we yield, the more powerful will be his deceptions over us. It is unsafe to enter into controversy or to parley with him. For every advantage that we give the enemy, he will claim more. Our only safety is in rejecting firmly the first approach to presumption. God has, through the merits of Christ, given us sufficient grace to withstand Satan and be more than conquerors. Resistance is success. "Resist the devil, and he will flee from you." James 4:7. Resistance must be firm and steadfast. We lose all we gain if we resist today only to yield tomorrow.

IMPORTANCE OF WOMEN'S WORK

The sin of this age is disregard of God's express commands. The power of influence in a wrong direction is very great. Eve had all that her wants required. There was nothing lacking to make her happy, but intemperate appetite desired the fruit of the only tree that God had withheld. She had no need of the fruit of the tree of knowledge, but she permitted her appetite and curiosity to control her reason. She was perfectly happy in her Eden home by her husband's side; but, like restless modern Eves, she was flattered that there was a higher sphere than that which God had assigned her. But in attempting to climb higher than her original position, she fell far below it. This will most assuredly be the result with the Eves of the present generation if they neglect to cheerfully take up their daily life duties in accordance with God's plan.

There is a work for women that is even more important and elevating than the duties of the king upon his throne. They may mold the minds of their children and shape their characters so that they may be useful in this world and that they may become sons and daughters of God. Their time should be considered too valuable to be passed in the ballroom or in needless labor. There is enough necessary and important labor in this world of need and suffering without wasting precious moments for ornamentation or display. Daughters of the heavenly King, members of the royal family, will feel a burden of responsibility to attain to a higher life, that they may be brought into close connection with heaven and work in unison with the Redeemer of the world. Those who are engaged in this work will not be satisfied with the fashions and follies which absorb the mind and affections of women in these last days. If they are indeed the daughters of God they will be partakers of the divine nature. They will be stirred with deepest pity, as was their divine Redeemer, as they see the corrupting influences in society. They will be in sympathy with Christ, and in their sphere, as they have ability and opportunity, will work to save perishing souls as Christ worked in His exalted sphere for the benefit of man.

MEN AND WOMEN CREATED EQUAL

A neglect on the part of woman to follow God's plan in her creation, an effort to reach for important positions which He has not qualified her to fill, leaves vacant the position that she could fill to acceptance. In getting out of her sphere, she loses true womanly dignity and nobility. When God created Eve, He designed that she should possess neither inferiority nor superiority to the man, but that in all things she should be his equal. The holy pair were to have no interest independent of each other; and yet each had an individuality in thinking and acting. But after Eve's sin, as she was first in the transgression, the Lord told her that Adam should rule over her. She was to be in subjection to her husband, and this was a part of the curse. In many cases the curse has made the lot of woman very grievous and her life a burden. The superiority which God has given man he has abused in many respects by exercising arbitrary power. Infinite wisdom devised the plan of redemption, which places the race on a second probation by giving them another trial.

A WARNING TO MINISTERS

Satan uses men as his agents to lead to presumption those who love God; especially is this the case with those who are deluded by spiritualism. Spiritualists generally do not accept Christ as the Son of God, and through their infidelity they lead many souls to presumptuous sins. They even claim superiority over Christ as did Satan in contesting with the Prince of life. Spiritualists whose souls are dyed with sins of a revolting character, and whose consciences are seared, dare to take the name of the spotless Son of God in their polluted lips and blasphemously unite His most exalted name with the vileness which marks their own polluted natures.

Men who bring in these damnable heresies will dare those who teach the word of God to enter into controversy with them, and some who teach the truth have not had the courage to withstand a challenge from this class, who are marked characters in the word of God. Some of our ministers have not had the moral courage to say to these men: God has warned us in His word in regard to you. He has given us a faithful description of your character and of the heresies which you hold. Some of our ministers, rather than give this class any occasion to triumph or to charge them with cowardice, have met them in open discussion. But in discussing with spiritualists they do not meet man merely, but Satan and his angels. They place themselves in communication with the powers of darkness and encourage evil angels about them.

Spiritualists desire to give publicity to their heresies; and ministers who advocate Bible truth help them to do this when they consent to engage in discussion with them. They improve their opportunities to get their heresies before the people, and in every discussion with them some will be deceived. The very best course for us to pursue is to avoid them.

PRESUMPTION is a common temptation, and as Satan assails men with this, he obtains the victory nine times out of ten. Those who *profess* to be followers of Christ, and claim by their faith to be enlisted in the warfare against all evil in their nature, frequently plunge without thought into temptations from which it would require a miracle to bring them forth unsullied. Meditation and prayer would have preserved them and led them to shun the critical, dangerous position in which they placed themselves when they gave Satan the advantage over them. The promises of God are not for us rashly to claim while we rush on recklessly into danger, violating the laws of nature and disregarding prudence and the judgment with which God has endowed us. This is the most flagrant presumption.—1876, vol. 4, pp. 44, 45.

Power of Appetite

One of the strongest temptations that man has to meet is upon the point of appetite. Between the mind and the body there is a mysterious and wonderful relation. They react upon each other. To keep the body in a healthy condition to develop its strength, that every part of the living machinery may act harmoniously, should be the first study of our life. To neglect the body is to neglect the mind. It cannot be to the glory of God for His children to have sickly bodies or dwarfed minds. To indulge the taste at the expense of health is a wicked abuse of the senses. Those who engage in any species of intemperance, either in eating or drinking, waste their physical energies and weaken moral power. They will feel the retribution which follows the transgression of physical law.

The Redeemer of the world knew that the indulgence of appetite would bring physical debility, and so deaden the perceptive organs that sacred and eternal things would not be discerned. Christ knew that the world was given up to gluttony and that this indulgence would pervert the moral powers. If the indulgence of appetite was so strong upon the race that, in order to break its power, the divine Son of God, in behalf of man, was required to fast nearly six weeks, what a work is before the Christian in order that he may overcome even as Christ overcame! The strength of the temptation to indulge perverted appetite can be measured only by the inexpressible anguish of Christ in that long fast in the wilderness.

Christ knew that in order to successfully carry forward the plan of salvation He must commence the work of redeeming man just where the ruin began. Adam fell by the indulgence of appetite. In order to impress upon man his obligations to

1875, vol. 3, pp. 485-492.

obey the law of God, Christ began His work of redemption by reforming the physical habits of man. The declension in virtue and the degeneracy of the race are chiefly attributable to the indulgence of perverted appetite.

There is a solemn responsibility upon all, especially upon ministers who teach the truth, to overcome upon the point of appetite. Their usefulness would be much greater if they had control of their appetites and passions, and their mental and moral powers would be stronger if they combined physical labor with mental exertion. With strictly temperate habits, and with mental and physical labor combined, they could accomplish a far greater amount of labor and preserve clearness of mind. If they would pursue such a course, their thoughts and words would flow more freely, their religious exercises would be more energized, and the impressions made upon their hearers would be more marked.

INTEMPERANCE IN EATING

Intemperance in eating, even of food of the right quality, will have a prostrating influence upon the system and will blunt the keener and holier emotions. Strict temperance in eating and drinking is highly essential for the healthy preservation and vigorous exercise of all the functions of the body. Strictly temperate habits, combined with exercise of the muscles as well as of the mind, will preserve both mental and physical vigor, and give power of endurance to those engaged in the ministry, to editors, and to all others whose habits are sedentary. As a people, with all our profession of health reform, we eat too much. Indulgence of appetite is the greatest cause of physical and mental debility, and lies at the foundation of the feebleness which is apparent everywhere.

Intemperance commences at our tables in the use of unhealthful food. After a time, through continued indulgence, the digestive organs become weakened, and the food taken does not satisfy the appetite. Unhealthy conditions are established, and there is a craving for more stimulating food. Tea, coffee, and flesh meats produce an immediate effect. Under the influence of these poisons the nervous system is excited, and, in some cases, for the time being, the intellect seems to be invigorated and the imagination to be more vivid. Because these stimulants produce for the time being such agreeable results, many conclude that they really need them and continue their use. But there is always a reaction. The nervous system, having been unduly excited, borrowed power for present use from its future resources of strength. All this temporary invigoration of the system is followed by depression. In proportion as these stimulants temporarily invigorate the system will be the letting down of the power of the excited organs after the stimulus has lost its force. The appetite is educated to crave something stronger which will have a tendency to keep up and increase the agreeable excitement, until indulgence becomes habit, and there is a continual craving for stronger stimulus, as tobacco, wines, and liquors. The more the appetite is indulged, the more frequent will be its demands and the more difficult of control. The more debilitated the system becomes and the less able to do without unnatural stimulus, the more the passion for these things increases, until the will is overborne, and there seems to be no power to deny the unnatural craving for these indulgences.

THE ONLY SAFE COURSE

The only safe course is to touch not, taste not, handle not, tea, coffee, wines, tobacco, opium, and alcoholic drinks. The necessity for the men of this generation to call to their aid the power of the will, strengthened by the grace of God, in order to withstand the temptations of Satan and resist the least indulgence of perverted appetite is twice as great as it was several generations ago. But the present generation have less power of self-control than had those who lived then. Those who have indulged the appetite for these stimulants have transmitted their depraved appetites and passions to their children, and greater moral power is required to resist intemperance in all its forms. The only perfectly safe course to pursue is to stand firmly on the side of temperance and not venture in the path of danger.

The great end for which Christ endured that long fast in the wilderness was to teach us the necessity of self-denial and temperance. This work should commence at our tables and should be strictly carried out in all the concerns of life. The Redeemer of the world came from heaven to help man in his weakness, that, in the power which Jesus came to bring him, he might become strong to overcome appetite and passion, and might be victor on every point.

Many parents educate the tastes of their children and form their appetites. They indulge them in eating flesh meats and in drinking tea and coffee. The highly seasoned flesh meats and the tea and coffee, which some mothers encourage their children to use, prepare the way for them to crave stronger stimulants, as tobacco. The use of tobacco encourages the appetite for liquor, and the use of tobacco and liquor invariably lessens nerve power.

If the moral sensibilities of Christians were aroused upon the subject of temperance in *all things,* they could, by their example, commencing at their tables, help those who are weak in self-control, who are almost powerless to resist the cravings of appetite. If we could realize that the habits we form in this life will affect our eternal interests, that our eternal destiny depends upon strictly temperate habits, we would work to the point of strict temperance in eating and drinking. By our example and personal effort we may be the means of saving many souls from the degradation of intemperance, crime, and death. Our sisters can do much in the great work for the salvation of others by spreading their tables with only healthful, nourishing food. They may employ their precious time in educating the tastes and appetites of their children, in forming habits of temperance in all things, and in encouraging self-denial and benevolence for the good of others.

Notwithstanding the example that Christ gave us in the wilderness of temptation by denying appetite and overcoming its power, there are many Christian mothers who by their example and by the education which they are giving their children are preparing them to become gluttons and winebibbers. Children are frequently indulged in eating what they choose and when they choose, without reference to health. There are many children who are educated gourmands from their babyhood. Through indulgence of appetite they are made dyspeptics at an early age. Self-indulgence and intemperance in eating grow with their growth and strengthen with their strength. Mental and physical vigor are sacrificed through the indulgence of parents. A taste is formed for certain articles of food from which they can receive no benefit, but only injury; and as the system is taxed, the constitution becomes debilitated.

BENEFITS OF PHYSICAL EXERCISE

Ministers, teachers, and students do not become as intelligent as they should in regard to the necessity of physical exercise in the open air. They neglect this duty, which is most essential for the preservation of health. They closely apply their minds to books and eat the allowance of a laboring man. Under such habits some grow corpulent, because the system is clogged. Others become lean, feeble, and weak because their vital powers are exhausted in throwing off the excess of food; the liver becomes burdened and unable to throw off the impurities in the blood, and sickness is the result. If physical exercise were combined with mental exertion, the blood would be quickened in its circulation, the action of the heart would be more perfect, impure matter would be thrown off, and new life and vigor would be experienced in every part of the body. . . .

When the minds of ministers, schoolteachers, and students are continually excited by study, and the body is allowed to be inactive, the nerves of emotion are taxed, while the nerves of motion are inactive. The wear being all upon the mental organs, they become overworked and enfeebled, while the muscles lose their vigor for want of employment. There is no inclination to exercise the muscles by engaging in physical labor, because exertion seems to be irksome.

MINISTERS TO BE EXAMPLES

Ministers of Christ, professing to be His representatives, should follow His example, and above all others should form habits of strictest temperance. They should keep the life and example of Christ before the people by their own lives of self-denial, self-sacrifice, and active benevolence. Christ overcame appetite in man's behalf, and in His stead they are to set others an example worthy of imitation. Those who do not feel the necessity of engaging in the work of overcoming upon the point of appetite will fail to secure precious victories which they might have gained and will become slaves to appetite and lust, which are filling the cup of iniquity of those who dwell upon the earth.

Men who are engaged in giving the last message of warning to the world, a message which is to decide the destiny of souls, should make a practical application in their own lives of the truths they preach to others. They should be examples to the people in their eating, in their drinking, and in their chaste conversation and deportment. Gluttony, indulgence of the baser passions, and grievous sins are hidden under the garb of sanctity by many professed representatives of Christ throughout our world. There are men of excellent natural ability whose labor does not accomplish half what it might if they were temperate in all things. Indulgence of appetite and passion beclouds the mind, lessens physical strength, and weakens moral power. Their thoughts are not clear. Their words are not spoken in power, are not vitalized by the Spirit of God so as to reach the hearts of the hearers.

As our first parents lost Eden through the indulgence of appetite, our only hope of regaining Eden is through the firm denial of appetite and passion. Abstemiousness in diet and control of all the passions will preserve the intellect and give mental and moral vigor, enabling men to bring all their propensities under the control of the higher powers and to discern between right and wrong, the sacred and the common. All who have a true sense of the sacrifice made by Christ in leaving His home in heaven to come to this world that He might by His own life show man how to resist temptation will cheerfully deny self and choose to be partakers with Christ of His sufferings.

CONTROLLED BY AN ENLIGHTENED CONSCIENCE

The fear of the Lord is the beginning of wisdom. Those who overcome as Christ overcame will need to constantly guard themselves against the temptations of Satan. The appetite and passions should be restricted and under the control of enlightened conscience, that the intellect may be unimpaired, the perceptive powers clear, so that the workings of Satan and his snares may not be interpreted to be the providence of God. Many desire the final reward and victory which are to be given to overcomers, but are not willing to endure toil, privation, and denial of self, as did their Redeemer. It is only through obedience and continual effort that we shall overcome as Christ overcame.

The controlling power of appetite will prove the ruin of thousands, when, if they had conquered on this point, they would have had moral power to gain the victory over every other temptation of Satan. But those who are slaves to appetite will fail in perfecting Christian character. The continual transgression of man for six thousand years has brought sickness, pain, and death as its fruits. And as we near the close of time, Satan's temptation to indulge appetite will be more powerful and more difficult to overcome.

Begin at Home. The work of temperance must begin in our families, at our tables. Mothers have an important work to do that they may give to the world, through correct discipline and education, children who will be capable of filling almost any position, and who can also honor and enjoy the duties of domestic life.

The work of the mother is very important and sacred. She should teach her children from the cradle to practice habits of self-denial and self-control. If her time is mostly occupied with the follies of this degenerate age, if dress and parties engage her precious time, her children fail to receive that education which it is essential they should have in order that they may form correct characters. The anxiety of the Christian mother should not be in regard to the external merely, but that her children may have healthy constitutions and good morals.

Many mothers who deplore the intemperance which exists everywhere do not look deep enough to see the cause. They are daily preparing a variety of dishes and highly seasoned food which tempt the appetite and encourage overeating. The tables of our American people are generally prepared in a manner to make drunkards. Appetite is the ruling principle with a large class. Whoever will indulge appetite in eating too often, and food not of a healthful quality, is weakening his power to resist the clamors of appetite and passion in other respects in proportion as he has strengthened the propensity to incorrect habits of eating. Mothers need to be impressed with their obligation to God and to the world to furnish society with children having well-developed characters. Men and women who come upon the stage of action with firm principles will be fitted to stand unsullied amid the moral pollutions of this corrupt age.—1875, vol. 3, pp. 562, 563.

WHILE a healthy state of mind depends upon the normal condition of the vital forces, what care should be exercised that neither stimulants nor narcotics be used.

Tobacco is a slow, insidious poison, and its effects are more difficult to cleanse from the system than those of liquor. What power can the tobacco devotee have to stay the progress of intemperance? There must be a revolution in our world upon the subject of tobacco before the ax is laid at the root of the tree. We press the subject still closer. Tea and coffee are fostering the appetite which is developing for stronger stimulants, as tobacco and liquor. And we come still closer home, to the daily meals, the tables spread in Christian households. Is temperance practiced in all things? Are the reforms which are essential to health and happiness carried out there?

Every true Christian will have control of his appetite and passions. Unless he is free from the bondage and slavery of appetite he cannot be a true, obedient servant of Christ. It is the indulgence of appetite and passion which makes the truth of none effect upon the heart. It is impossible for the spirit and power of the truth to sanctify a man, soul, body, and spirit, when he is controlled by appetite and passion.—1875, vol. 3, pp. 569, 570.

All should guard the senses, lest Satan gain victory over them; for these are the avenues to the soul.—1875, vol. 3, p. 507.

As a people we profess to be reformers, to be light bearers in the world, to be faithful sentinels for God, guarding every avenue whereby Satan could come in with his temptations to pervert the appetite. Our example and influence must be a power on the side of reform. We must abstain from any practice which will blunt the conscience or encourage temptation. We must open no door that will give Satan access to the mind of one human being formed in the image of God. If all would be vigilant and faithful in guarding the little openings made by the moderate use of the so-called harmless wine and cider, the highway to drunkenness would be closed up. What is needed in every community is firm purpose, and a will to touch not, taste not, handle not; then the temperance reformation will be strong, permanent, and thorough.—1885, vol. 5, p. 360.

The Discipline of Trial

"And He shall sit as a refiner and purifier of silver: and He shall purify the sons of Levi, and purge them as gold and silver, that they may offer unto the Lord an offering in righteousness. Then shall the offering of Judah and Jerusalem be pleasant unto the Lord, as in the days of old, and as in former years." Malachi 3:3, 4. This is the process, the refining, purifying process, which is to be carried on by the Lord of hosts. The work is most trying to the soul, but it is only through this process that the rubbish and defiling impurities can be removed. Our trials are all necessary to bring us close to our heavenly Father, in obedience to His will, that we may offer to the Lord an offering in righteousness.

To each whose name is here mentioned,* God has given capabilities, talents to improve. You each need a new and living experience in the divine life in order to do the will of God. No amount of past experience will suffice for the present nor strengthen us to overcome the difficulties in our path. We must have new grace and fresh strength daily in order to be victorious.

We are seldom, in all respects, placed in the same circumstances twice. Abraham, Moses, Elijah, Daniel, and many others were all sorely tried, but not in the same way. Everyone has his individual tests and trials in the drama of life, but the very same trials seldom come twice. Each has his own experience, peculiar in its character and circumstances, to accomplish

1875, vol. 3, pp. 541-544 (Man's Duty to His Fellow Men).

*Note: This chapter on the discipline of trial, is drawn from a lengthy testimony addressed to several individuals and families, consequently there are several references to those particularly addressed. [White Trustees.]

a certain work. God has a work, a purpose, in the life of each of us. Every act, however small, has its place in our life experience. We must have the continual light and experience that come from God. We all need these, and God is more than willing that we should have them if we will take them. He has not closed the windows of heaven to your prayers, but you have felt satisfied to pass on without the divine help you so much need.

How little you know the bearing of your daily acts upon the history of others. You may think that what you do or say is of little consequence, when the most important results for good or evil are the consequence of our words and actions. The words and actions looked upon as so small and unimportant are links in the long chain of human events. You have not felt the need of God's manifesting His will to us in all the acts of our daily life. With our first parents the desire for a single gratification of appetite opened the floodgate of woe and sin upon the world. Would that you, my dear sisters, might feel that every step you take may have a lasting and controlling influence upon your own lives and the characters of others. Oh, how much need, then, of communion with God! What need of divine grace to direct every step and show us how to perfect Christian characters!

A PROGRESSIVE EXPERIENCE

Christians will have new scenes and new trials to pass through where past experience cannot be a sufficient guide. We have greater need to learn of the divine Teacher now than at any other period of our lives. And the more experience we gain, the nearer we draw toward the pure light of heaven, the more shall we discern in ourselves that needs reforming. We may all do a good work in blessing others if we will seek counsel of God and follow on in obedience and faith. The path of the just is progressive, from strength to strength, from grace to grace, and from glory to glory. The divine illumination will increase more and more, corresponding with our onward movements, qualifying us to meet the responsibilities and emergencies before us.

When trials press you, when despondency and dark unbelief control your thoughts, when selfishness molds your actions, you do not see your need of God and of a deep and thorough knowledge of His will. You know not the will of God, neither can you know it while you live for self. You rely upon your good intentions and resolutions, and the principal sum of life is composed of resolutions made and resolutions broken. What you all need is to die to self, cease clinging to self, and surrender to God.

Gladly would I comfort you if I could. Gladly would I praise your good qualities, good purposes, and good acts; but God was not pleased to show me these. He presented before me the hindrances to your gaining the noble, elevated character of holiness needful for you to have that you may not lose the heavenly rest and immortal glory He would have you attain. Look away from yourselves to Jesus. He is all and in all. The merits of the blood of a crucified and risen Saviour will avail to cleanse from the least and greatest sin. In trusting faith commit the keeping of your souls to God as unto a faithful Creator. Be not continually in fear and apprehension that God will leave you. He never will unless you depart from Him. Christ will come in and dwell with you if you will open the door of your hearts to Him. There may be perfect harmony between you and the Father and His Son if you will die to self and live unto God.

How few are aware that they have darling idols, that they have cherished sins! God sees these sins to which you may be blinded, and He works with His pruning knife to strike deep and separate these cherished sins from you. You all want to choose for yourselves the process of purification. How hard it is for you to submit to the crucifixion of self; but when the work is all submitted to God, to Him who knows our weakness and our sinfulness, He takes the very best way to bring about the desired results.

It was through constant conflict and simple faith that Enoch walked with God. You may all do the same. You may be thoroughly converted and transformed, and be indeed children of God, enjoying not only the knowledge of His will, but, by your example, leading others in the same path of humble obedience and consecration. Real godliness is diffusive and communicative. The psalmist says: "I have not hid Thy righteousness within my heart; I have declared Thy faithfulness and Thy salvation: I have not concealed Thy loving-kindness and Thy truth from the great congregation." Psalm 40:10. Wherever the love of God is, there is always a desire to express it.

May God help you all to make earnest efforts to gain everlasting life and to lead others in the path of holiness.

"Cannot Come Down"

"I AM doing a great work," says Nehemiah, "so that I cannot come down: why should the work cease, whilst I leave it, and come down to you?" Nehemiah 6:3.

I was shown, January 3, 1875,* that God's people should not for one moment relax their watchfulness or their vigilance. Satan is upon our track. He is determined to overcome God's commandment-keeping people with his temptations. If we give no place to him, but resist his devices, steadfast in the faith, we shall have strength to depart from all iniquity. Those who keep the commandments of God will be a power in the land if they live up to their light and privileges. They may be patterns of piety, holy in heart and in conversation. We shall not have ease, that we may cease watchfulness and prayer. As the time draws near for Christ to be revealed in the clouds of heaven, Satan's temptations will be brought to bear with greater power upon those who keep God's commandments, for he knows that his time is short.

The work of Satan will be carried on through agents. Ministers who hate the law of God will employ any means to lead

1875, vol. 3, pp. 570-575.

*It is a pleasure here to state relative to the gracious manifestation of the Holy Spirit to Mrs. White on the eve of January 3, 1875, that she had been sick with severe influenza, and confined to her room and bed for one week, till the physicians at the Health Institute had become anxious in her case. In this condition she followed the directions given in the fifth chapter of the Epistle of James, and after a great stretch of faith, like the man in the gospel who stretched forth his withered hand, she reached the point of deliverance from pain and sickness, and was soon in vision, which lasted ten minutes. She then dressed for meeting, walked to the church, and spoke to the crowded assembly twenty minutes, and walked home. Since that time she has written very much, and has spoken to the people with freedom. She is now preparing for the long journey to the Pacific Coast. JAMES WHITE.

souls from their loyalty to God. Our bitterest foes will be among the first-day Adventists. Their hearts are fully determined to make war against those who keep the commandments of God and have the faith of Jesus. This class feel that it is a virtue to talk, write, and act out the most bitter hatred against us. We need not look for fair dealing or for justice at their hands. Many of them are inspired by Satan with insane madness against those who are keeping the commandments of God. We shall be maligned and misrepresented; all our motives and actions will be misjudged, and our characters will be attacked. The wrath of the dragon will be manifested in this manner. But I saw that we should not be in the least discouraged. Our strength is in Jesus, our Advocate. If in humility we trust in God and hold fast to His promises, He will give us grace and heavenly wisdom to withstand all the wiles of Satan and to come off victors.

In my recent view I saw that it will not increase our influence, or bring us into favor with God, to retaliate or come down from our great work to their level in meeting their slanders. There are those who will resort to any species of deception and gross falsehood to gain their object and deceive souls, and to cast stigma upon the law of God and those who love to obey it. They will repeat the most inconsistent and vile falsehoods, over and over, until they make themselves believe that they are truth. These are the strongest arguments they have to use against the Sabbath of the fourth commandment. We should not allow our feelings to control us and divert us from the work of warning the world.

NEHEMIAH'S EXAMPLE

The case of Nehemiah was presented before me. He was engaged in building the walls of Jerusalem, and the enemies of God were determined that the walls should not be built. "But it came to pass, that when Sanballat, and Tobiah, and the Arabians, and the Ammonites, and the Ashdodites, heard that the walls of Jerusalem were made up, and that the breaches began to be stopped, then they were very wroth, and conspired all of them together to come and to fight against Jerusalem, and to hinder it." Nehemiah 4:7, 8.

In this case a spirit of hatred and opposition to the Hebrews formed the bond of union and created a mutual sympathy among different bodies of men who might otherwise have warred with one another. This well illustrates what we frequently witness in our day in the existing union of men of different denominations to oppose present truth, men whose only bond seems to be that which is dragonic in its nature, manifesting bitterness and hatred against the remnant who keep the commandments of God. This is especially seen in the first-day, no-day, and all-days-alike Adventists, who seem to be famous for hating and slandering one another, when they can spare time from their efforts to misrepresent, slander, and in every way abuse Seventh-day Adventists.

"Nevertheless we made our prayer unto our God, and set a watch against them day and night, because of them." Verse 9. We are in constant danger of becoming self-sufficient, relying upon our own wisdom, and not making God our strength. Nothing disturbs Satan so much as our knowledge of his devices. If we feel our dangers we shall feel the need of prayer, as did Nehemiah, and like him we shall obtain that sure defense that will give us security in peril. If we are careless and indifferent, we shall surely be overcome by Satan's devices. We must be vigilant. While, like Nehemiah, we resort to prayer, taking all our perplexities and burdens to God, we should not feel that we have nothing to do. We are to watch as well as pray. We should watch the work of our adversaries, lest they gain advantage in deceiving souls. We should, in the wisdom of Christ, make efforts to defeat their purposes, while, at the same time, we do not suffer them to call us from our great work. Truth is stronger than error. Righteousness will prevail over wrong.

OPPOSITION TO BE EXPECTED

The Lord's people are seeking to heal the breach which has been made in the law of God. "And they that shall be of thee shall build the old waste places: thou shalt raise up the foundations of many generations; and thou shalt be called, The repairer of the breach, The restorer of paths to dwell in. If thou turn away thy foot from the Sabbath, from doing thy pleasure on My holy day; and call the Sabbath a delight, the holy of the Lord, honorable; and shalt honor Him, not doing thine own ways, nor finding thine own pleasure, nor speaking thine own words: then shalt thou delight thyself in the Lord; and I will cause thee to ride upon the high places of the earth, and feed thee with the heritage of Jacob thy father: for the mouth of the Lord hath spoken it." Isaiah 58:12-14.

This disturbs the enemies of our faith, and every means is employed to hinder us in our work. And yet the broken-down wall is going steadily up. The world is being warned, and many are turning away from trampling under their feet the Sabbath of Jehovah. God is in this work, and man cannot stop it. Angels of God are working with the efforts of His faithful servants, and the work steadily advances. We shall meet with opposition of every description, as did the builders of the walls of Jerusalem; but if we watch and pray and work, as they did, God will fight our battles for us and give us precious victories.

Nehemiah "clave to the Lord, and departed not from following Him, but kept His commandments, which the Lord commanded Moses. And the Lord was with him." 2 Kings 18:6, 7. Messengers were sent repeatedly, soliciting a conference with Nehemiah; but he refused to meet them. Bold threats were made of what they proposed to do, and messengers were sent to harangue the people engaged in the work of building. These presented flattering inducements and promised the builders freedom from restraint, and wonderful privileges, if they would unite their interest with them and cease their work of building.

But the people were commanded not to engage in controversy with their enemies and to answer them not a word, that no advantage of words might be given them. Threatenings and ridicule were resorted to. They said: "Even that which they build, if a fox go up, he shall even break down their stone wall." Sanballat "was wroth, and took great indignation, and mocked the Jews." Nehemiah prayed: "Hear, O our God; for we are despised: and turn their reproach upon their own head." Nehemiah 4:3, 1, 4.

"And I sent messengers unto them, saying, I am doing a great work, so that I cannot come down: why should the work cease, whilst I leave it, and come down to you? Yet they sent unto me four times after this sort; and I answered them after the same manner. Then sent Sanballat his servant unto me in like manner the fifth time with an open letter in his hand." Nehemiah 6:3-5.

We shall receive the most fierce opposition from the Adventists who oppose the law of God. But, like the builders of the walls of Jerusalem, we should not be diverted and hindered from our work by reports, by messengers desiring discussion or controversy, or by intimidating threats, the publication of falsehoods, or any of the devices that Satan may instigate. Our answer should be: We are engaged in a great work, and we cannot come down. We shall sometimes be perplexed to know what course we should pursue to preserve the honor of the cause of God and to vindicate His truth.

CONFIDENCE IN GOD

The course of Nehemiah should have a strong bearing upon our minds as to the manner of meeting this kind of opponents. We should take all these things to the Lord in prayer, as Nehemiah made his supplication to God, while his own spirit was humbled. He clung to God with unwavering faith. This is the course that we should pursue. Time is too precious to be devoted by the servants of God to vindicating their character, blackened by those who hate the Sabbath of the Lord. We should move forward with unwavering confidence, believing that God will give His truth great and precious victories. In humility, meekness, and purity of life, relying upon Jesus, we should carry a convincing power with us that we have the truth.

We do not understand, as is our privilege, the faith and confidence that we may have in God, and the great blessings which faith will give us. An important work is before us. We are to obtain a moral fitness for heaven. Our words and our example are to tell upon the world. Angels of God are actively engaged in ministering to the children of God. Precious promises are upon record on condition of our obedience to God's requirements. Heaven is full of the richest of blessings, all waiting to be communicated to us. If we feel our need, and come to God in sincerity and in earnest faith, we shall be brought into close connection with heaven and shall be channels of light to the world.

The warning needs to be often sounded: "Be sober, be vigilant; because your adversary the devil, as a roaring lion, walketh about, seeking whom he may devour." 1 Peter 5:8.

Bible Biographies

The lives recorded in the Bible are authentic histories of actual individuals. From Adam down through successive generations to the times of the apostles we have a plain, unvarnished account of what actually occurred and the genuine experience of real characters. It is a subject of wonder to many that inspired history should narrate in the lives of good men facts that tarnish their moral characters. Infidels seize upon these sins with great satisfaction and hold their perpetrators up to ridicule. The inspired writers did not testify to falsehoods to prevent the pages of sacred history being clouded by the record of human frailties and faults. The scribes of God wrote as they were dictated by the Holy Spirit, having no control of the work themselves. They penned the literal truth, and stern, forbidding facts are revealed for reasons that our finite minds cannot fully comprehend.

It is one of the best evidences of the authenticity of the Scriptures that the truth is not glossed over nor the sins of its chief characters suppressed. Many will urge that it is an easy matter to relate what has occurred in an ordinary life. But it is a proved fact that it is a human impossibility to give an impartial history of a contemporary; and it is almost as difficult to narrate, without deviating from the exact truth, the story of any person or people with whose career we have become acquainted. The human mind is so subject to prejudice that it is almost impossible for it to treat the subject impartially. Either the faults of the person under review stand out in glaring relief, or his virtues shine with undimmed luster, just as the writer is prejudiced for or against him. However

1876, vol. 4, pp. 9-15.

impartial the historian may design to be, all critics will agree that it is a very difficult matter to be truly so.

But divine unction, lifted above the weaknesses of humanity, tells the simple, naked truth. How many biographies have been written of faultless Christians, who, in their ordinary home life and church relations, shone as examples of immaculate piety. No blemish marred the beauty of their holiness, no fault is recorded to remind us that they were common clay and subject to the ordinary temptations of humanity. Yet had the pen of inspiration written their histories, how different would they have appeared. There would have been revealed human weaknesses, struggles with selfishness, bigotry, and pride, hidden sins perhaps, and the continual warfare between the spirit and the flesh.

Even private journals do not reveal on their pages the writer's sinful deeds. Sometimes the conflicts with evil are recorded, but usually only when the right has gained the victory. But they may contain a faithful account of praiseworthy acts and noble endeavors; this, too, when the writer honestly intends to keep a faithful journal of his life. It is next to a human impossibility to lay open our faults for the possible inspection of our friends.

Had our good Bible been written by uninspired persons, it would have presented quite a different appearance and would have been a discouraging study to erring mortals, who are contending with natural frailties and the temptations of a wily foe. But as it is, we have a correct record of the religious experiences of marked characters in Bible history. Men whom God favored, and to whom He entrusted great responsibilities, were sometimes overcome by temptation and committed sins, even as we of the present day strive, waver, and frequently fall into error. But it is encouraging to our desponding hearts to know that through God's grace they could gain fresh vigor to again rise above their evil natures; and, remembering this, we are ready to renew the conflict ourselves.

ISRAEL'S EXPERIENCE A WARNING

The murmurings of ancient Israel and their rebellious discontent, as well as the mighty miracles wrought in their favor and the punishment of their idolatry and ingratitude, are recorded for our benefit. The example of ancient Israel is given as a warning to the people of God, that they may avoid unbelief and escape His wrath. If the iniquities of the Hebrews had been omitted from the Sacred Record, and only their virtues recounted, their history would fail to teach us the lesson that it does.

Infidels and lovers of sin excuse their crimes by citing the wickedness of men to whom God gave authority in olden times. They argue that if these holy men yielded to temptation and committed sins, it is not to be wondered at that they, too, should be guilty of wrongdoing; and intimate that they are not so bad after all, since they have such illustrious examples of iniquity before them.

The principles of justice required a faithful narration of facts for the benefit of all who should ever read the Sacred Record. Here we discern the evidences of divine wisdom. We are required to obey the law of God, and are not only instructed as to the penalty of disobedience, but we have narrated for our benefit and warning the history of Adam and Eve in Paradise, and the sad results of their disobedience of God's commands. The account is full and explicit.

The law given to man in Eden is recorded, together with the penalty accruing in case of its disobedience. Then follows the story of the temptation and fall, and the punishment inflicted upon our erring parents. Their example is given us as a warning against disobedience, that we may be sure that the wages of sin is death, that God's retributive justice never fails, and that He exacts from His creatures a strict regard for His commandments. When the law was proclaimed at Sinai, how definite was the penalty annexed, how sure was punishment to follow the transgression of that law, and how plain are the cases recorded in evidence of that fact!

The pen of inspiration, true to its task, tells us of the sins that overcame Noah, Lot, Moses, Abraham, David, and Solomon, and that even Elijah's strong spirit sank under temptation during his fearful trial. Jonah's disobedience and Israel's idolatry are faithfully recorded. Peter's denial of Christ, the sharp contention of Paul and Barnabas, the failings and infirmities of the prophets and apostles, are all laid bare by the Holy Ghost, who lifts the veil from the human heart. There before us lie the lives of the believers, with all their faults and follies, which are intended as a lesson to all the generations following them. If they had been without foible they would have been more than human, and our sinful natures would despair of ever reaching such a point of excellence. But seeing where they struggled and fell, where they took heart again and conquered through the grace of God, we are encouraged, and led to press over the obstacles that degenerate nature places in our way.

God has ever been faithful to punish crime. He sent His prophets to warn the guilty, denounce their sins, and pronounce judgment upon them. Those who question why the word of God brings out the sins of His people in so plain a manner for scoffers to deride and saints to deplore, should consider that it was all written for their instruction, that they may avoid the evils recorded and imitate only the righteousness of those who served the Lord.

We need just such lessons as the Bible gives us, for with the revelation of sin is recorded the retribution which follows. The sorrow and penitence of the guilty, and the wailing of the sin-sick soul, come to us from the past, telling us that man was then, as now, in need of the pardoning mercy of God. It teaches us that while He is a punisher of crime, He pities and forgives the repenting sinner.

In His providence the Lord has seen fit to teach and warn

His people in various ways. By direct command, by the sacred writings, and by the spirit of prophecy has He made known unto them His will. My work has been to speak plainly of the faults and errors of God's people. Because the sins of certain individuals have been brought to light, it is no evidence that they are worse in the sight of the Lord than many whose failings are unrecorded. But I have been shown that it is not mine to choose my work, but humbly to obey the will of God. The errors and wrongdoings in the lives of professed Christians are recorded for the instruction of those who are liable to fall into the same temptations. The experience of one serves as a beacon light to warn others off the rocks of danger.

Thus are revealed the snares and devices of Satan, the importance of perfecting Christian character, and the means by which this result may be obtained. Thus God indicates what is necessary to secure His blessing. There is a disposition on the part of many to let rebellious feelings arise if their peculiar sins are reproved. The spirit of this generation is: "Speak unto us smooth things." Isaiah 30:10. But the spirit of prophecy speaks only the truth. Iniquity abounds, and the love of many who profess to follow Christ waxes cold. They are blind to the wickedness of their own hearts and do not feel their weak and helpless condition. God in mercy lifts the veil and shows them that there is an eye behind the scenes that discerns their hidden guilt and the motives of their actions.

The sins of the popular churches are whitewashed over. Many of the members indulge in the grossest vices and are steeped in iniquity. Babylon is fallen and has become the cage of every foul and hateful bird! The most revolting sins of the age find shelter beneath the cloak of Christianity. Many proclaim the law of God abolished, and surely their lives are in keeping with their faith. If there is no law, then there is no transgression, and therefore no sin; for sin is the transgression of the law.

The carnal mind is enmity against God, and it rebels against His will. Let it once throw off the yoke of obedience and it slips unconsciously into the lawlessness of crime. Iniquity abounds among those who talk grandly of pure and perfect religious liberty. Their conduct is abhorrent to the Lord, and they are co-workers with the adversary of souls. The light of revealed truth is turned from their sight, and the beauties of holiness are but as shadows to them.

It is astonishing to see upon what flimsy foundations very many build their hopes of heaven! They rail at the law of the Infinite One as though they would defy Him and make His word null. Even Satan with his knowledge of the divine law would not dare to make the speeches which some law-hating ministers make from the pulpit, yet he exults in their blasphemy.

I have been shown what man is without a knowledge of the will of God. Crimes and iniquity fill up the measure of his life. But when the Spirit of God reveals to him the full meaning of the law, what a change takes place in his heart! Like Belshazzar, he reads intelligently the handwriting of the Almighty, and conviction takes possession of his soul. The thunders of God's word startle him from his lethargy, and he calls for mercy in the name of Jesus. And to that humble plea God always listens with a willing ear. He never turns the penitent away comfortless.

The Lord has seen fit to give me a view of the needs and errors of His people. Painful though it has been to me, I have faithfully set before the offenders their faults and the means of remedying them, according to the dictates of the Spirit of God. This has, in many instances, excited the tongue of slander and embittered against me those for whom I have labored and suffered. But I have not been turned from my course because of this. God has given me my work, and, upheld by His sustaining strength, I have performed the painful duties He has set before me. Thus has the Spirit of God pronounced warnings and judgments, withholding not, however, the sweet promise of mercy.

If God's people would recognize His dealings with them and accept His teachings, they would find a straight path for their feet and a light to guide them through darkness and discouragement. David learned wisdom from God's dealings with him and bowed in humility beneath the chastisement of the Most High. The faithful portrayal of his true state by the prophet Nathan made David acquainted with his own sins and aided him to put them away. He accepted counsel meekly and humiliated himself before God. "The law of the Lord," he exclaims, "is perfect, converting the soul." Psalm 19:7.

NO OCCASION FOR DESPAIR

Repentant sinners have no cause to despair because they are reminded of their transgressions and warned of their danger. These very efforts in their behalf show how much God loves them and desires to save them. They have only to follow His counsel and do His will, to inherit eternal life. God sets the sins of His erring people before them, that they may behold them in all their enormity under the light of divine truth. It is then their duty to renounce them forever.

God is as powerful to save from sin today as He was in the times of the patriarchs, of David, and of the prophets and apostles. The multitude of cases recorded in sacred history where God has delivered His people from their own iniquities should make the Christian of this time eager to receive divine instruction and zealous to perfect a character that will bear the close inspection of the judgment.

Bible history stays the fainting heart with the hope of God's mercy. We need not despair when we see that others have struggled through discouragements like our own, have fallen into temptations even as we have done, and yet have recovered their ground and been blessed of God. The words of inspiration comfort and cheer the erring soul. Although the patriarchs and apostles were subject to human frailties, yet through faith they obtained a good report, fought their battles in the strength of the Lord, and conquered gloriously. Thus may we trust in the virtue of the atoning sacrifice and be overcomers in the name of Jesus. Humanity is humanity the world over from the time of Adam down to the present generation, and the love of God through all ages is without a parallel.

Responsibility of Church Membership

DEAR BRETHREN: As all the different members of the human system unite to form the entire body, and each performs its office in obedience to the intelligence that governs the whole, so the members of the church of Christ should be united in one symmetrical body, subject to the sanctified intelligence of the whole.

The advancement of the church is retarded by the wrong course of its members. Uniting with the church, although an important and necessary act, does not make one a Christian nor ensure salvation. We cannot secure a title to heaven by having our names enrolled upon the church book while our hearts are alienated from Christ. We should be His faithful representatives on earth, working in unison with Him. "Beloved, now are we the sons of God." 1 John 3:2. We should keep in mind this holy relationship and do nothing to bring dishonor upon our Father's cause.

Our profession is an exalted one. As Sabbathkeeping Adventists we profess to obey all God's commandments and to be looking for the coming of our Redeemer. A most solemn message of warning has been entrusted to God's faithful few. We should show by our words and works that we recognize the great responsibility laid upon us. Our light should shine so clearly that others can see that we glorify the Father in our daily lives; that we are connected with heaven and are joint heirs with Jesus Christ, that when He shall appear in power and great glory, we shall be like Him.

We should all feel our individual responsibility as members of the visible church and workers in the vineyard of the Lord.

1876, vol. 4, pp. 16-20 (Unity of the Church).

We should not wait for our brethren, who are as frail as ourselves, to help us along; for our precious Saviour has invited us to join ourselves to Him and unite our weakness with His strength, our ignorance with His wisdom, our unworthiness with His merit. None of us can occupy a neutral position; our influence will tell for or against. We are active agents for Christ or for the enemy. We either gather with Jesus or scatter abroad. True conversion is a radical change. The very drift of the mind and bent of the heart should be turned and life become new again in Christ.

GOD LEADING OUT A PEOPLE

God is leading out a people to stand in perfect unity upon the platform of eternal truth. Christ gave Himself to the world that He might "purify unto Himself a peculiar people, zealous of good works." Titus 2:14. This refining process is designed to purge the church from all unrighteousness and the spirit of discord and contention, that they may build up instead of tear down, and concentrate their energies on the great work before them. God designs that His people should all come into the unity of the faith. The prayer of Christ just prior to His crucifixion was that His disciples might be one, even as He was one with the Father, that the world might believe that the Father had sent Him. This most touching and wonderful prayer reaches down the ages, even to our day; for His words were: "Neither pray I for these alone, but for them also which shall believe on Me through their word." John 17:20.

How earnestly should the professed followers of Christ seek to answer this prayer in their lives. Many do not realize the sacredness of church relationship and are loath to submit to restraint and discipline. Their course of action shows that they exalt their own judgment above that of the united church, and they are not careful to guard themselves lest they encourage a spirit of opposition to its voice. Those who hold responsible positions in the church may have faults in common with other people and may err in their decisions; but notwithstanding this, the church of Christ on earth has given to them an authority that cannot be lightly esteemed. Christ, after His resurrection, delegated power unto His church, saying: "Whosesoever sins ye remit, they are remitted unto them; and whosesoever sins ye retain, they are retained." John 20:23.

Church relationship is not to be lightly canceled; yet when the path of some professed followers of Christ is crossed, or when their voice has not the controlling influence which they think it deserves, they will threaten to leave the church. True, in leaving the church they would themselves be the greatest sufferers; for in withdrawing beyond the pale of its influence, they subject themselves to the full temptations of the world.

WHOLEHEARTED SUPPORTERS

Every believer should be wholehearted in his attachment to the church. Its prosperity should be his first interest, and unless he feels under sacred obligations to make his connection with the church a benefit to it in preference to himself, it can do far better without him. It is in the power of all to do something for the cause of God. There are those who spend a large amount for needless luxuries; they gratify their appetites, but feel it a great tax to contribute means to sustain the church. They are willing to receive all the benefit of its privileges, but prefer to leave others to pay the bills.

Those who really feel a deep interest in the advancement of the cause will not hesitate to invest money in the enterprise whenever and wherever it is needed. They should also feel it a solemn duty to illustrate in their characters the teachings of Christ, being at peace one with another and moving in perfect harmony as an undivided whole. They should defer their individual judgment to the judgment of the body of the church. Many live for themselves alone. They look upon their lives with great complacency, flattering themselves that they are blameless, when in fact they are doing nothing for God and are living in direct opposition to His expressed word. The observance of external forms will never meet the great want of the human soul. A profession of Christ is not enough to enable one to stand the test of the day of judgment. There should be a perfect trust in God, a childlike dependence upon His promises, and an entire consecration to His will.

God has always tried His people in the furnace of affliction in order to prove them firm and true, and purge them from all unrighteousness. After Abraham and his son had borne the severest test that could be imposed upon them, God spoke through His angel unto Abraham: "Now I know that thou fearest God, seeing thou hast not withheld thy son, thine only son from Me." Genesis 22:12. This great act of faith causes the character of Abraham to shine forth with remarkable luster. It forcibly illustrates his perfect confidence in the Lord, from whom he withheld nothing, not even his son by promise.

There is nothing too precious for us to give to Jesus. If we return to Him the talents of means which He has entrusted to our keeping, He will give more into our hands. Every effort we make for Christ will be rewarded by Him, and every duty we perform in His name will minister to our own happiness. God surrendered His dearly beloved Son to the agonies of the crucifixion, that all who believe on Him might become one through the name of Jesus. When Christ made so great a sacrifice to save men and bring them into unity with one another, even as He was united with the Father, what sacrifice is too great for His followers to make in order to preserve that unity?

THE WITNESS OF A UNITED CHURCH

If the world sees a perfect harmony existing in the church of God, it will be a powerful evidence to them in favor of the

Christian religion. Dissensions, unhappy differences, and petty church trials dishonor our Redeemer. All these may be avoided if self is surrendered to God and the followers of Jesus obey the voice of the church. Unbelief suggests that individual independence increases our importance, that it is weak to yield our own ideas of what is right and proper to the verdict of the church; but to yield to such feelings and views is unsafe and will bring us into anarchy and confusion. Christ saw that unity and Christian fellowship were necessary to the cause of God, therefore He enjoined it upon His disciples. And the history of Christianity from that time until now proves conclusively that in union only is there strength. Let individual judgment submit to the authority of the church.

The apostles felt the necessity of strict unity, and they labored earnestly to this end. Paul exhorted his brethren in these words: "Now I beseech you, brethren, by the name of our Lord Jesus Christ, that ye all speak the same thing, and that there be no divisions among you; but that ye be perfectly joined together in the same mind and in the same judgment." 1 Corinthians 1:10.

He also wrote to his Philippian brethren: "If there be therefore any consolation in Christ, if any comfort of love, if any fellowship of the Spirit, if any bowels and mercies, fulfill ye my joy, that ye be like-minded, having the same love, being of one accord, of one mind. Let nothing be done through strife or vainglory; but in lowliness of mind let each esteem other better than themselves. Look not every man on his own things, but every man also on the things of others. Let this mind be in you, which was also in Christ Jesus." Philippians 2:1-5.

To the Romans he wrote: "Now the God of patience and consolation grant you to be like-minded one toward another according to Christ Jesus: that ye may with one mind and one mouth glorify God, even the Father of our Lord Jesus Christ. Wherefore receive ye one another, as Christ also received us to the glory of God." Romans 15:5-7. "Be of the same mind one toward another. Mind not high things, but condescend to men of low estate. Be not wise in your own conceits." Romans 12:16.

Peter wrote to the churches scattered abroad: "Finally, be ye all of one mind, having compassion one of another, love as brethren, be pitiful, be courteous: not rendering evil for evil, or railing for railing: but contrariwise blessing; knowing that ye are thereunto called, that ye should inherit a blessing." 1 Peter 3:8, 9.

And Paul, in his Epistle to the Corinthians, says: "Finally, brethren, farewell. Be perfect, be of good comfort, be of one mind, live in peace; and the God of love and peace shall be with you." 2 Corinthians 13:11.

As far as possible, you should come into harmony with your brethren and sisters. You should surrender yourselves to God and cease to manifest sternness and a disposition to find fault. You should yield your own spirit and take in its place the spirit of the dear Saviour. Reach up and grasp His hand, that the touch may electrify you and charge you with the sweet properties of His own matchless character. You may open your hearts to His love, and let His power transform you and His grace be your strength. Then will you have a powerful influence for good. Your moral strength will be equal to the closest test of character. Your integrity will be pure and sanctified. Then will your light break forth as the morning.—1876, vol. 4, p. 63.

The religion of Christ does not require us to lose our identity of character, but merely to adapt ourselves, in some measure, to the feelings and ways of others. Many people may be brought together in a unity of religious faith whose opinions, habits, and tastes in temporal matters are not in harmony; but if they have the love of Christ glowing in their bosoms, and are looking forward to the same heaven as their eternal home, they may have the sweetest and most intelligent communion together, and a unity the most wonderful. There are scarcely two whose experience is alike in every particular. The trials of one may not be the trials of another, and our hearts should ever be open to kindly sympathy and all aglow with the love that Jesus had for all His brethren.—1876, vol. 4, pp. 65, 66.

Go Forward

THE history of the children of Israel is written for the instruction and admonition of all Christians. When the Israelites were overtaken by dangers and difficulties, and their way seemed hedged up, their faith forsook them, and they murmured against the leader whom God had appointed for them. They blamed him for bringing them into peril, when he had only obeyed the voice of God.

The divine command was: "Go forward." They were not to wait until the way was made plain, and they could comprehend the entire plan of their deliverance. God's cause is onward, and He will open a path before His people. To hesitate and murmur is to manifest distrust in the Holy One of Israel. God in His providence brought the Hebrews into the mountain fastnesses, with the Red Sea before them, that He might work out their deliverance and forever rid them of their enemies. He might have saved them in any other way, but He chose this method in order to test their faith and strengthen their trust in Him.

We cannot charge Moses with being at fault because the people murmured against his course. It was their own rebellious, unsubdued hearts that led them to censure the man whom God had delegated to lead His people. While Moses moved in the fear of the Lord, and according to His direction, having full faith in His promises, those who should have upheld him became discouraged, and could see nothing before them but disaster, defeat, and death.

The Lord is now dealing with His people who believe present truth. He designs to bring about momentous results, and while in His providence He is working toward this end, He

1876, vol. 4, pp. 25-28.

says to His people: "Go forward." True, the path is not yet opened; but when they move on in the strength of faith and courage, God will make the way plain before their eyes. There are ever those who will complain, as did ancient Israel, and charge the difficulties of their position upon those whom God has raised up for the special purpose of advancing His cause. They fail to see that God is testing them by bringing them into strait places, from which there is no deliverance except by His hand.

There are times when the Christian life seems beset by dangers, and duty seems hard to perform. The imagination pictures impending ruin before, and bondage or death behind. Yet the voice of God speaks clearly above all discouragements: "Go forward." We should obey this command, let the result be what it may, even though our eyes cannot penetrate the darkness and though we feel the cold waves about our feet.

ADVANCE BY FAITH

The Hebrews were weary and terrified; yet if they had held back when Moses bade them advance, if they had refused to move nearer to the Red Sea, God would never have opened the path for them. In marching down to the very water, they showed that they had faith in the word of God as spoken by Moses. They did all that it was in their power to do, and then the Mighty One of Israel performed His part, and divided the waters to make a path for their feet.

The clouds that gather about our way will never disappear before a halting, doubting spirit. Unbelief says: "We can never surmount these obstructions; let us wait until they are removed, and we can see our way clearly." But faith courageously urges an advance, hoping all things, believing all things. Obedience to God is sure to bring the victory. It is only through faith that we can reach heaven.

There is great similarity between our history and that of

the children of Israel. God led His people from Egypt into the wilderness, where they could keep His law and obey His voice. The Egyptians, who had no regard for the Lord, were encamped close by them; yet what was to the Israelites a great flood of light, illuminating the whole camp, and shedding brightness upon the path before them, was to the hosts of Pharaoh a wall of clouds, making blacker the darkness of night.

So, at this time, there is a people whom God has made the depositaries of His law. To those who obey them, the commandments of God are as a pillar of fire, lighting and leading the way to eternal salvation. But unto those who disregard them, they are as the clouds of night. "The fear of the Lord is the beginning of wisdom." Psalm 111:10. Better than all other knowledge is an understanding of the word of God. In keeping His commandments there is great reward, and no earthly inducement should cause the Christian to waver for a moment in his allegiance. Riches, honor, and worldly pomp are but as dross that shall perish before the fire of God's wrath.

The voice of the Lord bidding His faithful ones "go forward" frequently tries their faith to the uttermost. But if they should defer obedience till every shadow of uncertainty was removed from their understanding, and there remained no risk of failure or defeat, they would never move on at all. Those who think it impossible for them to yield to the will of God and have faith in His promises until all is made clear and plain before them, will never yield at all. Faith is not certainty of knowledge; it "is the substance of things hoped for, the evidence of things not seen." Hebrews 11:1. To obey the commandments of God is the only way to obtain His favor. "Go forward" should be the Christian's watchword.

Co-workers With Christ

It was an important time for —— during and after the tent meeting in 1874. Had there been a pleasant and commodious house of worship there, more than double the number that were really gained would have taken their stand for the truth. God works with our efforts. We may close the way for sinners by our negligence and selfishness. There should have been great diligence in seeking to save those who were still in error, yet interested in the truth. Just as wise generalship is needed in the service of Christ as is needed over the battalions of an army that protects the life and liberty of the people. It is not everyone who can labor judiciously for the salvation of souls. There is much close thinking to be done. We must not enter into the Lord's work haphazard and expect success. The Lord needs men of mind, men of thought. Jesus calls for co-workers, not blunderers. God wants right-thinking and intelligent men to do the great work necessary to the salvation of souls.

Mechanics, lawyers, merchants, men of all trades and professions, educate themselves that they may become masters of their business. Should the followers of Christ be less intelligent, and while professedly engaged in His service be ignorant of the ways and means to be employed? The enterprise of gaining everlasting life is above every earthly consideration. In order to lead souls to Jesus there must be a knowledge of human nature and a study of the human mind. Much careful thought and fervent prayer are required to know how to approach men and women upon the great subject of truth.

Some rash, impulsive, yet honest souls, after a pointed dis-

1876, vol. 4., pp. 67-73.

course has been given, will accost those who are not with us in a very abrupt manner, and make the truth, which we desire them to receive, repulsive to them. "The children of this world are in their generation wiser than the children of light." Luke 16:8. Business men and politicians study courtesy. It is their policy to make themselves as attractive as possible. They study to render their address and manners such that they may have the greatest influence over the minds of those about them. They use their knowledge and abilities as skillfully as possible in order to gain this object.

There is a vast amount of rubbish brought forward by professed believers in Christ, which blocks up the way to the cross. Notwithstanding all this, there are some who are so deeply convicted that they will come through every discouragement and will surmount every obstacle in order to gain the truth. But had the believers in the truth purified their minds by obeying it, had they felt the importance of knowledge and of refinement of manners in Christ's work, where one soul has been saved there might have been twenty.

NEW CONVERTS TO BE ENCOURAGED

Again, after individuals have been converted to the truth, they need to be looked after. The zeal of many ministers seems to fail as soon as a measure of success attends their efforts. They do not realize that these newly converted ones need nursing—watchful attention, help, and encouragement. These should not be left alone, a prey to Satan's most powerful temptations; they need to be educated in regard to their duties, to be kindly dealt with, to be led along, and to be visited and prayed with. These souls need the meat apportioned to every man in due season.

No wonder that some become discouraged, linger by the way, and are left for wolves to devour. Satan is upon the track of all. He sends his agents forth to gather back to his ranks the souls he has lost. There should be more fathers and mothers to take these babes in the truth to their hearts, and to encourage them and pray for them, that their faith be not confused.

Preaching is a small part of the work to be done for the salvation of souls. God's Spirit convicts sinners of the truth, and He places them in the arms of the church. The ministers may do their part, but they can never perform the work that the church should do. God requires His church to nurse those who are young in faith and experience, to go to them, not for the purpose of gossiping with them, but to pray, to speak unto them words that are "like apples of gold in pictures of silver."

We all need to study character and manner that we may know how to deal judiciously with different minds, that we may use our best endeavors to help them to a correct understanding of the word of God and to a true Christian life. We should read the Bible with them, and draw their minds away from temporal things to their eternal interests. It is the duty of God's children to be missionaries for Him, to become acquainted with those who need help. If one is staggering under temptation, his case should be taken up carefully and managed wisely; for his eternal interest is at stake, and the words and acts of those laboring for him may be a savor of life unto life, or of death unto death.

Sometimes a case presents itself that should be made a prayerful study. The person must be shown his true character, understand his own peculiarities of disposition and temperament, and see his infirmities. He should be judiciously handled. If he can be reached, if his heart can be touched by this wise and patient labor, he can be bound with strong cords to Christ and led to trust in God. Oh, when a work like this is done, all the heavenly courts look and rejoice; for a precious soul has been rescued from Satan's snare and saved from death! Oh, will it not pay to work intelligently for the salvation of souls? Christ paid the price of His own life for them, and shall His followers ask: "Am I my brother's keeper?"

Shall we not work in unison with the Master? Shall we not appreciate the worth of souls for whom our Saviour died?

WORK FOR THE CHILDREN

Some efforts have been made to interest children in the cause, but not enough. Our Sabbath schools should be made more interesting. The public schools have of late years greatly improved their methods of teaching. Object lessons, pictures, and blackboards are used to make difficult lessons clear to the youthful mind. Just so may present truth be simplified and made intensely interesting to the active minds of the children.

Parents who can be approached in no other way are frequently reached through their children. Sabbath school teachers can instruct the children in the truth, and they will, in turn, take it into the home circle. But few teachers seem to understand the importance of this branch of the work. The modes of teaching which have been adopted with such success in the public schools could be employed with similar results in the Sabbath schools and be the means of bringing children to Jesus and educating them in Bible truth. This will do far more good than religious excitement of an emotional character, that passes off as rapidly as it comes.

The love of Christ should be cherished. More faith is needed in the work which we believe is to be done before the coming of Christ. There should be more self-denying, self-sacrificing labor in the right direction. There should be thoughtful, prayerful study how to work to the best advantage. Careful plans should be matured. There are minds among us that can invent and carry out if they are only put to use. Great results would follow well-directed and intelligent efforts.

INTERESTING PRAYER MEETINGS

The prayer meetings should be the most interesting gatherings that are held, but these are frequently poorly managed.

Many attend preaching, but neglect the prayer meeting. Here, again, thought is required. Wisdom should be sought of God, and plans should be laid to conduct the meetings so that they will be interesting and attractive. The people hunger for the bread of life. If they find it at the prayer meeting they will go there to receive it.

Long, prosy talks and prayers are out of place anywhere, and especially in the social meeting. Those who are forward and ever ready to speak are allowed to crowd out the testimony of the timid and retiring. Those who are most superficial generally have the most to say. Their prayers are long and mechanical. They weary the angels and the people who listen to them. Our prayers should be short and right to the point. Let the long, tiresome petitions be left for the closet, if any have such to offer. Let the Spirit of God into your hearts, and it will sweep away all dry formality.

POWER OF GOOD MUSIC

Music can be a great power for good, yet we do not make the most of this branch of worship. The singing is generally done from impulse or to meet special cases, and at other times those who sing are left to blunder along, and the music loses its proper effect upon the minds of those present. Music should have beauty, pathos, and power. Let the voices be lifted in songs of praise and devotion. Call to your aid, if practicable, instrumental music, and let the glorious harmony ascend to God, an acceptable offering.

But it is sometimes more difficult to discipline the singers and keep them in working order than to improve the habits of praying and exhorting. Many want to do things after their own style; they object to consultation, and are impatient under leadership. Well-matured plans are needed in the service of God. Common sense is an excellent thing in the worship of the Lord. The thinking powers should be consecrated to Christ, and ways and means should be devised to serve Him best. The church of God who are trying to do good by living out the truth and seeking to save souls, can be a power in the world if they will be disciplined by the Spirit of the Lord. They must not feel that they can work carelessly for eternity.

SYMPATHY AND SOCIABILITY

As a people, we lose much by lack of sympathy and sociability with one another. He who talks of independence and shuts himself up to himself is not filling the position that God designed he should. We are children of God, mutually dependent upon one another for happiness. The claims of God and of humanity are upon us. We must all act our part in this life. It is the proper cultivation of the social elements of our nature that brings us into sympathy with our brethren and affords us happiness in our efforts to bless others. The happiness of heaven will consist in the pure communion of holy beings, the harmonious social life with the blessed angels and with the redeemed who have washed their robes and made them white in the blood of the Lamb. We cannot be happy while we are wrapped up in our interest for ourselves. We should live in this world to win souls to the Saviour. If we injure others, we injure ourselves also. If we bless others, we also bless ourselves; for the influence of every good deed is reflected upon our own hearts.

We are in duty bound to help one another. It is not always that we are brought in contact with social Christians, those who are amiable and mild. Many have not received a proper education; their characters are warped, they are hard and gnarled, and seem to be crooked in every way. While we help these to see and correct their defects, we must be careful not to become impatient and irritable over our neighbor's faults. There are disagreeable ones who profess Christ; but the beauty of Christian grace will transform them if they will set diligently about the work of obtaining the meekness and gentleness of Him whom they follow, remembering that "none of us liveth to himself." Co-workers with Christ! What an exalted position!

Where are to be found the self-sacrificing missionaries in these large cities? The Lord needs workers in His vineyard. We should fear to rob Him of the time He claims from us; we should fear to spend it in idleness or in the adornment of the body, appropriating to foolish purposes the precious hours God has given us to be devoted to prayer, to becoming conversant with our Bibles, and to laboring for the good of our fellow beings, thus fitting ourselves and them for the great work devolving upon us.

Mothers spend unnecessary labor upon garments with which to beautify the persons of themselves and their children. It is our duty to dress ourselves plainly and to clothe our children neatly, without useless ornamentation, embroidery, or display, taking care not to foster in them a love of dress that will prove their ruin, but seeking rather to cultivate the Christian graces. None of us can be excused from our responsibilities, and in no case can we stand clear before the throne of God unless we do the work that the Master has left for us to do.

Missionaries for God are wanted, faithful men and women who will not shirk responsibility. Judicious labor will accomplish good results. There is real work to be done. The truth should be brought before people in a careful manner by those who unite meekness with wisdom. We should not hold ourselves aloof from our fellow men, but come close to them; for their souls are as precious as our own. We can carry the light into their homes, with a softened and subdued spirit plead with them to come up to the exalted privilege offered them, pray with them when it seems proper, and show them that there are higher attainments that they may reach, and then guardedly speak to them of the sacred truths for these last days.

There are more gatherings for singing than for prayer among our people; but even these gatherings can be conducted in so reverential yet cheerful a manner that they may exert a good influence. There is, however, too much jesting, idle conversation, and gossiping to make these seasons beneficial, to elevate the thoughts and refine the manners.

Sensational Revivals

There has been too much of a divided interest in ——. When a new excitement is raised, there are some who cast their influence on the wrong side. Every man and woman should be on guard when there are deceptions abroad calculated to lead away from the truth. There are those who are ever ready to see and hear some new and strange thing; and the enemy of souls has, in these large cities, plenty to inflame the curiosity and keep the mind diverted from the great and sanctifying truths for these last days.

If every fluctuating religious excitement leads some to neglect to fully sustain, by their presence and influence, the minority who believe unpopular truth, there will be much weakness in the church where there should be strength. Satan employs various means by which to accomplish his purposes; and if, under the guise of popular religion, he can lead off vacillating and unwary ones from the path of truth, he has accomplished much in dividing the strength of the people of God. This fluctuating revival enthusiasm, that comes and goes like the tide, carries a delusive exterior that deceives many honest persons into believing it to be the true Spirit of the Lord. It multiplies converts. Those of excitable temperaments, the weak and yielding, flock to its standard; but when the wave recedes, they are found stranded on the beach. Be not deceived by false teachers, nor led by vain words. The enemy of souls is sure to have enough dishes of pleasing fables to suit the appetites of all.

There will ever be flashing meteors to arise; but the trail of light they leave immediately goes out in darkness that seems denser than it was before. These sensational religious

1876, vol. 4, pp. 73-76 (Co-workers With Christ).

excitements that are created by the relation of anecdotes and the exhibition of eccentricities and oddities are all surface work, and those of our faith who are charmed and infatuated by these flashes of light will never build up the cause of God. They are ready to withdraw their influence upon the slightest occasion and to induce others to attend those gatherings where they hear that which weakens the soul and brings confusion to the mind. It is this withdrawal of the interest from the work that makes the cause of God languish. We must be steadfast in the faith; we must not be movable. We have our work before us, which is to cause the light of truth, as revealed in the law of God, to shine in upon other minds and lead them out of darkness. This work requires determined, persevering energy and a fixed purpose to succeed.

STEADFASTNESS NEEDED

There are some in the church who need to cling to the pillars of our faith, to settle down and find rock bottom, instead of drifting on the surface of excitement and moving from impulse. There are spiritual dyspeptics in the church. They are self-made invalids; their spiritual debility is the result of their own wavering course. They are tossed about here and there by the changing winds of doctrine, and are often confused and thrown into uncertainty because they move entirely by feeling. They are sensational Christians, ever hungering for something new and diverse; strange doctrines confuse their faith, and they are worthless to the cause of truth.

God calls for men and women of stability, of firm purpose, who can be relied upon in seasons of danger and trial, who are as firmly rooted and grounded in the truth as the eternal hills, who cannot be swayed to the right or to the left, but who move straight onward and are always found on the right side. There are some, who, in time of religious peril, may almost always be looked for in the ranks of the enemy; if they have any influence, it is on the wrong side. They do not feel under moral obligation to give all their strength to the truth they profess. Such will be rewarded according to their works.

Those who do little for the Saviour in the salvation of souls, and in keeping themselves right before God, will gain but little spiritual muscle. We need continually to use the strength we have that it may develop and increase. As disease is the result of the violation of natural laws, so is spiritual declension the result of a continued transgression of the law of God. And yet the very transgressors may profess to keep all of God's commandments.

We must come nearer to God, place ourselves in closer connection with heaven, and carry out the principles of the law in the minutest actions of our everyday lives in order to be spiritually whole. God has given His servants ability, talents to be used for His glory, not to lie idle or be wasted. He has given them light and a knowledge of His will to be communicated to others, and in imparting to others we become living channels of light. If we do not exercise our spiritual strength we become feeble, as the limbs of the body become powerless when the invalid is compelled to remain long inactive. It is use that gives power.

MINISTERING TO OTHERS

Nothing will give greater spiritual strength and a greater increase of earnestness and depth of feeling than visiting and ministering to the sick and the desponding, helping them to see the light and to fasten their faith upon Jesus. There are disagreeable duties that somebody must do or souls will be left to perish. Christians will find a blessing in doing these duties, however unpleasant they may be. Christ took the disagreeable task upon Himself of coming from the abode of purity and unsurpassed glory, to dwell, a man among men, in a world seared and blackened by crime, violence, and iniquity. He did this to save souls; and shall the objects of such amazing love and unparalleled condescension excuse their lives of selfish ease? shall they choose their own pleasure, follow their own inclinations, and leave souls to perish in darkness because they will meet with disappointment and rebuffs if they labor to save them? Christ paid an infinite price for man's redemption, and shall he say: "My Lord, I will not labor in Thy vineyard; I pray Thee have me excused"?

God calls for those who are at ease in Zion to be up and doing. Will they not listen to the Master's voice? He wants prayerful, faithful workers who will sow beside all waters. Those who labor thus will be surprised to find how trials, resolutely borne in the name and strength of Jesus, will give firmness to the faith and renew the courage. In the path of humble obedience is safety and power, comfort and hope; but the reward will finally be lost by those who do nothing for Jesus. Weak hands will be unable to cling to the Mighty One, feeble knees will fail to support in the day of adversity. Bible readers and Christian workers will receive the glorious prize, and hear the "Well done, thou good and faithful servant: . . . enter thou into the joy of thy Lord." Matthew 25:21.

Withholding Means

THE blessing of God will rest upon those in —— who have the cause of Christ at heart. The freewill offerings of our brethren and sisters, made in faith and love to the crucified Redeemer, will bring back blessings to them; for God marks and remembers every act of liberality on the part of His saints. In preparing a house of worship, there must be a great exercise of faith and trust in God. In business transactions those who venture nothing make but little advancement; why not have faith also in an enterprise for God and invest in His cause?

Some, when in poverty, are generous with their little; but as they acquire property, they become penurious. The reason they have so little faith is that they do not keep moving forward as they prosper, and give to the cause of God even at a sacrifice.

In the Jewish system it was required that beneficence should first be shown to the Lord. At the harvest and the vintage the first fruits of the field—the corn, the wine, and the oil—were to be consecrated as an offering to the Lord. The gleanings and the corners of the fields were reserved for the poor. Our gracious heavenly Father did not neglect the wants of the poor. The first fruits of the wool when the sheep were shorn, of the grain when the wheat was threshed, were to be offered to the Lord; and it was commanded that the poor, the widows, the orphans, and the strangers, be invited to their feasts. At the close of every year all were required to make solemn oath whether or not they had done according to the command of God.

1876, vol. 4, pp. 76-83 (Co-workers With Christ).

This arrangement was made by the Lord to impress upon the people that in every matter He must be first. By this system of benevolence they were to bear in mind that their gracious Master was the true proprietor of their fields, their flocks, and their herds; that the God of heaven sent them sunshine and rain for their seedtime and harvest, and that everything they possessed was of His creation. All was the Lord's, and He had made them stewards of His goods.

The liberality of the Jews in the construction of the tabernacle and the erection of the temple illustrates a spirit of benevolence which has not been equaled by Christians of any later date. They had just been freed from their long bondage in Egypt and were wanderers in the wilderness; yet scarcely were they delivered from the armies of the Egyptians who pursued them in their hasty journey, when the word of the Lord came to Moses, saying: "Speak unto the children of Israel, that they bring Me an offering: of every man that giveth it willingly with his heart ye shall take My offering." Exodus 25:2.

His people had small possessions and no flattering prospect of adding to them; but an object was before them—to build a tabernacle for God. The Lord had spoken, and they must obey His voice. They withheld nothing. All gave with a willing hand, not a certain amount of their increase, but a large portion of their actual possessions. They devoted it gladly and heartily to the Lord, and pleased Him by so doing. Was it not all His? Had He not given them all they possessed? If He called for it, was it not their duty to give back to the Lender His own?

No urging was needed. The people brought even more than was required, and were told to desist, for there was already more than could be appropriated. Again, in building the temple, the call for means met with a hearty response. The people did not give reluctantly. They rejoiced in the prospect of a building being erected for the worship of God, and donated more than enough for the purpose. David blessed the Lord before all the congregation, and said: "But who am I, and what is my people, that we should be able to offer so willingly after this sort? for all things come of Thee, and of Thine own have we given Thee." 1 Chronicles 29:14. Again in his prayer David gave thanks in these words: "O Lord our God, all this store that we have prepared to build Thee an house for Thine holy name cometh of Thine hand, and is all Thine own." Verse 16.

David well understood from whom came all his bounties. Would that those of this day who rejoice in a Saviour's love could realize that their silver and gold are the Lord's and should be used to promote His glory, not grudgingly retained to enrich and gratify themselves. He has an indisputable right to all that He has lent His creatures. All that they possess is His.

There are high and holy objects that require means, and money thus invested will yield to the giver more elevated and permanent enjoyment than if it were expended in personal gratification or selfishly hoarded for greed of gain. When God calls for our treasure, whatever the amount may be, the willing response makes the gift a consecrated offering to Him and lays up for the giver a treasure in heaven that moth cannot corrupt, that fire cannot consume, nor thieves break in and steal. The investment is safe. The money is placed in bags that have no holes; it is secure.

Can Christians, who boast of a broader light than had the Hebrews, give less than they? Can Christians living near the close of time be satisfied with their offerings when not half so large as were those of the Jews? Their liberality was to benefit their own nation; the work in these last days extends to the entire world. The message of truth is to go to all nations, tongues, and people; its publications, printed in many different languages, are to be scattered abroad like the leaves of autumn.

CROSS REVEALS PRINCIPLE OF SACRIFICE

It is written: "Forasmuch then as Christ hath suffered for us in the flesh, arm yourselves likewise with the same mind." 1 Peter 4:1. And again: "He that saith he abideth in Him ought himself also so to walk, even as He walked." 1 John 2:6. Let us inquire: What would our Saviour have done in our circumstances? what would have been His efforts for the salvation of souls? This question is answered by the example of Christ. He left His royalty, laid aside His glory, sacrificed His riches, and clothed His divinity with humanity, that He might reach men where they were. His example shows that He laid down His life for sinners.

Satan told Eve that a high state of felicity could be gained through the gratification of unlicensed appetite, but the promise of God to man is through denial of self. When upon the shameful cross Christ was suffering in agony for man's redemption, human nature was exalted. Only by the cross can the human family be elevated to connect with heaven. Self-denial and crosses meet us at every step on our heavenward journey.

The spirit of liberality is the spirit of heaven; the spirit of selfishness is the spirit of Satan. Christ's self-sacrificing love is revealed upon the cross. He gave all He had, and then gave Himself, that man might be saved. The cross of Christ appeals to the benevolence of every follower of the blessed Saviour. The principle there illustrated is to give, give. This, carried out in actual benevolence and good works, is the true fruit of the Christian life. The principle of worldlings is to get, get, and thus they expect to secure happiness; but, carried out in all its bearings, the fruit is misery and death.

To carry the truth to the inhabitants of the earth, to rescue them from their guilt and indifference, is the mission of the followers of Christ. Men must have the truth in order to be sanctified through it, and we are the channels of God's light. Our talents, our means, our knowledge, are not merely for our own benefit; they are to be used for the salvation of souls, to elevate man from his life of sin and bring him, through Christ, to the infinite God.

We should be zealous workers in this cause, seeking to lead sinners, repenting and believing, to a divine Redeemer, and to impress them with an exalted sense of God's love to man. "God so loved the world, that He gave His only-begotten Son, that whosoever believeth in Him should not perish, but have everlasting life." John 3:16. What an incomparable love is this! A theme for the most profound meditation! The amazing love of God for a world that did not love Him! The thought has a subduing power upon the soul and brings the mind into captivity to the will of God. Men who are crazy for gain, and are disappointed and unhappy in their pursuit of the world, need the knowledge of this truth to quiet the restless hungering and thirsting of their souls.

THE CURSE OF SELFISHNESS

Missionaries for God are wanted in your large city to carry light to those who sit in the shadow of death. Experienced hands are needed, in the meekness of wisdom and the strength of faith, to lift weary souls to the bosom of a compassionate Redeemer. Oh, selfishness! What a curse! It prevents us from engaging in the service of God. It prevents us from perceiving the claims of duty, which should set our hearts aglow with fervent zeal. All our energies should be turned to the obedience of Christ. To divide our interest with the leaders of error is aiding the wrong side and giving advantage to our foes. The truth of God knows no compromise with sin, no connection with artifice, no union with transgression. Soldiers are wanted who will always answer to the roll call and be ready for immediate action, not those who, when needed, are found aiding the enemy.

Ours is a great work. Yet there are many who profess to believe these sacred truths, who are paralyzed by the sophistry of Satan, and are doing nothing for, but rather hinder, God's cause. When will they act like those who wait for the Lord? When will they show a zeal in accordance with their faith? Many people selfishly retain their means, and soothe their conscience with a plan for doing some great thing for the cause of God after their death. They make a will donating a large sum to the church and its various interests, and then settle down with a feeling that they have done all that is required of them. Wherein have they denied self by this act? They have, on the contrary, exhibited the true essence of selfishness. When they have no longer any use for their money they propose to give it to God. But they will retain it as long as they can, till they are compelled to relinquish it by a messenger that cannot be turned aside.

Such a will is often an evidence of real covetousness. God has made us all His stewards, and in no case has He authorized us to neglect our duty or leave it for others to do. The call for means to advance the cause of truth will never be more urgent than now. Our money will never do a greater amount of good than at the present time. Every day of delay in rightly appropriating it, is limiting the period in which it will do good in saving souls. If we leave others to accomplish that which God has left for us to do, we wrong ourselves and Him who gave us all we have. How can others do *our* work of benevolence any better than we can do it ourselves? God would have every man, during his lifetime, the executor of his own will in this matter. Adversity, accident, or intrigue may forever cut off meditated acts of benevolence, when he who has accumulated a fortune is no longer by to guard it. It is sad that so many neglect the present golden opportunity to do good, and wait to be cast out of their stewardship before giving back to the Lord the means which He has lent them to be used for His glory.

"BEWARE OF COVETOUSNESS"

One marked feature in the teachings of Christ is the frequency and earnestness with which He rebuked the sin of covetousness and pointed out the danger of worldly acquisitions and inordinate love of gain. In the mansions of the rich, in the temple and in the streets, He warned those who inquired after salvation: "Take heed, and beware of covetousness." Luke 12:15. "Ye cannot serve God and mammon." Matthew 6:24; Luke 16:13.

It is this increasing devotion to money getting, the selfishness which the desire for gain begets, that removes the favor of God from the church and deadens its spirituality. When the head and hands are constantly occupied with planning and toiling for the accumulation of riches, the claims of God and humanity are forgotten. If God has blessed us with prosperity, it is not that our time and attention should be diverted from Him and given to that which He has lent us. The giver is greater than the gift. We are not our own; we have been bought with a price. Have we forgotten that infinite price paid for our redemption? Is gratitude dead in the heart? Does not the cross of Christ put to shame a life of selfish ease and indulgence?

What if Christ, becoming weary of the ingratitude and abuse that met Him on every side, had left His work! What if He had never reached that period when He said: "It is finished." What if He had returned to heaven, discouraged by His reception! What if He had never passed through that soul agony in the garden of Gethsemane that forced from His pores great drops of blood!

Christ was influenced in His labor for the redemption of the race by a love that is without parallel, and a devotion to the Father's will. He toiled for the good of man up to the very hour of His humiliation. He spent His life in poverty and self-denial for the degraded sinner. In a world that was

His own He had no place to lay His weary head. We are reaping the fruits of this infinite self-sacrifice; and yet when labor is to be done, when our money is wanted to aid the work of the Redeemer in the salvation of souls, we shrink from duty and pray to be excused. Ignoble sloth, careless indifference, and wicked selfishness seal our senses to the claims of God.

Oh, must Christ, the Majesty of heaven, the King of glory, bear the heavy cross, wear the thorny crown, and drink the bitter cup, while we recline at ease, glorifying ourselves and forgetting the souls He died to redeem by His precious blood? No; let us give while we have the power. Let us do while we have the strength. Let us work while it is day. Let us devote our time and means to the service of God, that we may have His approbation and receive His reward.

The Testing Process

Our cases are pending in the court of heaven. We are rendering our accounts there day by day. Everyone will be rewarded according to his works. Burnt offerings and sacrifices were not acceptable to God in ancient times unless the spirit was right with which the gift was offered. Samuel said: "Hath the Lord as great delight in burnt offerings and sacrifices, as in obeying the voice of the Lord? Behold, to obey is better than sacrifice, and to hearken than the fat of rams." 1 Samuel 15:22. All the money on earth cannot buy the blessing of God nor ensure you a single victory.

Many would make any and every sacrifice but the very one they *should* make, which is to yield themselves, to submit their wills to the will of God. Said Christ to His disciples: "Except ye be converted, and become as little children, ye shall not enter into the kingdom of heaven." Matthew 18:3. Here is a lesson in humility. We must all become humble as little children in order to inherit the kingdom.

Our heavenly Father sees the hearts of men, and He knows their characters better than they themselves know them. He sees that some have susceptibilities and powers, which, directed in the right channel, might be used to His glory to aid in the advancement of His work. He puts these persons on trial and in His wise providence brings them into different positions and under a variety of circumstances, testing them that they may reveal what is in their hearts and the weak points in their characters which have been concealed from their own knowledge. He gives them opportunities to correct these weaknesses, to polish off the rough corners of their natures, and to fit themselves for His service, that when He calls

1876, vol. 4, pp. 84-94.

them to action they will be ready, and that angels of heaven may unite their labor with human effort in the work that must be done upon the earth.

To men whom God designs shall fill responsible positions, He in mercy reveals their hidden defects, that they may look within and examine critically the complicated emotions and exercises of their own hearts, and detect that which is wrong; thus they may modify their dispositions and refine their manners. The Lord in His providence brings men where He can test their moral powers and reveal their motives of action, that they may improve what is right in themselves and put away that which is wrong. God would have His servants become acquainted with the moral machinery of their own hearts. In order to bring this about, He often permits the fire of affliction to assail them that they may become purified. "But who may abide the day of His coming? and who shall stand when He appeareth? for He is like a refiner's fire, and like fullers' soap: and He shall sit as a refiner and purifier of silver: and He shall purify the sons of Levi, and purge them as gold and silver, that they may offer unto the Lord an offering in righteousness." Malachi 3:2, 3.

The purification of the people of God cannot be accomplished without their suffering. God permits the fires of affliction to consume the dross, to separate the worthless from the valuable, that the pure metal may shine forth. He passes us from one fire to another, testing our true worth. If we cannot bear these trials, what will we do in the time of trouble? If prosperity or adversity discover falseness, pride, or selfishness in our hearts, what shall we do when God tries every man's work as by fire, and lays bare the secrets of all hearts?

True grace is willing to be tried; if we are loath to be searched by the Lord, our condition is serious indeed. God is the refiner and purifier of souls; in the heat of the furnace the dross is separated forever from the true silver and gold of the Christian character. Jesus watches the test. He knows what is needed to purify the precious metal that it may reflect the radiance of His divine love.

JESUS LED THE WAY

God brings His people near Him by close, testing trials, by showing them their own weakness and inability, and by teaching them to lean upon Him as their only help and safeguard. Then His object is accomplished. They are prepared to be used in every emergency, to fill important positions of trust, and to accomplish the grand purposes for which their powers were given them. God takes men upon trial; He proves them on the right hand and on the left, and thus they are educated, trained, disciplined. Jesus, our Redeemer, man's representative and head, endured this testing process. He suffered more than we can be called upon to suffer. He bore our infirmities and was in all points tempted as we are. He did not suffer thus on His own account, but because of our sins; and now, relying on the merits of our Overcomer, we may become victors in His name.

God's work of refining and purifying must go on until His servants are so humbled, so dead to self, that, when called into active service, their eye will be single to His glory. He will then accept their efforts; they will not move rashly, from impulse; they will not rush on and imperil the Lord's cause, being slaves to temptations and passions, and followers of their own carnal minds set on fire by Satan. Oh, how fearfully is the cause of God marred by man's perverse will and unsubdued temper! How much suffering he brings upon himself by following his own headstrong passions! God brings men over the ground again and again, increasing the pressure until perfect humility and a transformation of character bring them into harmony with Christ and the spirit of heaven, and they are victors over themselves.

God has called men from different states, and has been testing and proving them to see what characters they would develop, to see if they could be trusted to keep the fort at ——, and to see whether or not they would supply the deficiencies of the men already there, and, seeing the failures that these men have made, would shun the example of those who are not fit to engage in the most sacred work of God. He has followed men at —— with continual warnings, reproof, and counsel. He has poured great light about those who officiate in His cause there, that the way may be plain before them. But if they prefer to follow after their own wisdom, scorning the light, as did Saul, they will surely go astray and involve the cause in perplexity. Light and darkness have been set before them, but they have too often chosen the darkness.

THE LAODICEAN MESSAGE

The Laodicean message applies to the people of God who profess to believe present truth. The greater part are lukewarm professors, having a name but no zeal. God signified that He wanted men at the great heart of the work to correct the state of things existing there and to stand like faithful sentinels at their post of duty. He has given them light at every point, to instruct, encourage, and confirm them, as the case required. But notwithstanding all this, those who should be faithful and true, fervent in Christian zeal, of gracious temper, knowing and loving Jesus earnestly, are found aiding the enemy to weaken and discourage those whom God is using to build up the work. The term "lukewarm" is applicable to this class. They profess to love the truth, yet are deficient in Christian fervor and devotion. They dare not give up wholly and run the risk of the unbeliever, yet they are unwilling to die to self and follow out closely the principles of their faith.

The only hope for the Laodiceans is a clear view of their standing before God, a knowledge of the nature of their disease. They are neither cold nor hot; they occupy a neutral position, and at the same time flatter themselves that they are in need of nothing. The True Witness hates this lukewarmness. He loathes the indifference of this class of persons. Said He: "I would thou wert cold or hot." Revelation 3:15. Like lukewarm water, they are nauseous to His taste. They are neither unconcerned nor selfishly stubborn. They do not engage thoroughly and heartily in the work of God, identifying themselves with its interests; but they hold aloof and are ready to leave their posts when their worldly personal interests demand it. The internal work of grace is wanting in their hearts; of such it is said: "Thou sayest, I am rich, and increased with goods, and have need of nothing; and knowest not that thou art wretched, and miserable, and poor, and blind, and naked." Verse 17.

GOD'S REMEDY

Faith and love are the true riches, the pure gold which the True Witness counsels the lukewarm to buy. However rich we may be in earthly treasure, all our wealth will not enable us to buy the precious remedies that cure the disease of the soul called lukewarmness. Intellect and earthly riches were powerless to remove the defects of the Laodicean church, or to remedy their deplorable condition. They were blind, yet felt that they were well off. The Spirit of God did not illumine their minds, and they did not perceive their sinfulness; therefore they did not feel the necessity of help.

To be without the graces of the Spirit of God is sad indeed; but it is a more terrible condition to be thus destitute of spirituality and of Christ, and yet try to justify ourselves by telling those who are alarmed for us that we need not their fears and pity. Fearful is the power of self-deception on the human mind! What blindness! setting light for darkness and darkness for light! The True Witness counsels us to buy of Him gold tried in the fire, white raiment, and eyesalve.

The gold here recommended as having been tried in the fire is faith and love. It makes the heart rich; for it has been purged until it is pure, and the more it is tested the more brilliant is its luster. The white raiment is purity of character, the righteousness of Christ imparted to the sinner. This is indeed a garment of heavenly texture, that can be bought only of Christ for a life of willing obedience. The eyesalve is that wisdom and grace which enables us to discern between the evil and the good, and to detect sin under any guise. God has given His church eyes which He requires them to anoint with wisdom, that they may see clearly; but many would put out the eyes of the church if they could; for they would not have their deeds come to the light, lest they should be reproved. The divine eyesalve will impart clearness to the understanding. Christ is the depositary of all graces. He says: "Buy of Me."

SOME SHAKEN OUT

Some may say it is exalting our own merits to expect favor from God through our good works. True, we cannot buy one victory with our good works; yet we cannot be victors without them. The purchase which Christ recommends to us is only complying with the conditions He has given us. True grace, which is of inestimable value, and which will endure the test of trial and adversity, is only obtained through faith and humble, prayerful obedience. Graces that endure the proofs of affliction and persecution, and evidence their soundness and sincerity, are the gold which is tried in the fire and found genuine. Christ offers to sell this precious treasure to man: "Buy of Me gold tried in the fire." Verse 18. The dead, heartless performance of duty does not make us Christians. We must get out of a lukewarm condition and experience a true conversion, or we shall fail of heaven.

I was pointed to the providence of God among His people and was shown that every trial made by the refining, purifying process upon professed Christians proves some to be dross. The fine gold does not always appear. In every religious crisis some fall under temptation. The shaking of God blows away multitudes like dry leaves. Prosperity multiplies a mass of professors. Adversity purges them out of the church. As a class, their spirits are not steadfast with God. They go out from us because they are not of us; for when tribulation or persecution arises because of the word, many are offended.

Let these look back a few months to the time when they were sitting on the cases of others who were in a condition similar to that which they now occupy. Let them carefully call to mind the exercise of their minds in regard to those tempted ones. Had anyone told them then that notwithstanding their zeal and labor to set others right, they would at length be found in a similar position of darkness, they would have said, as did Hazael to the prophet: "Is thy servant a dog, that he should do this great thing?" 2 Kings 8:13.

Self-deception is upon them. During the calm, what firmness they manifest! what courageous sailors they make! But when the furious tempests of trial and temptation come, lo! their souls are shipwrecked. Men may have excellent gifts, good ability, splendid qualifications; but one defect, one secret sin indulged, will prove to the character what the worm-eaten plank does to the ship—utter disaster and ruin! . . .

NEED FOR CONSTANT ADVANCEMENT

Men in responsible positions should improve continually. They must not anchor upon an old experience and feel that it is not necessary to become scientific workers. Man, although the most helpless of God's creatures when he comes into the world, and the most perverse in his nature, is nevertheless capable of constant advancement. He may be enlightened by science, ennobled by virtue, and may progress in mental and moral dignity, until he reaches a perfection of intelligence and a purity of character but little lower than the perfection and purity of angels. With the light of truth shining upon the minds of men, and the love of God shed abroad in their hearts, we cannot conceive what they may become nor what great work they may do.

I know that the human heart is blind to its own true condition, but I cannot leave you without making an effort to help you. We love you, and we want to see you pressing on to victory. Jesus loves you. He died for you, and He wants you to be saved. We have no disposition to hold you in ——; but we do want you to make thorough work with your own soul, to right every wrong there, and make every effort to master self, lest you miss heaven. This you cannot afford to do. For Christ's sake, resist the devil, and he will flee from you.

The work of pruning and purifying to fit us for heaven is a great work and will cost us much suffering and trial, because our wills are not subjected to the will of Christ. We must go through the furnace till the fires have consumed the dross and we are purified and reflect the divine image. Those who follow their inclinations and are governed by appearances are not good judges of what God is doing. They are filled with discontent. They see failure where there is indeed triumph, a great loss where there is gain; and, like Jacob, they are ready to exclaim, "All these things are against me" (Genesis 42:36), when the very things whereof they complain are all working together for their good.

No cross, no crown. How can one be strong in the Lord without trials? To have strength we must have exercise. To have strong faith, we must be placed in circumstances where our faith will be exercised. The apostle Paul, just before his martyrdom, exhorted Timothy: "Be thou partaker of the afflictions of the gospel according to the power of God." 2 Timothy 1:8. It is through much tribulation that we are to enter the kingdom of God. Our Saviour was tried in every possible way, and yet He triumphed in God continually. It is our privilege to be strong in the strength of God under all circumstances and to glory in the cross of Christ.—1872, vol. 3, p. 67.

The Efficacy of Christ's Blood

The children of Israel were anciently commanded to make an offering for the entire congregation to purify them from ceremonial defilement. This sacrifice was a red heifer and represented the more perfect offering that should redeem from the pollution of sin. This was an occasional sacrifice for the purification of all those who had necessarily or accidentally touched the dead. All who came in contact with death in any way were considered ceremonially unclean. This was to forcibly impress the minds of the Hebrews with the fact that death came in consequence of sin and therefore is a representative of sin. The *one* heifer, the *one* ark, the *one* brazen serpent, impressively point to the *one* great offering, the sacrifice of Christ.

This heifer was to be red, which was a symbol of blood. It must be without spot or blemish, and one that had never borne a yoke. Here, again, Christ was typified. The Son of God came voluntarily to accomplish the work of atonement. There was no obligatory yoke upon Him, for He was independent and above all law. The angels, as God's intelligent messengers, were under the yoke of obligation; no personal sacrifice of theirs could atone for the guilt of fallen man. Christ alone was free from the claims of the law to undertake the redemption of the sinful race. He had power to lay down His life and to take it up again. "Who, being in the form of God, thought it not robbery to be equal with God." Philippians 2:6.

Yet this glorious Being loved the poor sinner and took upon Himself the form of a servant, that He might suffer and die in man's behalf. Jesus might have remained at His Father's right hand, wearing His kingly crown and royal

1876, vol. 4, pp. 120-123 (A Divided Interest).

robes. But He chose to exchange all the riches, honor, and glory of heaven for the poverty of humanity, and His station of high command for the horrors of Gethsemane and the humiliation and agony of Calvary. He became a man of sorrows and acquainted with grief, that by His baptism of suffering and blood He might purify and redeem a guilty world. "Lo, I come," was the joyful assent, "to do Thy will, O My God." Psalm 40:7, 8.

The sacrificial heifer was conducted without the camp and slain in the most imposing manner. Thus Christ suffered without the gates of Jerusalem, for Calvary was outside the city walls. This was to show that Christ did not die for the Hebrews alone, but for all mankind. He proclaims to a fallen world that He has come to be their Redeemer and urges them to accept the salvation He offers them. The heifer having been slain in a most solemn manner, the priest, clothed in pure white garments, took the blood in his hands as it issued from the body of the victim and cast it toward the temple seven times. "And having an high priest over the house of God; let us draw near with a true heart in full assurance of faith, having our hearts sprinkled from an evil conscience, and our bodies washed with pure water." Hebrews 10:21, 22.

The body of the heifer was burned to ashes, which signified a whole and ample sacrifice. The ashes were then gathered up by a person uncontaminated by contact with the dead and placed in a vessel containing water from a running stream. This clean and pure person then took a cedar stick with scarlet cloth and a bunch of hyssop, and sprinkled the contents of the vessel upon the tent and the people assembled. This ceremony was repeated several times in order to be thorough and was done as a purification from sin.

Thus Christ, in His own spotless righteousness, after shedding His precious blood, enters into the holy place to cleanse the sanctuary. And there the crimson current is brought into the service of reconciling God to man. Some may look upon this slaying of the heifer as a meaningless ceremony, but it was done by the command of God and bears a deep significance that has not lost its application to the present time.

The priest used cedar and hyssop, dipping them into the cleansing water and sprinkling the unclean. This symbolized the blood of Christ spilled to cleanse us from moral impurities. The repeated sprinklings illustrate the thoroughness of the work that must be accomplished for the repenting sinner. All that he has must be consecrated. Not only should his own soul be washed clean and pure, but he should strive to have his family, his domestic arrangements, his property, and his entire belongings consecrated to God.

After the tent had been sprinkled with hyssop, over the door of those cleansed was written: I am not my own; Lord, I am Thine. Thus should it be with those who profess to be cleansed by the blood of Christ. God is no less exacting now than He was in olden times. The psalmist, in his prayer, refers to this symbolic ceremony when he says: "Purge me with hyssop, and I shall be clean: wash me, and I shall be whiter than snow." "Create in me a clean heart, O God; and renew a right spirit within me." "Restore unto me the joy of Thy salvation; and uphold me with Thy free spirit." Psalm 51:7, 10, 12.

The blood of Christ is efficacious, but it needs to be applied continually. God not only wants His servants to use the means He has entrusted to them for His glory, but He desires them to make a consecration of *themselves* to His cause. If you, my brethren, have become selfish and are withholding from the Lord that which you should cheerfully give to His service, then you need the blood of sprinkling thoroughly applied, consecrating you and all your possessions to God.

Willing Obedience

Abraham was an old man when he received the startling command from God to offer up his son Isaac for a burnt offering. Abraham was considered an old man even in his generation. The ardor of his youth had faded away. It was no longer easy for him to endure hardships and brave dangers. In the vigor of youth man may breast the storm with a proud consciousness of strength and rise above discouragements that would cause his heart to fail later in life, when his steps are faltering toward the grave.

But in His providence God reserved His last most trying test for Abraham until the burden of years was heavy upon him and he longed for rest from anxiety and toil. The Lord spoke unto him, saying: "Take now thy son, thine only son Isaac, whom thou lovest," "and offer him . . . for a burnt offering." Genesis 22:2. The heart of the old man stood still with horror. The loss of such a son by disease would have been most heart-rending to the fond father, it would have bowed his whitened head with sorrow; but now he is commanded to shed the precious blood of that son with his own hand. It seemed to him a fearful impossibility.

Yet God had spoken, and His word must be obeyed. Abraham was stricken in years, but this did not excuse him from duty. He grasped the staff of faith and in dumb agony took by the hand his child, beautiful in the rosy health of youth, and went out to obey the word of God. The grand old patriarch was human; his passions and attachments were like ours, and he loved his boy, who was the solace of his old age, and to whom the promise of the Lord had been given.

1876, vol. 4, pp. 144-148.

But Abraham did not stop to question how God's promises could be fulfilled if Isaac were slain. He did not stay to reason with his aching heart, but carried out the divine command to the very letter, till, just as the knife was about to be plunged into the quivering flesh of the child, the word came: "Lay not thine hand upon the lad;" "for now I know that thou fearest God, seeing thou hast not withheld thy son, thine only son from Me." Verse 12.

This great act of faith is penciled on the pages of sacred history to shine forth upon the world as an illustrious example to the end of time. Abraham did not plead that his old age should excuse him from obeying God. He did not say: "My hairs are gray, the vigor of my manhood is gone; who will comfort my waning life when Isaac is no more? How can an aged father spill the blood of an only son?" No; God had spoken, and man must obey without questioning, murmuring, or fainting by the way.

We need the faith of Abraham in our churches today, to lighten the darkness that gathers around them, shutting out the sweet sunlight of God's love and dwarfing spiritual growth. Age will never excuse us from obeying God. Our faith should be prolific of good works, for faith without works is dead. Every duty performed, every sacrifice made in the name of Jesus, brings an exceeding great reward. In the very act of duty, God speaks and gives His blessing. But He requires of us an entire surrender of the faculties. The mind and heart, the whole being, must be given to Him, or we fall short of becoming true Christians.

God has withheld nothing from man that can secure to him eternal riches. He has clothed the earth with beauty and furnished it for his use and comfort during his temporal life. He has given His Son to die for the redemption of a world that had fallen through sin and folly. Such matchless love, such infinite sacrifice, claims our strictest obedience, our holiest love, our unbounded faith. Yet all these virtues, exercised to their fullest extent, can never be commensurate with the great sacrifice that has been offered for us.

UNQUESTIONING OBEDIENCE

God requires prompt and unquestioning obedience of His law; but men are asleep or paralyzed by the deceptions of Satan, who suggests excuses and subterfuges, and conquers their scruples, saying as he said to Eve in the garden: "Ye shall not surely die." Genesis 3:4. Disobedience not only hardens the heart and conscience of the guilty one, but it tends to corrupt the faith of others. That which looked very wrong to them at first, gradually loses this appearance by being constantly before them, till finally they question whether it is really sin and unconsciously fall into the same error.

Through Samuel, God commanded Saul to go and smite the Amalekites and utterly destroy all their possessions. But Saul only partially obeyed the command; he destroyed the inferior cattle, but reserved the best and spared the wicked king. The next day he met the prophet Samuel with flattering self-congratulations. Said he: "Blessed be thou of the Lord: I have performed the commandment of the Lord." But the prophet immediately answered: "What meaneth then this bleating of the sheep in mine ears, and the lowing of the oxen which I hear?" 1 Samuel 15:13, 14.

Saul was confused and sought to shirk responsibility by answering: "*They* have brought them from the Amalekites: for the *people* spared the best of the sheep and of the oxen, to sacrifice unto the Lord thy God; and the rest we have utterly destroyed." Verse 15. Samuel then reproved the king, reminding him of the explicit command of God directing him to destroy all things belonging to Amalek. He pointed out his transgression and declared that he had disobeyed the Lord. But Saul refused to acknowledge that he had done wrong; he again excused his sin by pleading that he had reserved the best cattle to sacrifice unto the Lord.

Samuel was grieved to the heart by the persistency with which the king refused to see and confess his sin. He sorrowfully asked: "Hath the Lord as great delight in burnt offerings and sacrifices, as in obeying the voice of the Lord? Behold, to obey is better than sacrifice, and to hearken than the fat of rams. For rebellion is as the sin of witchcraft, and stubbornness is as iniquity and idolatry. Because thou hast rejected the word of the Lord, He hath also rejected thee from being king." Verses 22, 23.

DANGER IN DELAY

We should not look in the face of duty and delay meeting its demands. Such delay gives time for doubts; unbelief creeps in, the judgment is perverted, the understanding darkened. At length the reproofs of God's Spirit do not reach the heart of the deluded person, who has become so blinded as to think that they cannot possibly be intended for him or apply to his case.

The precious time of probation is passing, and few realize that it is given them for the purpose of preparing for eternity. The golden hours are squandered in worldly pursuits, in pleasure, in absolute sin. God's law is slighted and forgotten, yet every statute is nonetheless binding. Every transgression will bring its punishment. Love of worldly gain leads to desecration of the Sabbath, yet the claims of that holy day are not abrogated or lessened. God's command is clear and unquestionable on this point; He has peremptorily forbidden us to labor upon the seventh day. He has set it apart as a day sanctified to Himself.

Many are the hindrances that lie in the path of those who would walk in obedience to the commandments of God. There are strong and subtle influences that bind them to the ways of the world, but the power of the Lord can break these chains. He will remove every obstacle from before the feet of His faithful ones or give them strength and courage to conquer every difficulty, if they earnestly beseech His help. All hindrances will vanish before an earnest desire and persistent effort to do the will of God at any cost to self, even if life itself is sacrificed. Light from heaven will illuminate the darkness of those, who, in trial and perplexity, go forward, looking unto Jesus as the Author and Finisher of their faith.

In ancient times God spoke to men by the mouth of prophets and apostles. In these days He speaks to them by the *Testimonies* of His Spirit. There was never a time when God instructed His people more earnestly than He instructs them now concerning His will and the course that He would have them pursue. But will they profit by His teachings? will they receive His reproofs and heed His warnings? God will accept of no partial obedience; He will sanction no compromise with self.

Criticizing Burden Bearers

The church is suffering for want of unselfish Christian workers. If all who are, as a rule, unable to resist temptation and are too weak to stand alone would remain away from ——, there would be a much purer spiritual atmosphere in that place. Those who live upon the husks of others' failings and deficiencies, and who gather to themselves the unwholesome miasma of their neighbors' neglects and shortcomings, making themselves church scavengers, are no advantage to the society of which they form a part, but are an actual burden to the community upon which they inflict themselves.

The church is in need, not of burdens, but of earnest workers; not of faultfinders, but of builders in Zion. Missionaries are really needed at the great heart of the work—men who will keep the fort, who will be true as steel to preserve the honor of those whom God has placed at the head of His work, and who will do their utmost to sustain the cause in all its departments, even at the sacrifice of their own interests and lives, if need be. But I was shown that there are but few who have the truth wrought into their very souls, who can bear the searching test of God. There are many who have taken hold of the truth, but the truth has not taken hold of them, to transform their hearts and cleanse them from all selfishness. There are those who come to —— to help in the work, as well as many of the old members, who have a fearful account to render to God for the hindrance they have been to the work through their self-love and unconsecrated lives.

Religion has no saving virtue if the characters of those professing it do not correspond with their profession. God has graciously given great light to His people in ——; but Satan

1876, vol. 4, pp. 193-196 (Faithful Reproofs Necessary).

has his work to accomplish, and he brings his power to bear most strongly at the great heart of the work. He seizes men and women who are selfish and unconsecrated, and makes of them sentinels to watch the faithful servants of God, to question their words, their actions, and their motives, and to find fault and murmur at their reproofs and warnings. Through them he creates suspicion and jealousy, and seeks to weaken the courage of the faithful, to please the unsanctified, and to bring to nought the labors of God's servants.

THE FRUIT OF CRITICISM

Satan has had great power over the minds of parents through their undisciplined children. The sin of parental neglect stands marked against many Sabbathkeeping parents. The spirit of gossip and talebearing is one of Satan's special agencies to sow discord and strife, to separate friends, and to undermine the faith of many in the truthfulness of our positions. Brethren and sisters are too ready to talk of the faults and errors that they think exist in others, and especially in those who have borne unflinchingly the messages of reproof and warning given them of God.

The children of these complainers listen with open ears and receive the poison of disaffection. Parents are thus blindly closing the avenues through which the hearts of the children might be reached. How many families season their daily meals with doubt and questionings. They dissect the characters of their friends, and serve them up as a dainty dessert. A precious bit of slander is passed around the board to be commented upon, not only by adults, but by children. In this God is dishonored. Jesus said: "Inasmuch as ye have done it unto one of the least of these My brethren, ye have done it unto Me." Matthew 25:40. Therefore Christ is slighted and abused by those who slander His servants.

The names of God's chosen servants have been handled with disrespect, and in some cases with absolute contempt, by certain persons whose duty it is to uphold them. The children have not failed to hear the disrespectful remarks of their parents in reference to the solemn reproofs and warnings of God's servants. They have understood the scornful jests and depreciatory speeches that from time to time have met their ears, and the tendency has been to bring sacred and eternal interests, in their minds, on a level with the common affairs of the world. What a work are these parents doing in making infidels of their children even in their childhood! This is the way that children are taught to be irreverent and to rebel against Heaven's reproof of sin.

Spiritual declension can but prevail where such evils exist. These very fathers and mothers, blinded by the enemy, marvel why their children are so inclined to unbelief and to doubt the truth of the Bible. They wonder that it is so difficult to reach them by moral and religious influences. Had they spiritual eyesight, they would at once discover that this deplorable condition of things is the result of their own home influence, the offspring of their jealousy and distrust. Thus many infidels are educated in the family circles of professed Christians.

There are many who find special enjoyment in discoursing and dwelling upon the defects, whether real or imaginary, of those who bear heavy responsibilities in connection with the institutions of God's cause. They overlook the good that has been accomplished, the benefits that have resulted from arduous labor and unflinching devotion to the cause, and fasten their attention upon some apparent mistake, some matter that, after it has been done and the consequences have followed, they fancy could have been done in a better manner with fairer results; when the truth is, had they been left to do the work, they would either have refused to move at all under the attending discouragements of the case, or would have managed more indiscreetly than those who did do the work, following the opening of God's providence.

But these unruly talkers will fasten upon the more disagreeable features of the work, even as the lichen clings to the roughness of the rock. These persons are spiritually dwarfed by continually dwelling upon the failings and faults of others. They are morally incapable of discerning good and noble actions, unselfish endeavors, true heroism, and self-sacrifice. They are not becoming nobler and loftier in their lives and hopes, more generous and broad in their ideas and plans. They are not cultivating that charity that should characterize the Christian's life. They are degenerating every day and are becoming narrower in their prejudices and views. Littleness is their element, and the atmosphere that surrounds them is poisonous to peace and happiness.

Christians should be careful in regard to their words. They should never carry unfavorable reports from one of their friends to another, especially if they are aware that there is a lack of union between them. It is cruel to hint and insinuate, as though you knew a great deal in regard to this friend or that acquaintance of which others are ignorant. Such hints go further, and create more unfavorable impressions, than to frankly relate the facts in an unexaggerated manner. What harm has not the church of Christ suffered from these things! The inconsistent, unguarded course of her members has made her weak as water. Confidence has been betrayed by members of the same church, and yet the guilty did not design to do mischief. Lack of wisdom in the selection of subjects of conversation has done much harm.

The conversation should be upon spiritual and divine things; but it has been otherwise. If the association with Christian friends is chiefly devoted to the improvement of the mind and heart, there will be no after regrets, and they can look back on the interview with a pleasant satisfaction. But if the hours are spent in levity and vain talking, and the precious time is employed in dissecting the lives and character of others, the friendly intercourse will prove a source of evil, and your influence will be a savor of death unto death.—1868, vol. 2, pp. 186, 187.

We are not to allow our perplexities and disappointments to eat into our souls and make us fretful and impatient. Let there be no strife, no evil thinking or evilspeaking, lest we offend God. My brother, if you open your heart to envy and evil surmising, the Holy Spirit cannot abide with you. Seek for the fullness that is in Christ. Labor in His lines. Let every thought and word and deed reveal Him. You need a daily baptism of the love that in the days of the apostles made them all of one accord. This love will bring health to body, mind, and soul. Surround your soul with an atmosphere that will strengthen spiritual life. Cultivate faith, hope, courage, and love. Let the peace of God rule in your heart.—1904, vol. 8, p. 191.

The Lord lives and reigns. Soon He will arise in majesty to shake terribly the earth. A special message is now to be borne, a message that will pierce the spiritual darkness and convict and convert souls. "Haste thee, flee for thy life," is the call to be given to those dwelling in sin. We must now be terribly in earnest. We have not a moment to spend in criticism and accusation. Let those who have done this in the past fall on their knees in prayer, and let them beware how they put their words and their plans in the place of God's words and God's plans.—1904, vol. 8, p. 36.

Sacredness of God's Commandments

Much-respected Brother K: In January, 1875, I was shown that there are hindrances in the way of the spiritual prosperity of the church. The Spirit of God is grieved because many are not right in heart and life; their professed faith does not harmonize with their works. The sacred rest day of Jehovah is not observed as it should be. Every week God is robbed by some infringement upon the borders of His holy time; and the hours that should be devoted to prayer and meditation are given to worldly employments.

God has given us His commandments, not only to be believed in, but to be obeyed. The great Jehovah, when He had laid the foundations of the earth, had dressed the whole world in the garb of beauty, and had filled it with things useful to man,—when He had created all the wonders of the land and the sea,—instituted the Sabbath day and made it holy. God blessed and sanctified the seventh day, because He rested upon it from all His wondrous work of creation. The Sabbath was made for man, and God would have him put by his labor on that day, as He Himself rested after His six days' work of creation.

Those who reverence the commandments of Jehovah will, after light has been given them in reference to the fourth precept of the Decalogue, obey it without questioning the feasibility or convenience of such obedience. God made man in His own image and then gave him an example of observing the seventh day, which He sanctified and made holy. He designed that upon that day man should worship Him and engage in no secular pursuits. No one who disregards the fourth commandment, after becoming enlightened concern-

1876, vol. 4, pp. 247-254.

ing the claims of the Sabbath, can be held guiltless in the sight of God.

Brother K, you acknowledge the requirements of God to keep the Sabbath, but your works do not harmonize with your declared faith. You give your influence to the side of the unbeliever, insofar as you transgress the law of God. When your temporal circumstances seem to require attention, you violate the fourth commandment without compunction. You make the keeping of God's law a matter of convenience, obeying or disobeying as your business or inclination indicates. This is not honoring the Sabbath as a sacred institution. You grieve the Spirit of God and dishonor your Redeemer by pursuing this reckless course.

PARTIAL OBEDIENCE NOT ACCEPTABLE

A partial observance of the Sabbath law is not accepted by the Lord and has a worse effect upon the minds of sinners than if you made no profession of being a Sabbathkeeper. They perceive that your life contradicts your belief, and lose faith in Christianity. The Lord means what He says, and man cannot set aside His commands with impunity. The example of Adam and Eve in the garden should sufficiently warn us against any disobedience of the divine law. The sin of our first parents in listening to the specious temptations of the enemy brought guilt and sorrow upon the world, and led the Son of God to leave the royal courts of heaven and take a humble place on earth. He was subjected to insult, rejection, and crucifixion by the very ones He came to bless. What infinite expense attended that disobedience in the Garden of Eden! The Majesty of heaven was sacrificed to save man from the penalty of his crime.

God will not pass over any transgression of His law more lightly now than in the day when He pronounced judgment against Adam. The Saviour of the world raises His voice in protest against those who regard the divine commandments with carelessness and indifference. Said He: "Whosoever therefore shall break one of these least commandments, and shall teach men so, He shall be called the least in the kingdom of heaven: but whosoever shall do and teach them, the same shall be called great in the kingdom of heaven." Matthew 5:19. The teaching of our lives is wholly for or against the truth. If your works seem to justify the transgressor in his sin, if your influence makes light of breaking the commandments of God, then you are not only guilty yourself, but you are to a certain extent responsible for the consequent errors of others.

At the very beginning of the fourth precept, God said, *"Remember,"* knowing that man, in the multitude of his cares and perplexities, would be tempted to excuse himself from meeting the full requirements of the law or, in the press of worldly business, would forget its sacred importance. "Six days shalt thou labor, and do all thy work" (Exodus 20:9), the usual business of life, for worldly profit or pleasure. These words are very explicit; there can be no mistake.

Brother K, how dare you venture to transgress a commandment so solemn and important? Has the Lord made an exception by which you are absolved from the law He has given to the world? Are your transgressions omitted from the book of record? Has He agreed to excuse your disobedience when the nations come before Him for judgment? Do not for a moment deceive yourself with the thought that your sin will not bring its merited punishment. Your transgressions will be visited with the rod, because you have had the light, yet have walked directly contrary to it. "That servant, which knew his Lord's will, and prepared not himself, neither did according to His will, shall be beaten with many stripes." Luke 12:47.

God has given man six days in which to do his own work and carry on the usual business of life; but He claims one day, which He has set apart and sanctified. He gives it to man as a day in which he may rest from labor and devote himself to worship and the improvement of his spiritual condition.

What a flagrant outrage it is for man to steal the one sanctified day of Jehovah and appropriate it to his own selfish purposes!

It is the grossest presumption for mortal man to venture upon a compromise with the Almighty in order to secure his own petty, temporal interests. It is as ruthless a violation of the law to occasionally use the Sabbath for secular business as to entirely reject it; for it is making the Lord's commandments a matter of convenience. "I the Lord thy God am a jealous God," is thundered from Sinai. No partial obedience, no divided interest, is accepted by Him who declares that the iniquities of the fathers shall be visited upon the children to the third and fourth generation of them that hate Him, and that He will show mercy unto thousands of them that love Him and keep His commandments. It is not a small matter to rob a neighbor, and great is the stigma attached to one who is found guilty of such an act; yet he who would scorn to defraud his fellow man will without shame rob his heavenly Father of the time that He has blessed and set apart for a special purpose.

My dear brother, your works are at variance with your professed faith, and your only excuse is the poor plea of convenience. The servants of God in past times have been called upon to lay down their lives in vindication of their faith. Your course illy harmonizes with that of the Christian martyrs, who suffered hunger and thirst, torture and death, rather than renounce their religion or yield the principles of truth.

FAITH AND OBEDIENCE

It is written: "What doth it profit, my brethren, though a man say he hath faith, and have not works? can faith save him?" James 2:14. Every time you put your hands to labor on the Sabbath day, you virtually deny your faith. The Holy Scriptures teach us that faith without works is dead, and that the testimony of one's life proclaims to the world whether or not he is true to the faith he professes. Your conduct lessens

God's law in the estimation of your worldly friends. It says to them: "You may or may not obey the commandments. I believe that the law of God, is, in a manner, binding upon men; but, after all, the Lord is not very particular as to a strict observance of its precepts, and an occasional transgression is not visited with severity on His part."

Many excuse themselves for violating the Sabbath by referring to your example. They argue that if so good a man, who believes the seventh day is the Sabbath, can engage in worldly employments on that day when circumstances seem to require it, surely they can do the same without condemnation. Many souls will face you in the judgment, making your influence an excuse for their disobedience of God's law. Although this will be no apology for their sin, yet it will tell fearfully against you.

God has spoken, and He means that man shall obey. He does not inquire if it is convenient for him to do so. The Lord of life and glory did not consult His convenience or pleasure when He left His station of high command to become a man of sorrows and acquainted with grief, accepting ignominy and death in order to deliver man from the consequence of his disobedience. Jesus died, not to save man *in* his sins, but *from* his sins. Man is to leave the error of his ways, to follow the example of Christ, to take up his cross and follow Him, denying self, and obeying God at any cost.

Said Jesus: "No man can serve two masters: for either he will hate the one, and love the other; or else he will hold to the one, and despise the other. Ye cannot serve God and mammon." Matthew 6:24. If we are true servants of God, there should be no question in our minds as to whether we will obey His commandments or consult our own temporal interests. If the believers in the truth are not sustained by their faith in these comparatively peaceful days, what will uphold them when the grand test comes and the decree goes forth against all those who will not worship the image of the beast and receive his mark in their foreheads or in their hands? This solemn period is not far off. Instead of becoming weak and irresolute, the people of God should be gathering strength and courage for the time of trouble.

Jesus, our great Exemplar, in His life and death taught the strictest obedience. He died, the just for the unjust, the innocent for the guilty, that the honor of God's law might be preserved and yet man not utterly perish. Sin is the transgression of the law. If the sin of Adam brought such inexpressible wretchedness, requiring the sacrifice of God's dear Son, what will be the punishment of those, who, seeing the light of truth, set at nought the fourth commandment of the Lord?

CIRCUMSTANCES NO EXCUSE

Circumstances will not justify anyone in working upon the Sabbath for the sake of worldly profit. If God excuses one man, He may excuse all. Why may not Brother L, who is a poor man, work upon the Sabbath to earn means for a livelihood when he might by so doing be better able to support his family? Why may not other brethren, or all of us, keep the Sabbath only when it is convenient to do so? The voice from Sinai makes answer: "Six days shalt thou labor, and do all thy work: but the seventh day is the Sabbath of the Lord thy God." Exodus 20:9, 10.

Wrongs perpetrated by believers in the truth bring great weakness upon the church. They are stumbling blocks in the way of sinners and prevent them from coming to the light. Brother, God calls you to come out fully upon His side and let your works show that you regard His precepts and keep inviolate the Sabbath. He bids you wake up to your duty and be true to the responsibilities that devolve upon you. These solemn words are addressed to you: "If thou turn away thy foot from the Sabbath, from doing thy pleasure on My holy day; and call the Sabbath a delight, the holy of the Lord, honorable; and shalt honor Him, not doing thine own ways, nor finding thine own pleasure, nor speaking thine own words: then shalt thou delight thyself in the Lord; and I will cause thee to ride upon the high places of the earth, and feed thee with the heritage of Jacob thy father: for the mouth of the Lord hath spoken it." Isaiah 58:13, 14.

Like many of our brethren, you are becoming entangled with the transgressors of God's law, viewing matters in their light and falling into their errors. God will visit with His judgments those who are professedly serving Him, yet *really* serving mammon. Those who disregard the Lord's express injunction for their personal advantage are heaping future woe upon themselves. The church in —— should inquire closely if they have not, like the Jews, made the temple of God a place of merchandise. Christ said: "It is written, My house shall be called the house of prayer; but ye have made it a den of thieves." Matthew 21:13.

Are not many of our people falling into the sin of sacrificing their religion for the sake of worldly gain; preserving a form of piety, yet giving all the mind to temporal pursuits? God's law must be considered first of all and obeyed in spirit and in letter. If God's word, spoken in awful solemnity from the holy mountain, is lightly regarded, how will the *Testimonies* of His Spirit be received? Minds that are so darkened as not to recognize the authority of the Lord's commandments given directly to man can receive little good from a feeble instrument whom He has chosen to instruct His people.

AGE NO EXCUSE

Your age does not excuse you from obeying the divine commands. Abraham was sorely tested in his old age. The words of the Lord seemed terrible and uncalled-for to the stricken old man, yet he never questioned their justice or hesitated in his obedience. He might have pleaded that he was old and feeble, and could not sacrifice the son who was the joy of his life. He might have reminded the Lord that this command conflicted with the promises that had been given in regard to this son. But the obedience of Abraham was without a murmur or a reproach. His trust in God was implicit.

The faith of Abraham should be our example, yet how few will patiently endure a simple test of reproof for the sins which imperil their eternal welfare. How few receive reproof with humility, and profit by it. God's claim upon our faith, our services, our affections, should meet with a cheerful response. We are infinite debtors to the Lord and should unhesitatingly comply with the least of His requirements. In order to be a commandment breaker it is not necessary that we should trample upon the whole moral code. If one precept is disregarded, we are transgressors of the sacred law. But if we would be true commandment keepers we should strictly observe every requirement that God has enjoined upon us.

GOD'S CONSTANT CARE

God allowed His own Son to be put to death in order to answer the penalty of the transgression of the law; then how will He deal with those who, in the face of all this evidence, dare venture upon the path of disobedience, after having received the light of truth? Man has no right to urge his convenience or wants in this matter. God will provide; He who fed Elijah by the brook, making a raven His messenger, will not suffer His faithful ones to want for food.

The Saviour asked His disciples, who were pressed with poverty, why they were anxious and troubled in regard to what they should eat or how they should be clothed. Said He: "Behold the fowls of the air: for they sow not, neither do they reap, nor gather into barns; yet your heavenly Father feedeth them. Are ye not much better than they?" Matthew 6:26. He pointed to the lovely flowers, formed and tinted by a divine hand, saying: "And why take ye thought for raiment? Consider the lilies of the field, how they grow; they toil not, neither do they spin: and yet I say unto you, That even Solomon in all his glory was not arrayed like one of these. Wherefore, if God so clothe the grass of the field, which today is, and tomorrow is cast into the oven, shall He not much more clothe you, O ye of little faith?" Verses 28-30.

Where is the faith of God's people? Why are they so unbelieving and distrustful of Him who provides for their wants and upholds them by His strength? The Lord will test the faith of His people; He will send rebukes, which will be followed by afflictions if these warnings are not heeded. He will break the fatal lethargy of sin at any cost to those who have departed from their allegiance to Him, and awaken them to their sense of duty.

My brother, your soul must be quickened and your faith enlarged. You have so long excused yourself in your disobedience on one plea or another that your conscience has been lulled to rest and ceases to remind you of your errors. You have so long followed your own convenience in regard to keeping the Sabbath that your mind has been rendered unimpressible as to your course of disobedience; yet you are nonetheless responsible, for you have brought yourself into this condition. Begin at once to obey the divine commandments, and trust in God. Provoke not His wrath, lest He visit you with terrible punishment. Return to Him before it is too late, and find pardon for your transgressions. He is rich and abundant in mercies; He will give you His peace and approbation if you come to Him in humble faith.

I pray that thy Word of truth shall burn there to the inner most depths of the heart to clear the channel that love and truth in Christ may flow out

---

that the light of Thy Word may shine and lighten to the very deep recesses of the heart of man to receive Thy truth

Ph. Bontragers

Preparation for Christ's Coming

In the late vision given me at Battle Creek during our general camp meeting, I was shown our danger, as a people, of becoming assimilated to the world rather than to the image of Christ. We are now upon the very borders of the eternal world, but it is the purpose of the adversary of souls to lead us to put far off the close of time. Satan will in every conceivable manner assail those who profess to be the commandment-keeping people of God and to be waiting for the second appearing of our Saviour in the clouds of heaven with power and great glory. He will lead as many as possible to put off the evil day and become in spirit like the world, imitating its customs. I felt alarmed as I saw that the spirit of the world was controlling the hearts and minds of many who make a high profession of the truth. Selfishness and self-indulgence are cherished by them, but true godliness and sterling integrity are not cultivated.

The angel of God pointed to those who profess the truth, and in a solemn voice repeated these words: "And take heed to yourselves, lest at any time your hearts be overcharged with surfeiting, and drunkenness, and cares of this life, and so that day come upon you unawares. For as a snare shall it come on all them that dwell on the face of the whole earth. Watch ye therefore, and pray always, that ye may be accounted worthy to escape all these things that shall come to pass, and to stand before the Son of man." Luke 21:34-36.

In consideration of the shortness of time we as a people should watch and pray, and in no case allow ourselves to be diverted from the solemn work of preparation for the great event before us. Because the time is apparently extended,

1879, vol. 4, pp. 306-313.

many have become careless and indifferent in regard to their words and actions. They do not realize their danger and do not see and understand the mercy of our God in lengthening their probation, that they may have time to form characters for the future, immortal life. Every moment is of the highest value. Time is granted them, not to be employed in studying their own ease and becoming dwellers on the earth, but to be used in the work of overcoming every defect in their own characters and in helping others, by example and personal effort, to see the beauty of holiness. God has a people upon the earth who in faith and holy hope are tracing down the roll of fast-fulfilling prophecy and are seeking to purify their souls by obeying the truth, that they may not be found without the wedding garment when Christ shall appear.

INFLUENCE OF TIME SETTING

Many who have called themselves Adventists have been time setters. Time after time has been set for Christ to come, but repeated failures have been the result. The definite time of our Lord's coming is declared to be beyond the ken of mortals. Even the angels who minister unto those who shall be heirs of salvation know not the day nor the hour. "But of that day and hour knoweth no man, no, not the angels of heaven, but My Father only." Matthew 24:36. Because the times repeatedly set have passed, the world is in a more decided state of unbelief than before in regard to the near advent of Christ. They look upon the failures of the time setters with disgust; and because men have been so deceived, they turn from the truth substantiated by the word of God that the end of all things is *at hand*.

Those who so presumptuously preach definite time, in so doing gratify the adversary of souls; for they are advancing infidelity rather than Christianity. They produce Scripture and by false interpretation show a chain of argument which apparently proves their position. But their failures show that they are false prophets, that they do not rightly interpret the language of inspiration. The word of God is truth and verity, but men have perverted its meaning. These errors have brought the truth of God for these last days into disrepute. Adventists are derided by ministers of all denominations, yet God's servants must not hold their peace. The signs foretold in prophecy are fast fulfilling around us. This should arouse every true follower of Christ to zealous action.

Those who think they must preach definite time in order to make an impression upon the people do not work from the right standpoint.* The feelings of the people may be stirred and their fears aroused, but they do not move from principle. An excitement is created; but when the time passes, as it has done repeatedly, those who moved out upon time fall back into coldness, darkness, and sin, and it is almost impossible to arouse their consciences without some great excitement.

In Noah's day the inhabitants of the old world laughed to scorn what they termed the superstitious fears and forebodings of the preacher of righteousness. He was denounced as a visionary character, a fanatic, an alarmist. "As it was in the days of Noah, so shall it be also in the days of the Son of man." Luke 17:26. Men will reject the solemn message of warning in our day, as they did in Noah's time. They will refer to those false teachers who have predicted the event and set the definite time, and will say that they have no more faith in our warning than in theirs. This is the attitude of the world today. Unbelief is widespread, and the preaching of Christ's coming is mocked at and derided. This makes it all the more essential

---

*Time has not been a test since 1844, and it will never again be a test. The Lord has shown me that the message of the third angel must go, and be proclaimed to the scattered children of the Lord, but it must not be hung on time. I saw that some were getting a false excitement, arising from preaching time; but the third angel's message is stronger than time can be. I saw that this message can stand on its own foundation, and needs not time to strengthen it; and that it will go in mighty power, and do its work, and will be cut short in righteousness.—1851, *Early Writings*, page 75.

that those who believe present truth should show their faith by their works. They should be sanctified through the truth which they profess to believe; for they are a savor of life unto life or of death unto death.

Noah preached to the people of his time that God would give them one hundred and twenty years in which to repent of their sins and find refuge in the ark, but they refused the gracious invitation. Abundant time was given them to turn from their sins, overcome their bad habits, and develop righteous characters. But inclination to sin, though weak at first with many, strengthened through repeated indulgence and hurried them on to irretrievable ruin. The merciful warning of God was rejected with sneers, with mockery and derision; and they were left in darkness to follow the course that their sinful hearts had chosen. But their unbelief did not hinder the predicted event. It came, and great was the wrath of God which was seen in the general ruin.

These words of Christ should sink into the hearts of all who believe present truth: "And take heed to yourselves, lest at any time your hearts be overcharged with surfeiting, and drunkenness, and cares of this life, and so that day come upon you unawares." Our danger is presented before us by Christ Himself. He knew the perils we should meet in these last days, and would have us prepare for them. "As it was in the days of Noah, so shall it be also in the days of the Son of man." They were eating and drinking, planting and building, marrying and giving in marriage, and knew not until the day that Noah entered into the ark, and the Flood came and swept them all away.

The day of God will find men absorbed in like manner in the business and pleasures of the world, in feasting and gluttony, and in indulging perverted appetite in the defiling use of liquor and the narcotic tobacco. This is already the condition of our world, and these indulgences are found even among God's professed people, some of whom are following the customs and partaking of the sins of the world. Lawyers, mechanics, farmers, traders, and even ministers from the pulpit are crying, "Peace and safety," when destruction is fast coming upon them.

BELIEF AND DILIGENCE

Belief in the near coming of the Son of man in the clouds of heaven will not cause the true Christian to become neglectful and careless of the ordinary business of life. The waiting ones who look for the soon appearing of Christ will not be idle, but diligent in business. Their work will not be done carelessly and dishonestly, but with fidelity, promptness, and thoroughness. Those who flatter themselves that careless inattention to the things of this life is an evidence of their spirituality and of their separation from the world are under a great deception. Their veracity, faithfulness, and integrity are tested and proved in temporal things. If they are faithful in that which is least they will be faithful in much.

I have been shown that here is where many will fail to bear the test. They develop their true character in the management of temporal concerns. They manifest unfaithfulness, scheming, dishonesty, in dealing with their fellow men. They do not consider that their hold upon the future, immortal life depends upon how they conduct themselves in the concerns of this life, and that the strictest integrity is indispensable to the formation of a righteous character. Dishonesty is practiced all through our ranks, and this is the cause of lukewarmness on the part of many who profess to believe the truth. They are not connected with Christ and are deceiving their own souls. I am pained to make the statement that there is an alarming lack of honesty even among Sabbathkeepers.

KNOWN BY THEIR FRUITS

I was referred to Christ's Sermon on the Mount. Here we have the injunction of the Great Teacher: "All things whatsoever ye would that men should do to you, do ye even so to them: for this is the law and the prophets." Matthew 7:12. This command of Christ is of the highest importance and should be strictly obeyed. It is like apples of gold in pictures of silver. How many carry out in their lives the principle Christ has here enjoined, and deal with others just as they would wish to be dealt with under similar circumstances? Reader, please answer.

An honest man, according to Christ's measurement, is one who will manifest unbending integrity. Deceitful weights and false balances, with which many seek to advance their interests in the world, are abomination in the sight of God. Yet many who profess to keep the commandments of God are dealing with false weights and false balances. When a man is indeed connected with God, and is keeping His law in truth, his life will reveal the fact; for all his actions will be in harmony with the teachings of Christ. He will not sell his honor for gain. His principles are built upon the sure foundation, and his conduct in worldly matters is a transcript of his principles. Firm integrity shines forth as gold amid the dross and rubbish of the world. Deceit, falsehood, and unfaithfulness may be glossed over and hidden from the eyes of man, but not from the eyes of God. The angels of God, who watch the development of character and weigh moral worth, record in the books of heaven these minor transactions which reveal character. If a workman in the daily vocations of life is unfaithful and slights his work, the world will not judge incorrectly if they estimate his standard in religion according to his standard in business.

"He that is faithful in that which is least is faithful also in much: and he that is unjust in the least is unjust also in much." Luke 16:10. It is not the magnitude of the matter that makes it fair or unfair. As a man deals with his fellow men, so will he deal with God. He that is unfaithful in the mammon of unrighteousness, will never be entrusted with the true riches. The children of God should not fail to remember that in all their business transactions they are being proved, weighed in the balances of the sanctuary.

Christ has said: "A good tree cannot bring forth evil fruit, neither can a corrupt tree bring forth good fruit." "Wherefore by their fruits ye shall know them." Matthew 7:18, 20. The deeds of a man's life are the fruit he bears. If he is unfaithful and dishonest in temporal matters he is bringing forth briers and thorns; he will be unfaithful in the religious life and will rob God in tithes and offerings.

The Bible condemns in the strongest terms all falsehood, false dealing, and dishonesty. Right and wrong are plainly stated. But I was shown that God's people have placed themselves on the enemy's ground; they have yielded to his temptations and followed his devices until their sensibilities have become fearfully blunted. A slight deviation from truth, a little variation from the requirements of God, is thought to be, after all, not so very sinful, when pecuniary gain or loss is involved. But sin is sin, whether committed by the possessor of millions or by the beggar in the streets. Those who secure property by false representations are bringing condemnation on their souls. All that is obtained by deceit and fraud will be only a curse to the receiver.

Adam and Eve suffered the terrible consequences of disobeying the express command of God. They might have reasoned: This is a very small sin, and will never be taken into account. But God treated the matter as a fearful evil, and the woe of their transgression will be felt through all time. In the times in which we live, sins of far greater magnitude are often committed by those who profess to be God's children. In the transaction of business, falsehoods are uttered and acted by God's professed people that bring His frown upon them and a reproach upon His cause. The least departure from truthfulness and rectitude is a transgression of the law of God. Continual indulgence in sin accustoms the person to a habit of wrongdoing, but does not lessen the aggravated character of the sin. God has established immutable principles, which He cannot change without a revision of His whole nature. If the word of God were faithfully studied by all who profess to believe the truth, they would not be dwarfs in spiritual things. Those who disregard the requirements of God in this life would not respect His authority were they in heaven.

THE BIBLE AN UNERRING GUIDE

Every species of immorality is plainly delineated in the word of God and its result spread before us. The indulgence of the lower passions is presented before us in its most revolting character. No one, however dark may be his understanding, need to err. But I have been shown that this sin is cherished by many who profess to be walking in all the commandments of God. God will judge every man by His word.

Said Christ: "Search the Scriptures; for in them ye think ye have eternal life: and they are they which testify of Me." John 5:39. The Bible is an unerring guide. It demands perfect purity in word, in thought, and in action. Only virtuous and spotless characters will be permitted to enter the presence of a pure and holy God. The word of God, if studied and obeyed, would lead the children of men, as the Israelites were led by a pillar of fire by night and a pillar of cloud by day. The Bible is God's will expressed to man. It is the only perfect standard of character, and marks out the duty of man in every circumstance of life. There are many responsibilities resting upon us in this life, a neglect of which will not only cause suffering to ourselves, but others will sustain loss in consequence.

Men and women professing to revere the Bible and follow its teachings fail in many respects to perform its requirements. In the training of children they follow their own perverse natures rather than the revealed will of God. This neglect of duty involves the loss of thousands of souls. The Bible lays down rules for the correct discipline of children. Were these requirements of God heeded by parents, we should today see a different class of youth coming upon the stage of action. But parents who profess to be Bible readers and Bible followers are going directly contrary to its teachings. We hear the cry of sorrow and anguish from fathers and mothers who bewail the conduct of their children, little realizing that they are bringing this sorrow and anguish upon themselves, and ruining their children, by their mistaken affection. They do not realize their God-given responsibilities to train their children to right habits from their babyhood.

Parents, you are in a great degree responsible for the souls of your children. Many neglect their duty during the first years of their children's lives, thinking that when they get older they will then be very careful to repress wrong and educate them in the right. But the very time for them to do this work is when the children are babes in their arms. It is not right for parents to pet and humor their children; neither is it right for them to abuse them. A firm, decided straightforward course of action will be productive of the best results.

Grafted Into Christ

Christ, in teaching His disciples, said: "I am the True Vine, and My Father is the Husbandman. Every branch in Me that beareth not fruit He taketh away: and every branch that beareth fruit, He purgeth it [pruneth it], that it may bring forth more fruit." John 15:1, 2. He who is united to Christ, partaking of the sap and nourishment of the Vine, will work the works of Christ. The love of Christ must be in him or he cannot be in the Vine. Supreme love to God, and love to your neighbor equal to that which you bear to yourself, is the basis of true religion.

Christ inquires of everyone professing His name: "Lovest thou Me?" If you love Jesus you will love the souls for whom He died. A man may not bear the most pleasant exterior, he may be deficient in many respects; but if he has a reputation for straightforward honesty, he will gain the confidence of others. The love of truth, the dependence and confidence which men can place in him, will remove or overbear objectionable features in his character. Trustworthiness in your place and calling, a willingness to deny self for the purpose of benefiting others, will bring peace of mind and the favor of God.

Those who will walk closely in the footsteps of their self-sacrificing, self-denying Redeemer will have the mind of Christ reflected in their minds. Purity and the love of Christ will shine forth in their daily lives and characters, while meekness and truth will guide their way. Every fruitful branch is pruned, that it may bring forth more fruit. Even fruitful branches may display too much foliage and appear what they really are not. The followers of Christ may be doing some

1879, vol. 4, pp. 353-355 (Uprightness in Deal).

work for the Master and yet not be doing half what they might do. He then prunes them, because worldliness, self-indulgence, and pride are cropping out in their lives. Husbandmen clip off the surplus tendrils of the vines that are grasping the rubbish of earth, thus making them more fruitful. These hindering causes must be removed and the defective overgrowth cut away, to give room for the healing beams of the Sun of Righteousness.

God purposed through Christ that fallen man should have another trial. Many misunderstand the object for which they were created. It was to bless humanity and glorify God, rather than to enjoy and glorify self. God is constantly pruning His people, cutting off profuse, spreading branches, that they may bear fruit to His glory and not produce leaves only. God prunes us with sorrow, with disappointment and affliction, that the outgrowth of strong, perverse traits of character may be weakened and that the better traits may have a chance to develop. Idols must be given up, the conscience must become more tender, the meditations of the heart must be spiritual, and the entire character must become symmetrical. Those who really desire to glorify God will be thankful for the exposure of every idol and every sin, that they may see these evils and put them away; but the divided heart will plead for indulgence rather than denial.

The apparently dry branch, by being connected with the living vine, becomes a part of it. Fiber by fiber, and vein by vein, it adheres to the vine till it derives its life and nourishment from the parent stock. The graft buds, blossoms, and produces fruit. The soul, dead in trespasses and sins, must experience a similar process in order to be reconciled to God and to become a partaker of Christ's life and joy. As the graft receives life when united to the vine, so the sinner partakes of the divine nature when connected with Christ. Finite man is united with the infinite God. When thus united, the words of Christ *abide* in us, and we are not actuated by a spasmodic feeling, but by a living, abiding principle. The words of Christ must be meditated upon and cherished and enshrined in the heart. They should not be repeated, parrot-like, finding no place in the memory and having no influence over the heart and life.

As the branch must abide in the vine to obtain the vital sap which causes it to flourish, so those who love God and keep all His sayings must abide in His love. Without Christ we cannot subdue a single sin or overcome the smallest temptation. Many need the Spirit of Christ and His power to enlighten their understanding, as much as blind Bartimaeus needed his natural sight. "As the branch cannot bear fruit of itself, except it abide in the vine; no more can ye, except ye abide in Me." Verse 4. All who are really in Christ will experience the benefit of this union. The Father accepts them in the Beloved, and they become objects of His solicitude and tender, loving care. This connection with Christ will result in the purification of the heart and in a circumspect life and faultless character. The fruit borne upon the Christian tree is "love, joy, peace, long-suffering, gentleness, goodness, faith, meekness, temperance." Galatians 5:22, 23.

A Lesson in Humility

Jesus, the dear Saviour, has given marked lessons in humility to all, but especially to the gospel minister. In His humiliation, when His work upon earth was nearly finished and He was about to return to His Father's throne whence He had come, with all power in His hands and all glory upon His head, among His last lessons to His disciples was one upon the importance of humility. While His disciples were contending as to who should be greatest in the promised kingdom, He girded Himself as a servant and washed the feet of those who called Him Lord and Master.

His ministry was nearly completed; He had only a few more lessons to impart. And that they might never forget the humility of the pure and spotless Lamb of God, the great and efficacious Sacrifice for man humbled Himself to wash the feet of His disciples. It will do you good, and our ministers generally, to frequently review the closing scenes in the life of our Redeemer. Here, beset with temptations as He was, we may all learn lessons of the utmost importance to us.

It would be well to spend a thoughtful hour each day reviewing the life of Christ from the manger to Calvary. We should take it point by point and let the imagination vividly grasp each scene, especially the closing ones of His earthly life. By thus contemplating His teachings and sufferings, and the infinite sacrifice made by Him for the redemption of the race, we may strengthen our faith, quicken our love, and become more deeply imbued with the spirit which sustained our Saviour.

If we would be saved at last we must all learn the lesson of

1879, vol. 4, pp. 373-375 (Consecration in Ministers).

penitence and faith at the foot of the cross. Christ suffered humiliation to save us from everlasting disgrace. He consented to have scorn, mockery, and abuse fall upon Him in order to shield us. It was our transgression that gathered the veil of darkness about His divine soul and extorted the cry from Him, as of one smitten and forsaken of God. He bore our sorrows; He was put to grief for our sins. He made Himself an offering for sin, that we might be justified before God through Him. Everything noble and generous in man will respond to the contemplation of Christ upon the cross.

I long to see our ministers dwell more upon the cross of Christ, their own hearts, meanwhile, softened and subdued by the Saviour's matchless love, which prompted that infinite sacrifice. If, in connection with the theory of the truth, our ministers would dwell more upon practical godliness, speaking from a heart imbued with the spirit of truth, we should see many more souls flocking to the standard of truth; their hearts would be touched by the pleadings of the cross of Christ, the infinite generosity and pity of Jesus in suffering for man. These vital subjects, in connection with the doctrinal points of our faith, would effect much good among the people. But the heart of the teacher must be filled with the experimental knowledge of the love of Christ.

The mighty argument of the cross will convict of sin. The divine love of God for sinners, expressed in the gift of His Son to suffer shame and death that they might be ennobled and endowed with everlasting life, is the study of a lifetime. I ask you to study anew the cross of Christ. If all the proud and vainglorious, whose hearts are panting for the applause of men and for distinction above their fellows, could rightly estimate the value of the highest earthly glory in contrast with the value of the Son of God, rejected, despised, spit upon, by the very ones whom He came to redeem, how insignificant would appear all the honor that finite man can bestow.

Duties are laid down in God's word, the performance of which will keep the people of God humble and separate from the world, and from backsliding, like the nominal churches. The washing of feet and partaking of the Lord's Supper should be more frequently practiced. Jesus set us the example, and told us to do as He had done. I saw that His example should be as exactly followed as possible; yet brethren and sisters have not always moved as judiciously as they should in washing feet, and confusion has been caused. It should be introduced into new places with carefulness and wisdom, especially where the people are not informed relative to the example and teachings of our Lord on this point, and where they have prejudice against it. Many honest souls, through the influence of former teachers in whom they had confidence, are much prejudiced against this plain duty, and the subject should be introduced to them in a proper time and manner.*—1854, *Early Writings,* pages 116, 117.

---

*This call for the celebration of the ordinances "more frequently" and for uniformity in practice to replace the "confusion" that then existed in some places was given in 1853. It led to the establishment of the present quarterly celebration of the communion services in Seventh-day Adventist churches, conducted with order and decorum. [White Trustees.]

The Judgment

On the morning of October 23, 1879, about two o'clock, the Spirit of the Lord rested upon me, and I beheld scenes in the coming judgment. Language fails me in which to give an adequate description of the things which passed before me and of the effect they had upon my mind.

The great day of the execution of God's judgment seemed to have come. Ten thousand times ten thousand were assembled before a large throne, upon which was seated a person of majestic appearance. Several books were before Him, and upon the covers of each was written in letters of gold, which seemed like a burning flame of fire: "Ledger of Heaven." One of these books, containing the names of those who claim to believe the truth, was then opened. Immediately I lost sight of the countless millions about the throne, and only those who were professedly children of the light and of the truth engaged my attention. As these persons were named, one by one, and their good deeds mentioned, their countenances would light up with a holy joy that was reflected in every direction. But this did not seem to rest upon my mind with the greatest force.

Another book was opened, wherein were recorded the *sins* of those who profess the truth. Under the general heading of selfishness came every other sin. There were also headings over every column, and underneath these, opposite each name, were recorded, in their respective columns, the lesser sins.

Under covetousness came falsehood, theft, robbery, fraud, and avarice; under ambition came pride and extravagance; jealousy stood at the head of malice, envy, and hatred; and intemperance headed a long list of fearful crimes, such as

1880, vol. 4, pp. 384-387.

lasciviousness, adultery, indulgence of animal passions, etc. As I beheld I was filled with inexpressible anguish and exclaimed: "Who can be saved? who will stand justified before God? whose robes are spotless? who are faultless in the sight of a pure and holy God?"

As the Holy One upon the throne slowly turned the leaves of the ledger, and His eyes rested for a moment upon individuals, His glance seemed to burn into their very souls, and at the same moment every word and action of their lives passed before their minds as clearly as though traced before their vision in letters of fire. Trembling seized them, and their faces turned pale. Their first appearance when around the throne was that of careless indifference. But how changed their appearance now! The feeling of security is gone, and in its place is a nameless terror. A dread is upon every soul, lest he shall be found among those who are wanting. Every eye is riveted upon the face of the One upon the throne; and as His solemn, searching eye sweeps over that company, there is a quaking of heart; for they are self-condemned without one word being uttered. In anguish of soul each declares his own guilt and with terrible vividness sees that by sinning he has thrown away the precious boon of eternal life.

CUMBERERS OF THE GROUND

One class were registered as cumberers of the ground. As the piercing eye of the Judge rested upon these, their sins of neglect were distinctly revealed. With pale, quivering lips they acknowledged that they had been traitors to their holy trust. They had had warnings and privileges, but they had not heeded nor improved them. They could now see that they had presumed too much upon the mercy of God. True, they had not such confessions to make as had the vile and basely corrupt; but, like the fig tree, they were cursed because they bore no fruit, because they had not put to use the talents entrusted to them.

This class had made *self* supreme, laboring only for selfish interests. They were not rich toward God, not having responded to His claims upon them. Although professing to be servants of Christ, they brought no souls to Him. Had the cause of God been dependent on their efforts, it would have languished; for they not only withheld the means lent them of God, but they withheld themselves. But these could now see and feel that in occupying an irresponsible position in reference to the work and cause of God they had placed themselves on the left hand. They had had opportunity, but would not do the work that they could and should have done.

The names of all who profess the truth were mentioned. Some were reproved for their unbelief, others for having been slothful servants. They had allowed others to do the work in the Master's vineyard, and to bear the heaviest responsibilities, while they were selfishly serving their own temporal interests. Had they cultivated the abilities God had given them, they could have been reliable burden bearers, working for the interest of the Master. Said the Judge: "All will be justified by their 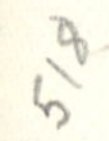 faith and judged by their works." How vividly then appeared their neglect, and how wise the arrangement of God in giving to every man a work to do to promote the cause and save his fellow men. Each was to demonstrate a living faith in his family and in his neighborhood, by showing kindness to the poor, sympathizing with the afflicted, engaging in missionary labor, and by aiding the cause of God with his means. But, like Meroz, the curse of God rested upon them for what they had not done. They had loved that work which would bring the greatest profit in this life; and opposite their names in the ledger devoted to good works there was a mournful blank.

FOUND WANTING

The words spoken to these were most solemn: "You are weighed in the balances, and found wanting. You have neglected spiritual responsibilities because of busy activity in temporal matters, while your very position of trust made it necessary that you should have more than human wisdom and greater than finite judgment. This you needed in order to perform even the mechanical part of your labor; and when you disconnected God and His glory from your business, you turned from His blessing."

The question was then asked: "Why have you not washed your robes of character and made them white in the blood of the Lamb? God sent His Son into the world, not to condemn the world, but that through Him it might be saved. My love for you has been more self-denying than a mother's love. It was that I might blot out your dark record of iniquity, and put the cup of salvation to your lips, that I suffered the death of the cross, bearing the weight and curse of your guilt. The pangs of death, and the horrors of the darkness of the tomb, I endured, that I might conquer him who had the power of death, unbar the prison house, and open for you the gates of life. I submitted to shame and agony because I loved you with an infinite love, and would bring back my wayward, wandering sheep to the paradise of God, to the tree of life. That life of bliss which I purchased for you at such a cost, you have disregarded. Shame, reproach, and ignominy, such as your Master bore for you, you have shunned. The privileges He died to bring within your reach have not been appreciated. You would not be partaker of His sufferings, and you cannot now be partaker with Him of His glory." Then were uttered these solemn words: "He that is unjust, let him be unjust still: and he that is righteous, let him be righteous still: and he that is holy, let him be holy still." The book then closed, and the mantle fell from the Person on the throne, revealing the terrible glory of the Son of God.

The scene then passed away, and I found myself still upon the earth, inexpressibly grateful that the day of God had not yet come, and that precious probationary time is still granted us in which to prepare for eternity.

Every hour's work passes in review before God and is registered for faithfulness or unfaithfulness. The record of wasted moments and unimproved opportunities must be met when the judgment shall sit and the books shall be opened and everyone shall be judged according to the things written in the books. Selfishness, envy, pride, jealousy, idleness, or any other sin which is cherished in the heart, will exclude one from the blessedness of heaven. "To whom ye yield yourselves servants to obey, his servants ye are."—1880, vol. 4, p. 453.

Christ's Ambassadors

Ambassadors for Christ have a solemn and important work, which rests upon some altogether too lightly. While Christ is the minister in the sanctuary above, He is also, through His delegates, the minister of His church on earth. He speaks to the people through chosen men, and carries forward His work through them, as when in the days of His humiliation He moved visibly upon the earth. Although centuries have passed, the lapse of time has not changed His parting promise to His disciples: "Lo, I am with you alway, even unto the end of the world." Matthew 28:20. From Christ's ascension to the present day, men ordained of God, deriving their authority from Him, have become teachers of the faith. Christ, the True Shepherd, superintends His work through the instrumentality of these undershepherds. Thus the position of those who labor in word and doctrine becomes very important. In Christ's stead they beseech the people to be reconciled to God.

The people should not regard their ministers as mere public speakers and orators, but as Christ's ambassadors, receiving their wisdom and power from the great Head of the church. To slight and disregard the word spoken by Christ's representative is not only showing disrespect to the man, but also to the Master who has sent him. He is in Christ's stead; and the voice of the Saviour should be heard in His representative.

PREACH CHRIST

Many of our ministers have made a great mistake in giving discourses which were wholly argumentative. There are souls who listen to the theory of the truth and are impressed with the evidences brought out, and then if a portion of the dis-

1880, vol. 4, pp. 393-404.

course presents Christ as the Saviour of the world, the seed sown may spring up and bear fruit to the glory of God. But in many discourses the cross of Christ is not presented before the people. Some may be listening to the last sermon they will ever hear, and some will never again be so situated that they can have the chain of truth brought before them and a practical application made of it to their hearts. That golden opportunity lost is lost forever. Had Christ and His redeeming love been exalted in connection with the theory of truth, it might have balanced them on His side.

There are more souls longing to understand how they may come to Christ than we imagine. Many listen to popular sermons from the pulpit and know no better than before they listened how to find Jesus and the peace and rest which their souls desire. Ministers who preach the last message of mercy to the world should bear in mind that Christ is to be exalted as the sinner's refuge. Many ministers think that it is not necessary to preach repentance and faith, with a heart all subdued by the love of God; they take it for granted that their hearers are perfectly acquainted with the gospel, and that matters of a different nature must be presented in order to hold their attention. If their hearers are interested, they take it as evidence of success. The people are more ignorant in regard to the plan of salvation and need more instruction upon this all-important subject than upon any other.

Those who assemble to listen to the truth should expect to be profited, as did Cornelius and his friends: "Now therefore are we all here present before God, to hear all things that are commanded thee of God." Acts 10:33.

Theoretical discourses are essential, that all may know the form of doctrine and see the chain of truth, link after link, uniting in a perfect whole. But no discourse should ever be delivered without presenting Christ and Him crucified as the foundation of the gospel, making a practical application of the truths set forth, and impressing upon the people the fact that the doctrine of Christ is not Yea and Nay, but Yea and Amen in Christ Jesus.

After the theory of truth has been presented, then comes the laborious part of the work. The people should not be left without instruction in the practical truths which relate to their everyday life. They must see and feel that they are sinners and need to be converted to God. What Christ said, what He did, and what He taught should be brought before them in the most impressive manner.

The work of the minister is but commenced when the truth is opened to the understanding of the people. Christ is our Mediator and officiating High Priest in the presence of the Father. He was shown to John as a Lamb that had been slain, as in the very act of pouring out His blood in the sinner's behalf. When the law of God is set before the sinner, showing him the depth of his sins, he should then be pointed to the Lamb of God, that taketh away the sin of the world. He should be taught repentance toward God and faith toward our Lord Jesus Christ. Thus will the labor of Christ's representative be in harmony with His work in the heavenly sanctuary.

TEACH PRACTICAL GODLINESS

Ministers would reach many more hearts if they would dwell more upon practical godliness. Frequently, when efforts are made to introduce the truth into new fields, the labor is almost entirely theoretical. The people are unsettled. They see the force of truth and are anxious to obtain a sure foundation. When their feelings are softened is the time, above all others, to urge the religion of Christ home upon the conscience; but too often the course of lectures has been allowed to close without that work being done for the people which they needed. That effort was too much like the offering of Cain; it had not the sacrificial blood to make it acceptable to God. Cain was right in making an offering, but he left out all that made it of any value—the blood of the atonement.

It is a sad fact that the reason why many dwell so much on theory and so little on practical godliness is that Christ is not abiding in their hearts. They do not have a living connection with God. Many souls decide in favor of the truth from the weight of evidence, without being converted. Practical discourses were not given in connection with the doctrinal, that as the hearers should see the beautiful chain of truth they might fall in love with its Author and be sanctified through obedience. The minister's work is not done until he has urged home upon his hearers the necessity of a change of character in accordance with the pure principles of the truth which they have received.

A formal religion is to be dreaded, for in it is no Saviour. Plain, close, searching, practical discourses were given by Christ. His ambassadors should follow His example in every discourse. Christ and His Father were one; in all the Father's requirements Christ cheerfully acquiesced. He had the mind of God. The Redeemer was the perfect Pattern. Jehovah was manifested in Him. Heaven was enshrined in humanity, and humanity enclosed in the bosom of Infinite Love.

If ministers will in meekness sit at the feet of Jesus, they will soon obtain right views of God's character and will be able to teach others also. Some enter the ministry without deep love to God or to their fellow men. Selfishness and self-indulgence will be manifested in the lives of such; and while these unconsecrated, unfaithful watchmen are serving themselves instead of feeding the flock and attending to their pastoral duties, the people perish for want of proper instruction.

PRESENT FERVENT APPEALS

In every discourse fervent appeals should be made to the people to forsake their sins and turn to Christ. The popular sins and indulgences of our day should be condemned and practical godliness enforced. The minister should be deeply in earnest himself, feeling from the heart the words he utters and unable to repress his feeling of concern for the souls of men and women for whom Christ died. Of the Master it was said: "The zeal of Thine house hath eaten Me up." Psalm 69:9. The same earnestness should be felt by His representatives.

An infinite sacrifice has been made for man, and made in vain for every soul who will not accept of salvation. How important, then, that the one who presents the truth shall do so under a full sense of the responsibility resting upon him. How tender, pitiful, and courteous should be all his conduct in dealing with the souls of men, when the Redeemer of the world has shown that He values them so highly. The question is asked by Christ: "Who then is a faithful and wise servant, whom his lord hath made ruler over his household?" Matthew 24:45. Jesus asks, Who? and every minister of the gospel should repeat the question to his own heart. As he views the solemn truths, and his mind beholds the picture drawn of the faithful and wise steward, his soul should be stirred to the very depths.

DOERS OF THE WORD

To every man is given his work; not one is excused. Each has a part to act according to his capacity; and it devolves upon the one who presents the truth to carefully and prayerfully learn the ability of all who accept the truth, and then to instruct them and lead them along, step by step, letting them realize the burden of responsibility resting upon them to do the work that God has for them to do. It should be urged upon them again and again that no one will be able to resist temptation, to answer the purpose of God, and to live the life of a Christian unless he shall take up his work, be it great or small, and do that work with conscientious fidelity. There is something for all to do besides going to church and listening to the word of God. They must practice the truth heard, carrying its principles into their everyday life. They must be doing work for Christ constantly, not from selfish motives, but with an eye single to the glory of Him who made every sacrifice to save them from ruin.

Ministers should impress upon those who accept the truth that they must have Christ in their homes; that they need grace and wisdom from Him in guiding and controlling their children. It is a part of the work which God has left for them to do, to educate and discipline these children, bringing them into subjection. Let the kindness and courtesy of the minister be seen in his treatment of children. He should ever bear in mind that they are miniature men and women, younger members of the Lord's family. These may be very near and dear to the Master, and, if properly instructed and disciplined, will do service for Him, even in their youth. Christ is grieved with every harsh, severe, and inconsiderate word spoken to children. Their rights are not always respected, and they are frequently treated as though they had not an individual character which needs to be properly developed, that it may not be warped and the purpose of God in their lives prove a failure.

From a child, Timothy knew the Scriptures, and his knowledge was a safeguard to him against the evil influences surrounding him and the temptation to choose pleasure and selfish gratification before duty. Such a safeguard all our children need, and it should be a part of the work of parents and of Christ's ambassadors to see that the children are properly instructed in the word of God.

PERFECTION IN CHRIST

If the minister would meet the approval of his Lord, he must labor with fidelity to present every man perfect in Christ. He should not, in his manner of labor, carry the impression that it is of little consequence whether men do or do not accept the truth and practice true godliness; but the faithfulness and self-sacrifice manifested in his life should be such as to convince the sinner that eternal interests are at stake and that his soul is in peril unless he responds to the earnest labor put forth in his behalf. Those who have been brought from error and darkness to truth and light have great changes to make, and unless the necessity of thorough reform is pressed home upon the conscience, they will be like the man who looked into the mirror, the law of God, and discovered the defects in his moral character, but went away and forgot what manner of man he was. The mind must be kept awake to a sense of responsibility or it will settle back into a state of even more careless inattention than before it was aroused.

The work of the ambassadors for Christ is far greater and more responsible than many dream of. They should not be at all satisfied with their success until they can, by their earnest labors and the blessing of God, present to Him serviceable Christians who have a true sense of their responsibility and will do their appointed work. The proper labor and instruction will result in bringing into working order those men and women whose characters are strong and their convictions so firm that nothing of a selfish character is permitted to hinder them in their work, to lessen their faith, or to deter them from duty.

If the minister has properly instructed those under his care, when he leaves for other fields of labor the work left will not ravel out, for it will be bound off so firmly as to be secure. Unless those who receive the truth are thoroughly converted and there is a radical change in their life and character, the soul is not riveted to the eternal Rock; and after the labor of the minister ceases, and the novelty is gone, the impression soon wears away, the truth loses its power to charm, and they exert no holier influence, and are no better for their profession of the truth.

I am astonished that with the examples before us of what

man may be, and what he may do, we are not stimulated to greater exertion to emulate the good works of the righteous. All may not occupy a position of prominence; yet all may fill positions of usefulness and trust, and may, by their persevering fidelity, do far more good than they have any idea that they can do. Those who embrace the truth should seek a clear understanding of the Scriptures and an experimental knowledge of a living Saviour. The intellect should be cultivated, the memory taxed. All intellectual laziness is sin, and spiritual lethargy is death.

DIRECT MINDS TO JESUS

Oh, that I could command language of sufficient force to make the impression I wish to make upon my fellow laborers in the gospel! My brethren, you are handling the words of life; you are dealing with minds that are capable of the highest development, if directed in the right channel. But there is too much exhibition of self in the discourses given. Christ crucified, Christ ascended into the heavens, Christ coming again, should so soften, gladden, and fill the mind of the minister of the gospel that he will present these truths to the people in love and deep earnestness. The minister will then be lost sight of and Jesus magnified. The people will be so impressed with these all-absorbing subjects that they will talk of them and praise them, instead of praising the minister, the mere instrument. But if the people, while they praise the minister, have little interest in the word preached, he may know that the truth is not sanctifying his own soul. He does not speak to his hearers in such a manner that Jesus is honored and His love magnified.

Said Christ: "Let your light so shine before men, that they may see your good works, and glorify your Father which is in heaven." Matthew 5:16. Let your light so shine that the glory will redound to God instead of to yourselves. If the praise comes to you, well may you tremble and be ashamed, for the great object is defeated; it is not God, but the servant, that is magnified. Let your light *so shine;* be careful, minister of Christ, in what manner your light shines. If it flashes heavenward, revealing the excellence of Christ, it shines aright. If it is turned upon yourself, if you exhibit yourself, and attract the people to admire you, it would be better for you to hold your peace altogether: for your light shines in the wrong way.

LIVING REPRESENTATIVES OF CHRIST

Ministers of Christ, you may be connected with God if you will watch and pray. Let your words be seasoned with salt, and let Christian courtesy and true elevation pervade your demeanor. If the peace of God is ruling within, its power will not only strengthen, but soften your hearts, and you will be living representatives of Christ. The people who profess the truth are backsliding from God. Jesus is soon to come, and they are unready. The minister must reach a higher standard himself, a faith marked with greater firmness, an experience that is living and vivid, not dull and commonplace, like that of the nominal professors.

The word of God sets a high mark before you. Will you, through fasting and prayerful effort, attain to the completeness and consistency of Christian character? You should make straight paths for your feet, lest the lame be turned out of the way. A close connection with God will bring to you in your labor that vital power which arouses the conscience, and convicts the sinner of sin, leading him to cry: "What shall I do to be saved?"

The commission which Christ gave to the disciples just prior to His ascension to heaven was: "Go ye therefore, and teach all nations, baptizing them in the name of the Father, and of the Son, and of the Holy Ghost: teaching them to observe all things whatsoever I have commanded you: and, lo, I am with you alway, even unto the end of the world."

Matthew 28:19, 20. "Neither pray I for these alone, but for them also which shall believe on Me through their word." John 17:20. The commission reaches those who shall believe on His word through His disciples. And all who are called of God to stand as ambassadors for Him should take the lessons upon practical godliness given them by Christ in His word and teach them to the people.

Christ opened the Scriptures to His disciples, beginning at Moses and the prophets, and instructed them in all things concerning Himself, and also explained to them the prophecies. The apostles in their preaching went back to Adam's day and brought their hearers down through prophetic history and ended with Christ and Him crucified, calling upon sinners to repent and turn from their sins to God. The representatives of Christ in our day should follow their example and in every discourse magnify Christ as the Exalted One, as all and in all.

A CONVERTED MINISTRY

Not only is formality taking possession of the nominal churches, but it is increasing to an alarming extent among those who profess to be keeping the commandments of God and looking for the soon appearing of Christ in the clouds of heaven. We should not be narrow in our views and limit our facilities for doing good; yet while we extend our influence and enlarge our plans as Providence opens the way, we should be more earnest to avoid the idolatry of the world. While we make greater efforts to increase our usefulness, we must make corresponding efforts to obtain wisdom from God to carry on all the branches of the work after His own order, and not from a worldly standpoint. We should not pattern after the customs of the world, but make the most of the facilities which God has placed within our reach to get the truth before the people.

When as a people our works correspond with our profession, we shall see very much more accomplished than now. When we have men as devoted as Elijah, and possessing the faith which he possessed, we shall see that God will reveal Himself to us as He did to holy men of old. When we have men who, while they acknowledge their deficiencies, will plead with God in earnest faith as did Jacob, we shall see the same results. Power will come from God to man in answer to the prayer of faith.

There is but little faith in the world. There are but few who are living near to God. And how can we expect more power and that God will reveal Himself to men, when His word is handled negligently and when hearts are not sanctified through the truth? Men who are not half converted, who are self-confident and self-sufficient in character, preach the truth to others. But God does not work with them, for they are not holy in heart and life. They do not walk humbly with God. We must have a converted ministry, and then we shall see the light of God and His power aiding all our efforts.

The watchmen anciently placed upon the walls of Jerusalem and other cities occupied a most responsible position. Upon their faithfulness depended the safety of all within those cities. When danger was apprehended, they were not to keep silent day nor night. Every few moments they were required to call to one another to see if all were awake and no harm had come to any. Sentinels were stationed upon some eminence overlooking the important posts to be guarded, and the cry of warning or of good cheer was sounded from them. This was borne from one to another, each repeating the words, till it went the entire rounds of the city.

These watchmen represent the ministry, upon whose fidelity depends the salvation of souls. The stewards of the mysteries of God should stand as watchmen upon the walls of Zion; and if they see the sword coming, they should sound the note of warning. If they are sleepy sentinels, and their spiritual senses are so benumbed that they see and realize no danger, and the people perish, God will require their blood at the watchmen's hands.

SACRED RESPONSIBILITY OF WATCHMEN

"O son of man, I have set thee a watchman unto the house of Israel; therefore thou shalt hear the word at My mouth, and warn them from Me." Ezekiel 33:7. The watchmen will need to live very near to God, to hear His word and be impressed with His Spirit, that the people may not look to them in vain. "When I say unto the wicked, O wicked man, thou shalt surely die; if thou dost not speak to warn the wicked from his way, that wicked man shall die in his iniquity; but his blood will I require at thine hand. Nevertheless, if thou warn the wicked of his way to turn from it; if he do not turn from his way, he shall die in his iniquity; but thou hast delivered thy soul." Verses 8, 9. Ambassadors of Christ should take heed that they do not, through their unfaithfulness, lose their own souls and the souls of those who hear them.

I was shown the churches in different states that profess to be keeping the commandments of God and looking for the second coming of Christ. There is an alarming amount of indifference, pride, love of the world, and cold formality existing among them. And these are the people who are fast coming to resemble ancient Israel, so far as the want of piety is concerned. Many make high claims to godliness and yet are destitute of self-control. Appetite and passion bear sway; self is made prominent. Many are arbitrary, dictatorial, overbearing, boastful, proud, and unconsecrated. Yet some of these persons are ministers, handling sacred truths. Unless they repent, their candlestick will be removed out of its place. The Saviour's curse pronounced upon the fruitless fig tree is a sermon to all formalists and boasting hypocrites who stand forth to the world in pretentious leaves, but are devoid of fruit. What a rebuke to those who have a form of godliness, while in their unchristian lives they deny the power thereof! He who treated with tenderness the very chief of sinners, He who never spurned true meekness and penitence, however great the guilt, came down with scathing denunciations upon those who made high professions of godliness, but in works denied their faith.

Duty of Parents to the College

Our brethren and sisters abroad should feel it their duty to sustain this institution which God has devised. Some of the students return home with murmuring and complaints, and parents and members of the church give an attentive ear to their exaggerated, one-sided statements. They would do well to consider that there are two sides to the story; but instead, they allow these garbled reports to build up a barrier between them and the college. They then begin to express fears, questionings, and suspicions in regard to the way the college is conducted. Such an influence does great harm. The words of dissatisfaction spread like a contagious disease, and the impression made upon minds is hard to efface. The story enlarges with every repetition, until it becomes of gigantic proportions, when investigation would reveal the fact that there was no fault with teachers or professors. They were simply doing their duty in enforcing the rules of the school, which must be carried out or the school will become demoralized.

Parents do not always move wisely. Many are very exacting in wishing to bring others to their ideas, and become impatient and overbearing if they cannot do this; but when their own children are required to observe rules and regulations at school, and these children fret under the necessary restraint, too often their parents, who profess to love and fear God, join with the children instead of reproving them and correcting their faults. This often proves the turning point in the character of their children. Rules and order are broken down, and discipline is trampled underfoot. The children despise restraint and are allowed to speak disparagingly of

1880, vol. 4, pp. 428, 429 (Our College).

the institutions at Battle Creek. If parents would only reflect, they would see the evil result of the course they are pursuing. It would indeed be a most wonderful thing if, in a school of four hundred students, managed by men and women subject to the frailties of humanity, every move should be so perfect, so exact, as to challenge criticism.

If parents would place themselves in the position of the teachers and see how difficult it must necessarily be to manage and discipline a school of hundreds of students of every grade and class of minds, they might upon reflection see things differently. They should consider that some children have never been disciplined at home. Having always been indulged and never trained to obedience, it would be greatly for their advantage to be removed from their injudicious parents and placed under as severe regulations and drilling as soldiers in an army. Unless something shall be done for these children who have been so sadly neglected by unfaithful parents, they will never be accepted of Jesus; unless some power of control shall be brought to bear upon them, they will be worthless in this life and will have no part in the future life.

In heaven there is perfect order, perfect obedience, perfect peace and harmony. Those who have had no respect for order or discipline in this life would have no respect for the order which is observed in heaven. They can never be admitted into heaven, for all worthy of an entrance there will love order and respect discipline. The characters formed in this life will determine the future destiny. When Christ shall come, He will not change the character of any individual. Precious, probationary time is given to be improved in washing our robes of character and making them white in the blood of the Lamb. To remove the stains of sin requires the work of a lifetime. Every day renewed efforts in restraining and denying self are needed. Every day there are new battles to fight and victories to be gained. Every day the soul should be called out in earnest pleading with God for the mighty victories of the cross. Parents should neglect no duty on their part to benefit their children. They should so train them that they may be a blessing to society here and may reap the reward of eternal life hereafter.

College Students

Those students who profess to love God and obey the truth should possess that degree of self-control and strength of religious principle that will enable them to remain unmoved amid temptations and to stand up for Jesus in the college, at their boardinghouses, or wherever they may be. Religion is not to be worn merely as a cloak in the house of God, but religious principle must characterize the entire life. Those who are drinking at the fountain of life will not, like the worldling, manifest a longing desire for change and pleasure. In their deportment and character will be seen the rest and peace and happiness that they have found in Jesus by daily laying their perplexities and burdens at His feet. They will show that there is contentment and even joy in the path of obedience and duty. Such will exert an influence over their fellow students which will tell upon the entire school. Those who compose this faithful army will refresh and strengthen the teachers and professors in their efforts by discouraging every species of unfaithfulness, of discord, and of neglect to comply with the rules and regulations. Their influence will be saving, and their works will not perish in the great day of God, but will follow them into the future world; and the influence of their life here will tell throughout the ceaseless ages of eternity. One earnest, conscientious, faithful young man in school is an inestimable treasure. Angels of heaven look lovingly upon him. His precious Saviour loves him, and in the Ledger of Heaven will be recorded every work of righteousness, every temptation resisted, every evil overcome. He will thus be laying up a good foundation against the time to come, that he may lay hold on eternal life. . . .

Upon Christian youth depend in a great measure the

1880, vol. 4, pp. 432-435 (The Cause in Iowa).

preservation and perpetuity of the institutions which God has devised as means by which to advance His work. This grave responsibility rests upon the youth of today who are coming upon the stage of action. Never was there a period when results so important depended upon a generation of men; then how important that the young should be qualified for the great work, that God may use them as His instruments. Their Maker has claims upon them which are paramount to all others.

It is God that has given life and every physical and mental endowment they possess. He has bestowed upon them capabilities for wise improvement, that they may be entrusted with a work which will be as enduring as eternity. In return for His great gifts He claims a due cultivation and exercise of their intellectual and moral faculties. He did not give them these faculties merely for their amusement, or to be abused in working against His will and His providence, but that they might use them to advance the knowledge of truth and holiness in the world. He claims their gratitude, their veneration and love, for His continued kindness and infinite mercies. He justly requires obedience to His laws and to all wise regulations which will restrain and guard the youth from Satan's devices and lead them in paths of peace. If youth could see that in complying with the laws and regulations of our institutions they are only doing that which will improve their standing in society, elevate the character, ennoble the mind, and increase their happiness, they would not rebel against just rules and wholesome requirements, nor engage in creating suspicion and prejudice against these institutions. Our youth should have a spirit of energy and fidelity to meet the demands upon them, and this will be a guaranty of success. The wild, reckless character of many of the youth in this age of the world is heartsickening. Much of the blame lies upon their parents at home. Without the fear of God no one can be truly happy.

Sacredness of Vows

The brief but terrible history of Ananias and Sapphira is traced by the pen of inspiration for the benefit of all who profess to be the followers of Christ. This important lesson has not rested with sufficient weight upon the minds of our people. It will be profitable for all to thoughtfully consider the nature of the grievous offense for which these guilty ones were made an example. This one marked evidence of God's retributive justice is fearful, and should lead all to fear and tremble to repeat sins which brought such a punishment. Selfishness was the great sin which had warped the characters of this guilty couple.

With others, Ananias and his wife Sapphira had the privilege of hearing the gospel preached by the apostles. The power of God attended the word spoken, and deep conviction rested upon all present. The softening influence of the grace of God had the effect upon their hearts to cause them to release their selfish hold upon their earthly possessions. While under the direct influence of the Spirit of God, they made a pledge to give to the Lord certain lands; but when they were no longer under this heavenly influence, the impression was less forcible, and they began to question and draw back from fulfilling the pledge which they had made. They thought that they had been too hasty, and wished to reconsider the matter. Thus a door was opened by which Satan at once entered and gained control of their minds.

This case should be a warning to all to guard against the first approach of Satan. Covetousness was first cherished; then, ashamed to have their brethren know that their selfish

1880, vol. 4, pp. 462-476.

souls grudged that which they had solemnly dedicated and pledged to God, deception was practiced. They talked the matter over together and deliberately decided to withhold a part of the price of the land. When convicted of their falsehood, their punishment was instant death. They knew that the Lord, whom they had defrauded, had searched them out; for Peter said: "Why hath Satan filled thine heart to lie to the Holy Ghost, and to keep back part of the price of the land? Whiles it remained, was it not thine own? and after it was sold, was it not in thine own power? why hast thou conceived this thing in thine heart? thou hast not lied unto men, but unto God." Acts 5:3, 4.

A special example was necessary to guard the young church from becoming demoralized; for their numbers were rapidly increasing. A warning was thus given to all who professed Christ at that time, and to all who should afterward profess His name, that God requires faithfulness in the performance of vows. But notwithstanding this signal punishment of deception and lying, the same sins have often been repeated in the Christian church and are widespread in our day. I have been shown that God gave this example as a warning to all who should be tempted to act in a similar manner. Selfishness and fraud are practiced daily in the church, in withholding from God that which He claims, thus robbing Him and conflicting with His arrangements to diffuse the light and knowledge of truth throughout the length and breadth of the land.

SUSTAINING THE WORK OF GOD

God in His wise plans has made the advancement of His cause dependent upon the personal efforts of His people and upon their freewill offerings. By accepting the co-operation of man in the great plan of redemption, He has placed a signal honor upon him. The minister cannot preach except he be sent. The work of dispensing light does not rest upon ministers alone. Every person, upon becoming a member of the church, pledges himself to be a representative of Christ by living out the truth he professes. The followers of Christ should carry forward the work which He left for them to do when He ascended into heaven.

Institutions that are God's instruments to carry forward His work on the earth must be sustained. Churches must be erected, schools established, and publishing houses furnished with facilities for doing a great work in the publication of the truth to be sent to all parts of the world. These institutions are ordained of God and should be sustained by tithes and liberal offerings. As the work enlarges, means will be needed to carry it forward in all its branches. Those who have been converted to the truth and been made partakers of His grace may become co-workers with Christ by making voluntary sacrifices and freewill offerings to Him. And when the members of the church wish in their hearts that there would be no more calls for means, they virtually say that they are content that the cause of God shall not progress.

EXPERIENCE OF JACOB

"And Jacob vowed a vow, saying, If God will be with me, and will keep me in this way that I go, and will give me bread to eat, and raiment to put on, so that I come again to my father's house in peace; then shall the Lord be my God: and this stone, which I have set for a pillar, shall be God's house: and of all that Thou shalt give me I will surely give the tenth unto Thee." Genesis 28:20-22. The circumstances which prompted Jacob to vow to the Lord were similar to those which prompt men and women to vow to the Lord in our time. He had by a sinful act obtained the blessing which he knew had been promised him by the sure word of God. In doing this he showed great lack of faith in God's power to carry out His purposes, however discouraging present appearances might be. Instead of placing himself in the position he coveted, he was obliged to flee for his life from the wrath of Esau. With only his staff in his hand he must travel hundreds of miles through a desolate country. His courage was gone, and he was filled with remorse and timidity, seeking to avoid men, lest he should be traced by his angry brother. He had not the peace of God to comfort him, for he was harrassed with the thought that he had forfeited divine protection.

The second day of his journey is drawing to a close. He is weary, hungry, and homeless, and he feels that he is forsaken of God. He knows that he has brought this upon himself by his own wrong course. Dark clouds of despair enclose him, and he feels that he is an outcast. His heart is filled with a nameless terror, and he hardly dares to pray. But he is so utterly lonely that he feels the need of protection from God as he has never felt it before. He weeps and confesses his sin before God, and entreats for some evidence that He has not utterly forsaken him. But his burdened heart finds no relief. He has lost all confidence in himself, and he fears that the God of his fathers has cast him off. But God, the merciful God, pities the desolate, sorrow-stricken man, who gathers the stones for his pillow and has only the canopy of heaven for his covering.

In a vision of the night he sees a mystic ladder, its base resting upon the earth and its top reaching above the starry host to the highest heavens. Angel messengers are ascending and descending this ladder of shining brightness, showing him the pathway of communication between earth and heaven. A voice is heard by him, renewing the promise of mercy and protection and of future blessings. When Jacob awoke from his dream, he said: "Surely the Lord is in this place; and I knew it not." Verse 16. He looked about him as if expecting to see the heavenly messengers; but only the dim outline of earthly objects, and the heavens above, brilliant with the gems of light, met his earnest, wondering gaze. The ladder and the bright messengers were gone, and the glorious Majesty above it he could see only in imagination.

Jacob was awed with the deep stillness of the night and with the vivid impression that he was in the immediate presence of God. His heart was full of gratitude that he was not destroyed. There was no more sleep for him that night; gratitude deep and fervent, mingled with holy joy, filled his soul. "And Jacob rose up early in the morning, and took the stone that he had put for his pillows, and set it up for a pillar, and poured oil upon the top of it." Verse 18. And here he made his solemn vow to God.

KEEPING OF THE VOW

Jacob made his vow while refreshed by the dews of grace and invigorated by the presence and assurance of God. After the divine glory had passed away, he had temptations, like men in our time; but he was faithful to his vow and would not harbor thoughts as to the possibility of being released from the pledge which he had made. He might have reasoned much as men do now, that this revelation was only a dream, that he was unduly excited when he made his vow, and that therefore it need not be kept; but he did not.

Long years intervened before Jacob dared to return to his own country, but when he did he faithfully discharged his debt to his Master. He had become a wealthy man, and a very large amount of property passed from his possessions to the treasury of the Lord.

Many in our day fail where Jacob made a success. Those to whom God has given the greatest amount have the strongest inclination to retain what they have, because they must give a sum proportionate to their property. Jacob gave the tenth of all that he had, and then reckoned the use of the tenth, and gave the Lord the benefit of that which he had used for his own interest during the time he was in a heathen land and could not pay his vow. This was a large amount, but he did not hesitate; that which he had vowed to God he did not regard as his, but as the Lord's.

AS GOD HATH PROSPERED

According to the amount bestowed will be the amount required. The larger the capital entrusted, the more valuable is the gift which God requires to be returned to Him. If a Christian has ten or twenty thousand dollars, God's claims are imperative upon him, not only to give his proportion according to the tithing system, but to present his sin offerings and thank offerings to God. The Levitical dispensation was distinguished in a remarkable manner by the sanctification of property.

When we speak of the tithe as the standard of the Jewish contributions to religious purposes, we do not speak understandingly. The Lord kept His claims paramount, and in almost every article they were reminded of the Giver by being required to make returns to Him. They were required to pay a ransom for their firstborn son, for the first fruits of their flocks, and for the first gathering of the harvest. They were required to leave the corners of their harvest fields for the destitute. Whatever dropped from their hands in reaping was left for the poor, and once in every seven years their lands were allowed to produce spontaneously for the needy. Then there were the sacrificial offerings, the trespass offerings, the sin offerings, and the remission of all debts every seventh year. There were also numerous expenses for hospitalities and gifts to the poor, and there were assessments upon their property.

At stated periods, in order to preserve the integrity of the law, the people were interviewed as to whether they had faithfully performed their vows or not. A conscientious few made returns to God of about one third of all their income for the benefit of religious interests and for the poor. These exactions were not from a particular class of the people, but from *all,* the requirement being proportioned according to the amount possessed. Besides all these systematic and regular donations there were special objects calling for freewill offerings, such as the tabernacle built in the wilderness and the temple erected at Jerusalem. These drafts were made by God upon the people for their own good, as well as to sustain His service.

AN AWAKENING TO DUTY

There must be an awakening among us as a people upon this matter. There are but few men who feel conscience-stricken if they neglect their duty in beneficence. But few feel remorse of soul because they are daily robbing God. If a Christian deliberately or accidently underpays his neighbor, or refuses to cancel an honest debt, his conscience, unless seared, will trouble him; he cannot rest although no one may know but himself. There are many neglected vows and unpaid pledges, and yet how few trouble their minds over the matter; how few feel the guilt of this violation of duty. We must have new and deeper convictions on this subject. The conscience must be aroused, and the matter receive earnest attention; for an account must be rendered to God in the last day, and His claims must be settled.

The responsibilities of the Christian businessman, however large or small his capital, will be in exact proportion to his gifts from God. The deceitfulness of riches has ruined thousands and tens of thousands. These wealthy men forget that they are stewards, and that the day is fast approaching when it shall be said to them: "Give an account of thy stewardship." Luke 16:2. As shown by the parable of the talents, every man is responsible for the wise use of the gifts bestowed. The poor man in the parable, because he had the least gift, felt the least responsibility and made no use of the talent entrusted to him; therefore he was cast into outer darkness.

Said Christ: "How hardly shall they that have riches enter into the kingdom of God!" Mark 10:23. And His disciples were astonished at His doctrine. When a minister who has labored successfully in securing souls to Jesus Christ abandons his sacred work in order to secure temporal gain, he is called an apostate, and he will be held accountable to God for the talents that he has misapplied. When men of business, farmers, mechanics, merchants, lawyers, etc., become members of the church, they become servants of Christ; and although their talents may be entirely different, their responsibility to advance the cause of God by personal effort, and with their means, is no less than that which rests upon the minister. The woe which will fall upon the minister if he preach not the gospel, will just as surely fall upon the businessman, if he, with his different talents, will not be a co-worker with Christ in accomplishing the same results. When this is brought home to the individual, some will say, "This is an hard saying;" nevertheless it is true, although continually contradicted by the practice of men who profess to be followers of Christ.

EQUALITY OF SYSTEMATIC BENEVOLENCE

God provided bread for His people in the wilderness by a miracle of mercy, and He could have provided everything necessary for religious service; but He did not, because in His infinite wisdom He saw that the moral discipline of His people depended upon their co-operating with Him, every one of them doing something. As long as the truth is progressive, the claims of God rest upon men to give of that which He has entrusted to them for this very purpose. God, the Creator of man, by instituting the plan of systematic benevolence, has made the work bear equally upon all according to their several abilities.

Everyone is to be his own assessor and is left to give as he purposes in his heart. But there are those who are guilty of the same sin as Ananias and Sapphira, thinking that if they withhold a portion of what God claims in the tithing system the brethren will never know it. Thus thought the guilty couple whose example is given us as a warning. God in this case proves that He searches the heart. The motives and purposes of man cannot be hidden from Him. He has left a perpetual warning to Christians of all ages to beware of the sin to which the hearts of men are continually inclined.

Although no visible marks of God's displeasure follow the repetition of the sin of Ananias and Sapphira now, yet the sin is just as heinous in the sight of God and will as surely be visited upon the transgressor in the day of judgment, and many will feel the curse of God even in this life. When a pledge is made to the cause, it is a vow made to God and should be sacredly kept. In the sight of God it is no better than sacrilege to appropriate to our own use that which has been once pledged to advance His sacred work.

SACREDNESS OF PLEDGES

When a verbal or written pledge has been made in the presence of our brethren to give a certain amount, they are the visible witnesses of a contract made between ourselves and God. The pledge is not made to man, but to God, and is as a written note given to a neighbor. No legal bond is more binding upon the Christian for the payment of money than a pledge made to God.

Persons who thus pledge to their fellow men do not generally think of asking to be released from their pledges. A vow made to God, the Giver of all favors, is of still greater importance; then why should we seek to be released from our vows to God? Will man consider his promise less binding because made to God? Because his vow will not be put to trial in courts of justice, is it less valid? Will a man who professes to be saved by the blood of the infinite sacrifice of Jesus Christ, "rob God"? Are not his vows and his actions weighed in the balances of justice in the heavenly courts?

Each of us has a case pending in the court of heaven. Shall our course of conduct balance the evidence against us? The case of Ananias and Sapphira was of the most aggravated character. In keeping back part of the price, they lied to the Holy Ghost. Guilt likewise rests upon every individual in proportion to like offenses.

When the hearts of men are softened by the presence of the Spirit of God, they are more susceptible to impressions of the Holy Spirit, and resolves are made to deny self and to sacrifice for the cause of God. It is when divine light shines into the chambers of the mind with unusual clearness and power that the feelings of the natural man are overcome, that selfishness loses its power upon the heart, and that desires are awakened to imitate the Pattern, Jesus Christ, in practicing self-denial and benevolence. The disposition of the naturally selfish man then becomes kind and pitiful toward lost sinners, and he makes a solemn pledge to God, as did Abraham and Jacob. Heavenly angels are present on such occasions. The love of God and love for souls triumphs over selfishness and love of the world. Especially is this the case when the speaker, in the Spirit and power of God, presents the plan of redemption, laid by the Majesty of heaven in the sacrifice of the cross. By the following scriptures we may see how God regards the subject of vows:

"And Moses spake unto the heads of the tribes concerning the children of Israel, saying, This is the thing which the Lord hath commanded. If a man vow a vow unto the Lord, or swear an oath to bind his soul with a bond; he shall not break his word, he shall do according to all that proceedeth out of his mouth." Numbers 30:1, 2. "Suffer not thy mouth to cause thy flesh to sin; neither say thou before the angel, that it was an error: wherefore should God be angry at thy voice, and destroy the work of thine hands?" Ecclesiastes 5:6. "I will go into Thy house with burnt offerings: I will pay Thee my vows, which my lips have uttered, and my mouth hath spoken, when I was in trouble." Psalm 66:13, 14. "It is a snare to the man who devoureth that which is holy, and after vows to make inquiry." Proverbs 20:25. "When thou shalt vow a vow unto the Lord thy God, thou shalt not slack to pay it: for the Lord thy God will surely require it of thee; and it would be sin in thee. But if thou shalt forbear to vow, it shall be no sin in thee. That which is gone out of thy lips thou shalt keep and perform; even a freewill offering, according as thou hast vowed unto the Lord thy God, which thou hast promised with thy mouth." Deuteronomy 23:21-23.

"Vow, and pay unto the Lord your God: let all that be round about Him bring presents unto Him that ought to be feared." Psalm 76:11. "But ye have profaned it, in that ye say, The table of the Lord is polluted; and the fruit thereof, even His meat, is contemptible. Ye said also, Behold, what a weariness is it! and ye have snuffed at it, saith the Lord of hosts; and ye brought that which was torn, and the lame, and the sick; thus ye brought an offering: should I accept this of your hand? saith the Lord. But cursed be the deceiver, which hath in his flock a male, and voweth, and sacrificeth unto the Lord a corrupt thing: for I am a great King, saith the Lord of hosts, and My name is dreadful among the heathen." Malachi 1:12-14.

"When thou vowest a vow unto God, defer not to pay it; for He hath no pleasure in fools: pay that which thou hast vowed. Better is it that thou shouldest not vow, than that thou shouldest vow and not pay." Ecclesiastes 5:4, 5.

God has given man a part to act in accomplishing the salvation of his fellow men. He can work in connection with Christ by doing acts of mercy and beneficence. But he cannot redeem them, not being able to satisfy the claims of insulted justice. This the Son of God alone can do, by laying aside His honor and glory, clothing His divinity with humanity, and coming to earth to humiliate Himself and shed His blood in behalf of the human race.

In commissioning His disciples to go "into all the world, and preach the gospel to every creature," Christ assigned to men the work of spreading the gospel. But while some go forth to preach, He calls upon others to answer to His claims upon them for tithes and offerings with which to support the ministry and to spread the printed truth all over the land. This is God's means of exalting man. It is just the work which he needs, for it will stir the deepest sympathies of his heart and call into exercise the highest capabilities of the mind.

MAN—GOD'S INSTRUMENTALITY

Every good thing of earth was placed here by the bountiful hand of God as an expression of His love to man. The poor are His, and the cause of religion is His. He has placed means in the hands of men, that His divine gifts may flow through human channels in doing the work appointed us in saving our fellow men. Everyone has his appointed work in the great field; and yet none should receive the idea that God is dependent upon man. He could speak the word, and every son of poverty would be made rich. In a moment of time He could heal the human race of all their diseases. He might dispense with ministers altogether and make angels the ambassadors of His truth. He might have written the truth upon the firmament, or imprinted it upon the leaves of the trees and upon the flowers of the field; or He might with an audible voice have proclaimed it from heaven. But the all-wise God did not choose any of these ways. He knew that man must have something to do in order that life might be a blessing to him. The gold and silver are the Lord's, and He could rain them from heaven if He chose; but instead of this He has made man His steward, entrusting him with means, not to be hoarded, but to be used in benefiting others. He thus makes man the medium through which to distribute His blessings on earth. God planned the system of beneficence in order that man might become, like his Creator, benevolent and unselfish in character, and finally be a partaker with Him of the eternal, glorious reward.

God works through human instrumentalities; and whoever shall awaken the consciences of men, provoking them to good works and a real interest in the advancement of the cause of truth, does not do it of himself, but by the Spirit of God which worketh in him. Pledges made under these circumstances are of a sacred character, being the fruit of the work of the Spirit of God. When these pledges are canceled, Heaven accepts the offering, and these liberal workers are credited for so much treasure invested in the bank of heaven. Such are laying up a good foundation against the time to come, that they may lay hold on eternal life.

But when the immediate presence of the Spirit of God is not so vividly felt, and the mind becomes exercised in the temporal concerns of life, then they are tempted to question the force of the obligation which they voluntarily assumed; and, yielding to Satan's suggestions, they reason that undue pressure was brought to bear upon them and they acted under the excitement of the occasion; that the demand for means to use in the cause of God was overstated; and that they were induced to pledge under false pretenses, without fully understanding the subject, and therefore they wish to be released. Have ministers the power to accept their excuses and say: "You shall not be holden to your pledge; you are released from your vow"? If they venture to do this, they become partakers of the sin of which the withholder is guilty. . . .

A church is responsible for the pledges of its individual members. If they see that there is a brother who is neglecting to fulfill his vows, they should labor with him kindly but plainly. If he is not in circumstances which render it possible for him to pay his vow, and he is a worthy member and has a willing heart, then let the church compassionately help him. Thus they can bridge over the difficulty and receive a blessing themselves.

God would have the members of His church consider their obligations to Him as binding as their indebtedness to the merchant or the market. Let everyone review his past life and see if any unpaid, unredeemed pledges have been neglected, and then make extra exertions to pay "the uttermost farthing," for we must all meet and abide the final issue of a tribunal where nothing will stand the test but integrity and veracity.

Wills and Legacies

"Lay not up for yourselves treasures upon earth, where moth and rust doth corrupt, and where thieves break through and steal: but lay up for yourselves treasures in heaven, where neither moth nor rust doth corrupt, and where thieves do not break through nor steal." Matthew 6:19, 20. Selfishness is a soul-destroying sin. Under this head comes covetousness, which is idolatry. All things belong to God. All the prosperity we enjoy is the result of divine beneficence. God is the great and bountiful giver. If He requires any portion of the liberal supply He has given us, it is not that He may be enriched by our gifts, for He needs nothing from our hand; but it is that we may have an opportunity to exercise self-denial, love, and sympathy for our fellow men, and thus become highly exalted.

In every dispensation, from Adam's time to ours, God has claimed the property of man, saying: I am the rightful owner of the universe; therefore consecrate to Me thy first fruits, bring a tribute of loyalty, surrender to Me My own, thus acknowledging My sovereignty, and you shall be free to retain and enjoy My bounties, and My blessing shall be with you. "Honor the Lord with thy substance, and with the first fruits of all thine increase." Proverbs 3:9.

God's requirements come first. We are not doing His will if we consecrate to Him what is left of our income after all our imaginary wants have been supplied. Before any part of our earnings is consumed, we should take out and present to Him that portion which He claims. In the old dispensation an offering of gratitude was kept continually burning upon the altar, thus showing man's endless obligation to God. If

1880, vol. 4, pp. 476-485.

we have prosperity in our secular business, it is because God blesses us. A part of this income is to be devoted to the poor, and a large portion to be applied to the cause of God. When that which God claims is rendered to Him, the remainder will be sanctified and blessed to our own use. But when a man robs God by withholding that which He requires, His curse rests upon the whole.

God has made men the channels through which His gifts are to flow to sustain the work which He would have carried forward in the world. He has given them property to be wisely used, not selfishly hoarded or extravagantly expended in luxury and selfish gratification either in dress or in the embellishment of their houses. He has entrusted them with means with which to support His servants in their labor as preachers and missionaries, and to sustain the institutions He has established among us.

Those who rejoice in the precious light of truth should feel a burning desire to have it sent everywhere. There are a few faithful standard-bearers who never flinch from duty or shirk responsibilities. Their hearts and purses are always open to every call for means to advance the cause of God. Indeed, some seem ready to exceed their duty, as though fearful that they will lose an opportunity of investing their portion in the bank of heaven.

There are others who will do as little as possible. They hoard their treasure, or lavish means upon themselves, grudgingly doling out a mere pittance to sustain the cause of God. If they make a pledge or a vow to God, they afterward repent of it, and will avoid the payment of it as long as they can, if not altogether. They make their tithe as small as possible, as if afraid that that which they return to God is lost. Our various institutions may be embarrassed for means, but this class act as though it made no difference to them whether they prospered or not. And yet these are God's instrumentalities with which to enlighten the world.

STEWARDSHIP OF THE AGED

These institutions have not, like other institutions of the kind, received endowments or legacies. And yet God has greatly prospered and blessed them, and made them the means of great good. There are aged ones among us who are nearing the close of their probation; but for the want of wide-awake men to secure to the cause of God the means in their possession, it passes into the hands of those who are serving Satan. This means was only lent them of God to be returned to Him; but in nine cases out of ten these brethren, when passing from the stage of action, appropriate God's property in a way that cannot glorify Him, for not one dollar of it will ever flow into the Lord's treasury. In some cases these apparently good brethren have had unconsecrated advisers, who counseled from their own standpoint and not according to the mind of God. Property is often bequeathed to children and grandchildren only to their injury. They have no love for God or for the truth, and therefore this means, all of which is the Lord's, passes into Satan's ranks, to be controlled by him. Satan is much more vigilant, keen-sighted, and skillful in devising ways to secure means to himself than our brethren are to secure the Lord's own to His cause. Some wills are made in so loose a manner that they will not stand the test of the law, and thus thousands of dollars have been lost to the cause. Our brethren should feel that a responsibility rests upon them, as faithful servants in the cause of God, to exercise their intellect in regard to this matter, and secure to the Lord His own.

Many manifest a needless delicacy on this point. They feel that they are stepping upon forbidden ground when they introduce the subject of property to the aged or to invalids in order to learn what disposition they design to make of it. But this duty is just as sacred as the duty to preach the word to save souls. Here is a man with God's money or property in his hands. He is about to change his stewardship. Will he place the means which God has lent him to be used in His cause, in the hands of wicked men, just because they are his relatives? Should not Christian men feel interested and anxious for that man's future good as well as for the interest of God's cause, that he shall make a right disposition of his Lord's money, the talents lent him for wise improvement? Will his brethren stand by and see him losing his hold on this life and at the same time robbing the treasury of God? This would be a fearful loss to himself and to the cause; for, by placing his talent of means in the hands of those who have no regard for the truth of God, he would, to all intents and purposes, be wrapping it in a napkin and hiding it in the earth.

The Lord would have His followers dispense their means while they can do it themselves. Some may inquire: "Must we actually dispossess ourselves of everything which we call our own?" We may not be required to do this now; but we must be willing to do so for Christ's sake. We must acknowledge that our possessions are absolutely His, by using of them freely whenever means is needed to advance His cause.

Some close their ears to the calls made for money to be used in sending missionaries to foreign countries and in publishing the truth and scattering it like autumn leaves all over the world. Such excuse their covetousness by informing you that they have made arrangements to be charitable at death. They have considered the cause of God in their wills. Therefore they live a life of avarice, robbing God in tithes and in offerings, and in their wills return to God but a small portion of that which He has lent them, while a very large proportion is appropriated to relatives who have no interest in the truth. This is the worst kind of robbery. They rob God of His just dues, not only all through life, but also at death.

FOLLY IN DELAY

It is utter folly to defer to make a preparation for the future life until nearly the last hour of the present life. It is also a great mistake to defer to answer the claims of God for liberality to His cause until the time comes when you are to shift your stewardship upon others. Those to whom you entrust your talents of means may not do as well with them as you have done. How dare rich men run so great risks! Those who wait till death before they make a disposition of their property, surrender it to death rather than to God. In so doing many are acting directly contrary to the plan of God plainly stated in His word. If they would do good they must seize the present golden moments and labor with all their might, as if fearful that they may lose the favorable opportunity.

Those who neglect known duty by not answering to God's claims upon them in this life, and who soothe their consciences by calculating on making their bequests at death, will receive no words of commendation from the Master, nor will they receive a reward. They practiced no self-denial, but selfishly retained their means as long as they could, yielding it up only when death claimed them. That which many propose to defer until they are about to die, if they were Christians indeed they would do while they have a strong hold on life. They would devote themselves and their property to God, and, while acting as His stewards, they would have the satisfaction of doing their duty. By becoming their own executors, they could meet the claims of God themselves, instead of shifting the responsibility upon others.

We should regard ourselves as stewards of the Lord's property and God as the supreme proprietor, to whom we are to render His own when He shall require it. When He shall come to receive His own with usury, the covetous will see that instead of multiplying the talents entrusted to them, they have brought upon themselves the doom pronounced upon the unprofitable servant.

The Lord designs that the death of His servants shall be regarded as a loss because of the influence for good which they exerted and the many willing offerings which they bestowed to replenish the treasury of God. Dying legacies are a miserable substitute for living benevolence. The servants of God should be making their wills every day in good works and liberal offerings to God. They should not allow the amount given to God to be disproportionately small when compared with that appropriated to their own use. In making their wills daily, they will remember those objects and friends that hold the largest place in their affections. Their best friend is Jesus. He did not withhold His own life from them, but for their sakes became poor, that through His poverty they might be made rich. He deserves the whole heart, the property, all that they have and are.

But many professed Christians put off the claims of Jesus in life and insult Him by giving Him a mere pittance at death. Let all of this class remember that this robbery of God is not an impulsive action, but a well-considered plan which they preface by saying: "Being in sound mind." After having defrauded the cause of God through life they perpetuate the fraud after death. And this is with the full consent of all the powers of the mind. Such a will many are content to cherish for a dying pillow. Their will is a part of their preparation for death and is prepared so that their possessions shall not disturb their dying hours. Can these dwell with pleasure upon the requirement that will be made of them to give an account of their stewardship?

We must all be rich in good works in this life if we would secure the future, immortal life. When the judgment shall sit and the books shall be opened, every man will be rewarded according to his works. Many names are enrolled on the church book that have robbery recorded against them in the Ledger of Heaven. And unless these repent and work for the Master with disinterested benevolence, they will certainly share in the doom of the unfaithful steward.

It often happens that an active businessman is cut down without a moment's warning and on examination his business is found to be in a most perplexing condition. In the effort to settle his estate the lawyers' fees eat up a large share, if not all, of the property, while his wife and children and the cause of Christ are robbed. Those who are faithful stewards of the Lord's means will know just how their business stands, and, like wise men, they will be prepared for any emergency. Should their probation close suddenly, they would not leave such great perplexity upon those who are called to settle their estate.

Many are not exercised upon the subject of making their wills while they are in apparent health. But this precaution should be taken by our brethren. They should know their financial standing and should not allow their business to become entangled. They should arrange their property in such a manner that they may leave it at any time.

Wills should be made in a manner to stand the test of law. After they are drawn they may remain for years and do no harm, if donations continue to be made from time to time as the cause has need. Death will not come one day sooner, brethren, because you have made your will. In disposing of your property by will to your relatives, be sure that you do not forget God's cause. You are His agents, holding His property; and His claims should have your first consideration. Your wife and children, of course, should not be left destitute; provision should be made for them if they are needy. But do not, simply because it is customary, bring into your will a long line of relatives who are not needy.

Let it ever be kept in mind that the present selfish system of disposing of property is not God's plan, but man's device. Christians should be reformers and break up this present system, giving an entirely new aspect to the formation of wills. Let the idea be ever present that it is the Lord's property which you are handling. The will of God in this matter is law. If man had made you the executor of his property, would you not closely study the will of the testator, that the smallest amount might not be misapplied? Your heavenly Friend has entrusted you with property, and given you His will as to how it should be used. If this will is studied with an unselfish heart, that which belongs to God will not be misapplied. The Lord's cause has been shamefully neglected, when He has provided men with sufficient means to meet every emergency, if they only had grateful, obedient hearts.

CONTINUE TO DISTRIBUTE WISELY

Those who make their wills should not feel that when this is done they have no further duty; but they should be constantly at work, using the talents entrusted to them, for the upbuilding of the Lord's cause. God has devised plans that all may work intelligently in the distribution of their means. He does not propose to sustain His work by miracles. He has a few faithful stewards, who are economizing and using their means to advance His cause. Instead of self-denial and benevolence being an exception, they should be the rule. The growing necessities of the cause of God require means. Calls are constantly coming in from men in our own and foreign countries for messengers to come to them with light and truth. This will necessitate more laborers and more means to support them.

Only a small amount of means flows into the Lord's treasury to be appropriated to the saving of souls, and it is with hard labor that even this is obtained. If the eyes of all could be opened to see how prevailing covetousness has hindered the advancement of the work of God, and how much more might have been done had all acted up to God's plan in tithes and offerings, there would be a decided reform on the part of many; for they would not dare to hinder the work of advancing the cause of God as they have done. The church is asleep as to the work it might do if it would give up all for Christ. A true spirit of self-sacrifice would be an argument for the reality and power of the gospel which the world could not misunderstand or gainsay, and abundant blessings would be poured upon the church.

I call upon our brethren to cease their robbery of God. Some are so situated that wills must be made. But in doing this, care should be taken not to give to sons and daughters means which should flow into the treasury of God. These wills often become the subject of quarrels and dissensions. It is recorded to the praise of God's ancient people that He was not ashamed to be called their God; and the reason assigned is that instead of selfishly seeking for and coveting earthly possessions, or seeking their happiness in worldly pleasures, they placed themselves and all that they had in the hands of God. They lived only for His glory, declaring plainly that they sought a better country, even a heavenly. Of such a people God was not ashamed. They did not disgrace Him in the eyes of the world. The Majesty of heaven was not ashamed to call them brethren.

FREELY GIVE

There are many who urge that they cannot do more for God's cause than they now do; but they do not give according to their ability. The Lord sometimes opens the eyes blinded by selfishness by simply reducing their income to the amount they are willing to give. Horses are found dead in the field or stable, houses or barns are destroyed by fire, or crops fail. In many cases God tests man with blessings, and if unfaithfulness is manifested in rendering to Him tithes and offerings, His blessing is withdrawn. "He which soweth sparingly shall reap also sparingly." 2 Corinthians 9:6. By the mercies of Christ and the riches of His goodness, and for the honor of truth and religion, we beseech you who are followers of Christ to dedicate yourselves and your property anew to God. In view of the love and compassion of Christ, which brought Him from the royal courts to suffer self-denial, humiliation, and death, let each ask himself the question, "How much do

I owe my Lord?" and then let your grateful offerings be in accordance with your appreciation of the great gift of heaven in God's dear Son.

In determining the proportion to be given to the cause of God, be sure to exceed, rather than fall short, of the requirements of duty. Consider for whom the offering is to be made. This recollection will put covetousness to flight. Only consider the great love wherewith Christ has loved us, and our richest offerings will seem unworthy of His acceptance. When Christ is the object of our affections, those who have received His pardoning love will not stop to calculate the value of the alabaster box of precious ointment. Covetous Judas could do this; but the receiver of the gift of salvation will only regret that the offering has not a richer perfume and greater value. Christians must look upon themselves only as channels through which mercies and blessings are to flow from the Fountain of all goodness to their fellow men, by whose conversion they may send to heaven waves of glory in praise and offerings from those who thus become partakers with them of the heavenly gift.

The Relation of Church Membership

Every man who is striving to overcome will have his own weaknesses to contend with, but it is so much easier for persons to see the faults of their brethren than to see their own that they should be much more diligent and critical with themselves than with others.

All the members of the church, if they are sons and daughters of God, will have to undergo a process of discipline before they can be lights in the world. God will not make men and women channels of light while they are in darkness and are content to remain so, making no special efforts to connect with the Source of light. Those who feel their own need, and arouse themselves to the deepest thought and the most earnest, persevering prayer and action, will receive divine aid. There is much for each to unlearn with respect to himself, as well as much to learn. Old habits and customs must be shaken off, and it is only by earnest struggles to correct these errors, and a full reception of the truth in carrying out its principles, by the grace of God, that the victory can be gained.

I wish I could speak words which would impress us all that our only hope as individuals is to connect with God. Purity of soul must be obtained; and there is much heart searching to be done and much obstinacy and self-love to be overcome, which will require constant, earnest prayer.

CALMNESS AND SELF-CONTROL

Men who are harsh and censorious often excuse or try to justify their lack of Christian politeness because some of the Reformers worked with such a spirit, and they claim that the work for this time requires the same spirit; but this is not so.

1880, vol. 4, pp. 485-489.

A spirit which is calm and under perfect control is better in any place, even in the roughest company. A furious zeal does no good to anyone. God did not select the Reformers because they were overbearing, passionate men. He accepted them as they were, notwithstanding these traits of character; but He would have placed tenfold greater responsibilities upon them had they been of humble mind, having their spirits under control of reason. While ministers of Christ must denounce sin and ungodliness, impurity and falsehood, while they are sometimes called to rebuke iniquity among the high as well as the low, showing them that the indignation of God will fall upon the transgressors of His law, yet they should not be overbearing or tyrannical; they should manifest kindness and love, a spirit to save rather than to destroy.

The long-suffering of Jehovah teaches ministers and church members who aspire to be colaborers with Christ, unmistakable lessons of forbearance and love. Christ connected Judas and impulsive Peter with Himself, not because Judas was covetous and Peter passionate, but that they might learn of Him, their great Teacher, and become, like Him, unselfish, meek, and lowly of heart. He saw good material in both these men. Judas possessed financial ability and would have been of value to the church had he taken home to his heart the lessons which Christ was giving by rebuking all selfishness, fraud, and avarice, even in the little matters of life. These lessons were oft-repeated: "He that is faithful in that which is least is faithful also in much: and he that is unjust in the least is unjust also in much." Luke 16:10.

STRICT INTEGRITY

Our Saviour sought to impress upon His hearers that a man who would advantage himself by overreaching his neighbor in the smallest item would, if the opportunity were favorable, overreach in larger matters. The least departure from strict rectitude breaks down the barriers and prepares the heart to do greater injustice. Christ, by precept and example, taught that the strictest integrity should govern our actions toward our fellow men. "Whatsoever ye would that men should do to you, do ye even so to them." Matthew 7:12. Christ was continually portraying the defective lives of the Pharisees and reproving them. They professed to be keeping the law of God, yet in their daily acts were practicing iniquity. Many widows and orphans were robbed of their little all to gratify an avaricious desire for gain.

Judas might have been benefited by all these lessons had he possessed a desire to be right at heart; but his acquisitiveness overcame him, and the love of money became a ruling power. He carried the purse containing the means to be used in carrying forward the work of Christ, and little sums were from time to time applied to his own use. His selfish heart grudged the offering made by Mary of the alabaster box of ointment, and he reproved her for her imprudence. Thus, instead of being a learner, he would be a teacher and instruct our Lord in regard to the propriety of her action.

These two men alike had the opportunities and privileges of the continual lessons and example of Christ to correct their sinful traits of character. While they heard His withering rebukes and denunciations against hypocrisy and corruption, they saw that those so terribly denounced were the objects of solicitous and unwearied labor for their reformation. The Saviour wept because of their darkness and error. He yearned over them with unbounded compassion and love, exclaiming to Jerusalem: "How often would I have gathered thy children together, as a hen doth gather her brood under her wings, and ye would not!" Luke 13:34.

THE FORBEARANCE OF JESUS

Peter was prompt and zealous in action, bold and uncompromising; and Christ saw in him material that would be of great value to the church. He therefore connected Peter with Himself, that all which was good and valuable might be preserved, and that by His lessons and example He might soften whatever was harsh in his temper and smooth whatever was rugged in his deportment. If the heart were indeed transformed by divine grace, an external change would be seen in true kindness, sympathy, and courteousness. Jesus was never cold and unapproachable. The afflicted often broke in upon His retreat when He needed refreshment and rest, but He had a kind look and an encouraging word for all. He was a pattern of true courtesy. Peter denied his Lord, but afterward repented and was deeply humbled because of his great sin; and Christ showed that He forgave His erring disciple in condescending to mention him by name after His resurrection.

Judas yielded to the temptations of Satan and betrayed his best friend. Peter learned and profited by the lessons of Christ, and carried forward the work of reform which was left to the disciples when their Lord ascended on high. These two men represent the two classes that Christ connects with Himself, giving to them the advantages of His lessons and the example of His unselfish, compassionate life, that they may learn of Him.

The more man views his Saviour and becomes acquainted with Him, the more he will become assimilated to His image and work the works of Christ. The age in which we live calls for reformatory action. The light of truth which shines upon us calls for men of determined action and sterling moral worth to labor diligently and perseveringly to save the souls of all who will hear the invitation of the Spirit of God.

The love which should exist between church members frequently gives place to criticism and censure; and these appear, even in the religious exercises, in reflections and severe personal thrusts. Such things should not be countenanced by ministers, elders, or people. The services of the church should be carried forward with an eye single to the glory of God. When men with their peculiar organizations are brought together in church capacity, unless the truth of God softens and subdues the sharp points in the character, the church will be affected and its peace and harmony sacrificed to indulge these selfish, unsanctified traits. Many, in their close watch to discover the faults of their brethren, neglect the investigation of their own hearts and the purification of their own lives. This brings the displeasure of God. The individual members of the church should be jealous for their own souls, critically watching their own actions, lest they should move from selfish motives and be a cause of stumbling to their weak brethren.

God takes men as they are, with the human element in their character, and then trains them for His service if they will be disciplined and learn of Him. The root of bitterness, envy, distrust, jealousy, and even hatred, which exists in the hearts of some church members, is the work of Satan. Such elements have a poisonous influence upon the church. "A little leaven leaveneth the whole lump." 1 Corinthians 5:6. The religious zeal which is manifested in a raid upon brethren is a zeal not according to knowledge. Christ has nothing to do with such testimony.

Mental Dyspeptics

LOVE for your soul causes me to write at the present time. I am oppressed with the burden of responsibility which I now take upon myself in writing out these things for you. By your own course you are closing the gates of heaven against yourself and your children, for neither you nor they will ever enter there with your present defective characters. You, my sister, are playing a sad, losing game in life. Holy angels are watching you with sadness; and evil spirits are looking on with triumph as they see you losing, fast losing, the graces that adorn the Christian character, while in their place Satan is implanting his own evil traits.

You have indulged in novel and story reading until you live in an imaginary world. The influence of such reading is injurious to both the mind and the body; it weakens the intellect and brings a fearful tax upon the physical strength. At times your mind is scarcely sane because the imagination has been overexcited and diseased by reading fictitious stories. The mind should be so disciplined that all its powers will be symmetrically developed. A certain course of training may invigorate special faculties and at the same time leave other faculties without improvement so that their usefulness will be crippled. The memory is greatly injured by ill-chosen reading, which has a tendency to unbalance the reasoning powers and to create nervousness, weariness of the brain, and prostration of the entire system. If the imagination is constantly overfed and stimulated by fictitious literature, it soon becomes a tyrant, controlling all the other faculties of the mind and causing the taste to become fitful and the tendencies perverse.

You are a mental dyspeptic. Your mind has been crammed with knowledge of all sorts,—politics, history, theology, and

1880, vol. 4, pp. 497-499 (Importance of Self-Control).

anecdote,—only a part of which can be retained by the abused memory. Much less information, with a mind well disciplined, would be of far greater value. You have neglected to train your mind to vigorous action; therefore your will and inclination have controlled you and been your masters instead of your servants. The result is a loss of physical and mental power.

For years your mind has been like a babbling brook, nearly filled with rocks and weeds, the water running to waste. Were your powers controlled by high purposes, you would not be the invalid that you now are. You fancy you must be indulged in your caprice of appetite and in your excessive reading. I saw the midnight lamp burning in your room while you were poring over some fascinating story, thus stimulating your already overexcited brain. This course has been lessening your hold upon life and enfeebling you physically, mentally, and morally. Irregularity has created disorder in your house, and, if continued, will cause your mind to sink into imbecility. Your God-given probation has been abused, your God-given time wasted.

FRUIT OF IMPROPER READING

God bestows upon us talents for wise improvement, not for abuse. Education is but a preparation of the physical, intellectual, and moral powers for the best performance of all the duties of life. Improper reading gives an education that is false. The power of endurance, and the strength and activity of the brain, may be lessened or increased according to the manner in which they are employed. There is a work before you to dispose of your light reading. Remove it from your house. Do not have before you the temptation to pervert your imagination, to unbalance your nervous system, and to ruin your children. By much reading you are unfitting yourself for the duties of a wife and mother, and, in fact, are disqualifying yourself to do good anywhere.

The Bible is not studied as it should be; therefore you do not become wise in the Scriptures and are not thoroughly furnished unto all good works. Light reading fascinates the mind and makes the reading of God's word uninteresting. You seek to make others believe that you are conversant with the Scriptures; but this cannot be, for your mind is filled with rubbish. The Bible requires thought and prayerful research. It is not enough to skim over the surface. While some passages are too plain to be misunderstood, others are more intricate, demanding careful and patient study. Like the precious metal concealed in the hills and mountains, its gems of truth are to be searched out and stored in the mind for future use. Oh, that all would exercise their minds as constantly in searching for celestial gold as for the gold that perishes!

When you search the Scriptures with an earnest desire to learn the truth, God will breathe His Spirit into your heart and impress your mind with the light of His word. The Bible is its own interpreter, one passage explaining another. By comparing scriptures referring to the same subjects, you will see beauty and harmony of which you have never dreamed. There is no other book whose perusal strengthens and enlarges, elevates and ennobles the mind, as does the perusal of this Book of books. Its study imparts new vigor to the mind, which is thus brought in contact with subjects requiring earnest thought, and is drawn out in prayer to God for power to comprehend the truths revealed. If the mind is left to deal with commonplace subjects, instead of deep and difficult problems, it will become narrowed down to the standard of the matter which it contemplates and will finally lose its power of expansion.

God is displeased with those who are too careless or indolent to become efficient, well-informed workers. The Christian should possess more intelligence and keener discernment than the worldling. The study of God's word is continually expanding the mind and strengthening the intellect. There is nothing that will so refine and elevate the character, and give vigor to every faculty, as the continual exercise of the mind to grasp and comprehend weighty and important truths.

The human mind becomes dwarfed and enfeebled when dealing with commonplace matters only, never rising above the level of the things of time and sense to grasp the mysteries of the unseen. The understanding is gradually brought to the level of the subjects with which it is constantly familiar. The mind will contract its powers and lose its ability if it is not exercised to acquire additional knowledge and put to the stretch to comprehend the revelations of divine power in nature and in the Sacred Word.—1881, vol. 4, pp. 545, 546.

Unscriptural Marriages

We are living in the last days, when the mania upon the subject of marriage constitutes one of the signs of the near coming of Christ. God is not consulted in these matters. Religion, duty, and principle are sacrificed to carry out the promptings of the unconsecrated heart. There should be no great display and rejoicing over the union of the parties. There is not one marriage in one hundred that results happily, that bears the sanction of God, and places the parties in a position better to glorify Him. The evil consequences of poor marriages are numberless. They are contracted from impulse. A candid review of the matter is scarcely thought of, and consultation with those of experience is considered old-fashioned.

Impulse and unsanctified passion exist in the place of pure love. Many imperil their own souls, and bring the curse of God upon them, by entering into the marriage relation merely to please the fancy. I have been shown the cases of some who profess to believe the truth, who have made a great mistake by marrying unbelievers. The hope was cherished by them that the unbelieving party would embrace the truth; but after his object is gained, he is further from the truth than before. And then begin the subtle workings, the continued efforts, of the enemy to draw away the believing one from the faith.

INFLUENCE OF WORLDLY ALLIANCE

Many are now losing their interest and confidence in the truth because they have taken unbelief into close connection with themselves. They breathe the atmosphere of doubt, of

1880, vol. 4, pp. 503-508.

questioning, of infidelity. They see and hear unbelief, and finally they cherish it. Some may have the courage to resist these influences, but in many cases their faith is imperceptibly undermined and finally destroyed. Satan has then succeeded in his plans. He has worked through his agents so silently that the barriers of faith and truth have been swept away before the believing ones have had any thought of where they were drifting.

It is a dangerous thing to form a worldly alliance. Satan well knows that the hour that witnesses the marriage of many young men and women closes the history of their religious experience and usefulness. They are lost to Christ. They may for a time make an effort to live a Christian life, but all their strivings are made against a steady influence in the opposite direction. Once it was a privilege and joy to them to speak of their faith and hope; but they become unwilling to mention the subject, knowing that the one with whom they have linked their destiny takes no interest in it. As the result, faith in the precious truth dies out of the heart, and Satan insidiously weaves about them a web of skepticism.

It is carrying that which is lawful to excess that makes it a grievous sin. Those who profess the truth trample on the will of God in marrying unbelievers; they lose His favor and make bitter work for repentance. The unbelieving may possess an excellent moral character; but the fact that he or she has not answered to the claims of God, and has neglected so great salvation, is sufficient reason why such a union should not be consummated. The character of the unbelieving may be similar to that of the young man to whom Jesus addressed the words, "One thing thou lackest;" that was the one thing needful.

The plea is sometimes made that the unbeliever is favorable to religion and is all that could be desired in a companion except in one thing—he is not a Christian. Although the better judgment of the believer may suggest the impropriety of a union for life with an unbeliever, yet, in nine cases out of ten, inclination triumphs. Spiritual declension commences the moment the vow is made at the altar; religious fervor is dampened, and one stronghold after another is broken down, until both stand side by side under the black banner of Satan. Even in the festivities of the wedding, the spirit of the world triumphs against conscience, faith, and truth. In the new home the hour of prayer is not respected. The bride and bridegroom have chosen each other and dismissed Jesus.

At first the unbelieving one may make no show of opposition in the new relation; but when the subject of Bible truth is presented for attention and consideration, the feeling at once arises: "You married me, knowing that I was what I am; I do not wish to be disturbed. From henceforth let it be understood that conversation upon your peculiar views is to be interdicted." If the believer should manifest any special earnestness in regard to his faith, it might seem like unkindness toward the one who has no interest in the Christian experience.

The believing one reasons that in his new relation he must concede somewhat to the companion of his choice. Social, worldly amusements are patronized. At first there is great reluctance of feeling in doing this, but the interest in the truth becomes less and less, and faith is exchanged for doubt and unbelief. No one would have suspected that the once firm, conscientious believer and devoted follower of Christ could ever become the doubting, vacillating person that he now is. Oh, the change wrought by that unwise marriage!

CANDIDLY FACING THE ISSUE

What ought every Christian to do when brought into the trying position which tests the soundness of religious principle? With a firmness worthy of imitation he should say frankly: "I am a conscientious Christian. I believe the seventh day of the week to be the Sabbath of the Bible. Our faith and principles are such that they lead in opposite directions. We cannot be happy together, for if I follow on to gain a more perfect knowledge of the will of God, I shall become more and more unlike the world, and assimilated to the likeness of Christ. If you continue to see no loveliness in Christ, no attractions in the truth, you will love the world, which I cannot love, while I shall love the things of God, which you cannot love. Spiritual things are spiritually discerned. Without spiritual discernment you will be unable to see the claims of God upon me, or to realize my obligations to the Master whom I serve; therefore you will feel that I neglect you for religious duties. You will not be happy; you will be jealous on account of the affections which I give to God; and I shall be alone in my religious belief. When your views shall change, when your heart shall respond to the claims of God, and you shall learn to love my Saviour, then our relationship may be renewed."

The believer thus makes a sacrifice for Christ which his conscience approves, and which shows that he values eternal life too highly to run the risk of losing it. He feels that it would be better to remain unmarried than to link his interest for life with one who chooses the world rather than Jesus and who would lead away from the cross of Christ. But the danger of giving the affections to unbelievers is not realized. In the youthful mind, marriage is clothed with romance, and it is difficult to divest it of this feature, with which imagination covers it, and to impress the mind with a sense of the weighty responsibilities involved in the marriage vow. This vow links the destinies of the two individuals with bonds which nought but the hand of death should sever.

THEY CANNOT WALK TOGETHER

Shall one who is seeking for glory, honor, immortality, eternal life, form a union with another who refuses to rank with the soldiers of the cross of Christ? Will you who profess to choose Christ for your master and to be obedient to Him in all things, unite your interests with one who is ruled by the prince of the powers of darkness? "Can two walk together, except they be agreed?" Amos 3:3. "If two of you shall agree on earth as touching anything that they shall ask, it shall be done for them of My Father which is in heaven." Matthew 18:19. But how strange the sight! While one of those so closely united is engaged in devotion, the other is indifferent and careless; while one is seeking the way to everlasting life, the other is in the broad road to death.

Hundreds have sacrificed Christ and heaven in consequence of marrying unconverted persons. Can it be that the love and fellowship of Christ are of so little value to them that they prefer the companionship of poor mortals? Is heaven so little esteemed that they are willing to risk its enjoyments for one who has no love for the precious Saviour?

The happiness and prosperity of the married life depend upon the unity of the parties. How can the carnal mind harmonize with the mind that is assimilated to the mind of Christ? One is sowing to the flesh, thinking and acting in accordance with the promptings of his own heart; the other is sowing to the Spirit, seeking to repress selfishness, to overcome inclination, and to live in obedience to the Master, whose servant he professes to be. Thus there is a perpetual difference of taste, of inclination, and of purpose. Unless the believer shall, through his steadfast adherence to principle, win the impenitent, he will, as is much more common, become discouraged and sell his religious principles for the poor companionship of one who has no connection with heaven.

God strictly forbade the intermarrying of His ancient people with other nations. The plea is now offered that this prohibition was made in order to prevent the Hebrews from marrying idolaters and forming connections with heathen families. But the heathen were in a more favorable condition than are the impenitent in this age, who, having the light of truth, yet persistently refuse to accept it. The sinner of today is far more guilty than the heathen, because the light of the gospel shines clearly all around him. He violates conscience and is a deliberate enemy of God. The reason which God assigned for forbidding these marriages was: "For they will turn away thy son from following Me." Deuteronomy 7:4. Those among ancient Israel who ventured to disregard the prohibition of God did it at the sacrifice of religious principle. Take the case of Solomon for example. His wives turned away his heart from his God.

Faithful Workers

The peace of Christ, the peace of Christ—money cannot buy it, brilliant talent cannot command it, intellect cannot secure it; it is the gift of God. The religion of Christ—how shall I make all understand their great loss if they fail to carry its holy principles into the daily life? The meekness and lowliness of Christ is the Christian's power. It is indeed more precious than all things which genius can create or wealth can buy. Of all things that are sought, cherished, and cultivated, there is nothing so valuable in the sight of God as a pure heart, a disposition imbued with thankfulness and peace.

If the divine harmony of truth and love exists in the heart, it will shine forth in words and actions. The most careful cultivation of the outward proprieties and courtesies of life has not sufficient power to shut out all fretfulness, harsh judgment, and unbecoming speech. The spirit of genuine benevolence must dwell in the heart. Love imparts to its possessor grace, propriety, and comeliness of deportment. Love illuminates the countenance and subdues the voice; it refines and elevates the entire man. It brings him into harmony with God, for it is a heavenly attribute.

Many are in danger of thinking that in the cares of labor, in writing and practicing as physicians, or performing the duties of the various departments, they are excusable if they lay down prayer, neglect the Sabbath, and neglect religious service. Sacred things are thus brought down to meet their convenience, while duties, denials, and crosses are left untouched. Neither physicians nor helpers should attempt to perform their work without taking time to pray. God would be the helper of all who profess to love Him, if they would

1881, vol. 4, pp. 559-561.

come to Him in faith and, with a sense of their own weakness, crave His power. When they separate from God, their wisdom will be found to be foolishness. When they are small in their own eyes and lean heavily upon their God, then He will be the arm of their power, and success will attend their efforts; but when they allow the mind to be diverted from God, then Satan comes in and controls the thoughts and perverts the judgment.

None are in greater danger than he who feels that his mountain standeth sure. It is then that his feet will begin to slide. Temptations will come, one after another, and so imperceptible will be their influence upon the life and character, that, unless kept by divine power, he will be corrupted by the spirit of the world and will fail to carry out the purpose of God. All that man has, God has given him, and he who improves his abilities to God's glory will be an instrument to do good; but we can no more live a religious life without constant prayer and the performance of religious duties than we can have physical strength without partaking of temporal food. We must daily sit down at God's table. We must receive strength from the living Vine, if we are nourished.

The course which some have pursued, in using worldly policy to accomplish their purposes, is not in harmony with the will of God. They see evils which need correcting, but they do not wish to bring down reproach upon their own heads, and instead of courageously meeting these things, they throw the burden upon another and let him meet the difficulties which they have shunned and in too many cases the one who uses plain speech is made the great offender.

Brethren, I entreat you to move with an eye single to the glory of God. Let His power be your dependence, His grace your strength. By study of the Scriptures and earnest prayer seek to obtain clear conceptions of your duty, and then faithfully perform it. It is essential that you cultivate faithfulness in little things, and in so doing you will acquire habits of integrity in greater responsibilities. The little incidents of everyday life often pass without our notice, but it is these things that shape the character. Every event of life is great for good or for evil. The mind needs to be trained by daily tests, that it may acquire power to stand in any difficult position. In the days of trial and of peril you will need to be fortified to stand firmly for the right, independent of every opposing influence.

God is willing to do much for you, if you will only feel your need of Him. Jesus loves you. Ever seek to walk in the light of God's wisdom, and through all the changing scenes of life do not rest unless you know that your will is in harmony with the will of your Creator. Through faith in Him you may obtain strength to resist every temptation of Satan and thus increase in moral power with every test from God.

You may become men of responsibility and influence if, by the power of your will, united with divine strength, you earnestly engage in the work. Exercise the mental powers, and in no case neglect the physical. Let not intellectual slothfulness close up your path to greater knowledge. Learn to reflect as well as to study, that your minds may expand, strengthen, and develop. Never think that you have learned enough and that you may now relax your efforts. The cultivated mind is the measure of the man. Your education should continue during your lifetime; every day you should be learning and putting to practical use the knowledge gained.

Into the Maze of Skepticism

There is no excuse for doubt or skepticism. God has made ample provision to establish the faith of all men, if they will decide from the weight of evidence. But if they wait to have every seeming objection removed before they believe, they will never be settled, rooted, and grounded in the truth. God will never remove all seeming difficulties from our path. Those who wish to doubt may find opportunity; those who wish to believe will find plenty of evidence upon which to base their faith.

The position of some is unexplainable, even to themselves. They are drifting without an anchor, beating about in the fog of uncertainty. Satan soon seizes the helm and carries their frail bark wherever he pleases. They become subject to his will. Had these minds not listened to Satan, they would not have been deceived by his sophistry; had they been balanced on the side of God they would not have become confused and bewildered.

God and angels are watching with intense interest the development of character and are weighing moral worth. Those who withstand Satan's devices will come forth as gold tried in the fire. Those who are swept off their feet by the waves of temptation, imagine, as did Eve, that they are becoming wonderfully wise, outgrowing their ignorance and narrow conscientiousness; but, like her, they will find themselves sadly deceived. They have been chasing shadows, exchanging heavenly wisdom for frail human judgment. A little knowledge has made them self-conceited. A more deep and thorough knowledge of themselves and of God would make them again

1881, vol. 4, pp. 583-586 (Position and Work of the Sanitarium).

sane and sensible men, and would balance them on the side of truth, of angels, and of God.

The word of God will judge every one of us at the last great day. Young men talk about science and are wise above that which is written; they seek to explain the ways and work of God to meet their finite comprehension; but it is all a miserable failure. True science and Inspiration are in perfect harmony. False science is a something independent of God. It is pretentious ignorance. This deceptive power has captivated and enslaved the minds of many, and they have chosen darkness rather than light. They have taken their position on the side of unbelief, as though it were a virtue and the sign of a great mind to doubt, when it is the sign of a mind too weak and narrow to perceive God in His created works. They could not fathom the mystery of His providence should they study with all their power for a lifetime. And because the works of God cannot be explained by finite minds, Satan brings his sophistry to bear upon them and entangles them in the meshes of unbelief. If these doubting ones will come into close connection with God, He will make His purposes clear to their understanding.

Spiritual things are spiritually discerned. The carnal mind cannot comprehend these mysteries. If questioners and doubters continue to follow the great deceiver, the impressions and convictions of God's Spirit will grow less and less, the promptings of Satan more frequent, until the mind will fully submit to his control. Then that which appears to these bewildered minds as foolishness will be the power of God, and that which God regards as foolishness will be to them the strength of wisdom.

One of the great evils which has attended the quest of knowledge, the investigations of science, is that those who engage in these researches too often lose sight of the divine character of pure and unadulterated religion. The worldly-wise have attempted to explain upon scientific principles the influence of the Spirit of God upon the heart. The least advance in this direction will lead the soul into the mazes of skepticism. The religion of the Bible is simply the mystery of godliness; no human mind can fully understand it, and it is utterly incomprehensible to the unregenerate heart.

The son of God compared the operations of the Holy Spirit to the wind, which "bloweth where it listeth, and thou hearest the sound thereof, but canst not tell whence it cometh, and whither it goeth." John 3:8. Again, we read in the Sacred Record that the world's Redeemer rejoiced in spirit and said: "I thank Thee, O Father, Lord of heaven and earth, because Thou hast hid these things from the wise and prudent, and hast revealed them unto babes." Matthew 11:25.

The Saviour rejoiced that the plan of salvation is such that those who are wise in their own estimation, who are puffed up by the teachings of vain philosophy, cannot see the beauty, power, and hidden mystery of the gospel. But to all those who are of a humble heart, who have a teachable, honest, childlike desire to know and do the will of their heavenly Father, His word is revealed as the power of God to their salvation.

The Influence of Associates

In our institutions, where many are laboring together, the influence of association is very great. It is natural to seek companionship. Everyone will find companions or make them. And just in proportion to the strength of the friendship, will be the amount of influence which friends will exert over one another for good or for evil. All will have associates, and will influence and be influenced in their turn.

The link is a mysterious one which binds human hearts together, so that the feelings, tastes, and principles of two individuals are closely blended. One catches the spirit, and copies the ways and acts, of the other. As wax retains the figure of the seal, so the mind retains the impression produced by intercourse and association. The influence may be unconscious, yet it is no less powerful.

If the youth could be persuaded to associate with the pure, the thoughtful, and the amiable, the effect would be most salutary. If choice is made of companions who fear the Lord, the influence will lead to truth, to duty, and to holiness. A truly Christian life is a power for good. But, on the other hand, those who associate with men and women of questionable morals, of bad principles and practices, will soon be walking in the same path. The tendencies of the natural heart are downward. He who associates with the skeptic will soon become skeptical; he who chooses the companionship of the vile will most assuredly become vile. To walk in the counsel of the ungodly is the first step toward standing in the way of sinners and sitting in the seat of the scornful.

Let all who would form a right character choose associates who are of a serious, thoughtful turn of mind and who are

1881, vol. 4, pp. 587-591.

religiously inclined. Those who have counted the cost and wish to build for eternity must put good material into their building. If they accept of rotten timbers, if they are content with deficiencies of character, the building is doomed to ruin. Let all take heed how they build. The storm of temptation will sweep over the building, and unless it is firmly and faithfully constructed it will not stand the test.

A good name is more precious than gold. There is an inclination with the youth to associate with those who are inferior in mind and morals. What real happiness can a young person expect from a voluntary connection with persons who have a low standard of thoughts, feelings, and deportment? Some are debased in taste and depraved in habits, and all who choose such companions will follow their example. We are living in times of peril that should cause the hearts of all to fear. We see the minds of many wandering through the mazes of skepticism. The causes of this are ignorance, pride, and a defective character. Humility is a hard lesson for fallen man to learn. There is something in the human heart which rises in opposition to revealed truth on subjects connected with God and sinners, the transgression of the divine law, and pardon through Christ.

GUARD THE MIND

My brethren and sisters, old and young, when you have an hour of leisure, open the Bible and store the mind with its precious truths. When engaged in labor, guard the mind, keep it stayed upon God, talk less, and meditate more. Remember: "Every idle word that men shall speak, they shall give account thereof in the day of judgment." Matthew 12:36. Let your words be select; this will close a door against the adversary of souls. Let your day be entered upon with prayer; work as in God's sight. His angels are ever by your side, making a record of your words, your deportment, and the manner in which your work is done. If you turn from good counsel and choose to associate with those who you have reason to suspect are not religiously inclined, although they profess to be Christians, you will soon become like them. You place yourself in the way of temptation, on Satan's battleground, and will, unless constantly guarded, be overcome by his devices. There are persons who have for some time made a profession of religion, who are, to all intents and purposes, without God and without a sensitive conscience. They are vain and trifling; their conversation is of a low order. Courtship and marriage occupy the mind to the exclusion of higher and nobler thoughts.

ASSOCIATES DETERMINE OUR DESTINY

The associations chosen by the workers are determining their destiny for this world and the next. Some who were once conscientious and faithful have sadly changed; they have disconnected from God, and Satan has allured them to his side. They are now irreligious and irreverent, and they have an influence upon others who are easily molded. Evil associations are deteriorating character; principle is being undermined. "He that walketh with wise men shall be wise: but a companion of fools shall be destroyed." Proverbs 13:20.

The young are in danger; but they are blind to discern the tendencies and result of the course they are pursuing. Many of them are engaged in flirtation. They seem to be infatuated. There is nothing noble, dignified, or sacred in these attachments; as they are prompted by Satan, the influence is such as to please him. Warnings to these persons fall unheeded. They are headstrong, self-willed, defiant. They think the warning, counsel, or reproof does not apply to them. Their course gives them no concern. They are continually separating themselves from the light and love of God. They lose all discernment of sacred and eternal things, and while they may keep up a dry form of Christian duties they have no heart in these religious exercises. All too late these deceived souls will learn that "strait is the gate, and narrow is the way, which leadeth unto life, and few there be that find it." Matthew 7:14.

Words and actions and motives are recorded; but how little do these light, superficial heads and hard hearts realize that an angel of God stands writing down the manner in which their precious moments are employed. God will bring to light every word and every action. He is in every place. His messengers, although unseen, are visitors in the workroom and in the sleeping apartment. The hidden works of darkness will be brought to light. The thoughts, the intents and purposes of the heart, will stand revealed. All things are naked and open to the eyes of Him with whom we have to do.

MAKING OUR WORK ENNOBLING

The workers should take Jesus with them in every department of their labor. Whatever is done should be done with an exactness and thoroughness that will bear inspection. The heart should be in the work. Faithfulness is as essential in life's common duties as in those involving greater responsibility. Some may receive the idea that their work is not ennobling; but this is just as they choose to make it. They alone are capable of degrading or elevating their employment. We wish that every drone might be compelled to toil for his daily bread; for work is a blessing, not a curse. Diligent labor will keep us from many of the snares of Satan, who "finds some mischief still for idle hands to do."

None of us should be ashamed of work, however small and servile it may appear. Labor is ennobling. All who toil with head or hands are workingmen or workingwomen. And all are doing their duty and honoring their religion as much while working at the washtub or washing the dishes as they are in going to meeting. While the hands are engaged in the most common labor, the mind may be elevated and ennobled by pure and holy thoughts. When any of the workers manifest a lack of respect for religious things, they should be separated from the work. Let none feel that the institution is dependent upon them.

Those who have long been employed in our institutions should now be responsible workers, reliable in every place, as faithful to duty as the compass to the pole. Had they rightly improved their opportunities, they might now have symmetrical characters and a deep, living experience in religious things. But some of these workers have separated from God. Religion is laid aside. It is not an inwrought principle, carefully cherished wherever they go, into whatever society they are thrown, proving as an anchor to the soul. I wish all the workers carefully to consider that success in this life and success in gaining the future life depend largely upon faithfulness in little things. Those who long for higher responsibilities should manifest faithfulness in performing the duties just where God has placed them.

The perfection of God's work is as clearly seen in the tiniest insect as in the king of birds. The soul of the little child that believes in Christ is as precious in His sight as are the angels about His throne. "Be ye therefore perfect, even as your Father which is in heaven is perfect." Matthew 5:48. As God is perfect in His sphere, so man may be perfect in his sphere. Whatever the hand finds to do should be done with thoroughness and dispatch. Faithfulness and integrity in little things, the performance of little duties and little deeds of kindness, will cheer and gladden the pathway of life; and when our work on earth is ended, every one of the little duties performed with fidelity will be treasured as a precious gem before God.

The Church to Triumph

UNTIL Christ shall appear in the clouds of heaven with power and great glory, men will become perverse in spirit and turn from the truth to fables. The church will yet see troublous times. She will prophesy in sackcloth. But although she must meet heresies and persecutions, although she must battle with the infidel and the apostate, yet by the help of God she is bruising the head of Satan. The Lord will have a people as true as steel, and with faith as firm as the granite rock. They are to be His witnesses in the world, His instrumentalities to do a special, a glorious work in the day of His preparation.

The gospel message does not win a single soul to Christ, or make its way to a single heart, without wounding the head of Satan. Whenever a captive is wrenched from his grasp, delivered from his oppression, the tyrant is defeated. The publishing houses, the presses, are instrumentalities in God's hand to send out to every tongue and nation the precious light of truth. This light is reaching even to heathen lands, and is constantly making inroads upon superstition and every conceivable error.

Ministers who have preached the truth with all zeal and earnestness may apostatize and join the ranks of our enemies, but does this turn the truth of God into a lie? "Nevertheless," says the apostle, "the foundation of God standeth sure." 2 Timothy 2:19. The faith and feelings of men may change; but the truth of God, never. The third angel's message is sounding; it is infallible.

No man can serve God without uniting against himself evil men and evil angels. Evil spirits will be put upon the track of every soul that seeks to join the ranks of Christ, for Satan

1881, vol. 4, pp. 594-596 (The Tract Societies).

wishes to recover the prey taken from his grasp. Evil men will give themselves over to believe strong delusions, that they may be damned. These men will put on the garments of sincerity and deceive, if possible, the very elect.

CERTAINTY OF THE TRUTH

It is as certain that we have the truth as that God lives; and Satan, with all his arts and hellish power, cannot change the truth of God into a lie. While the great adversary will try his utmost to make of none effect the word of God, truth must go forth as a lamp that burneth.

The Lord has singled us out and made us subjects of His marvelous mercy. Shall we be charmed with the pratings of the apostate? Shall we choose to take our stand with Satan and his host? Shall we join with the transgressors of God's law? Rather let it be our prayer: "Lord, put enmity between me and the serpent." If we are not at enmity with his works of darkness, his powerful folds encircle us, and his sting is ready at any moment to be driven to our hearts. We should count him a deadly foe. We should oppose him in the name of Christ. Our work is still onward. We must battle for every inch of ground. Let all who name the name of Christ clothe themselves with the armor of righteousness.

Simplicity in Dress

In His Sermon on the Mount Christ exhorts His followers not to allow their minds to be absorbed in earthly things. He plainly says: "Ye cannot serve God and mammon. Therefore I say unto you, Take no thought for your life, what ye shall eat, or what ye shall drink; nor yet for your body, what ye shall put on. Is not the life more than meat, and the body than raiment?" "And why take ye thought for raiment? Consider the lilies of the field, how they grow; they toil not, neither do they spin: and yet I say unto you, That even Solomon in all his glory was not arrayed like one of these." Matthew 6:24, 25, 28, 29.

These words are full of meaning. They were applicable in the days of Christ, and they are applicable in our day. Jesus here contrasts the natural simplicity of the flowers of the field with the artificial adorning of raiment. He declares that the glory of Solomon could not bear comparison with one of the flowers in natural loveliness. Here is a lesson for all who desire to know and to do the will of God. Jesus has noticed the care and devotion given to dress, and has cautioned, yea, commanded, us not to bestow too much thought upon it. It is important that we give careful heed to His words. Solomon was so engrossed with thoughts of outward display that he failed to elevate his mind by a constant connection with the God of wisdom. Perfection and beauty of character were overlooked in his attempt to obtain outward beauty. He sold his honor and integrity of character in seeking to glorify himself before the world, and finally became a despot, supporting his extravagance by a grinding taxation upon the people. He first became corrupt at heart, then he apostatized from God, and finally became a worshiper of idols.

As we see our sisters departing from simplicity in dress,

1881, vol. 4, p. 628-648.

and cultivating a love for the fashions of the world, we feel troubled. By taking steps in this direction they are separating themselves from God and neglecting the inward adorning. They should not feel at liberty to spend their God-given time in the unnecessary ornamentation of their clothing. How much better might it be employed in searching the Scriptures, thus obtaining a thorough knowledge of the prophecies and of the practical lessons of Christ. . . .

God would be pleased to see our sisters clad in neat, simple apparel and earnestly engaged in the work of the Lord. They are not deficient in ability, and if they would put to a right use the talents they already have, their efficiency would be greatly increased. If the time they now spend in needless work were devoted to searching the word of God and explaining it to others, their own minds would be enriched with gems of truth, and they would be strengthened and ennobled by the effort made to understand the reasons of our faith. Were our sisters conscientious Bible Christians, seeking to improve every opportunity to enlighten others, we should see scores of souls embracing the truth through their self-sacrificing endeavors alone. Sisters, in the day when the accounts of all are balanced, will you feel a pleasure in reviewing your life, or will you feel that the beauty of the outward man was sought, while the inward beauty of the soul was almost entirely neglected?

Have not our sisters sufficient zeal and moral courage to place themselves without excuse upon the Bible platform? The apostle has given most explicit directions on this point: "I will therefore . . . that women adorn themselves in modest apparel, with shamefacedness and sobriety; not with broided hair, or gold, or pearls, or costly array; but (which becometh women professing godliness) with good works." 1 Timothy 2:8-10. Here the Lord, through His apostle, speaks expressly against the wearing of gold. Let those who have had experience see to it that they do not lead others astray on this point by their example. That ring encircling your finger may be very plain, but it is useless, and the wearing of it has a wrong influence upon others.

Especially should the wives of our ministers be careful not to depart from the plain teachings of the Bible on the point of dress. Many look upon these injunctions as too old-fashioned to be worthy of notice; but He who gave them to His disciples understood the dangers from the love of dress in our time and sent to us the note of warning. Will we heed the warning and be wise? Extravagance in dress is continually increasing. The end is not yet. Fashion is constantly changing, and our sisters follow in its wake, regardless of time or expense. There is a great amount of means expended upon dress, when it should be returned to God the giver. . . .

Those among Sabbathkeepers who have yielded to the influence of the world are to be tested. The perils of the last days are upon us, and a trial is before the professed people of God which many have not anticipated. The genuineness of their faith will be proved. Many have united with worldlings in pride, vanity, and pleasure seeking, flattering themselves that they could do this and still be Christians. But it is such indulgences that separate them from God and make them children of the world. Christ has given us no such example. Those only who deny self, and live a life of sobriety, humility, and holiness, are true followers of Jesus; and such cannot enjoy the society of the lovers of the world.

Many dress like the world in order to have an influence over unbelievers, but here they make a sad mistake. If they would have a true and saving influence, let them live out their profession, show their faith by their righteous works, and make the distinction plain between the Christian and the worldling. The words, the dress, the actions, should tell for God. Then a holy influence will be shed upon all around them, and even unbelievers will take knowledge of them that they have been with Jesus. If any wish to have their influence tell in favor of truth, let them live out their profession and thus imitate the humble Pattern.

Pride, ignorance, and folly are constant companions. The Lord is displeased with the pride manifested among His professed people. He is dishonored by their conformity to the unhealthful, immodest, and expensive fashions of this degenerate age.

Fashion rules the world; and she is a tyrannical mistress, often compelling her devotees to submit to the greatest inconvenience and discomfort. Fashion taxes without reason and collects without mercy. She has a fascinating power, and stands ready to criticize and ridicule the poor if they do not follow in her wake at any cost, even the sacrifice of life itself. Satan triumphs that his devices succeed so well, and Death laughs at the health-destroying folly and blind zeal of the worshipers at fashion's shrine. . . .

It is a shame to our sisters to so forget their holy character and their duty to God as to imitate the fashions of the world. There is no excuse for us except the perversity of our own hearts. We do not extend our influence by such a course. It is so inconsistent with our profession of faith that it makes us ridiculous in the eyes of worldlings.

Many a soul who was convinced of the truth has been led to decide against it by the pride and love of the world displayed by our sisters. The doctrine preached seemed clear and harmonious, and the hearers felt that a heavy cross must be lifted by them in taking the truth. When these persons have seen our sisters making so much display in dress, they have said: "This people dress fully as much as we do. They cannot really believe what they profess; and, after all, they must be deceived. If they really thought that Christ was soon coming, and the case of every soul was to be decided for eternal life or death, they could not devote time and money to dress according to the existing fashions." How little did those professedly believing sisters know of the sermon their dress was preaching!

Our words, our actions, and our dress are daily, living preachers, gathering with Christ or scattering abroad. This is no trivial matter to be passed off with a jest. The subject of dress demands serious reflection and much prayer. Many unbelievers have felt that they were not doing right in permitting themselves to be slaves of fashion; but when they see some, who make a high profession of godliness dressing as worldlings dress, enjoying frivolous society, they decide that there can be no wrong in such a course.

"We are," said the inspired apostle, "made a spectacle unto the world, and to angels, and to men." 1 Corinthians 4:9. All heaven is marking the daily influence which the professed followers of Christ exert upon the world. My sisters, your dress is telling either in favor of Christ and the sacred truth or in favor of the world. Which is it? Remember we must all answer to God for the influence we exert.

We would not by any means encourage carelessness in dress. Let the attire be appropriate and becoming. Though only a ten-cent calico, it should be kept neat and clean. If there are no ruffles, the wearer cannot only save something by making it herself, but she can save quite a little sum by washing and ironing it herself. Families bind heavy burdens upon themselves by dressing their children in accordance with the fashion. What a waste of time! The little ones would look very inviting in a dress without a ruffle or ornament, but kept sweet and clean. It is such a trifle to wash and iron a dress of this style that the labor is not felt to be a burden.

Why will our sisters rob God of the service due Him, and rob His treasury of money which they should give to His cause, to serve the fashions of this age? The first and best thoughts are given to dress; time is squandered and money wasted. The culture of the mind and heart is neglected. The character is considered of less importance than the dress. The ornament of a meek and quiet spirit is of infinite value, and it is the wickedest of folly to waste in frivolous pursuits our opportunities to secure this precious adorning of the soul.

Sisters, we may do a noble work for God if we will. Woman does not know her power. God did not intend that her capabilities should be all absorbed in questioning: What shall I eat? what shall I drink? and wherewithal shall I be clothed? There is a higher purpose for woman, a grander destiny. She should develop and cultivate her powers, for God can employ them in the great work of saving souls from eternal ruin. . . .

But the greatest evil is the influence upon the children and youth. Almost as soon as they come into the world they are subjected to fashion's demands. Little children hear more of dress than of their salvation. They see their mothers more earnestly consulting the fashion plates than the Bible. More visits are made to the dry goods dealer and the milliner than to the church. The outward display of dress is made of greater consequence than the adornment of the character. Sharp reprimands are called forth for soiling the fine clothing, and the mind becomes peevish and irritable under continual restraint.

A deformed character does not disturb the mother so much as a soiled dress. The child hears more of dress than of virtue, for the mother is more familiar with fashion than with her Saviour. Her example too often surrounds the young with a poisonous atmosphere. Vice, disguised in fashion's garb, intrudes itself among the children.

Simplicity of dress will make a sensible woman appear to the best advantage. We judge of a person's character by the style of dress worn. Gaudy apparel betrays vanity and weakness. A modest, godly woman will dress modestly. A refined taste, a cultivated mind, will be revealed in the choice of simple and appropriate attire.

There is an ornament that will never perish, that will promote the happiness of all around us in this life, and will shine with undimmed luster in the immortal future. It is the adorning of a meek and lowly spirit. God has bidden us wear the richest dress upon the soul. By every look into the mirror, the worshipers of fashion should be reminded of the neglected soul. Every hour squandered over the toilet should reprove them for leaving the intellect to lie waste. Then there might be a reformation that would elevate and ennoble all the aims and purposes of life. Instead of seeking golden ornaments for the exterior, an earnest effort would be put forth to secure that wisdom which is of more value than fine gold, yea, which is more precious than rubies.

Those who worship at fashion's altar have but little force of character and but little physical energy. They live for no great purpose, and their lives accomplish no worthy end. We meet everywhere women whose whole mind and heart are absorbed in their love of dress and display. The soul of womanhood is dwarfed and belittled, and her thoughts are centered upon her poor, despicable self. As a fashionably dressed young lady was passing several gentlemen on the street, one of them made some inquiries in regard to her. The answer was: "She makes a pretty ornament in her father's house, but otherwise she is of no use." It is deplorable that those who profess to be Christ's disciples should think it a fine thing to imitate the dress and manners of these useless ornaments.

Peter gives valuable instruction concerning the dress of Christian women: "Whose adorning let it not be that outward adorning of plaiting the hair, and of wearing of gold, or of putting on of apparel; but let it be the hidden man of the heart, in that which is not corruptible, even the ornament of a meek and quiet spirit, which is in the sight of God of great price. For after this manner in the old time the holy women also, who trusted in God, adorned themselves." 1 Peter 3:3-5. All that we urge is compliance with the injunctions of God's word. Are we Bible readers and followers of Bible teachings? Will we obey God, or conform to the customs of the world? Will we serve God or mammon? Can we expect to enjoy peace of mind and the approval of God while walking directly contrary to the teachings of His word?

The apostle Paul exhorts Christians not to be conformed to the world, but to be transformed by the renewing of the mind, "that ye may prove what is that good, and acceptable, and perfect, will of God." Romans 12:2. But many who profess to be children of God feel no scruples against conforming to the customs of the world in the wearing of gold and pearls and costly array. Those who are too conscientious to wear these things are regarded as narrow-minded, superstitious, and even fanatical. But it is God who condescends to give us these instructions; they are the declarations of Infinite Wisdom, and those who disregard them do so at their own peril and loss. Those who cling to the ornaments forbidden in God's word cherish pride and vanity in the heart. They desire to attract attention. Their dress says: Look at me; admire me. Thus the vanity inherent in human nature is steadily increasing by indulgence. When the mind is fixed upon pleasing God alone, all the needless embellishments of the person disappear.

The apostle places the outward adorning in direct contrast with a meek and quiet spirit and then testifies of the comparative value of the latter: "In the sight of God of great price." There is a decided contradiction between the love of outward adorning and the grace of meekness, the quiet spirit. It is only when we seek in all things to conform to the will of God that peace and joy will reign in the soul.

The love of dress endangers the morals and makes woman the opposite of the Christian lady characterized by modesty and sobriety. . . .

Christ is ashamed of His professed followers. Wherein do we bear any resemblance to Him? Wherein does our dress conform to the Bible requirements? I do not want the sins of the people upon me, and I will give the trumpet a certain sound. For years I have borne a plain and decided testimony upon this subject, in print and upon the speaker's stand. I have not shunned to declare the whole counsel of God. I must be clear of the blood of all. The fact that worldliness and pride bear almost universal sway is no excuse for one Christian to do as others do. God has said: "Thou shalt not follow a multitude to do evil." Exodus 23:2.

Do not, my sisters, trifle longer with your own souls and with God. I have been shown that the main cause of your backsliding is your love of dress. This leads to the neglect of grave responsibilities, and you find yourselves with scarcely a spark of the love of God in your hearts. Without delay, renounce the cause of your backsliding, because it is sin against your own soul and against God. Be not hardened by the deceitfulness of sin. Fashion is deteriorating the intellect and eating out the spirituality of our people. Obedience to fashion is pervading our Seventh-day Adventist churches and is doing more than any other power to separate our people from God. I have been shown that our church rules are very deficient. All exhibitions of pride in dress, which is forbidden in the word of God, should be sufficient reason for church discipline. If there is a continuance, in face of warnings and appeals and entreaties, to still follow the perverse will, it may be regarded as proof that the heart is in no way assimilated to Christ. Self, and only self, is the object of adoration, and one such professed Christian will lead many away from God.

There is a terrible sin upon us as a people, that we have permitted our church members to dress in a manner inconsistent with their faith. We must arise at once and close the door against the allurements of fashion. Unless we do this, our churches will become demoralized.

The Wedding Ring

SOME have had a burden in regard to the wearing of a marriage ring, feeling that the wives of our ministers should conform to this custom. All this is unnecessary. Let the ministers' wives have the golden link which binds their souls to Jesus Christ, a pure and holy character, the true love and meekness and godliness that are the fruit borne upon the Christian tree, and their influence will be secure anywhere. The fact that a disregard of the custom occasions remark is no good reason for adopting it. Americans can make their position understood by plainly stating that the custom is not regarded as obligatory in our country. We need not wear the sign, for we are not untrue to our marriage vow, and the wearing of the ring would be no evidence that we were true. I feel deeply over this leavening process which seems to be going on among us, in the conformity to custom and fashion. Not one penny should be spent for a circlet of gold to testify that we are married. In countries where the custom is imperative, we have no burden to condemn those who have their marriage ring; let them wear it if they can do so conscientiously; but let not our missionaries feel that the wearing of the ring will increase their influence one jot or tittle. If they are Christians, it will be manifest in their Christlikeness of character, in their words, in their works, in the home, in association with others; it will be evinced by their patience and long-suffering and kindliness. They will manifest the spirit of the Master, they will possess His beauty of character, His loveliness of disposition, His sympathetic heart.

Written from Australia, 1892, *Testimonies to Ministers and Gospel Workers,* pages 180, 181.

Forming Character

STRENGTH of character consists of two things—power of will and power of self-control. Many youth mistake strong, uncontrolled passion for strength of character; but the truth is that he who is mastered by his passions is a weak man. The real greatness and nobility of the man is measured by the power of the feelings that he subdues, not by the power of the feelings that subdue him. The strongest man is he, who, while sensitive to abuse, will yet restrain passion and forgive his enemies. Such men are true heroes.

Many have such meager ideas of what they may become that they will ever remain dwarfed and narrow, when, if they would improve the powers which God has given them, they might develop a noble character and exert an influence that would win souls to Christ. Knowledge is power; but intellectual ability, without goodness of heart, is a power for evil.

God has given us our intellectual and moral powers, but to a great extent every person is the architect of his own character. Every day the structure is going up. The word of God warns us to take heed how we build, to see that our building is founded upon the eternal Rock. The time is coming when our work will stand revealed just as it is. Now is the time for all to cultivate the powers which God has given them, that they may form characters for usefulness here and for a higher life hereafter.

Every act of life, however unimportant, has its influence in forming the character. A good character is more precious than worldly possessions, and the work of forming it is the noblest in which men can engage.

1881, vol. 4, pp. 656, 657 (Accountability to God).

Characters formed by circumstance are changeable and discordant—a mass of contraries. Their possessors have no high aim or purpose in life. They have no ennobling influence upon the characters of others. They are purposeless and powerless.

The little span of life allotted us here should be wisely improved. God would have His church a living, devoted, working church. But our people, as a body, are far from this now. God calls for strong, brave souls, for active, living Christians, who are following the true Pattern, and who will exert a decided influence for God and the right. The Lord has committed to us, as a sacred trust, most important and solemn truths, and we should show their influence upon our lives and characters.

In the Olympic games to which the apostle Paul calls our attention, those engaged in the races were required to make most thorough preparations. For months they were trained by different masters in the physical exercises calculated to give strength and vigor to the body. They were restricted to such food as would keep the body in the most healthy condition, and their clothing was such as would leave every organ and muscle untrammeled.

Now if those who were to engage in running a race for earthly honor were obliged to submit to such severe discipline in order to succeed, how much more necessary it is for those who are to engage in the work of the Lord to be thoroughly disciplined and prepared, if they would be successful! Their preparation should be as much more thorough, their earnestness and self-denying efforts as much greater, than were those of the aspirants for worldly honors, as heavenly things are of more value than earthly. The mind, as well as the muscles, should be trained to the most diligent and persevering efforts. The road to success is not a smooth way over which we are borne in palace cars, but it is a rugged path filled with obstacles which can be surmounted only by patient toil.—1889, vol. 5, p. 552.

How little we know of the bearing our acts will have upon the future history of ourselves and others. Many think it is of little importance what they do. It will do no harm for them to attend this concert, or unite with the world in that amusement, if they wish to do so. Thus Satan leads and controls their desires, and they do not consider that the results may be most momentous. It may be the link in the chain of events which binds a soul in the snare of Satan and determines his eternal ruin.

Every act, however small, has its place in the great drama of life. Consider that the desire for a single gratification of appetite introduced sin into our world, with its terrible consequences. Unhallowed marriages of the sons of God with the daughters of men resulted in apostasy which ended in the destruction of the world by a flood. The most trifling act of self-indulgence has resulted in great revolutions. This is the case now. There are very few who are circumspect. Like the children of Israel, they will not take heed to words of counsel, but follow their own inclination. They unite with a worldly element in attending gatherings where they will be brought into notice, and thus lead the way and others follow. What has been done once will be done again by themselves and many others. Every step these take makes a lasting impression, not only on their own consciences and habits, but upon those of others. This consideration gives awful dignity to human life.—1882, vol. 5, pp. 92, 93.

We shall be individually, for time and eternity, what our habits make us. The lives of those who form right habits, and are faithful in the performance of every duty, will be as shining lights, shedding bright beams upon the pathway of others; but if habits of unfaithfulness are indulged, if lax, indolent, neglectful habits are allowed to strengthen, a cloud darker than midnight will settle on the prospects in this life and forever debar the individual from the future life.—1880, vol. 4, p. 452.

The whole Bible is a revelation of the glory of God in Christ. Received, believed, obeyed, it is the great instrumentality in the transformation of character. And it is the only sure means of intellectual culture.—1904, vol. 8, p. 319.

The religion of Christ never degrades the receiver; it never makes him coarse or rough, discourteous or self-important, passionate or hardhearted. On the contrary, it refines the taste, sanctifies the judgment, and purifies and ennobles the thoughts, bringing them into captivity to Christ. God's ideal for His children is higher than the highest human thought can reach. He has given in His holy law a transcript of His character.—1904, vol. 8, p. 63.

The ideal of Christian character is Christlikeness. There is opened before us a path of constant advancement. We have an object to gain, a standard to reach, that includes everything good and pure and noble and elevated. There should be continual striving and constant progress onward and upward toward perfection of character.—1904, vol. 8, p. 64.

PACIFIC PRESS PUB ASSN
Satan - 117,
angelic work 356, 347.
Praise 400